5/24/22   4.⁰⁰

Surveillance or Security?

Surveillance or Security?

The Risks Posed by New Wiretapping Technologies

Susan Landau

The MIT Press
Cambridge, Massachusetts
London, England

For information about special quantity discounts, please email special_sales@mitpress .mit.edu

This book was set in Stone Sans and Stone Serif by Toppan Best-set Premedia Limited. Printed and bound in the United States of America.

Library of Congress Cataloging-in-Publication Data

Landau, Susan Eva.
Surveillance or security? : the risks posed by new wiretapping technologies / Susan Landau.
   p.   cm.
Includes bibliographical references and index.
ISBN 978-0-262-01530-1 (hardcover : alk. paper)
1. Telecommunication—Security measures—United States. 2. Wiretapping—United States. 3. Data encryption (Computer science)—Government policy—United States. 4. Electronic surveillance—Political aspects—United States. 5. Computer crimes—Risk assessment—United States. I. Title.
TK5102.85.L36   2011
363.25'2—dc22

10   9   8   7   6   5   4   3   2   1

This book is dedicated to Daniel, Emmy, and Ellie.

Contents

Author's Note

Throughout this book, when I say the *Internet*, I mean the packet-moving layered architecture described in chapter 2. The Internet does not include the applications—the Googles, Facebooks, and so on—that lie above this architecture. Often the public conflates these two. I owe the observation about the confusion to Stefan Savage, who pointed out that engineers and the public have two differing definitions of the Internet. While there are security problems in both Internets, the ones that make securing the Internet extremely difficult are the ones inherent in the packet-moving architecture. This book focuses on these problems.

Preface

Several years before this book was completed, I gave a talk at a company's annual meeting for its technologists. There was nothing particularly unusual about that; I was representing Sun Microsystems to technologists of a major customer. I spoke on new technologies being developed in Sun Labs. Someone from Microsoft also spoke, as did someone from Google, Intel, and so on. The meeting was held at a combination hotel/convention center. That, too, was not surprising. What was odd was the phalanx of hotel security guards who carefully monitored the meeting room as three hundred attendees trooped back and forth between talks, meals, and coffee breaks.

Because outsiders had been invited to attend the sessions, there was no company proprietary information presented at the talks. The hotel was somewhat isolated; it was a large complex on the edge of several four-lane roads. I did not really think much about the security guards until the evening a guard walked into the elevator as I was going up to my room. Except for the United States right after September 11, and traveling in the Soviet Union and China, I could not recall ever having been in a place with so many security personnel, and I commented on the large number of guards I had seen in the hotel.

"That's good," he replied. I thought about this a day later, as the hotel's shuttle service took me back to the airport. The driver had a uniform that included a white shirt with epaulettes. I have taken shuttles in more states of the union and to and from more airports than I care to count. Some shuttle services are more professional than others, but never before had I been driven to the airport by someone who looked like he worked for the military in a third-world dictatorship. That's when I began to reflect on the security guards who had stood before the conference room.

I am sure that the company whose meeting it was did not arrange for the guards. Rather it was the hotel that provided them as part of the service of running a conference. The service was unnecessary. Any determined "spy"—I say "spy" in quotes because no proprietary information was released during the conference—could have counterfeited a badge and gone to hear the presentations. The guards kept out the hordes on the street, except that the hotel was on an inaccessible four-lane roadway. There was no street and no hordes. The guards were completely superfluous, but they were required by the hotel contract. The money the company was spending on guards' salaries was money it was not spending on training additional security technicians, on upgrading its IT infrastructure, or on improving the security of its products (which included defense information systems sold to the U.S. government). These guards were not providing good security. The situation was even worse. The cost of this "security" prevented this company from protecting what mattered.

The guards provided what Bruce Schneier has called *security theater:* the appearance of security rather than the genuine article. There are thousands of examples of this, from TSA inspections of passengers and X-rays of their hand luggage without accompanying inspection of the parcels that ride in the bellies of the planes, to the ubiquitous closed-circuit TV (CCTV) cameras appearing everywhere with little evidence that their usage actually cuts crime.[1] The cost of CCTVs diverts money from such activities as community policing. As such, their use may actually be counterproductive.

Electronic communication is the lifeblood of modern society. Simultaneously, such communication can be central to how criminals and terrorists conduct their business. Not a day passes without another story of Internet insecurities, critical infrastructure being attacked, attacks from China on U.S. corporations, and Russian hackers targeting U.S. consumers or Estonian government sites. In the decade since the attacks of September 11, in an attempt to keep the nation safe, the U.S. government has embarked on an unprecedented effort to build surveillance capabilities into communication infrastructure.

Unlike the TSA and CCTV examples, the issue of who is defending what runs more deeply than the question of whether we are diverting funds from techniques that may provide better security. What are these communication surveillance systems? Who are the guards? Are they really protecting us? Or are they working for someone else? Could these surveillance capabilities be turned by trusted insiders for their own profit, or used by our enemies to access our secrets? The fundamental issue is whether, by housing wiretapping within communication infrastructure, we are creating serious security risks. Understanding whether building wiretapping into communication infrastructure keeps us safe requires that we understand the technology, economics, law, and policy issues of communication surveillance technologies. That is the point and purpose of this book.

I begin in chapter 1 by laying out the issues of communication and wiretapping within their social and legal contexts. In chapter 2, I discuss the development of communication networks, both the telephone and the Internet, while in chapter 3, I explain how the Internet came to be so insecure. These two chapters are more technical than the rest of the book and less technically trained readers may choose to skim them. I discuss legal aspects of wiretapping in chapter 4, effectiveness of communications surveillance in chapter 5, and evolving communications technologies in chapter 6. In chapter 7, I examine who is intruding on our communications, how they intrude, and what they are seeking. Having built that framework, in chapter 8, I look at the technology risks that arise when wiretapping is embedded within communications infrastructures, while in chapter 9, I look at the policy risks created by wiretapping technologies. In chapter 10, I examine how communication takes place during disasters; this gives different insights into communications security. I conclude in chapter 11 by discussing how we might get communications security and surveillance "right."

Note: Because my focus in this book is on whether widespread communications surveillance enhances or endangers national security, I am not addressing broader policy issues of U.S. national security. In particular, I will discuss only peripherally the role that the concentration of executive power over the last decades, and most particularly under the administration of President George W. Bush, has had in determining current U.S. communications surveillance policy. This issue—which has been the subject of many other publications—is beyond the scope of this book.

Acknowledgments

My thanks, first and foremost, go to my long-term collaborator, Whitfield Diffie, with whom I enjoyed many years of intellectual give-and-take. Much of my thinking on the issues of privacy, security, and surveillance has been influenced by our conversations. The direction my career has taken is no small part due to Whit, and I am very grateful to him.

Sun Microsystems was a great place to work: full of smart people and the ferment of ideas, and I was lucky to be there. I am particularly appreciative of Bob Sproull's strong encouragement and support for writing this book.

Dancing between policy and technology is complicated, and I owe many thanks to friends and colleagues who answered more questions than they imagined existed. I particularly want to thank Steve Bellovin, Matt Blaze, Clint Brooks, Jim Dempsey, Al Gidari, and Brian Snow. I very much appreciate Nancy Snyder's work on the illustrations for the book. I have benefited from meetings organized by Deirdre Mulligan and David Clark, and I would like to thank them for those as well as for many stimulating conversations. The following people generously shared their knowledge, read over sections, and translated text: Steve Babbage, Curt Barker, Jim Bidzos, Danny Cohen, Dennis Costa, Tom Cross, Gary Cutbill, George Danezis, Roger Dingledine, Chris Essid, Dickie George, John Gilmore, Andy Grosso, Ann Harrison, Paul Karger, Eleni Kosta, Leslie Lambert, Herb Lin, Steve Lipner, Nick McKeown, John Morris, John Nagengast, Peter Neumann, Hilarie Orman, Jon Peterson, Phil Reitinger, Jen Rexford, Ed Roback, Greg Rose, Ari Schwartz, Renee Stratulate, Paul Syverson, Lee Tien, and Jonathan Weinberg. I am very grateful to them all. In addition, there are a number of knowledgeable high government and private-sector sources whom I will have to thank anonymously.

Special thanks to Brown Kennedy, who told me to stop revising my outline and start writing. Without her, this book might still be a highly polished outline.

Everyone thanks their spouse or partner, and I am no exception. With great equanimity my husband, Neil Immerman, put up with my intense focus on surveillance, frequent travels to Washington, and a lifelong obsession, at least in pre-Internet days, with finding a copy of today's *New York Times*. He found me texts, read multiple drafts of this book, and even helped with typesetting.

It has been many years since I took a writing course with John McPhee and learned how the fact-checkers at the *New Yorker* insist on the accuracy of even the smallest fact.[1] My debt to John—and the legions of fact-checkers employed by the *New Yorker*—is enormous. I have done my best to apply the many lessons learned. Any errors in this book, however, are my own.

1 Introduction

Communication lies at the heart of being human. Communication can be private—the whispered conversations of two lovers, the secretive negotiations of politicians, the hushed deals of businesspeople—or highly public—marriage ceremonies, civic speeches, announcements of products and mergers.

The invention of electronic communications—the telegraph in 1844, followed by the telephone three decades later—enabled conversation at a distance and substantially changed the way people interact. Cell phones, the Internet, and other communication devices have so magnified this change that in the modern world it is quite likely that more "conversations" occur electronically than face to face. This has a critical impact on privacy. Or as the noted cryptographer Whitfield Diffie has put it, "In the 1790s, at the time the [U.S.] Bill of Rights was written, you could just walk off a few feet down the road and there were no tape recorders, no shotgun microphones, and you were having a private conversation in a way that nobody can be sure of today."[1] The freedom to communicate at a distance carries with it hidden risk: eavesdroppers may hear the conversation too.

Such risks have always existed, of course. The letters of Mary, Queen of Scots, for example, were intercepted and read, leading to her conviction for high treason and her death.[2] Thomas Jefferson worried about the interception of his communications; at times he avoided signing his letters—or even writing them.[3]

For many years, protecting confidential communications through encryption was a practice limited to governments; by and large, the public rarely attempted such efforts. The arrival of the public Internet, and its wide use by business, changed the situation. The risk of communications interception has spread to a large swath of society. In the 1990s a pitched battle ensued between the U.S. government, technologists, and academics over the public's right to use cryptography.

The government argued that, important as confidentiality was for some public business, the government's need for wiretapping was more critical; widespread access to encryption would impede this. The public's need won out. In 2000 the U.S. government began permitting most exports of strong cryptography[4] and thus indirectly enabling deployment and use of strong cryptography within the United States.[5] Technologists and academics had won the "Crypto Wars." Even the events of September 11, 2001, did not shake the U.S. government position. Shortly after the Al Qaeda attacks, New Hampshire senator Judd Gregg argued for the reinstatement of the cryptographic export controls, but there was no White House or NSA support of his position. Widespread availability of cryptography was here to stay.

While the code warriors[6] may have emerged victorious in the battle over confidential communications, there were signs of government efforts to thwart the privacy that encryption engenders. A 1994 law regulating telephone carriers that passed during the early days of the Internet boom may actually be the linchpin that undoes communications privacy.

The Communications Assistance for Law Enforcement Act (CALEA) requires that digitally switched telephone networks be built with wiretapping capabilities designed by the federal government. In 2003 the Federal Bureau of Investigation (FBI) pressed for CALEA's extension to instances of Voice over Internet Protocol (VoIP), voice communication that traverses the Internet, a position that was upheld by the U.S. Court of Appeals.

Events were occurring on other wiretapping fronts as well. In late 2005 and spring 2006 journalists at the *New York Times* and *USA Today* reported that, without any warrants, NSA was surveilling domestic communications. In the summer of 2007 Congress passed the controversial Protect America Act (PAA).[7] Valid for only six months, the PAA allowed warrantless wiretapping of communications if one end was "reasonably believed to be outside the United States." How the new law would be implemented was unclear—there had been minimal public discussion of the bill before it was passed—but the actions at an AT&T switching office in San Francisco gave hints. Large amounts of domestic traffic were being selected and shipped to a "central location";[8] presumably this was the NSA.

The 1990s battle over encryption has shifted from the public's ability to encrypt their communications to the government's requiring that surveillance capabilities be built directly into communications infrastructures. With the shift of usage from the telephone network to the Internet, it appears that the U.S. government is simply seeking to keep wiretapping capabilities current with modern communications technology. But the difference in techniques and scale is creating a substantial difference in kind.

CALEA applied to VoIP attempts to design the new communications world so that it satisfies the surveillance capabilities of the old. Objections to CALEA and the government's warrantless wiretapping have focused on threats to privacy and civil liberties, and on potential harm to innovation. There has been an implicit presumption that enabling such surveillance is good for security. Characterizing such wiretapping as an obvious win for security is a facile description of a complex problem and like many facile descriptions, it is wrong. Embedding surveillance capabilities deeply into communications infrastructures squarely pits surveillance against security, and may, in fact, endanger us far more than it secures us.

Wiretapping and location tracking will not be easy to implement in the Internet communications environment. On the surface, the circuit-switched telephone and the packet-switched Internet look alike: the communications networks use the same type of transmission facilities (often sharing the same cable), often delivering the same type of content (voice, data).[9] However, the Internet is a far more complex and diverse communications network than the telephone. The two have very different architectures.

Technologists have a snappy way to say this: the telephone network has dumb "terminals"—telephones—and smart networks while the Internet is the reverse. The fact is that while there is a great deal of cleverness in the switches and routers that direct the traffic on the Internet, the "smarts" are at the endpoints: the computers and applications they support that have given rise to a powerful new economy in the last decade and a half. The same "smarts at the edges" have important implications for privacy and security. The flexibility and dynamism that make possible Internet innovation also enable the network's vulnerabilities.

At the same time that the FBI was seeking CALEA jurisdiction over certain types of VoIP, over one hundred Greek government officials—*including the prime minister*—were being wiretapped for ten months by parties unknown.[10] Although this was the cell phone network that was wiretapped, and not the Internet, the underlying principle is the same. The danger in CALEA and other efforts to build wiretapping capabilities into the communications infrastructures is that the surveillance potential we are building will be turned and used against us.

In the old days, tapping a phone line was not particularly hard; you simply attached a pair of alligator clips[11] to the copper wires that constituted the phone line. But the case in Greece did not occur in the old days. The tapping was neither small in scale (e.g., of a single subscriber), nor did it occur only for a brief period. Rather the wiretapping went on for almost a year. The ability to eavesdrop undetected for such a long period arose from the ease of penetration into the communications network. That ease is the result of changes in communications technology that have occurred over the last fifty years, changes from electromechanical switching boxes to computer-mediated routing.

In 1960, in order to make a phone call from New York to London, you first had to book it, then use an operator to place the call.[12] In 2010, you neither have to book the call in advance nor use the services of any person employed by the phone company. You don't even need to use a telephone.

More has changed with communications technology in a half century than has remained the same. Fifty years ago the United States had a single long-distance carrier: AT&T. Now it has a plethora of companies providing such communications services, including cable companies and Internet service providers (ISPs). Fifty years ago, telephone service was provided through the Public Switched Telephone Network (PSTN), which assigned a circuit to each call that lasted for the duration of the call. Now calls can proceed through a variety of technologies, from POTS (plain old telephone service, e.g., the PSTN) to a combination Voice over IP (VoIP) and POTS (where the call is telephone service between the subscribers and the phone switch but VoIP across the network), to PANS (Pretty Advanced Network Services) such as is provided by Skype. Fifty years ago telephones were the "dumb terminals" of figure 1.1; now a telephone may be a cell phone, a laptop computer, a device that has aspects of both technologies in it (such as an iPhone), or just the same squat black box that worked in 1960.

The simplicity of dialing 011-44-20-7323-8000 from New York and reaching the British Museum in seconds belies the fact that the technologies making such a call possible have become increasingly complex. Many technical and policy hurdles had to be overcome to permit such simplicity.

Until the mid-1950s, overseas communications were transmitted by high-frequency radio; fading, interference, and noise made it essentially impossible to use automatic switching equipment to transmit the calls.[13] The first transatlantic cable was installed in 1956, but this did not in itself solve the problem. Just as at the beginning different national railroads each developed their own different—and thus incompatible—gauges for their tracks,[14] so did the national telephone companies develop diverse and incompatible signaling systems.

For automatic switching to occur, the differences in numbering schemes, switching and signaling systems, operating procedures, and transmission criteria had to be made compatible across different national systems.[15] Over

Figure 1.1
The "terminals" of the PSTN. Photo by Neil Immerman.

a period of years, AT&T and the British, French, and West German telephone systems agreed on a signaling system that would be compatible with
the North American and European systems.[16] One problem preventing
genuine direct dialing was that installed equipment could not handle the
increased number of digits needed for such a call.[17] By 1970 this was fixed
for calls between the United States and the United Kingdom;[18] international direct dialing from the United States to a number of other nations
followed rather quickly.[19]

Other changes were legal ones. In 1968 the Federal Communications
Commission ruled that it was permissible to connect a "Carterfone," essentially a two-way mobile radio, to the PSTN.[20] This ended the era when
AT&T was the sole judge of what could be connected to the telephone
network.[21] Consumers could use whatever device they wanted to connect
to the phone system so long as the device did not harm the network.[22]
Innovation resulted. Probably the most profound effect of the Carterfone
decision was on a different network entirely. By allowing the attachment

of various devices, including modems, to the telephone network, the Carterfone decision enabled digital communication with the same broad connectivity enjoyed by telephone communication. This included the Internet, ushering in a new era of communication.[23]

There is yet a third transformation ongoing as this book is being written, one that grew out of the other two and has so far occurred without much public notice: the conjoining of the PSTN and the Internet. The PSTN had telephones, or "dumb" terminals, as endpoints, while the Internet's endpoints were computers, "smart" terminals. If you consider Skype and the iPhone, it becomes clear that the PSTN and the Internet are converging. Computers have become telephones, and telephones, computers. In fact some of that convergence is happening within the network as well, as control mechanisms are moving to being based on Internet protocols. This convergence may be the most revolutionary transformation of all.

The Greek wiretapping case is one example of information security gone wrong. There is a good chance that the eavesdropping was professionally done, but even amateurs can easily succeed in the business. Anyone present at the 2008 trial of a Hollywood detective who had illegally tapped various celebrities could have learned how to wiretap using less than $50 worth of easily available electrical equipment.[24] It was not even necessary to go to the trial; *Wired* magazine's online wiki presented detailed instructions on telephone tapping.[25] The emergence of common switching worldwide simplifies the ability to wiretap at long distance.

Communications security is simply not easy with modern systems. In 2008 the FBI uncovered a major case of counterfeit Cisco equipment being imported into the United States from China;[26] the fake material included various forms of network switching equipment.[27] This has potentially serious national-security implications. The hardware had been sold to the Department of Defense and financial firms, defense contractors, and universities. Investigations showed that fortunately the fake equipment did not have secret back doors.[28] The United States appears to have been lucky—this time.

In the 1990s, we moved our mail online. A few years later we moved real-time chatting and conversations online. We moved control of much of our critical infrastructure online (either onto the Internet or onto private networks that employ Internet protocols). We have moved much of our business online. We are poised to move large numbers of our social and business meetings and collaborations online. In a globalized economy where "the product" is often not an object but its digital representation, in some sense, we have moved much of our manufacturing online. We are moving detailed data about our daily lives online as Radio Frequency Identification (RFID) tags[29] and sensor networks become ubiquitous. Indeed, the Internet is changing from a network supporting millions of users to one supporting billions and billions of devices.

Technology has changed, and usage patterns have evolved even more. We have become a mobile society, always on and always connected. Our communication devices travel with us. It is not unusual for someone to be carrying a BlackBerry, a cell phone, and a laptop. Communications are where we are, not where our home or office is. We text from our cell phone while riding the subway, we send mail from our iPhones while waiting on a plane, we read our email from our laptops while sitting at a coffeehouse. Without thinking about it, we communicate our whereabouts a thousand times a day while using our BlackBerrys, our cell phones, and our laptops, yet also without thinking about it, we frequently disguise our location—every time we use a phone card or borrow a friend's cell phone.

Law enforcement's job has become more challenging. When a telephone number determined a location—"this line belongs to that apartment"—wiretapping was straightforward. Now electronic surveillance is very different. If the target calls using his own cell phone, he is easy to track.[30] But when the target uses an Internet café, an anonymizing service, or VoIP, tracking in real time who is talking with whom is often not possible. This has created quite a shock for law enforcement.

Of course these advanced communications methods are not the first time new technologies have created complexities for law enforcement. From the telegraph to the telephone to the automobile, police have had to cope with the challenges posed by technical innovations, including inventions that allow criminals to move with abandon. Criminals and police officers both benefited from the mobility and connection that Alexander Graham Bell's device provided—just as both sides benefited from other forms of modern technology. The major difference for law enforcement between the new communications technologies and the older ones is that where the earlier generation of communications technologies took decades[31] before they were widely adopted by society and criminals,[32] the widespread adoption of Internet cafés, anonymizing services, and VoIP is happening in "Internet time." We have experienced a profound change in societal behavior in a matter of a few years—and sometimes even a matter of months—not the decades over which such adoption and change occurred previously.

Exacerbating this has been the fact that this time around the law enforcement community has been slow in adopting the new communications technologies themselves. This has created a serious problem when combating criminal activities—including terrorism—and an equally serious problem when advising lawmakers about law enforcement legislative needs regarding wiretapping.[33] The adage that generals always fight the last war comes to mind.

Law enforcement is seeking to hold on to the wiretapping capabilities it had during the era of circuit-switched telephony, capabilities that do not readily translate into the packet-switched era of Internet communications. The old paradigms do not easily fit the new technologies. During the Cold War we had a formidable enemy with vast technological capabilities of its own and with a population it sought to protect. During our current war, one that may go on for decades, we are faced with a shadowy enemy, one that not only has no discernible population base but that also relishes U.S. attacks on its supposed "base" for the new recruits such attacks create.

As a society, we have at least three fundamentally clashing concerns. We are in a world of mobile communications, which makes electronic surveillance far more complicated. We have critical infrastructure—electric power grid, banking, water, transportation, health services—moving onto IP-based networks; such networks are far more vulnerable than the circuit-switched networks of the past. And we face an elusive enemy, one that has created tremendous fear as a result of the attacks on New York, London, and Madrid. It is worth noting that there was a similar level of heightened fear in 1949 when the Soviet Union exploded its first atomic bomb.

This new enemy consists of loosely connected nonstate actors. Small cell size and lack of a consistent network make tracking these opponents exceedingly difficult. This argues for increased surveillance capabilities. Yet because of communications mobility and the migration of critical infrastructure to IP-based networks, the actual effect of such increased wiretapping capabilities may in the end play into our enemies' hands.

We are creating a massive communications network that will contain information about the billions and billions of actions—business, governmental, and personal—that we take each day. Our enemies are not just the terrorists that have been the focus of the extraordinary security precautions over the last decade, but other nation-states and organized crime.

Heavy U.S. reliance on information systems has left the nation highly exposed. A 2009 National Research Council study reports that the ease of cyberattack is increasing and warns that "the U.S. information technology infrastructure is likely to remain vulnerable to cyberattack for the foreseeable future."[34] Given the U.S. military might, opponents will seek to attack asymmetrically, and the information domain will be a prime target.[35] A number of governments are developing their information warfare capabilities. The issue of cyberwar is quite broad, and I will limit my attention in this book to the extent to which domestic wiretapping capabilities enable our opponents.

In embedding eavesdropping mechanisms in the very fabric of our lives, we are building tools to catch one set of enemies. Other antagonists may be well poised to turn these tools against us. We are, in fact, putting into place something for our enemies that they could not afford to do on their own. Rather than increasing our security, we may well be imperiling it. Melissa Hathaway, appointed by President Obama in 2009 to review the nation's cybersecurity strategy,[36] observed that "history has taught us that security, when pursued properly, enables innovation and growth and protects existing investments."[37] Communications surveillance *when pursued properly* will enable innovation and growth and protect the nation. The issue before us is whether our policies are doing that or creating a major security risk in the name of greater security.

In many national-security and foreign-intelligence cases, wiretaps provide important pieces of a complex puzzle. In other types of cases, including corruption and bribery, it is difficult to infiltrate the conspiracy, and wiretaps (and bugs) provide crucial and, sometimes, the only hard evidence of participation.[38] While it appears that electronic bugs may play a more important role in the prosecution of organized crime than do wiretaps,[39] the potential that law enforcement or national security may be wiretapping keeps criminals, as well as spies, terrorists, and others who would do harm, from using modern communications technologies. That alone is of sufficient benefit to keep these eavesdropping tools in the law enforcement and national-security arsenals. So my concern is not about legally authorized law enforcement and national-security wiretapping, but about the security risks of building surveillance into communications infrastructures.

In this book I have chosen to focus on the United States. There are three interlocking reasons for a national focus rather than an international one. The first is that wiretapping policy issues are very complex. It seems better to handle issues of one nation thoroughly than to provide a more superficial discussion of several. The second reason is that U.S. choices on wiretapping affect surveillance decisions in much of the rest of the world. Thus U.S. wiretap policy is a useful focus from which to understand global wiretapping efforts. Finally, communications intelligence—the flip side of communications security—has a great impact on economic matters. Since each nation has different economic self-interests, it is reasonable to take the perspective of one state, not many. So while at times the arguments here may seem nationalistic, it should not be hard for the reader to reinterpret the issues from the perspective of other nations.

The beginning for the United States is the Constitution and the Bill of Rights, which strictly limit the government's power. The First Amendment states:

"Congress shall make no law . . . abridging the freedom of speech, or of the press; or the right of the people peaceably to assemble, and to petition the Government for a redress of grievances."

At least insofar as it refers to communications, the First Amendment is about the press's right to publish. In order to publish, however, one must first gather information. As we know from various troubled times in U.S. history (e.g., the McCarthy period) as well as from difficult periods in the histories of other nations, such ability is often impeded by the government. Thus as we consider the issue of communications security and government surveillance, we must include the importance the U.S. constitution assigns to freedom of the press—and thus to freedom for journalistic investigations. This is a freedom that has not been without controversy.[40]

I have saved for last the most critical policy issue of all: privacy. Privacy is one of those ineffable matters, almost easier to define by its absence than its presence. Indeed, one could paraphrase Justice Potter Stewart's opinion on pornography:[41] one knows a privacy violation when one sees it. Yet despite its elusiveness, privacy is a fundamental aspect of a functioning human society, a clear necessity for human freedom and dignity. Privacy appears in Jewish law two thousand years ago, protecting the privacy inside a house by preventing neighbors from building in such a way that they may look in.[42]

Privacy includes the right to control information about yourself, the right to associate as you wish, as privately as you wish, to share confidence, in confidence, the right to enjoy solitude and intimacy. It includes the right to anonymity. It is not always possible to exercise these rights in modern society—of course, some of these rights were even more difficult to exercise in centuries past—but they are all aspects of the right to privacy.

For almost two centuries privacy was not explicitly part of U.S. jurisprudence; privacy is not, after all, distinctly discussed in the Constitution. The concept was not even part of legal discussion until it was framed in the famous Brandeis and Warren article written in 1890.[43] But over the last half century, the Supreme Court has recognized privacy as a basis for a number of court decisions. *NAACP v. Alabama*[44] protects the right to "privacy in one's associations"; the decision allowed members of the National Association for the Advancement of Colored People to keep their membership private at a time when public knowledge of their participation in the organization would have been dangerous. *Griswold v. Connecticut*[45] struck down the Connecticut law that prohibited the sale of contraceptives. The controversial *Roe v. Wade* decision[46] was based on the idea that the right of privacy was "broad enough to encompass a woman's decision whether or not to terminate her pregnancy."

Of course, what is of interest to us is communications privacy. Here the crucial protections are the Fourth and Fifth Amendments to the Constitution:

The right of the people to be secure in their persons, houses, papers, and effects, against unreasonable searches and seizures, shall not be violated, and no Warrants shall issue, but upon probable cause, supported by Oath or affirmation, and particularly describing the place to be searched, and the persons or things to be seized.

No person shall be held to answer for a capital, or otherwise infamous crime, unless on a presentment or indictment of a Grand Jury, except in cases arising in the land or naval forces, or in the Militia, when in actual service in time of War or public danger; nor shall any person be subject for the same offense to be twice put in jeopardy of life or limb; nor shall be compelled in any criminal case to be a witness against himself, nor be deprived of life, liberty, or property, without due process of law; nor shall private property be taken for public use, without just compensation.

On its face, the Fourth Amendment is about searching places, not such ephemera as conversation. But communication, whether oral, written, or, in the last century and a half, electronic, is fundamental to being human. The extension of constitutional protections to communications started with protections to written communications;[47] in 1937 the Supreme Court began extending similar protections to other forms of media. The right to privacy in electronic communications was firmly established in *Charles Katz v. United States*,[48] which protected the right to privacy of telephone calls.[49] This forms the backdrop of communication privacy protections for U.S. wiretap law.

Since the wiretapping case of Roy Olmstead in 1928,[50] the United States has been concerned with the threat that communications surveillance poses to civil liberties, with the discussion often coming down to a debate between security and freedom. I believe that this is an incorrect formulation of the issues, and that the appropriate one is between surveillance and security. The risks that communications surveillance pose to security are high indeed. It is to this subject I now turn, beginning with an introduction to communications networks and their security, continuing with a brief foray into U.S. wiretap law, then moving to the security risks that arise from building surveillance into communications infrastructures.

2 Communication Networks and Their Architectures

I have three telephones on my desk: a slim beige push-button model with redial and speed-dial buttons purchased in the late 1990s, a squat black 1950s "Modern Telephone"[1] with letters along the dial and a real bell inside, and a stripped-down Nokia cell phone. One phone is for my work line, one for my home line, and one for travel. Yet despite the diversity of devices and the half century that separates their manufacture, all work over the same network, commonly called the Public Switched Telephone Network or PSTN. While everyone knows that Alexander Graham Bell invented the telephone,[2] his more important work was the development of the network.

A telephone by itself is not worth much; its value lies in its ability to connect its user with others.[3] The Internet's broad functionality stretched the meaning of communications network. This chapter describes the history and technology of the Internet with two purposes in mind: explaining how it is that the network supports such a broad set of applications, and developing an understanding of why securing the network is so hard.

2.1 The Telephone Network

The first device to rely on a networked system was the telegraph. The telegraph functioned very differently from the telephone. For one thing, the telegraph was not for use by unskilled people; only experts (who knew Morse code among other things) could use the system.[4] As a result, although telegraphs were quickly taken up by businesses and other institutions,[5] they were not for home use. Nonetheless the networks for the two communications systems are similar.

Both are also similar to a network with a completely different purpose: the railroad. Such a similarity should not be surprising; the telegraph was not only modeled on the railroad, in many parts of the world early telegraph networks and railway systems were inseparable.[6] Telegraph wires traveled along railroad rights of way, railroad stations served as telegraph offices,[7] and the telegraph was used to let stations up the line know when the train would be in.

Telegraph networks were "decentralized": networks with hubs or clusters and with some, but limited, connectivity between the hubs.[8] Decentralized networks look like railroad connections between major cities and the suburbs. There are railway connections between a city and its suburbs, and between the cities, but typically there are no direct connections between one city's suburbs and another's. For example, all routes from Cold Spring Harbor, a Long Island suburb, to Boston require travel via New York City.

Decentralized systems, however, provide some redundancy of routes. To travel from New York to Boston, one could take the direct way through New Haven, or a completely distinct routing, perhaps through Albany and Springfield. (You might do the latter if the railroad bridge at New London were out.) A centralized system provides no redundancy; it is like a hotel switchboard. Everything—calls from one guest room to another, to the restaurant, front desk, concierge, and so on—is routed through the centralized switch. Figure 2.1 shows a centralized railway network and a decentralized subway network.

Initially networks were quite local. The subscriber would ring the local switch and tell the operator the name of the party with whom they wanted to speak. The first switches were manual, consisting of panels with jacks and cables between them. The operator would ring that party and then connect the two lines on the switchboard via patch cords. While the original operators were teenage boys, their antics soon made clear that more responsible people were needed, and young women became the telephone operators of choice.[9] A Missouri undertaker designed the first automated telephone switch.[10]

We tend to think of a phone number as the name of the phone at a particular location, but it is actually something else entirely. As Van Jacobson, one of the early designers of Internet protocols, once put it, "A phone number is not the name of your mom's phone; it's a program for the end-office switch fabric to build a path to the destination line card."[11]

Consider, for example, the U.S. telephone number: 212–930–0800. The first three digits—the area code—establish the general area of the phone number; in this case it is New York City. The next three digits, normally

Figure 2.1 (*opposite page*)
Centralized versus decentralized networks. Illustration by Nancy Snyder.

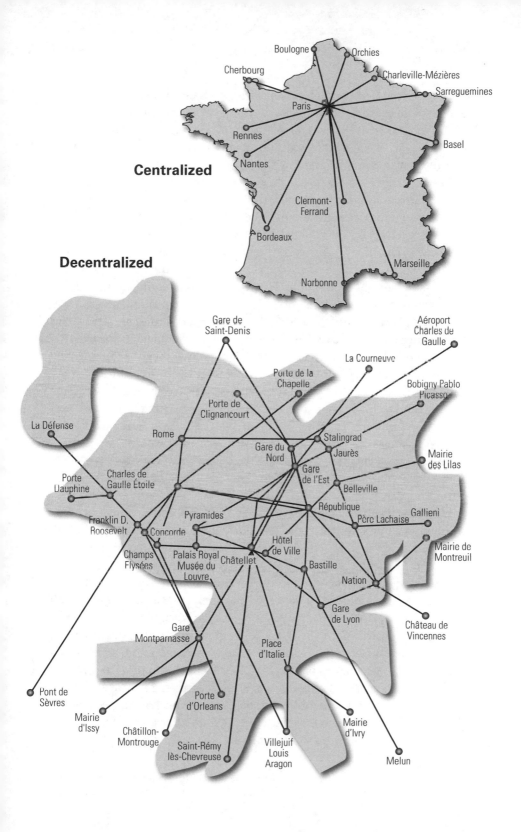

Centralized

Decentralized

called the telephone exchange, represent a smaller geographic area.[12] In our example the last four digits are, indeed, the local exchange's name for the phone. Taken as a whole, the set of ten digits constitute a route description; the switching equipment within the network interprets that information much like a program and uses it to form a connection.

The first thing a modern telephone—and I will start by describing just landline phones—must do is signal that it is "off hook" and thus ready to make a call. This happens when the receiver is lifted, which closes a circuit, creating a dial tone and signaling the *central office* (the local phone exchange). Then the subscriber can dial the phone number she wishes to reach ("dial," of course, being an anachronism from the era of rotary telephones). When the central office receives this number, its job is to determine where to route the call.

If the call is local—that is, within the same area code—then the switches at the central office need to determine which trunk line, or communication channel, should be used to route the call to an appropriate intermediate telephone exchange. This new exchange repeats the process, but this time connects to the recipient's local exchange. Since the first three digits denote the local exchange and are thus unnecessary, only the last four digits of the number are transmitted. The local exchange determines if the recipient's line is free; if so, it "rings" the line. If the recipient answers, her receiver closes a circuit to the local exchange, which establishes the call.[13] The speakers have a fixed circuit for the call, the one that was created during the call setup.

This is, of course, a simplified example: the call did not use an area code, let alone an international code. The other simplification is that the call described above had only two "hops"—that is, it only went through two telephone exchanges.

The key goal of the network design was to provide quality of voice service. Engineers needed to factor in that each time a call goes through an exchange, it needs to use a *repeater* to amplify the voice signal. Passing through a repeater causes the signal to change slightly. Thus the network needed to minimize the number of times a call would go through an exchange. The telephone company limits calls to five hops, after which it deems the degradation in voice quality unacceptable.[14] Digital signals do not face this problem and thus can travel through an arbitrary number of repeaters. This small engineering difference leads to a remarkable freedom in system design. Messages can traverse an arbitrarily long path[15] to reach a destination, enabling a more robust network.

The telephone system is built from highly reliable components. The telephone company believed in service that allowed a user's calls to go through ninety-nine times out of a hundred. Since central office switches served ten thousand lines, this meant "five 9s" reliability (otherwise the 1 percent blocking could not be satisfied). Of course, more than central office switches are needed to service a call that travels between two destinations with different central offices.

At the height of the Cold War, some engineers began thinking about reliability differently. After all, you might care less about talking to a particular person at a particular moment than about getting the message through eventually. That is, presuming the other party is in and willing to answer the phone, you might not be concerned about always being able to connect each time you dialed, but you might want to ensure that the message you are attempting to send eventually gets through. This was the problem that the designers of the Internet tried to solve.

2.2 Creating the Internet

In the 1960s, physicists had realized that the electromagnetic pulse from a high altitude nuclear explosion would disrupt, and quite possibly destroy, electrical systems in a large area. Any centralized communication network such as the phone system that the United States (and the rest of the world) used would be in trouble.[16] RAND researcher Paul Baran went to work on this problem.

Since the frequency of AM radio stations would not be disrupted by the blast, Baran realized the stations could be used to relay messages. He implemented this using a dozen radio stations.[17] Meanwhile, using digital networks, Donald Davies of the United Kingdom's National Physical Laboratory found another solution to the problem. Davies solved Baran's problem while trying to address a completely different question.

Davies was interested in transmitting large data files across networked computers.[18] The problem is different from voice communications. Data traffic is *bursty*: lots of data for a short time, then nothing, then lots again. Dedicating a telephone circuit to a data transfer did not make a lot of sense; the line would just not be used to its full extent[19] and, unlike with voice, a small delay is not a major issue in transmitting data files.

Both Baran and Davies hit upon the same solution. Redundancy in the network—multiple distinct ways of going between the sender and the recipient—was key. Such redundancy is surprisingly cheap to obtain. Say a network has redundancy 1 if there are exactly enough wires connecting the nodes so that there is one path between any two nodes; if there are twice as many wires, call that redundancy 2, and so on.[20] Trying experiments on more traditional communications networks, Baran ran simulations and discovered that with a redundancy level of about 3, "The enemy could destroy 50, 60, 70% of the targets or more and [the network] would still work."[21] The design resulted in a highly robust system.

The distributed networks that Davies and Baran had independently invented were to be even more decentralized than decentralized networks of earlier efforts. Network redundancy meant that paths might be much longer than the typical PSTN communication. Thus the communications signal had to be digital, not analog. That turned out to be a tremendous advantage. There was no need for the entire data transfer to occur in one large message; indeed, efficiency and reliability argued that the message should be split into small *packets*.

The idea was that when the packets were received the recipient's machine sent a message back to the sender saying, "OK; got it." If there was no acknowledgment, after a short period, the sender's machine would resend the packet. Of course, because the packets traveled by varied routes, they might arrive out of order. But the packets could be numbered, and the receiving end could simply sort them back into order.

One of the striking things about this proposed network was that while the network itself was to be extremely reliable, individual components need not achieve that same level of reliability. Instead the network depended on "structural reliability, rather than component reliability."[22] Small amounts of redundancy led to vastly increased reliability, a result surprising to the engineers.[23]

The Internet's decentralized control meant all machines on the network were, more or less, peers. No one computer was in charge; the machines were more or less equal and more or less capable of doing any of the communication tasks. A computer could be the initiator or recipient of a communication, or could simply pass a message through to a different machine. This is the essence of a *peer-to-peer* network, and very much the antithesis of the telephone company's hierarchical model of network communication.

In Britain, the telecommunications establishment supported Davies,[24] but in the United States Baran received a chilly reception from AT&T. Baran was turning all the ideas that AT&T had used to manage their system upside down. While scientists at the research arm of AT&T were quite excited by Baran's work, corporate headquarters viewed that approbation as the reaction of head-in-the-cloud scientists and refused to have anything to do with Baran's packet-switched network.[25] The odd thing about all this was that the new network was not actually a new network at all. Baran had built his network on top of the existing telephone network built by

Alexander Graham Bell and his successors. It "hooked itself together as a mesh,"[26] simply connecting everything in new ways.

Scientific and technological ideas often emerge when the time is ripe, and Baran and Davies were not the only ones to be considering packet-switched networks. (The actual term *packet* is due to Davies, who wanted to convey the idea of a small package.) In 1961, Leonard Kleinrock, then a graduate student at MIT, published the first of a series of papers analyzing the mathematical behavior of messages traveling on one-way links in a network. This analysis was critical for building a large-scale packet-switched network.

One could say, only partially tongue in cheek, that the Internet is due to Sputnik, the Soviet satellite that in 1957 startled the United States out of its scientific complacency. In response the U.S. government founded the Defense Advanced Research Projects Agency (DARPA), a Department of Defense agency devoted to developing advanced technology for military use.[27] The Internet grew out of an ARPANET project and was perhaps the most important civilian application that came from DARPA.

In 1966 DARPA hired MIT's Lawrence Roberts to build a network of different computers that all communicated with one another.[28] This would be a resource-sharing network. Each individual system would follow its own design with the only requirement being that the various networks be able to "internetwork" with one another[29] through the use of Interface Message Processors (IMPs). Designing the IMPs fell to a Cambridge, Massachusetts, consulting company, Bolt Beranak and Newman (BBN), one of whose researchers, Robert Kahn, moved to DARPA.

Kahn realized that only the IMPs would need a common language to communicate, and this greatly simplified the entire scheme. The other machines within the individual networks would not need to be transformed in any way in order to communicate with the rest of the system. These principles made so much sense that forty years later they still govern the Internet:

• Each individual network would stand on its own and would not need internal changes in order to connect to the internetwork.
• Communications were on a "best-effort" basis. If a communication did not go through, it would be retransmitted.
• The IMPs would connect the networks. These gateway machines (now known as routers and switches) did not store information about the packets that flowed through them, but simply directed the packets.
• All control would be local; there would be no centralized authority directing traffic.[30] (This model is essentially opposite to the PSTN architecture

of the time; there are many reasons for this difference, not all of them technical.[31])

With his colleague Vinton Cerf, Kahn developed the fundamental design principles and communication protocols for the network that became the Internet; they are the true "fathers of the Internet."

Kahn and Cerf developed the underlying protocol for end-to-end transmissions in 1973. It consisted of the Transmission Control Protocol (TCP) and the Internet Protocol (IP) and is usually simply abbreviated as TCP/IP. TCP determines whether a packet has reached its destination, while the IP address is a numeric address that locates a device on a computer network. Kahn and Cerf's original version of IP used 32 bits for the address; this is still in use today. As more and more devices connect to the Internet, the 32-bit address space, which allows for over four billion individual devices to be located on the Internet, is running out of room.[32] The new version of addressing, IPv6 (Internet Protocol version 6), has 128 bits for addressing, which increases the number of possible Internet addresses by a factor of 2^{96}, or more than a billion billion billion times as many.

Although the numbers used in an IP address are meaningful to a networking expert—to those in the know, an address of the form 18.*x.y.z*, where *x, y, z* are between 0 and 255, designates MIT—most people find the sequence of numbers largely incomprehensible. Instead people use names (such as www.mit.edu) rather than IP addresses to define Internet locations; machines around the Internet resolve these names into the numeric IP addresses.[33]

Internet routing is very different from PSTN routing. There is no restriction that a path take just five hops. More importantly, the routing of a communication is dynamic: packets travel whichever way is least congested and, in theory—though not often in practice—the different packets of a file transfer, VoIP call, email, or any other IP-based communication could each take different paths. Packet switching puts the destination address into each packet of data, and the Internet routers and switches constantly broadcast the best ways to get from here to there.[34]

The flexibility of the system engendered many uses. The original vision for the ARPANET was a resource-sharing research network, and users in one part of the network could employ a computer somewhere on the network to do their computation. By 1985, the network was not only a technology used for research and development, it was supporting forms of collaboration that the original designers had never anticipated.[35] Email was the surprising "killer app,"[36] an application of such great value that its use alone could be a reason for having the network.[37]

Network redundancy proved to be magic. "We had the realization that if there's an overload in one place, traffic will move around it," Baran recalled years later.[38] In other words, the network routes around problems. Redundancy provided even more. Increased size created increased reliability; indeed, redundancy increased exponentially with network size. No initial call setup work meant there was high efficiency at any bandwidth, holding time, or scale. And distributed routing could be deployed on any network topology (as long as all endpoints are connected to the network).[39] That last point means that anyone could deploy an Internet over an existing network. This was bad news for the telephone companies whose role was left to provide the physical infrastructure—and not much else.

2.3   Creating Other IP-Based Networks

ARPANET's success spurred the development of other networks,[40] some with quite different properties. The U.S. Department of Energy (DoE) set up MFENet for collaboration in magnetic fusion energy; DoE's high-energy physicists created one of their own: HEPNet. Academics started CSNET to enable academic collaboration. Other networks were developed with other purposes in mind. Two Duke University graduate students set up USENET, a forum for electronic discussion groups, while the Because It's There Net— BITNET—was started for universities to do email, file transfer, and so on. (CSNET, USENET, and BITNET are all "store-and-forward" networks, in which the data are stored in the transit machine until it receives an acknowledgment that the data has arrived at the next device in the network. This is unlike the Internet best-effort protocols.)[41]

In the mid-1980s the value of the ARPANET was clear, and it was time to bring the work to a new level. The U.S. National Science Foundation (NSF) had already connected the nation's supercomputing centers over what is now a very slow network: 56,000 bits per second. Now the NSF went a major step further: NSF built a high-speed national network connecting six supercomputing centers[42] to the ARPANET. (Supercomputers are machines that are super fast at the time they are introduced. They are often used for large scientific or military computations.) That was not all.

NSF decided to build a general-purpose research network,[43] and various existing regional and local academic networks connected to the system. The effort was an immediate success: in the first year the system needed an upgrade in order to cope with traffic. While it took the ARPANET ten years to reach a thousand computers, NSFNET went from two thousand computers at its start to more than two million in 1993.[44] NSFNET had one rule: traffic could be only for the purposes of research and education.

That limitation spurred private growth, including the development of companies like AOL, which provided a limited, "walled garden" approach to the Internet for the public. The growth inside and outside NSFNET demonstrated that commercialization was needed;[45] this occurred in the mid-1990s. This commercialized network—basically the same one we use today—is larger and faster than NSFNET, but relies on the same protocols.[46]

2.4 The Network Stack

To understand the insecurities of the network, it is necessary to delve a bit more deeply into the way communication occurs over the network. This section and related sections in the next chapter on security risks are more technical than other sections of the book, and some readers may choose to skip them.

Communications networks are described in terms of "layers," in which each layer has specific jobs (e.g., routing, transport). At their simplest, communications systems have two layers: physical and logical. The physical layer consists of the wires and cables that make up the communication system. These can be copper wires, fiber-optic cables, or even the wireless communications systems that are supplanting them in many parts of the world. (Many parts of the world had not built the wired infrastructure and so skipped over it in favor of completely wireless communications.) Both the PSTN and the Internet use this same type of physical layer. Indeed, they use the same type of transmission facilities, often sharing them, and they use the same type of electronic routing and switching devices to move communications through the network.

Recall that the two communications systems differ in the logical layers that direct how communications traverse the network. The PSTN establishes a circuit for a call and this circuit is used by the communication for the entire duration of the call. Internet communications are broken into packets and each packet is sent over the network individually. Packets from a single communication could follow different paths. They are subjected to the possibility of being subdivided into several smaller packets, or even dropped entirely, at the discretion of a router handling it. Because packets may arrive out of order, proper sequencing and reassembly of the packets into the original message are the responsibility of the receiving end, called a *network host* or simply a *host*.

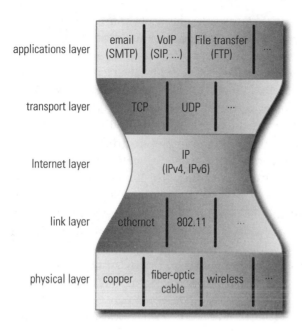

applications layer — email (SMTP) | VoIP (SIP, ...) | File transfer (FTP) | ...

transport layer — TCP | UDP | ...

Internet layer — IP (IPv4, IPv6)

link layer — ethernet | 802.11 | ...

physical layer — copper | fiber-optic cable | wireless | ...

Figure 2.2
Internet protocol stack. Illustration by Nancy Snyder.

Engineers talk about the Internet having a *protocol stack*; this model, shown in figure 2.2, simplifies envisioning the communication system. The bottom of the Internet protocol stack is the *physical layer*, consisting of the connections between nodes. Above this is the *link layer*, the logical layer that communicates with the actual physical hardware of the network. The link layer provides a simple program that moves data from one device in the network to the next. Then the question is which way a packet should exit a link. This is settled by the *Internet layer*, the next level of the protocol stack. There are various functionalities at the Internet layer,[47] but here I will focus only on packet routing. This is where the IP part of Cerf and Kahn's TCP/IP is implemented, using a device called a *router*.

A router is a simple computer connecting two or more networks. Each arriving packet has the numeric IP address of its source and destination. The router examines a packet's destination address and determines from this which link out of the router the packet should take. Of course, the router cannot possibly know all the best routes to all possible destinations (of which there are currently billions on the Internet). Instead the router knows something local: it knows the routers to which it is connected and it knows a little bit about where these are connected. The beauty of the

Cerf and Kahn protocol is that even though each router is mostly concerned only about the packet's next hop, packets make it to their destination efficiently.

Routers store routing information in routing tables. These tables are small databases, recording locations (addresses) of other network devices and the most efficient routes to them. Internet routing changes as new devices are added or taken off the network, new networks created, new ISPs linked to, communication links fail or are restored to service, and so on. Thus routing tables are constantly updated through the routers sharing new routing information with one another. (In this, the Internet differs from its predecessor, the PSTN, where such routing tables had been determined in advance by the phone company.) This on-the-fly updating provides a potential source of security problems, an issue I will discuss in the next chapter.

A typical routing table will have entries for many destination subnetworks. This table will include a cost for delivering the packet to a subnetwork via each of its neighboring routers. (There are many possible metrics for "cost," including bandwidth, number of hops, delay, reliability, and communications cost.) Because there are billions of potential destinations, routing tables cannot possibly list an entry for each possible destination. Instead they aggregate nodes into subnetworks that are numerically adjacent[48] and that share similar characteristics. This is sufficient to send the packet on its way to the next router, which is closer to the packet's destination. If the communication is TCP-based, the packets of a communication, whether it is email, Instant Messaging, or the contents of a web page, are numbered.

IP does routing on a best-effort basis; it does not guarantee packet delivery. Packets may be lost to congestion, insufficient bandwidth, and various hiccups in the network. IP also does not guarantee the packets will arrive in order. IP provides data transport without regard to the type of applications being supported or the type of communications technologies being used. The protocol constitutes the "narrow waist" of the Internet stack and this is its strength. By minimizing the number of service interfaces, the IP hourglass maximizes interoperability. This has been key to the innovation that has flourished on the network.[49]

TCP ensures reliability. TCP first determines whether all packets have arrived. It does so by gently letting the sender know about missed packets; if, for example, all packets up to number fifteen have arrived and then packet seventeen appears, TCP sends a message back to the source identifying packet fifteen as the highest-sequence number correctly received. Once all the packets are in, TCP reassembles the communication.[50] TCP monitors not only packet delivery but also network congestion. By examining what is happening to the connection between two machines, TCP can not only determine congestion, the protocol can do something about it. Once a TCP connection has been established, TCP controls the flow of data sent out to the network, increasing the flow when it appears that bandwidth is available, throttling back when it appears it is not. TCP does this through limiting the number of packets that it has sent out but for which it has not yet received an acknowledgment.[51]

Once packets are reassembled at the recipient's end, the user is in a position to do something with the transmission. But she needs a way to interact with the data—to read an email, transfer a file, browse a web page, Instant Message (IM). That is the role of an *application layer*. The programs to do so are developed by someone who does not have to know about transport on the Internet, or reassembling packets, or how the different devices sending the communications behaved (or even if the communication devices had changed from last month). All the application designer has to know is how to write a program to transform the packets into email, files, web pages, IMs, and so on. The simplicity embodied in the Internet's layered architecture means that applications can freely use the delivery functionality of the network while ignoring the mechanics of what is occurring at lower levels of the protocol stack.

2.5 Mobile Communications

When TCP/IP was being developed, there was no issue about IP addresses for portable devices: computers were big heavy objects that did not move. The IP address of a device stayed fixed because the device stayed fixed, and so did the network routes to it. The world has changed with the advent of laptop computers, tablets, and other portable devices. In many situations, the IP address for these devices is assigned dynamically, and it may be different each time the device connects to the network. This is true even if the device is connecting to the Internet from the same location; it happens because the local network through which the device is connecting is likely to have multiple addresses available to it.

While IP addressing can handle portability, it has some trouble with mobility. Being connected is a heavy-duty operation—it sends signals down the line that the IP address, which designates the physical location of the device, is such-and-such. An IP address, say for routing a piece of email or downloading a movie, needs to be stable for at least the duration of the data being transferred to it. That stability is quite complicated to achieve when the user is mobile, and the problem has not been fully solved yet. (What appears to be IP connectivity on a moving vehicle—for example, the web browsing now available on some planes—is actually a local IP network connecting to the Internet via a cell link. The IP address does not change as the device moves.)

If Internet communications have not fully sorted out how to handle highly mobile communications, another community had that problem— and solution—as its raison d'être. Cell phones allow users to communicate while moving. This is not always easy; for example, if the speaker is on a high-speed train, special technology is needed so that the call is not dropped.[52] There are two parts to enabling the mobility of cell phone users. Cell phones (called mobile phones in Europe) rely on a network of radio towers to transmit the communication. But a cell phone is not fixed in space and so the system also needs a way to determine that the user has paid for services. Thus each user is registered in a *Home Location Register* (HLR), a very large database that stores subscriber information (including to what services users are entitled) about all users in that home location. Users are assigned to a particular HLR based on their phone number.[53] That solves part of the problem, but, of course, cell phone subscribers are mobile. So as a subscriber moves about the network, information about the user's privileges on the network must also travel. Otherwise there is simply too much delay in completing calls while the network checks back with the HLR. In addition to the HLR there is a local, smaller database called the *Visitor Location Register* (VLR) that contains a portion of the subscriber's information.

Calls are handed from tower to tower as the phone subscriber moves during a conversation. These towers, or base stations, are divided into groups called *Location Areas*. When a cell phone is turned on, the phone identifies itself through its phone number to the nearest tower (note that unlike a telephone on the PSTN, a cell telephone number is definitely *not* a program used to define the phone's location). By checking in with the appropriate HLR (easy to determine from the phone number), the base station grants the phone service.

When a roaming phone is initially turned on, and maybe every thirty minutes after that, a signaling message is sent from the phone to the HLR.[54] This enables the HLR to route calls to the subscriber. The first time a roaming subscriber tries to make a call, the HLR is queried: to what services is the subscriber entitled? After that, the VLR is established in the new Location Area; all queries go to it, rather than the HLR. (This is why the initial call made while roaming may take longer to connect than subsequent ones.) A new VLR is created whenever a subscriber crosses into a new Location Area.

2.6 Voice on the Data Network

In the Internet, voice communications systems did not happen until several decades after written applications (such as email). There was one exception: in 1973 an engineering team led by Danny Cohen of the Information Sciences Institute (ISI) of the University of Southern California used the ARPANET to make calls between ISI and MIT Lincoln Lab in Lexington, Massachusetts.[55] At the time, the entire cross-capacity of the ARPANET was only two or three 56-kilobit lines, the equivalent of two or three dial-up modems. A voice call, which is very rich in data, could use up the entire capacity. Thus the issue was how to compress the data rate for voice calls way down. While current voice calls use about 64 kilobits for a call, the 1970s effort did the call using just 2 to 3 kilobits.[56] "Remember, the phone companies were looking over our shoulders laughing," Cohen recalled years later, "and our job was just to prove it could be done. We did."[57]

The network did not have reasonable bandwidth for voice calls until the mid-1990s. Speed was part of the problem. While emails can take a few seconds to transit their route and that presents no difficulty, people will drop a phone conversation if there is as much as a half second delay in transmission. Early versions of the network were too slow to support real-time voice compression that, in the 1970s, took two or three cabinets of cutting-edge electronics to achieve. Today's Internet is much faster than the ARPANET of three decades ago, and such compression is no longer needed. Voice communications over the Internet, known as VoIP, has arrived.

VoIP means that the voice conversation is routed over a network using the Internet Protocol. This network could be the Internet itself or it could be a smaller regional or local network. Though the communication is a real-time voice communication like a phone call, the technology is not like the PSTN. Unlike the dedicated circuit that is established for a telephone call, at some point during the call, a VoIP communication is converted into packets that are sent over an IP-based network and then reassembled at the endpoint.

The simplest form of VoIP—and the first to come onto the market—was transparent to the user. The caller uses a telephone to make the call which then travels, as it would normally, to the telephone company's central office. There the call is converted to a digital signal, sent over an IP-based network to its destination; at the final hop to the recipient, it may change to an analog signal (whether it does so depends on the type of phone and network being used). This is the model that Vonage employed.

Of course, there is no reason that the customer's telephone has to be an old-style voice phone; it could be a more modern IP-based telephone. To the user the device itself looks—and acts—like a telephone, but its innards and actions, as well as the connection to the outside world, are quite different. The telephone converts the signal from analog to digital and connects to a data network rather than the telephone network.

There is also a VoIP model that fully dispenses with the telephone; one uses a computer to make the call and the Internet is used for routing the communication (to another computer). This is how Skype[58] works, but Skype goes one step further. Skype is a fully peer-to-peer based VoIP system: any machine running Skype may be used in the transmission of another Skype user's call.[59] Skype is a realization of Baran's peer-to-peer model of communication. Just as the telephone company executives observed, this communication system turns the telephone network model upside down—leaving the utility to provide only the underlying wires.

The difference in networks means that the "phone" is not quite a telephone; this causes important differences. The telephone network is powered by electricity but because PSTN telephones are powered from the central office, the telephone network tends to stay up even when the electric power grid goes down. Another issue is that IP-based telephones can run into quality-of-service problems: if the network is being heavily used, communication quality can suffer. On the PSTN the situation is handled differently: either the call goes through and there is a steady connection or one hears: "All circuits are busy now. Please try your call again later." Yet another distinction is that Internet users do not necessarily know the IP address of the person they wish to "call" using VoIP. Because the Internet enables mobility, there is no "phone book" of IP addresses, which are often allocated dynamically. The user can have a different IP address each time they log on. In the space of an hour, the caller can move from a hotel lobby to a café to an airport lounge. Most VoIP systems use a rendezvous service that transforms a user identifier (e.g., a telephone number, screen name, email address) into the user's current IP address.[60]

2.7 Data on the Voice Network

While the Internet has enabled voice communications over what was originally a data network, the telephone network has gone the other way:

simplifying text transmission over a voice network. This is texting, also called SMS.[61] Texting arose from telephone signaling capabilities developed in the 1980s. Once call setup information traveled on the same channel as voice communications, but as communications systems moved to digital transmission, an out-of-band channel was needed for transmitting the signaling information. Thus Signaling System 6 (SS6), a packet-based digital protocol for network control, was developed in the 1970s; it has since been replaced by Signaling System 7 (SS7), which is more versatile. SS7 uses two conduits: a *Call Content Channel* (CCC) that is typically, though not necessarily, used for voice communications, and a separate call signaling channel, the *Call Data Channel* (CDC). This architecture enables such advanced telephony features as caller ID, call forwarding, and voice mail.

When the CDC is not in use, it could be put to other purposes. One such is enabling the transmission of short text messages between users; that is the essence of SMS.[62] SMS lets users send 140-character-long messages from the keypad of their cell phones.[63] It was introduced by European commercial carriers in 1993. The carriers did not use the same standard for texting, and originally text messages could not be sent between networks. Once that issue was resolved, texting took off. By 2003, over 70 percent of Europeans were using text messaging.[64] The telecommunications companies expected businesspeople to be the SMS users, but the biggest market for SMS turned out to be teenagers, a pattern echoed in other parts of the world.

Texting is popular in Asia, where adoption of personal computers lags far behind that of western Europe and the United States,[65] and the cell phone is the communications device of choice. One in three Chinese has a mobile phone, and China is responsible for over 300 billion SMS communications annually. The Asia-Pacific region and Japan sent an estimated 1.5 trillion messages in 2007,[66] and that number is only expected to grow. Everyone teenagers, families, businesspeople, commuters—uses text messaging. Japan was an early leader in texting. Japan's use is far broader than simple messages: five of 2007's bestselling novels were originally published via cell phones.[67] Japan's texting technology is, however, different from most other nations': it is IP-based rather than using cell phone technology.

Texting can be used for fun and games, but it is also used for business. That is its primary purpose in Africa. On a continent where transport and wired communications are unreliable, SMS technology is a true business enabler.[68] As is the case throughout the world, the asynchrony of text messaging is part of its attractiveness as a communications medium. Sometimes texting can be used for serious political business. In 2001, Philippine

President Joseph Estrada was ousted after hundreds of thousands of people, summoned to the streets by text messages, protested a vote that would have cleared the president of wrongdoing.[69] Even China, which carefully controls communication channels and political activities, has had political protests organized through texting.[70]

When it comes to text messaging, the United States is out of sync with the rest of the world. The U.S. marketplace-based approach to cell phones meant that unlike in Europe, there was no government mandate of a cell phone standard. Carrier interoperability for SMS messaging did not occur until 2002. Text messaging took off more slowly in the United States than it did in the rest of the world and is, relatively speaking, expensive.[71]

SMS is not without limitations. There is no guaranteed message delivery. Furthermore, depending on the type of routing the message takes, the text message may not receive the privacy protections of regular telephone communications but instead have only the lesser protections typical of email.[72]

2.8   Who Calls—and What Do They Communicate?

For a time, the telephone was the communications medium of choice. In 1960 people in the United States made about 100 billion domestic telephone calls[73] and only 42 million international ones annually.[74] By 1990 those numbers had increased to 402 billion and 984 million respectively.[75] In 2004, the increase was not particularly striking; the numbers went up, respectively, to 420 billion calls domestically and 10.9 billion overseas.[76] That was because Americans were turning to wireless: Americans used thirty-one billion minutes of wireless in 1995 and seventy times as much by 2008 (2.23 trillion minutes annually).[77] Meanwhile during the period from 1990 to 2004, more than 70 percent of the U.S. population began using the Internet.[78] Texting finally caught on, going from 75 billion text messages sent in 2005 to 600 billion in 2008.[79]

The design objective behind the PSTN was to maximize voice quality throughout the network. Depending on the language and emotions being expressed, human speech appears in many patterns, and the human voice in many timbres. Yet regardless of whether the conversation is in Chinese, Aramaic, English, or Hindi and whether the speaker is an adult male, a small child, a young woman, or an older one, speech and voices fall into a fixed acoustic range. The same PSTN equipment can be used in Beijing as in Bangalore without an effect on the quality of transmittal of the speaker's utterances. Data are simpler but more fluid. Bits are 0s or 1s, yet they can be used to represent nearly anything: a laundry list, an Instant

Message conversation, course grades in a database, a blueprint, a photo from Mars, the results from a search query, the census.

Because data varies tremendously, Kahn's design principles were simple: deliver the data and do so efficiently. Or to put it another way: assume the recipient herself will know how to maximize quality for her own particular application. That "the function in question can completely and correctly be implemented only with the knowledge and help of the application standing at the endpoints of the communication system"[80] came to be known as the *end-to-end* principle. It is the guiding principle of Internet design, and this essential idea underlies the network's versatility.

Application designers do not need to negotiate with the Internet developers or ISPs to launch an application; they just need a communications endpoint—a PC, a laptop, or even a cell phone—and they can be in business. Put another way, no changes were needed in the underlying Internet infrastructure to enable the most important Internet application of all: web browsers. All that took was the development of html, the computer language used to create documents on the web, and http, the protocol that enables linking and web browsing.[81] The same is true for other Internet applications, like VoIP, RSS feeds, and so on. And because html and http were made available patent and royalty free, in order to develop Amazon, Google, Flickr, or Facebook, engineers simply wrote code and launched.[82]

As a communications medium, the Internet has had an immediate and profound impact on public discourse. The network's decentralization of control means that anyone can publish. Indeed, the Internet makes possible Andy Warhol's claim that in the future everyone will be famous for fifteen minutes.[83] Similarly anyone can read. The Internet provides a forum for publication that virtually everyone in the world can access. By lowering the cost of participation, the Internet has changed the rules in virtually every domain of human commerce.

Instead of being a one-to-one communications channel as is supplied by the telephone,[84] the Internet allows one-to-many (blogs, YouTube, etc.) and many-to-many communication (Meetup.com). Of course the Internet did not introduce one-to-many communications—both radio and television broadcasts do that. The change the Internet has brought is that anyone with an Internet connection can be a broadcaster. The new technologies of publication such as blogs, photo-sharing sites, and so forth encourage the public to act as newsgatherers.[85] The general public has much more power and control than it had even a decade ago, although this is true only in nations where the Internet functions freely.[86] User-created content means that the voices of individuals are heard in a way unknown even a decade ago. Private citizens not only gather the news, they play a role in shaping it.[87]

The networking afforded by the Internet has enabled the growth of grassroots communities. One example of this in the United States is the political action committee MoveOn, which originated in 1998 as an email effort opposing President Bill Clinton's impeachment and quickly grew to an organization of three million.[88] Another involved priests who had sexually abused children over a period of years. New York University faculty member Clay Shirky looked at two cases, one in 1992 and one in 2002.[89] Both resulted in convictions, but the second created a national group of activist Catholics seeking fundamental change in the Church;[90] Shirky posits the Internet made the difference. The network simplified distribution of information and enabled members to network between meetings. Through lowered transactional costs—fast communications channels, uncomplicated one-to-many communications, an easy ability to share and forward information—the Internet is fundamentally changing society.

Various laws have been developed to describe this value—the value, of course, depends on what you choose to measure. A broadcast network, such as TV or AOL's network-based services, serves one user at a time, and so its value would be proportional to the number of users, or simply n for n members. Users interact with each other—they email, IM, and so on—and Metcalfe's law captures that aspect, describing the value of a network as proportional to the square of the number of users, or $n(n - 1)/2$.[91] Reed's law looks at the social groups that form, and claims the value of a network with n participants is 2^n, or the number of subgroups that can be created from this set of participants.[92]

A networking site can host all sorts of groups: people who live in Berkeley and like to play bridge, people who like to birdwatch at Tule Lake, and people who live in Berkeley, like to play bridge, and like to birdwatch at Tule Lake. (The ability of the networking site to easily create these groups is inherent in the flexibility of the Internet's end-to-end design.) Since the number of possible subgroups doubles each time a new member joins the site, this makes large networking sites very powerful. That easily draws in new members, but also makes it difficult for a competitor to pose a serious threat to an existing large site.

Network architecture enables new speakers and it encourages new connections. By erasing—figuratively and, of course, not completely—organizational boundaries, the network abets collaboration. Wikipedia, the online collaborative encyclopedia,[93] is one example. Perhaps an even more striking example is the open-source operating system Linux. (Open source means that the source code, which is written in a high-level language comprehensible to humans, is made public, enabling programmers to transform it if they so choose; closed-source programs, such as Apple's iPhone or the Microsoft operating system, show only the machine's "object code," which, because people find it incomprehensible, they cannot change.) Operating systems are huge, running to millions of lines of code. Until the early 1990s, these were developed by large teams of people. Linus Torvalds, at the time a twenty-year-old Finnish engineering student, changed that.

Torvalds posted to a mailing list that he was building an operating system kernel[94] (the central piece of the operating system that manages schedule calls, memory accesses, and the like) and could use some help. A month later the ten-thousand-line kernel was ready. Programmers liked the idea of collaborating on an open-source operating system. Linux[95] was developed through a collaborative effort started by Torvalds but with thousands of programmers across the world contributing code and bug fixes. By 2002, it was a system with over thirty million lines of code.[96] Linux arrived as the Internet was being transformed from a U.S.-based network supporting research and academic institutions to a much broader one.[97] New York University researchers Jac Yun Moon and Lee Sproull commented that "easy access to the Internet or its equivalent is a necessary precondition for the kind of distributed work represented by Linux."[98]

The Internet certainly enables large programming projects with thousands of contributors. The network's ability to aid production is broader than that. Worldwide access to the network allows a fundamental change in production of intellectual goods. It permits people to contribute even when their only reward is the pleasure of having done so. Of course, some problems are unlikely to particularly benefit from a very large set of contributors, but many other tasks—such as developing an open-source screen reader for people with visual impairments or finding cures for diseases— would be.[99]

As Yale law professor Yochai Benkler has observed, the Internet encourages nonmarket social production: "What characterizes the networked information economy is that decentralized individual action—specifically, new and important cooperative and coordinated action carried out through radically distributed, nonmarket mechanisms that do not depend on proprietary strategies—plays a much greater role than it did, or could have, in the industrial information economy."[100] The Internet has changed many playing fields.

2.9   Threats to the Network

The Internet has moved to the point where it is fundamentally changing modes of production. Just on the cusp of such bounty, the Internet's open architecture is under attack from multiple directions.

The network is being assailed by content owners—especially the music and movie industries—who find the combination of perfect copying that digital data makes possible with the ability to rapidly and broadly share that content a serious threat to their business. In a desire to hold onto a business and business model threatened by new technologies, some have sought to restrict the use of peer-to-peer communication systems.

In response to flourishing electronic crime and the difficulty of tracking criminals who may be halfway across the globe, a different set of concerns is being raised by law enforcement and lawmakers. They want to know who the bad guys are and shut their websites and computers down. In an effort to prosecute cyberintrusions and prevent new ones, some seek full attribution—knowing the party behind a communication—and authentication for network access.

The third objection to the Internet's design comes from national security and law enforcement. Their focus is on mobile, elusive enemies, who exploit the mobile and anonymous communications that the network enables. In an attempt to recreate the tools of the PSTN, they want to embed surveillance capabilities into communications infrastructure.

These are strong pressures. The Internet was once the playground of engineers, who could dismiss thoughts of criminal uses. The network's success has made it society's tool, increasingly under society's regulation. What will be the impact of these different pressures?

The challenge to peer-to-peer systems is unlikely to have much effect. Peer-to-peer architecture provides the Internet's robustness and enables the network to stay up during major disruption. The objections are not to peer-to-peer architectures, however, but to peer-to-peer file sharing. Any laws affecting peer-to-peer file sharing have to be carefully constructed, and that has not always been the case with proposed legislation.

While peer-to-peer file sharing enables the illegal sharing of music and movies, it also enables the distribution of large programs. BitTorrent, a program based on the clever idea of using downloaders of files as distribution sources, is used by NASA for dissemination of satellite images. It is also used by various computer companies for the distribution of large files such as operating systems; by established content providers including CBS, Twentieth Century Fox, and Sports Illustrated for delivering video programming to online viewers;[101] and by game companies for patch updates. The broad value of Internet peer-to-peer file sharing makes attempted legislative attacks on it unlikely to succeed.

The call for attribution is likely to have only a limited impact. Attribution compromises the openness of the network, and is likely to be valuable only in limited circumstances. As society debates whether to build surveillance capabilities into the Internet, we must weigh the costs. These include not only risks to civil liberties, privacy, and innovation, but also the serious danger that we will create serious security risks. It is time to explain why network security has been so difficult to achieve.

3 Securing the Internet Is Difficult

At a celebration marking the ARPANET's twentieth anniversary, Danny Cohen, one of the Internet "pioneers,"[1] provided a poetic description of the network's origins:

In the Beginning, ARPA created the ARPANET. And the ARPANET was without form and void. And darkness was upon the deep. And the spirit of ARPA moved upon the face of the network and ARPA said, "Let there be a protocol," and there was a protocol. And ARPA saw that it was good. And ARPA said, "Let there be more protocols," and it was so. And ARPA saw that it was good. And ARPA said, "Let there be more networks," and it was so.

Indeed it was so. Unfortunately rather more of the biblical story holds. Gaps in the network's security were a temptation in this Garden of Eden, and more than one user partook of the forbidden fruit. But I anticipate. Let the story unfold itself.

3.1 The Principles behind the Internet's Design

The network protocol was Kahn and Cerf's 1974 TCP/IP. Its simplicity enables complex procedures to be layered on top including protocols for web page exchange, secure communications, and downloads of audio and video. As I have described, with the ARPANET's success came other networks including the Internet.

Baran and Davies sought to build a reliable communications network for data transmission. They succeeded well beyond that. The network that developed from Baran, Davies, and Kleinrock's initial ideas augmented by Cerf and Kahn—and a host of others—has been transformed into a network on which society relies.

The Internet has become fundamental to business communication. Governments use the network to transmit information both internally and to the citizenry. The public uses the network multiple times a day to check a stock price, email or Instant Message a friend, or look up a restaurant review. Information in support of critical societal needs traverses the Internet. But the network of Baran and Davies lacks security, a problem that has come to haunt the Internet creators. The subject of this chapter is the inherent insecurity of the Internet's design and how this came to be.

3.2 Designing for Reliability and Availability

Cerf and Kahn do not mention security in their initial paper on the protocol enabling packet-switched networks to internetwork.[2] The two engineers were concerned about breakdowns, packet loss, drops in connection, and robustness.[3] The rationale for the network was that it would be a system linking researchers and scientists.

When Cerf and Kahn were initially developing TCP/IP, security was about reliability and availability, not targeted attacks. Security was not actually needed. Each computing company was using its own proprietary protocols on their internal networks. This provided a modicum of security: problems on one network could not easily propagate to become problems on another.[4] This is an instance of security through obscurity, a method of making attacks difficult by hiding how a system works. Security through obscurity is not considered a wise way to proceed, because experience has shown that the best method for finding a system's security flaws is through public examination.[5] The adoption of the TCP/IP protocol by a wider audience occurred in several steps. First TCP/IP was the protocol designed for transmission on the ARPANET. Then the National Science Foundation (NSF) decided to build a network to link scientific researchers with supercomputer centers around the country. This proved to be the tipping point for the Internet, though no one foresaw this at the time.

"We were building a research network for the U.S. research community, and perhaps also for the research community in industry," explained Dennis Jennings, who had been the program director for networking within NSF's Office of Advanced Scientific Computing during the building of NSFNET.[6] "Our budget was limited. What every researcher wanted us to do was build a network to his or her computer or workstation, but that didn't scale." NSF proposed a three-level hierarchy of networks: campus networks, regional networks, and a backbone network. This was a network of networks, as it were. While individual researchers were not pleased about connecting to a campus network, "interestingly campuses were thinking about networks and they all seized on this [idea]. The stuff took off like wildfire," said Jennings.

Only one protocol could link the networks in a way that allowed computers running different networking systems to communicate: Cerf and Kahn's TCP/IP. Some objected: researchers running IBM mainframes wanted to use the IBM networking protocol, while those running DEC VAX sought the use of DEC's protocol, and so on. NSF prevailed and TCP/IP was adopted.

No one envisioned that NSF's decision would lead to the Internet becoming a national network. TCP/IP's utilization by the larger constituency did not prompt any work on improving the protocol's security. DARPA's focus was on protecting communications on the Internet, rather than on protecting the network infrastructure itself.[7]

The security services that preoccupied DARPA at the time were confidentiality, protecting communications against eavesdropping; integrity, ensuring that communications had not been tampered with; and authenticity, ensuring that the sender being claimed is in fact the originator of the message.

A principal user of encrypted communications was the Navy, which found it far cheaper to use the Internet for communications between Washington and Hawaii than to rent a leased encrypted line.

There was no focus on such attacks as spam, viruses, and the like.[8] Trust was built in, in the sense that the network was a network for research and education, and everyone was viewed as everyone else's friend or colleague. This turned out to be a mistake. Or as retired NSA technical director Brian Snow[9] put it at a scientific meeting in 2007, "[With the Internet] there's malice out there trying to get you. When you build a refrigerator, you have to worry about random power surges. The problem is that [Internet] projects are designed assuming random malice rather than targeted attacks."[10]

Security was simply not viewed as a serious problem for the new communications systems. No one anticipated needing to protect the network against its users, and so no explicit mechanisms were built in to protect the network. After all, attacks had never been a serious problem on the telephone network. The fact that this did not carry over to the new network was because of the differences I have discussed in the two communication networks, but this was not considered at the time.

Essentially the only devices that could be connected to the PSTN were telephones. Because telephones are not multipurpose devices and cannot be programmed to do other tasks, the only serious network attacks the phone network suffered were "blue box" attacks: users, or devices, whistled in the phone receiver at the correct frequency,[11] tricking the network into providing free long-distance calls.[12] Signaling System 6 thwarts this through "out-of-band" signaling, in which the call-signaling information is transmitted through a different channel than the voice communication.

In contrast with telephones, computers are "smart" devices capable of being programmed to do many interesting things. That tremendous benefit can, however, be a problem when this malleability is turned against the network itself. This was not something that the ARPANET designers considered.

The PSTN designers opted to handle the problem that systems for data transfer, whether human speech or file transfer over an electronic network, are unreliable[13] by building a system out of highly reliable components. Early Internet architects went in the other direction and opted for reliability achieved through redundancy. TCP/IP assumes an unreliable data delivery mechanism, IP, and then uses a reliable delivery mechanism, TCP, on top of it. TCP has various mechanisms to ensure this reliability, including congestion control, managing the order of packets received to ensure none are missed, and opening the connection in the first place. The latter is worth discussing in some detail.

There is a handshake between the two connecting machines establishing their communication; there are messages that flow back and forth establishing that packets have been received; and the two machines measure the time elapsed between such acknowledgments, resending if there has not been a timely response.

Suppose user Alice wants to view an article from *Scientific American* on how magic fools the human brain.[14] Her machine, the client, makes a request to the computer hosting the *Scientific American* web page stating it wants to establish a connection (figure 3.1). This is the synchronization message, or *SYN*. The *Scientific American* server then responds with a synchronization acknowledgment: *SYN ACK*. If all is working correctly, Alice's machine replies with an acknowledgment of its own, *ACK*, and the connection is established. The server downloads the *Scientific American* home page onto Alice's client. The *Scientific American* home page contains more information, and this step is actually a sequence of many small steps: a large number of packets have to flow across the network from the *Scientific American* server to Alice's machine.

The *Scientific American* server starts sending packets and Alice's machine acknowledges receiving them. If the server does not receive packet acknowledgments within a fixed time window, the server resends the missing packets. Both machines have timers operating; if appropriate acknowledgments are not received in a timely fashion (a matter of milliseconds), then the packets (or request for packets) are automatically resent. Once the

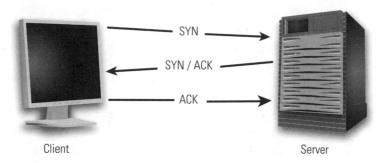

Figure 3.1
Client/server interaction. Illustration by Nancy Snyder.

Scientific American server has received an acknowledgment that the last packet has been received, it closes the connection to the client; that connection session is terminated.

Now that Alice has received the web page at her machine, she starts to search for the article she wants. Alice types in the appropriate keywords (e.g., magic brain) in the search field on the *Scientific American* web page. When she clicks on the "search" button on the web page, the connection process starts afresh. Alice's client opens a connection with the *Scientific American* server, sends it information ("Perform a search query on 'magic brain'"), and the connection process begins (handshake, connection establishment), followed by packet exchange and then connection teardown.

Note that the *Scientific American* server did not "know" Alice before establishing a connection with her machine. TCP does not require any form of authentication of the user before connections are established. For the research environment for which TCP was developed, this made good sense. The network's purpose was sharing information and authentication was an unnecessary complication that would have been difficult to implement. (By contrast, the phone company did care about authenticating the call originator because that is who pays for the call.) Authentication would also not easily scale. Requiring an introduction before a connection could be made would have prevented the growth that the network experienced between the early 1990s and the present.

The real point here is that while the Internet is a communications network, it is a communications network that behaves nothing like the telephone network. For some applications such as email, IM, and Voice over IP conversations, an introduction prior to communication might make sense. But many other applications function more like a store or library (a library with no requirement for signing out borrowed materials). For those, an introduction is not only not valuable, it is actually disruptive. Alice's browsing of the *Scientific American* website or her browsing of books and their reviews at Amazon, do not—and should not—require an introduction before the connection is established. Even the first examples I mentioned, email, IM, VoIP, would have difficulty with an introduction prior to establishing a TCP connection because of Internet-enabled mobility. The IP address Alice's machine has today in the coffee shop is different from the one it had yesterday at the airport, and it will be different again tomorrow even if Alice frequents the same coffee shop (unless the coffee shop has only one IP address available, an unlikely situation). Yet it is the IP address that is the identifier in the TCP/IP protocol. By contrast, Alice's mobile telephone has the same number[15] regardless of whether she is in Paris, Texas, or Paris, France.

In deciding to adopt TCP/IP for NSFNET, "Our ambition in 1985 was to have all three-hundred-and-four research universities connected to NSFNET by the end of 1986 or early 1987," said Dennis Jennings, who ran the NSF program that built NSFNET. In that respect, the NSF succeeded spectacularly. "Had we any idea that this would be the network for the world, we probably would have had to go to the PTTs [Public Telegraph and Telecommunications] or ISOs [International Standards Organizations]. Certainly the PTTs would have designed a hierarchical system and would have built in authentication."

Had that occurred, it is likely that the result would have been more secure than the current Internet. It is also likely that the resulting network would have lacked the openness and capability for innovation that have made the Internet so remarkably fruitful. Jennings observed that "had we known [what was to come], we'd have been terrified and the Internet [would never have happened]." Jennings paused as he reflected on those decisions made in the mid-1980s. "And we would have said, 'That's not within scope; we're building a research network for a research community.'"[16]

3.3   Cryptography to the Rescue?

For a long time people believed that once strong cryptography was available, the solution to Internet security would be at hand. While this is not true—security is much more than simply encryption—it is the case that cryptography is a basic tool for many Internet security problems. I will take a brief detour to describe aspects of cryptography that play a role in

Internet security; for learning the material in appropriate depth, the interested reader is urged to consult one of the large number of books on the subject.

Cryptography, encoding messages so that only the intended recipient can understand them, is nearly as old as written communication. A Mesopotamian scribe hid a formula for pottery glaze within cuneiform symbols, while a Greek at the Persian court used steganography, or hiding a message within another, to send a communication. The fourth century BCE Indian political classic, the *Arthasastra*, urged cryptanalysis as a means of obtaining intelligence. The Caesar cipher, used by Julius Caesar to communicate with his generals, shifts each letter of the alphabet some number of letters "to the right." Thus a Caesar shift of 3 would be: a $\rightarrow$ D, b $\rightarrow$ E, ..., y $\rightarrow$ B, z $\rightarrow$ C.

Cryptography holds within itself an inherent contradiction: the system must be made available to its users, yet widespread sharing of the system increases the risk that the system will be compromised. The solution is to minimize the secret part of the cryptosystem. A nineteenth-century cryptographer, Auguste Kerckhoffs, codified a basic tenet of cryptography: the cryptosystem's security should rely upon the secrecy of the key—and not upon the secrecy of the system's encryption algorithm.

The difficulty of breaking a secure system should roughly be the time it takes for an exhaustive search of the keys. The Caesar cipher, with its simple structure and simple key—if one can call the "3" of "shift three letters to the right" the key—is easy to break. More sophisticated ciphers, including transposition ciphers and more sophisticated substitution ciphers, were developed in the fifteenth century. By the nineteenth century, cryptography had become part of popular lore, turning up in such literature as "The Adventure of the Dancing Men" by Arthur Conan Doyle and "The Gold Bug" by Edgar Allen Poe. Despite its long history, cryptography was more a curiosity than a valuable tool. Radio and its transformation of warfare made cryptography important.

Radio's ability to essentially instantaneously traverse great distances gave military commanders tremendous flexibility. Generals and admirals no longer had to be in the thick of battle to learn what was occurring; they could be updated almost instantly from anywhere reachable by radio from the field. The advantage of radio communications was that one could transmit anywhere, but the disadvantage was large: anyone could listen in.[17] For radio to be beneficial to the military, all field communications had to be encrypted.

Ciphering was slow and backlogs of material were common;[18] the solution was mechanization. In the period after World War I, there were a number of inventions related to cryptographic encipherment. Gilbert Vernam, an AT&T engineer, designed a system in which the key was marked on a tape and fed into an enciphering mechanism, which automatically combined the key with the message.[19] The original system developed by Vernam had one flaw: too short a key. The system was vulnerable to frequency analysis, which relies on the fact that within each language there is a well-known distribution of letters.[20]

An Army major, Signals Corps member Joseph Mauborgne, modified Vernam's system to produce a very long key. Encrypting with this key, once and only once—it is known as a *one-time pad*—is a secure method of encryption;[21] it is truly unbreakable. This is because any message can be decrypted into any other of the same length. The reason one-time pads are not widely used is the problem of key distribution. The amount of key used in encoding a message is exactly the length of the message. If participants can securely share the key ahead of time and only a few, short messages need to be transmitted, one-time pads work exceedingly well. Otherwise they fail to solve the problem of secure communications.

German engineer Arthur Scherbius designed a rotor machine, an electromechanical device consisting of a set of rotors[22] or wheels with electrical contacts on each side of the rotor producing a complex substitution cipher. This was the famed Enigma. Multiple wheels gave *polyalphabetic substitution ciphers*, in which multiple substitution alphabets are used for encryption: the first alphabet is used to encode the first letter of the unencrypted message, the second for the second letter, and so on.[23] The complexity of the Enigma's encryption scheme seemed to make decryption impossible without the key.

Enigmas came into commercial use during the 1920s, but their important deployment occurred during World War II. Initially the German military used three-rotor Enigmas, later replacing them with four-rotor versions. The encryption provided by these devices was daunting for the Allies to break, but an impressive combination of mathematical skill, computational power, periodic German misuse of the machines, and some determined efforts to obtain encryption keys[24] meant that the British were able to decrypt a high percentage of Enigma-coded messages.

If radio was the driver for cryptography's use by the military, collection and distribution of sensitive, unclassified information by the U.S. government drove cryptography's adoption in the public sector. By the early 1970s, the U.S. government realized it needed to protect the sensitive civilian data that it was electronically transmitting and storing.[25] In the mid-1970s the Data Encryption Standard (DES) became a federal information processing standard. U.S. civilian agencies were to use the algorithm for secure transmission and storage of unclassified but sensitive data.

DES was an algorithm with a 56-bit key, a controversial choice at the time. A number of cryptographers argued that DES's 56-bit key size was too small.[26] If DES was, in fact, secure, then the time to break a DES-encrypted algorithm should have been about 2^{55} steps.[27] That was far too large a problem to be solved quickly in 1975, but Moore's law, which roughly says that computing power doubles every two years, spelled trouble for DES. By 1998, the speed of computing had sufficiently increased that the Electronic Frontier Foundation was able to build a $250,000 special-purpose computer that decrypted a DES-encoded message in fifty-six hours.[28] By then the U.S. government was taking steps to replace DES. In 1997 the National Institute of Standards and Technology announced a competition for a DES replacement and algorithms were submitted from around the world. The winner was the Belgian-designed Advanced Encryption Standard (AES), with key lengths of 128, 192, and 256 bits. This became DES's successor and has been widely adopted throughout the world.

DES and AES are *private-key* or *symmetric-key* cryptosystems; the same key is used for encryption and decryption. The problem of securely transmitting the key to cryptosystem users is a problem that has bedeviled many designers of encryption systems. It is one thing if the system is being developed for use in a known, relatively small, community, whose members have had some secure way of communicating prior to using the algorithm to encrypt the message (such was the case for the Navajo code talkers in the Pacific[29] or the resistance fighters flown into occupied Europe by the British in World War II[30]). It is quite another if the encryption system is to be utilized by a large, dynamically changing set of users—for example, people using the Internet for doing ecommerce with Amazon or eBay. In that case, there needs to be a way to exchange an encryption key, but how do you securely transmit a key if the network is subject to eavesdropping?

In 1976 computer scientists Whitfield Diffie and Martin Hellman proposed a remarkable solution: *public-key cryptography*. The method relies on two keys: a widely known *public key* issued for encryption, and a privately held one, the *private key*, used for decryption. Diffie and Hellman's idea is based on complexity: some mathematical problems are easy to compute but their inverse appears computationally difficult.[31] Integer multiplication and the inverse problem, factoring integers into their prime factors, seem to be one such pair. While multiplying two large prime numbers can be done quickly,[32] the time apparently required[33] to factor an integer into its prime factors is significantly greater.

Public-key cryptography allows two parties who have not previously communicated to establish a secure communication link over an insecure channel. If Alice is sending a message to Bob, she encrypts her message using a publicly known algorithm and Bob's public key. Bob uses his private key, *known only to him*, to decrypt the message. Public-key cryptography is the enabler of many things digital. Undoubtedly the widest use is for key exchange for secure web sessions (https). Other uses include encrypted email and virtual private networks (VPNs), which securely connect remote users to the inside of a protected network (they do this through creating a private, encrypted channel to a server on the protected network). While the Internet's dramatic expansion since the early 1990s is due to the openness of the TCP/IP architecture, the ability to secure communications, which public-key cryptography supports on an Internet-wide scale, was undoubtedly the network's ecommerce enabler—and thus its other driver.

Because it is easy to make a perfect copy of digital material, it is somewhat counterintuitive that there might be a message-dependent way to sign digital material that could not be forged. Diffie and Hellman's other achievement was digital signatures, electronic signatures that do exactly that.[34] These use public-key cryptography to provide authentication in a digital environment. To sign, Alice encrypts a cryptographically created shorter version of her message with her private key and appends this signature to the communication. When Bob receives the message, he uses Alice's public key to decrypt her message-dependent signature. Because only Alice has the key to enable signing this cryptographically shortened form of the message, only Alice was able to have signed the message. Thus Alice cannot successfully later deny that the signature is hers; this is called the property of *nonrepudiation*. By comparing the decrypted signature with his own computation of the cryptographically shortened version of the message, Bob can discover whether any alterations have been made to the message in transit, thus ensuring the message's integrity.

Having spent the 1970s through the 1990s first opposing public research in cryptography and later the deployment of strong cryptographic algorithms in nonclassified settings,[35] in June 2003 the NSA approved the use of AES as a "Type 1" algorithm, meaning it could be used in protecting classified information.[36] This development was quite striking. Given the ability to use AES for the protection of classified information, this meant security equipment manufacturers would now have two markets with systems supporting AES: the national security one[37] and the civilian one.

AES is one piece of securing a communications network, but to function effectively, the system must also have algorithms for establishing keys for the secure communication, for digital signatures (to ensure authenticity), and for performing message-integrity checks. In 2005 NSA put forward "Suite B," comprising a full set of algorithms to do exactly that. Suite B includes AES; Elliptic-Curve Diffie-Hellman, a public-key algorithm for securely establishing keys; Elliptic-Curve Digital Signature Algorithm, an algorithm for signing documents in a manner that cannot be repudiated; and the Secure Hash Algorithm, a function for converting variable-length inputs to fixed-length outputs that enables the establishment of message integrity.[38] Without fanfare, the NSA had endorsed the idea of widespread availability of end-to-end encryption for communications. It would take time to get there, of course. The public, while in principle wanting private communications, in practice appears willing to make it private only if the system is simple to use, does not affect the communications by slowing them down or degrading quality, and cheap (as in little or no cost to the user). Thus, for example, when the default settings for Google's gmail were for unsecured communications—a situation that changed in January 2010—few people bothered to turn on encryption and secure their email even though doing so took minimal effort.

During the period when DES became a standard and public-key cryptography was developed, concerns were over communications security: protecting the confidentiality, integrity, and authenticity of the transmission of messages. Time was to show, however, that attacks on the Internet had a completely different—and quite unexpected—flavor. Public-key cryptography could not solve, at least on its own, the problem of authenticity: How could you know with whom you are communicating? If you have a way of connecting Alice with her public key, you can ask Alice to sign her messages. What if you have never met Alice? How do you know that it really is Alice, and not A1ice (the second "Alice" actually has a "1" instead of an "l" as the second "letter" in her name)? This issue of establishing identity, only rarely a problem for the PSTN,[39] turned out to be a more complicated problem for the Internet than any of the original DARPA engineers might have imagined.

3.4   Attacks on the Internet

As the network moved from being a small DARPA effort to supporting a much broader NSF constituency, the researchers were caught short by an unexpected event: the 1988 "Morris worm."[40] Written by Cornell University graduate student Robert Morris Jr.,[41] the worm was a self-replicating program that spread from machine to machine. The resulting congestion brought down about 10 percent of the network as it then existed.[42]

The program was designed so that as soon as the worm was on one computer, it would attempt to open a connection to another. That it could do so was the result of Cerf and Kahn's internetworking. Once the program succeeded in opening a connection, it would find one of several vulnerabilities and copy itself to the new computer. Then it would repeat the process. Unlike some worms, which corrupt and may even destroy other files on the system, the Morris worm was relatively benign. But although it did not attack files, its self-replication caused an exponential increase in the number of copies, and this clogged the system.

Whether the Morris worm was an experiment gone awry or something with more sinister intent, it nonetheless marked a "boundary between the largely trusting Internet of the time and the heterogeneous, dangerous worldwide Internet of today."[43] Morris's attack on the network thrust both him and the Internet out of Eden.[44]

Since then attacks have proliferated. Solutions to prevent them are not easy to come by. Attacks like the Morris worm rely on unpatched vulnerabilities in the network hosts (endpoint computers) and simply use the Internet as a distribution method. Another type of attack is on the Internet infrastructure itself. Routers are one source of such problems. Keeping routers functioning properly is fundamental to the Internet's smooth running.

Recall that routers continually update each other with the best routes to distant hosts. If a routing table is deliberately misconfigured—poisoned—this error will propagate to other routers, so packets will be misrouted through the network. The system ends up with too many packets on a particular link or packets going round in an infinite loop, repeating and repeating their path. The network becomes congested and unreliable.[45]

Yet another source of problems arises from the popularity of the network and the difficulty of knowing addresses of all the sites one may have occasion to visit. IP addresses are very difficult for people to remember. Originally the mapping of names to addresses was done by having a copy of a file on every computer on the network listing all computers and their corresponding IP addresses. This was not sustainable once the network grew.

Name lookup turns out to be a surprisingly difficult problem. It is also an extremely important one to get right. If you enter your name and password on a site purporting to be bankofamerica.com but actually is a criminal fake to which you have been misdirected, the result could be quite unfortunate. Because of the importance of doing such name direction correctly, I will explain this issue in some detail.

In 1983 Paul Mockapetris developed the Domain Name Servers (DNS) system to enable names to be translated to IP addresses (and vice versa).[46] Propagating that information through the network, which is necessary if your machine is to communicate with an arbitrary one on the network, requires a complex infrastructure to do the translation. DNS introduced hierarchical domain names and a system for distributing the mappings between host names and IP addresses.

To manage the mappings between names and IP addresses, DNS allows the mappings to be divided into contiguous regions called *zones*. Zones can be subdivided into smaller zones. This means that zones are a naturally hierarchical construct.[47] When a zone is created, responsibility for the mappings it holds are delegated to multiple nameservers, which are *authoritative* for the zone. Servers authoritative for a zone assert that the mappings that they have for a zone are correct.

Nameservers can store the mappings for multiple zones (some authoritatively, some not), as well as individual mappings that are stored as a result of earlier lookups. Because of the size of the network, the number of mappings that exist is extremely large, so it would be impossible for any one nameserver to hold all such mappings at once. Instead, nameservers have the ability to traverse the known parts of the hierarchy and find the parts they need.

At the top of the hierarchy are replicated nameservers for the "dot" or "." domain. These are called the *root nameservers*, and they are authoritative for "top-level domains," such as .com, .gov, .org, .jp, and .uk. In turn, there are top-level DNS nameservers, which are authoritative for their own zones. Thus, for example, the .com nameservers will be authoritative for the IP addresses for the various .com domains (e.g., amazon.com, cnn.com, google.com, etc.), while the .uk nameserver will be authoritative for the various .uk domains (ac.uk, co.uk, etc.). The google.com nameserver would be authoritative for the IP addresses for the various google.com domains (e.g., images.google.com, mail.google.com, maps.google.com, etc.). The model recurses down.

The model in figure 3.2 is called a "distributed hierarchical database" because each DNS nameserver holds a database mapping DNS names to their IP addresses. In 2009 there were, for example, thirteen root servers. As shown in figure 3.3, ten were in the United States, one in the United Kingdom, one in Sweden, and one in Japan.[48]

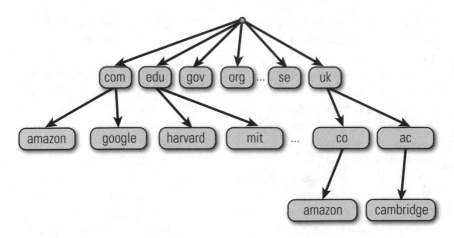

Figure 3.2
Distributed DNS hierarchy. Illustration by Nancy Snyder.

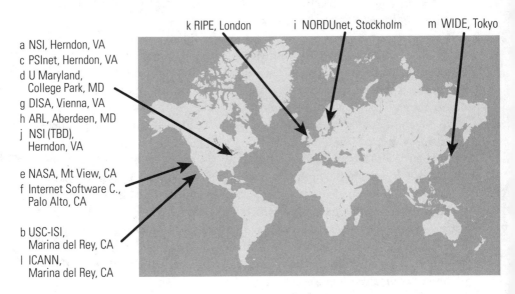

Figure 3.3
Location of root DNS servers (nonreplicated). Illustration by Nancy Snyder.

The astute reader will have noticed a problem. It cannot be the case that the root nameservers are consulted each time the DNS nameserver seeks a numeric IP address for a domain name. Instead, each lookup is cached—stored—for a certain period of time[49] and the cached result is used for other queries that occur during that period.

If the user (or really, the user's application) wants the IP address of maps .google.com, the query goes to a *DNS resolver*, a machine that resolves the URLs into IP addresses, within the user's local system. In the case of a home user, this would be the ISP; in the case of a user at a large business, it is likely to be a DNS resolver within the local network. If this DNS resolver has the IP address cached, the DNS resolver will respond with that address. Otherwise the resolver has a list of DNS nameservers it can query. It picks one[50] and sends a query to a local DNS nameserver. If the local DNS nameserver has the address for maps.google.com, it will supply the address to the DNS resolver, which then returns it to the application. Otherwise the local DNS nameserver will query a DNS nameserver with authoritative information about "google.com" for the address of "maps.google.com."[51] A nameserver that is authoritative for google.com[52] will have the IP addresses for all google.com subzones, including maps.google.com, images .google.com, mail.google.com, and so on.

The local DNS nameserver may not know how to reach an authoritative server for the google.com zone. Then the local DNS nameserver will go "up" one level in the hierarchy and send a query to a DNS nameserver that is authoritative for the .com zone,[53] asking for the IP address of google. com. If the local DNS nameserver somehow did not know how to reach an authoritative nameserver for the .com zone—this is unlikely, but possible—the local DNS nameserver would continue up the hierarchy. It would go to the authoritative "root" DNS nameserver, called the server for "dot" or ".", and ask for the IP address of the authoritative ".com" DNS server.[54] Finally the DNS nameserver would recurse back through its own unanswered queries, resolving them. First it asks the authoritative.com DNS nameserver for the IP address of google.com. Then the local nameserver uses the answer to that query and asks the authoritative nameserver for google.com for the IP address for maps.google.com. Finally it would return that IP address to the local DNS resolver, which in turn would provide the response to the application. Despite the complexity of the algorithm, the local resolver will typically have the answer in under a few seconds.

Even so, not everything is rosy in this solution. Caching of IP addresses creates a potential security problem, indeed a very serious one.[55] There are various ways a DNS nameserver can be fooled into accepting a false IP address for a site. A survey reported by David Dagon et al. found that 2.4 percent of the DNS servers they examined responded with incorrect answers.[56] This is surprisingly high, but the number should be viewed in context. In China, for example, DNS resolution is correct only 81.5 percent of the time[57] (this was the largest fraction of incorrect responses; it is clearly not accidental). Some of the misdirections are to protect the user—for example, OpenDNS prevents users from going to known phishing sites.[58] Regardless of whether the misdirection is actually in the user's interest, that the user can be secretly misdirected is highly disturbing.

DNS misdirections are possible because messages to DNS servers are not digitally signed (thus proving they came from a legitimate site). If a user types in a URL, say www.bankofamerica.com, but encounters a DNS name-server whose cache has been poisoned, the user could end up not at the Bank of America website but at a web page that looks as if it is the Bank of America website, but is in fact a bogus site. Such a fake site could be set up to collect password and account information.

Of course, the same problem could conceivably happen in the physical world: a customer could walk into a storefront that looked like a Bank of America branch, but that was actually a fake banking office. In practice, the latter situation is highly improbable. The cost of building such an office, the permits that would be needed, and so on, make such an event unlikely.[59] An extension to the DNS protocol, DNSSEC, eliminates the problem of spoofing the IP address; a number of implementation issues have prevented DNSSEC from being widely deployed.

Another problem, not with the Internet protocols themselves, but rather with the difficulty of transferring human experience to an online world, arises from the spoofing that can occur when a fake address mimics a well-known site, such as www.paypa1.com for www.paypal.com. Such spoofing is often the basis of a *phishing attack*[60] in which the user receives an email with a link purportedly to the genuine site—PayPal—but that is actually a link to its mimic. The user who clicks on the link is taken to something that looks like the PayPal site and can thus be fooled into submitting passwords and other valuable data on the rogue website.

Routers have operating systems, and thus they themselves are vulnerable to attack. As early as 2000, for example, a number of Cisco routers were attacked in a way that caused the routers to crash.[61] This can be really disruptive to communications. In 2003, over two thousand Cisco routers whose passwords were poorly chosen (*cisco* was a common choice) were attacked. If a router is taken over, it can be programmed to do many nefarious things. Fortunately these were low-end routers and there was not much damage.

If a high-end router at a network peering point—a location where networks connect and freely exchange traffic[62]—were to be so compromised, it would be in a position to do a great deal of damage. Routers can be programmed to *sniff packets*—that is, read the contents of the packets as they transit the router—or to launch a *denial-of-service* (DoS) attack, in which a network resource is bombarded by so many packets attempting to connect to it that legitimate users cannot, and the resource is inaccessible. Typically DoS attacks are against a website but even Internet root nameservers have been so targeted. Attacks on routers are serious business indeed.

The attacks just described are on devices in the Internet "cloud," but the vulnerabilities inherent in TCP/IP can also directly disrupt Internet hosts. One such vulnerability arises from the SYN flood attack. Recall that under TCP, a client and server establish a connection through a "three-way" SYN, SYN ACK, and ACK handshake. If the client is using a spoofed IP address—and nothing in TCP/IP checks to see that the IP address is genuine—then the server's message is not acknowledged. The server is left waiting. If too many of these falsified connections occur at once, the server is not available for new connections. Thus, purely as a result of TCP/IP's lack of an authentication requirement, the server is vulnerable to a denial-of-service attack.

A *distributed denial-of-service* (DDoS) attack occurs when previously compromised hosts band together to perform a concerted attack on a targeted system. The attackers are called a *botnet* or *zombies*. DDoS attacks can employ thousands of machines to send messages to a target machine (e.g., to establish a connection such as opening a web page stored on the target machine), saturating the target and preventing it from communicating. A 2007 DDoS attack against Estonia shut down numerous government and business websites in the Baltic nation for several days. Note that a DDoS attack combines the insecurities inherent in Internet protocols with the insecurities of the endpoints, and thus is a combination of the two previous forms of attack.

3.5 Attacks on the Hosts

End hosts face attacks from three types of malicious software, or malware:

• Worms, which are self-replicating programs that spread throughout a machine or between machines.

• Viruses, which are self-replicating program fragments (rather than complete programs); these must be inserted into a program in order to work.

• Trojan horses, which are programs that hide some malicious behavior within an attractive functionality; the attractive aspect often tempts the user to download the program. Trojan horses can be used to deliver viruses or worms.

Such malware can enter a user's machine in various ways. It may arrive unbidden via the Internet, as the Morris worm did, or via removable media such as a floppy disk, which is how the first such virus spread in 1982.[63] It may be downloaded as an attachment in an email and then opened; that is how both the 1999 Melissa and the 2000 ILOVEYOU viruses[64] arrived on users' machines.

Commonly users are attacked only by Trojan-horse programs that they have explicitly downloaded to their machine (typically the user downloads the program because of some attractive functionality; the user is unaware of the other functionality—such as random shutdowns, or redirecting the browser to a pornography site—that might occur once the Trojan horse is installed). But users can also be threatened by a more insidious form of Trojan-horse attack, referred to as "drive-by download," which arrives when the user visits an infected web page. Small pieces of code can be embedded within the code of vulnerable websites. This code then invisibly and automatically installs malware on any vulnerable machine whose user visits the infected site. The malware gains control over the compromised system, perhaps stealing sensitive information (e.g., banking passwords when the user is visiting a banking website), perhaps sending out spam, and so forth.[65]

Different sets of vulnerabilities are exploited in this type of attack: the website has vulnerabilities allowing malware to be installed in its html code, and this malware installs other software on a vulnerable network host. Such a dual-level attack reflects a different level of sophistication than previous attacks on user machines.

One might ask how users' machines came to be so vulnerable to subversion. The answer starts with the fact that decades ago when personal computers were first designed, they were standalone machines. The model was that the user should have full access to all functions on the machine. This has distinct advantages; in particular, it allows the user to do anything she wants on the machine. But such a model becomes problematic when the machine is networked. If the user can do anything she wants on her machine, then if her computer is not properly secured, anyone else having access to her machine can also do anything they want to it. Add to this situation the fact that securing computers is not easy. Computer operating systems are highly complex systems. It is very difficult to completely eliminate mistakes in the millions of lines of code in them, but it is possible to do better than present systems. NASA's shuttle software, for example, has a rather remarkable record.[66]

The business model for high tech conspires against security. Being first to market is extremely important, and security concerns have often been relegated to a backwater to be fixed in "version 2.0." Often version 2.0 never comes. In any case, by the time it does, it is often too late—too many machines with poor security paradigms have already been purchased and deployed.

One might imagine that somewhere on the network it would be possible to examine packets before they arrive at a vulnerable machine and thus stop attacks before they start. Firewalls are a step in this direction. A firewall is a device interposed between an internal network (e.g., home, university, corporate, etc.) and the rest of the network; it filters traffic based on a set of rules defined by the user. Its job can be to prevent traffic to or from a certain IP address (though this can be defeated by IP address spoofing) or to prevent certain applications from transferring data.[67] Some firewalls block the file transfer protocol, while others have been known to block such applications as YouTube.[68] Firewalls are useful in stopping the spread of known worms and viruses, but are less useful in preventing unknown bad programs from entering a user's machine.

Firewalls interpose a censor between the user and the communication and break the Internet communications model that allows any endpoint to send a message to any other without first having an "introduction." Despite that, such censors are being deployed. One is the "Great Firewall of China," which examines IP addresses and blocks incoming and outgoing packets to China on that basis.[69] Although the censorship is not perfect, it is sufficient to disrupt human rights activities. Such censorship has also been documented closer to home. In 2005 Canada's second largest telecommunications company blocked its subscribers and smaller ISPs that depended on the network from reaching the site of the Telecommunications Workers Union.[70]

It may well be appropriate to use intrusive packet inspection or censorship to prevent network attacks such as DDoS, yet clearly the potential for abuse using such monitoring is high. I return to this issue later.

3.6 The Security Problems Are Inherent

The list above of Internet security holes is not exhaustive—indeed, the nature of the problem is that new vulnerabilities continue to be uncovered—but the description captures the essence of the problem. Security issues are inherent in any fully open packet-switching network with smart hosts. Whenever a data-manipulating device is sufficiently multipurpose so as to be programmable (in other words, to be a computer), such a device will have flaws and be a security risk. And whenever a computer connects to a network, the machine will be at risk from other computers on the network and the whole network itself will be at risk.

Unless the endpoint hosts are fully secured, they leave the network in a highly vulnerable state. The fact is, however, that the security of users' machines is in a terrible state; most machines are unpatched and open to attack. We are in a situation in which the very strength of the Internet—a network connecting smart endpoints—creates its weakness. The network hosts can be compromised, with the Internet providing the delivery system for compromise.

Here the Internet architecture comes into play. TCP/IP is about "conversations." You can secure the channels over which the TCP/IP communications occur, but the layered nature of the Internet means that that information within packets does not leak into other layers of the network. Van Jacobson described it this way: "Channels are secured, but not data, so there's no way to know if what you get is complete, consistent, or even what you asked for."[71] There is no way for the network to know what the content looks like until it reaches the endpoint, a user's computer.

Into this mix comes a large population with diverse interests (including developing many applications that the original Internet designers had never considered). One gets the enormous burst of creativity that has produced the Internet post the mid-1990s: This creative energy is what Harvard law professor Jonathan Zittrain terms the "generative Internet": the network's ability to produce unprompted change because of its "large, varied, and uncoordinated audience."[72] The generative Internet provides a large panoply of services, from ecommerce and ecollaboration to social networks. One does not necessarily obtain secure applications.

The peer-to-peer nature of the network further complicates control. Many users are familiar with the client/server model, in which a "client" initiates an action, such as accessing a web page or requesting a file, and the "server" provides that service. Internet architecture supports a peer-to-peer network, in which nodes function as both clients and servers to other nodes (in other words, as peers). The peer-to-peer model relies on the robust connectivity of the Internet and is extremely efficient for file distribution, whether for illegal copyrighted music or legal downloads (such as music under Creative Commons licenses),[73] or some open-source operating systems.

Skype is an example of a peer-to-peer program that takes security seriously. The program encrypts all calls end to end. This prevents computers routing the call from eavesdropping on the conversation as well as preventing the call itself from corrupting any machines through which it travels.[74] Such careful attention to security is not the norm for peer-to-peer systems.

Underlying peer-to-peer systems is the idea that the user is accessing useful information from an unknown source. While the server is also something of an unknown entity in a client/server interaction, it is generally the case that servers are better protected than random nodes on the network. Because the average user does not know and does not check what is being downloaded onto her system, it is entirely possible that a malicious node on the peer-to-peer system has included a virus among its shared files. And because the average user does not know how peer-to-peer applications work, and does not know to protect her own machine, many of the user's files can be "shared" while on a peer-to-peer connection. In 2007, a U.S. House of Representatives committee examined possible consequences of using a peer-to-peer file-sharing program:

We used the most popular P2P [peer-to-peer] program, LimeWire, and ran a series of basic searches. What we found was astonishing: personal bank records and tax forms, attorney/client communications, the corporate strategies of Fortune 500 companies, confidential corporate accounting documents, internal documents from political campaigns, government emergency response plans, and even military operations orders.[75]

The risks created by peer-to-peer file sharing have raised concerns in Congress. The circulation of copyrighted material via peer-to-peer networks has induced some to propose controls to eliminate P2P file sharing. While the intent is that such schemes apply only to application-layer peer-to-peer networking (rather than IP layer routing), experience indicates that such legislation would sow confusion in the networking world. In any case, laws restricting P2P file sharing undoubtedly would be disruptive to the development of many beneficial P2P applications. Such legislation is rarely proposed by anyone who understands why the network works so very well.

3.7 Attribution and Authentication

One idea that often seems attractive and that has periodically been proposed is that all Internet communications include attribution. Packets would authenticate themselves before being received by an endpoint; in some proposals, network users would also authenticate themselves before using the network.[76] While this would not preclude anonymous network communication,[77] it would certainly make such forms of communication more difficult.

In fact, attribution is quite complex, and several problems are being mixed together. We might want to know the IP address of the host that initiated the DDoS attack, identify an originator's email address for attacks carried out by email (e.g., phishing), establish the physical location of the source of an attack, or identify the individual who launched the attack.[78] These differing needs argue for different types of attribution: machine, human, digital identity.

Packet-level attribution identifies the machine, but not the user. While packet attribution might specify which machine is launching a DDoS attack, it does nothing to establish who was actually responsible for the DDoS attack being on the machine—or even who was using the machine at the time it launched the attack. Application-level authentication could identify the user, but not the machine. It can do so only if the form of user authentication can be trusted. We are far from such a situation. User-name/password is easily spoofed. Even systems requiring such biometrics as fingerprints can be scammed; in 2002 researchers showed that a jelly print of a fingerprint can fool a fingerprint reader.[79] So if someone with access to a good copy of your fingerprint also had your laptop, they would be able to open files that are protected by your fingerprint. The real complication for attribution is that the type of attribution varies with the type of entity for which we are seeking the attribution.

A further complication is that in many cases, a level of anonymity for the network host is more appropriate. This may be for privacy or security reasons, or it may simply be an artifact of network design. For example, while it may be possible to identify the machine initiating the connection, it is very difficult to identify the machine being accessed. That is because when so many users want to simultaneously access a site, the content is often transparently "mirrored" on other sites.[80] The user who requested a connection is typically unaware that this substitution has occurred and that her machine is receiving packets from a different IP address. Thus a system design that has a "whitelist" of IP addresses may refuse content from a site that has the very content it is seeking, a confused response to a complex networking solution. A host that requires attribution before it will accept packets and that has certain expectations as to the source of the packets must take into account the myriad legitimate disruptions that might occur; this is exceedingly hard to do, and especially difficult to do dynamically.

Attribution was a natural fit for the telephone network, which originally did not attempt to establish connections between two entities that had not yet met (telemarketing was not big in the 1890s). But attribution is not a natural fit for the Internet, which is many networks at once. The current Internet is open: users can link to the New Zealand government, to Amazon.co.uk, to Google, and even, apparently, to the U.S. electric power grid.[81] While there is every reason for the subnetwork controlling the power grid to prevent open connections—it would be appropriate for the subnetwork controlling the power grid to seek attribution and strong forms of authentication for every packet that transits into that network— there is little reason why the New Zealand government, Amazon.co.uk, or Google should seek to limit connections by insisting on packet source attribution or user authentication first.

3.8   Efforts to Secure Communications

Securing communications can take several different tacks. There are efforts to protect against electrical, mechanical, or acoustic emissions that may reveal information about the communication. Computers leak electromagnetic radiation, which reveals information about the data being processed. This has been known for quite some time and systems with sensitive data have metal shields to prevent such leaks. The U.S. government program to provide such emission security is called TEMPEST.[82]

The entire communications link may be encrypted. This prevents an interceptor from gaining any information on communications transiting the link and was done on a number of AT&T trunk lines in the 1970s (New York, Washington, and San Francisco) in order to protect against Soviet interception.[83] The encryption is *between* switches, which permits routing and interception at the switches.

Individual messages may be encrypted end to end, from the sender to the receiver. This is what Skype does. It has the advantage of completely protecting the communication contents from any interception but, unlike link encryption, it has the disadvantage that addressing information is visible to interceptors. Secure web browsing using https is another example of communications using end-to-end encryption.

Cryptography is no silver bullet. It provides security only for the communications contents. In particular, the transactional information—who is communicating with whom when—is not encrypted. It is often the case that transactional information is more valuable than content, but this somewhat private information may be public even when the communications contents are hidden. Transactional data are remarkably revealing: it can indicate that a company merger is about to occur, that nation-states are engaged in negotiation, that someone is having an affair. Yet because routers do need to know where packets are going, hiding such transactional information is quite difficult.[84]

It has become a national, indeed, international, priority to increase network security (by which I mean the security of the communications network itself). This is not an easy matter. It is made more difficult by the fact that any solution must be *backward compatible:* changes to the protocols must be made in such a way that the new version works seamlessly with products that have not been so updated. Securing the network is not the same as securing the communications that travel on it, though the two are closely related; securing the network includes communications security, but also ensuring availability and nonrepudability of communications.

3.9 Efforts to Secure the Internet

Internet protocols were designed to provide network reliability and availability, and they do so well. They were not designed to provide security and, in general, they do not (one exception is the protocol SSL/TLS, which encrypts transport-layer communications). Some aspects of security can be relatively easily handled. Cryptography, for example, can ensure the end-to-end confidentiality, authenticity, and integrity of a communication. Cryptography itself cannot ensure network security; more infrastructure is needed. There are currently a number of different efforts to accomplish this.

Fundamental to the correct functioning of the network is assurance: ensuring that the communication arrives at the correct network destination. This is harder than it sounds. Recall that DNS—the mechanism that associates a domain name, such as www.bankofamerica.com, with an IP address—can be spoofed, sending a user to a bogus website. Domain Name System Security Extensions (DNSSEC) is a protocol for guaranteeing that DNS resolvers receive correct IP addresses for their queries. DNSSEC provides two things:

Source authentication A DNS resolver can verify that the information it received originally came from a DNS authoritative nameserver (one that the DNS resolver can "trust").

Integrity verification A DNS resolver can determine that the information it has received from a DNS nameserver has not been tampered with during transit from the original authoritative nameserver.

When a DNS resolver receives an IP address via DNSSEC lookup, it validates the response through verifying that an authoritative nameserver has signed the response. Under DNSSEC, each DNS nameserver generates a public/private key pair for using in public-key cryptography. The nameserver publishes the public key and places a cryptographically shortened version of the public key—this is called a hash—in its parent DNS nameserver. Using its private key, the nameserver signs its zone's records connecting domain names with their IP addresses. Of course, the resolver needs to know that the local DNS server has fully checked the authenticity of the information (and that the local DNS server is not being spoofed). If its parent zone has signed its record, and the parent zone is authoritative, then that is proof.

But it may be that the resolver does not have proof that the parent DNS nameserver is authoritative.

So the question can recurse all the way "up the chain" of DNS nameservers to the root nameserver, which is the *trust anchor*—the one party you have to trust, regardless—in most DNSSEC implementations.

The trust anchor has signed its record connecting the top-level zone nameserver to its IP address, making the top-level nameserver authoritative. Then the top-level nameserver has signed its records using its own private key to show that the nameserver for the next zone down is authoritative (to know that the names.google.com nameserver is authoritative requires knowing that the google.com nameserver is authoritative, which in turn requires that the.com nameserver is authoritative). This is complicated. DNSSEC works only if all the DNS nameservers in the lookup chain are DNSSEC-enabled; if one of them is not, then there cannot be a trusted chain of authenticity.

Of course, there needs to be a way for the DNS resolver to check the validity of the DNS root. In theory—in practice this has not yet been done—there is a key for the root that each DNS resolver has, which it has received *not through the network but by some other means*.

The other difficulty with DNSSEC is complexity. Beginning with the root nameserver, the resolver has to go through the DNS nameserver chain and (1) find the authoritative IP address for the next level down the chain, as well as (2) verifying the public key of the signature of the zone so that the resolver knows that the IP address of the next DNS resolver in the chain is valid (e.g., the chain for maps.google.com would be the "." DNS nameserver—the root, the .com DNS nameserver, and the google.com DNS nameserver). It should be no surprise that this algorithm is complex to implement.

It should also be no surprise that thus, despite its importance, DNSSEC deployment has been slow. One cause is political—the root trust anchor determines which sites are authentic and which are not, and that has presented policy problems as to who should control Internet trust anchors. For a number of years there was conflict over who should sign the "." server. There were a number of contenders, including the Internet Corporation for Assigned Names and Numbers, the nonprofit organization established in 1998 to run Internet-related tasks that previously the U.S. government had done; the U.S. Department of Commerce, which believed it had the authority to do so (recall that although the Internet is now an international network, it had its origins in the United States);[85] and the International Telecommunications Union, which was preferred by some since it is a United Nations agency. In 2009, the issue was resolved in favor of VeriSign, a U.S. company that operates two of the Internet's root nameservers, as well as the top-level domains of .com and .net.

The other problem is technical. DNS is difficult to implement, and DNSSEC even more so. What makes the situation worse is that DNSSEC only works if the DNS nameservers in a lookup chain are *all* DNSSEC enabled; just updating the local DNS nameserver to DNSSEC will not solve the problem. In some sense, the difference between a DNS and DNSSEC response resembles the difference between obtaining a notarized signature and a signature guarantee;[86] the former is a witnessing of the signature, the latter, a financial institution guarantee that the signature is genuine.[87] The challenges in setting up DNSSEC are large, and given that attacks are still rare, the difficulty involved in setting up DNSSEC can make deploying the protocol a risky proposition. Deployment was slow until a particularly destructive attack on DNS surfaced in the summer of 2008;[88] after this, the pace of adoption picked up.

DNS is not the only problem that the security network faces. When the original DARPA network was set up, 32 bits seemed more than ample for network addresses; after all, that provides for over four billion distinct addresses. Three decades later, the crunch is apparent. The network is not only being used for people; it is being used for billions and billions of devices. Hence the move to IPv6, or version 6 of the Internet Protocol.[89] This allows for 128-bit, or over 3×10^{28}, distinct addresses, enough for every human on earth to have an Internet address for every word they have time to utter.

IPv6 has some security features as well. IPsec, a protocol for key establishment and mutual authentication, enables packet-level encryption.[90] But IPsec is quite limited in scope. In particular, it does not solve the fundamental problem of authenticity: Is the connection to the real site? (For example, is http://www.lloydstsb.com/ the Lloyds Bank website or a fraudulent site reached as a result of a poisoned DNS cache?) Thus IPsec is mostly useful for establishing a virtual private network,[91] a virtual network established over a public one (such as the Internet) that securely connects remote users with an organization. The implementation of IPv6 has been remarkably slow, with the result that IPsec has also been implemented in IPv4.

By the late 1990s, it was apparent that the Internet was an experiment that had escaped the lab. While the network is no Frankenstein, the problems that have already arisen leave no doubt about the need for improved security.[92] Bolting on security afterward is exceedingly difficult, and because attribution, authentication, and identity are social concerns as well as technical ones, solutions will not simply be a matter of a patch here and a patch there. Fundamental design must be examined, with the intent of bringing protocols to the network that are "secure by design." The European Commission, the United States, Korea, Japan, and several other nations have launched research projects on that effort. These efforts will not bear fruit for some time. I examine them in chapter 11.

4 Wiretaps and the Law

It is well known that human perception and actual events are often at odds. That dissonance is particularly notable in our perceptions of the patterns of our daily lives. Once certain practices have been present for a period of time, it becomes difficult to recall that things were ever different. Whether this is our present reliance on cell phones, or law enforcement and national security reliance on wiretapping, our belief systems would have us think that circumstances were always like this.

In the case of cell phones and legalized wiretapping, such beliefs are false, of course. Cell phones became common beginning only in the late 1990s, while the legal basis for law enforcement and national-security wiretapping was, at least in the United States, established only about a generation earlier.

The first U.S. wiretapping law was the 1968 Omnibus Crime Control and Safe Streets Act of 1968,[1] which established warrant procedures for wiretaps in criminal investigations. (The U.S. law for electronic surveillance in national security cases, the Foreign Intelligence Surveillance Act, came into existence ten years later.) The current discussion of wiretapping accepts as a given that electronic surveillance is necessary for law enforcement and national-security investigations. The reality is that the tool is only relatively recent and is used in ways that were not necessarily expected. In this chapter, I discuss wiretapping laws as well as the inextricably linked subject of how they are applied.

Wiretapping law is a subject about which much has been written, of course. My coverage will be a quick tour; those who wish a longer exegesis are urged to consult one of the large number of books on the subject. In particular, Whitfield Diffie and I wrote about wiretapping law in *Privacy on the Line: The Politics of Wiretapping and Encryption.*

4.1   The Antecedents of U.S. Wiretapping Law

The Fourth Amendment to the Constitution was written in reaction to the British writs of assistance, general search warrants used in the American colonies. The writs' lack of specificity in the "persons, houses, papers, and effects" to be searched and seized were viewed as instruments of arbitrary power.[2] The writs were a main grievance against the British. Thus the Fourth Amendment requires that warrants shall particularly describe "the place to be searched, and the persons or things to be seized."

In the early days of the colonies, mail delivery was dependent on the kindness of strangers, often done with the help of a traveler or merchant along the route. Privacy was certainly not assured. Even after postal delivery was somewhat regularized in the early eighteenth century, communications privacy remained a problem. Such leaders as Benjamin Franklin and Thomas Jefferson worried that their written messages were less than private, although from early on, privacy of the mails was built into U.S. law. The 1792 act[3] establishing the U.S. Postal Service included two important features: low rates for newspapers (to enable the populace to participate in political activity) and privacy of the mails. Postal officials were prohibited from opening letters. In establishing these features as part of the postal system, the United States set itself apart from England and France, where the post was used as an instrument of government surveillance. But what was law was not necessarily practice, and there were multiple instances of snooping on the mails.[4] Postal privacy protections were strengthened with an 1878 Supreme Court ruling that a warrant was required before the government could open first-class mail.[5]

Government wiretapping started with the telegraph. Electronic eavesdropping was in use during the Civil War, when a tapper traveled with General Jeb Stuart.[6] In 1895, when there was less than one telephone per 200 people, New York City police were using wiretapping in criminal investigations.[7] The first concerted use of wiretapping for these investigations occurred during Prohibition—the period from 1919 to 1933, when the production, sale, and transportation of alcohol was illegal.

Wiretapping was the principal means of investigation by Prohibition enforcement officers.[8] This should be no surprise. The illegal production, sale, and transport of alcohol—especially the sale and transport—require a complex organization that typically will pay off the police as part of its work plan. Penetrating organized crime of this nature is difficult, and wiretapping is a particularly effective tool to obtain information about a closed conspiracy. Such electronic eavesdropping was used to gather evidence in the case of Roy Olmstead, a Seattle bootlegger who had been running a vast operation. Using the telephone to handle orders, Olmstead and his co-conspirators worked out of an office in downtown Seattle. Four federal Prohibition officers tapped the office line as well as phone wires outside the homes of several participants.

Olmstead's lawyers argued that the warrantless wiretaps violated his constitutional rights against illegal search and seizure. The court did not agree and Olmstead was convicted of participating in "a conspiracy of amazing magnitude to import, possess and sell liquor unlawfully."[9] Olmstead appealed, and the case made its way to the U.S. Supreme Court.

The Supreme Court was closely divided but ruled that the warrantless wiretaps had not involved trespass. Thus neither the Fourth, nor therefore the Fifth, Amendment was violated. Five justices, a majority, concurred that the Fourth Amendment's protections were only for tangibles.[10]

The most famous opinion in the Olmstead case is, however, not the majority one, but the dissent provided by Justice Louis Brandeis. He argued that protections provided by the Bill of Rights should operate in a world of electronic communications:

Whenever a telephone line is tapped, the privacy of the persons at both ends of the line is invaded, and all conversations between them upon any subject, and although proper, confidential and privileged, may be overheard. Moreover, the tapping of one man's telephone line involves the tapping of the telephone of every other person whom he may call, or who may call him. As a means of espionage, writs of assistance and general warrants are but puny instruments of tyranny and oppression when compared with wiretapping.[11]

Unhappy with the Supreme Court's decision, Congress considered several bills to make wiretapping illegal, but in the end, passed nothing expressly addressing the issue. However, in 1934 the Federal Communications Act (FCA)[12] was enacted, section 605 of which prohibited the unauthorized "interception and divulgence" of wired communications.

In 1937 another bootlegging case came to the Supreme Court, that of Carmine Nardone. The U.S. government had wiretapped Nardone, but Nardone did not try a constitutional argument against warrantless wiretapping. Instead he claimed that the FCA prohibition of "interception and divulgence" of wired communications applied to law enforcement officers. Nardone won.[13] What is interesting to note is that the law that preceded the Federal Communications Act, the Radio Act of 1927, had similar wording regarding the legality of the interception and divulgence of radio communications. Olmstead's lawyers had chosen instead to argue their case on the basis of the constitution. That was not a winning strategy in 1928.

Two years later Nardone was back in court, concerned about the "fruit of the poisoned tree": was evidence derived from the warrantless wiretaps admissible in court? The Court said no.[14] Quoting an earlier case involving illegal search and seizure,[15] the Court noted, "The essence of a provision forbidding the acquisition of evidence in a certain way is that not merely evidence so acquired shall not be used before the court, but that it shall not be used at all."

With a court ruling in hand that the Federal Communications Act also applied to intrastate communication,[16] U.S. Attorney General Robert Jackson ordered the end of FBI wiretapping. Despite the order, FBI warrantless wiretapping was to continue for over three decades. Two things made that happen: the Department of Justice's (DoJ) interpretation of the *Nardone* decision and FBI Director J. Edgar Hoover. The Department of Justice construed the *Nardone* decision to mean that the combination of interception *and* divulgence of wired communications was illegal but that interception itself was permitted. This odd viewpoint allowed the federal government to wiretap so long as the contents were not divulged outside the administration.[17]

Although the department's interpretation of interception meant that the government was already able to conduct intelligence surveillance, the start of World War II gave FBI Director Hoover an opportunity to seek permission from the president to conduct electronic surveillance against potential spies. In a fateful decision, Roosevelt granted explicit permission to conduct electronic surveillance in situations that would now be called nationalsecurity cases. While the president's order limited wiretapping "insofar as possible" to aliens,[18] within a few years the limitation disappeared.[19] For the next thirty years, the FBI wiretapped with little supervision.

The Department of Justice's belief that it could not prosecute in any case in which wiretapping had occurred created a complex state of affairs. The FBI, the nation's premier law enforcement agency, hid any evidence of its wiretaps,[20] for disclosure would end a case.[21] Besides targeting criminals, the bureau wiretapped citizens and groups exercising their civil and political rights,[22] including the November 1969 anti–Vietnam War groups' March on Washington,[23] journalists,[24] such civic groups as the Los Angeles Chamber of Commerce, and critics and opponents of various administrations[25]—and the FBI hid that too. Even members of the government were wiretapped.[26]

The FBI wiretapping was a well-known secret in Washington. This made legislative oversight of the agency[27] highly problematic—a situation that did not escape the wily Hoover. For example, in 1965, Missouri Senator

Edward Long sought to investigate the government's use of electronic surveillance. Two senior FBI officials met with Long and dissuaded him from doing so. When the senator was unable—or unwilling—to write a press release saying that he was satisfied with FBI usage of wiretaps and microphones, the bureau agents wrote one for him (it was released under the senator's name). A year later, Long introduced a bill limiting FBI wiretapping to national-security cases. This time the FBI did not meet and write a press release; instead, the national magazine *Life* ran a story that Long had received $48,000 from Jimmy Hoffa's counsel (Hoffa was a corrupt Teamster's Union official). The article implied the money was a bribe to help Hoffa. Long lost a state primary shortly afterward, and his political career ended.[28] Such lessons were not lost on other legislators.

The FBI ran an extensive wiretapping and bugging operation on the civil rights leader Martin Luther King Jr. In its counterintelligence operations, it sought to use information the bureau learned about his extramarital affairs to discredit him.[29] The bureau also shared information about King's political activities with President Johnson, who was at odds with the civil rights leader during the 1964 Democratic Party convention.[30] During the Nixon years, journalists who crossed the president were tapped; this included reporters from CBS News, the *London Sunday Times*, and the *New York Times*.[31]

The widespread FBI wiretapping became public knowledge in the 1970s, when the Senate, in response to the abuses uncovered during the Watergate investigations, examined governmental domestic surveillance abuses. This was done by the Senate Select Committee to Study Governmental Operations with respect to Intelligence Activities, which became known as the Church Committee, after its chairman, Senator Frank Church. The committee found a train of wiretap abuses as far back as the 1940s and the presidency of Harry Truman;[32] these abuses continued through the 1970s and the Nixon era. Some of the abuses occurred with the knowledge of the White House, but many did not.

In U.S. law the term *electronic surveillance* refers not only to wiretaps, but also to bugs or covert listening devices, typically quite small, whose transmissions travel through radio waves. Even though bugs are used to capture face-to-face conversations, and the topic of this book is wiretapping and secure telecommunications, because U.S. law unifies these two technologies, a brief discussion of the legal aspects of bugging is in order.

The 1934 Federal Communications Act referred only to the interception of wired communications, an omission that left the bugging of conversations unaffected by the *Nardone* rulings. At first the Supreme Court traveled the *Olmstead* path on bugging. In 1942, in *Goldman v. United States*,[33] the Supreme Court ruled that law enforcement officers could plant a bugging device on a wall adjoining that of a suspect's office—no warrant needed. In 1954, in *Irvine v. California*,[34] the Court considered evidence from microphones concealed in walls of the defendants' homes; the devices had been installed during warrantless break-ins by the police. The Court expressed concern about this:

Each of these repeated entries of petitioner's home without a search warrant or other process was a trespass. . . . That officers of the law would break and enter a home, secrete such a device, even in a bedroom, and listen to the conversation of the occupants for over a month would be almost incredible if it were not admitted. Few police measures have come to our attention that more flagrantly, deliberately, and persistently violated the fundamental principle declared by the Fourth Amendment.

The case was a California prosecution for a state crime and the Court chose to accept the evidence. Then in 1961, in *Julius Silverman et al. v. United States*,[35] the Court changed direction. In a District of Columbia case, police investigating gambling pushed a foot-long microphone into the space under the suspect's apartment from the house next door. The Court ruled that a search, in the meaning of the Fourth Amendment, occurred whenever a bug was used. It took one more case to end the situation of warrantless bugs. This was *Charles Katz v. United States*.[36]

Charles Katz was a Los Angeles gambler who used a public phone booth to place his bets. Police had placed a listening device on the outside of the booth. The Court ruled that the fact that the booth was public and that the bug was on the outside of the booth was not important:

The Fourth Amendment protects people, not places.[37] . . .What [Katz] sought to exclude when he entered the [telephone] booth was not the intruding eye—it was the uninvited ear. . . . [A] person in a telephone booth may rely upon the protection of the Fourth Amendment. One who occupies it, shuts the door behind him, and pays the toll that permits him to place a call is surely entitled to assume that the words he utters into the mouthpiece will not be broadcast to the world. To read the Constitution more narrowly is to ignore the vital role that the public telephone has come to play in private communication.[38]

With this ruling, the Supreme Court had come full circle on the *Olmstead* decision. The Court held that the Fourth Amendment protections apply to such ephemera as communications. The *Katz* decision did not rule out wiretaps and bugs; indeed the ruling makes clear that a "procedure of antecedent justification"[39] would have legalized the Katz search.[40] It was time for Congress to fix the wiretap problem.

4.2 How Wiretapping Works

Wiretapping simply means intercepting a call. It can involve a person listening in or it can involve taping for future use, or both. If the recipient of the call permits the eavesdropping (e.g., in a kidnapping case), the interception is called a *consensual overhear*; under U.S. law such interception does not require a court order. But the same freedom does not apply to such eavesdropping by private parties. Some U.S. states permit one-party consent for the taping of a call, but others are *two-party consent* states, in which both parties must acquiesce in order for a call to be taped.

Wiretapping can be done anywhere along the communication path, including in the phone itself. The decision on where to tap is a trade-off between stealth and ease of installation.[41] Using an electronic *bug*, a small device capable of sending radio signals, allows tapping within the phone itself. This has the drawback of needing to do a *black-bag* job—a break-in—to hide the bug, but after that, as long as the battery-operated device has sufficient power and the suspect has no inkling that he is being tapped, this solution has the advantage of being perfectly hidden. It is essentially invisible, and its operation does not involve telephone-company personnel.

Old film noir movies have the wiretapper in the basement of an apartment building, using alligator clips to connect into the phone lines and listening through a headset. Indeed, taps can be placed at a phone junction box or on a telephone pole. Such locations have the disadvantage, however, that they are publicly visible. These locations are subject to maintenance by the telephone-company personnel, who may discover the tap and disable it.[42]

The next most likely place for a tap is at the telephone company's central office. That is where the pair of wires associated with the subscriber's phone, known as the *local loop*, are placed onto a *frame*, where they are sorted into numerical order. From here they go to a switch to be connected to outgoing lines. Because a phone circuit has many possible paths—during busy times a call from New York to Washington may go by way of Chicago—it is impossible to predict exactly which path a call may take. In the predigital age, the frame was the last possible place to ensure that a wiretap picked up all communications to/from a particular number. This was done through placing a *loop extender*, a tap that created a logical fork on the subscriber's line, bridging it to a so-called *friendly circuit*, a line from the loop extender that fed directly into a secure location for monitoring.[43]

The frame was the location preferred by law enforcement—but it was a location that would prove problematic once more advanced switching technology appeared. The difficulty is that the local loop receives exactly the information that passes through the loop, no more, no less. Some advanced services, such as call forwarding, work at the switch, and never pass information through the local loop.[44] This was the set of problems for which the FBI sought resolution in the early 1990s.

Surveillance for intelligence purposes may be for a specific target, in which case, if agents have access to communications facilities, the collection works as previously described. (If agents do not have such access, they have to break in one way or another.) Or it may be a broader intercept capable of accessing all communication through a pipe. Such interception facilities may be in the air, on the ground, or on ships (all intercepting signals from the air), from submarines (which can tap into underwater fiber-optic cables), from satellites, or from such covert locations as embassies, including, it is alleged, not just the U.S. embassy, but also other friendly ones. But the capability for total access does not mean that national security collects all signals that are available. Collecting all communications from a country, from a small city, or even from a single 4ESS[45] switch is simply overwhelming: there is far too much to process.

The issue is locating the traffic of interest. Choices about collection must be made in fractions of a second. Such decisions may be determined by the transactional information of the communication—the phone number, the URL, the email address, the serial number of the phone card—or by content—a particular voice, language, words, the text in an email or fax. If the traffic is interesting, it is recorded.

This is simply gathering and storage, or, as is called in the trade, access and collection. In a sense, it is the easy part of the job. The work of intelligence and counterintelligence—analysis, processing, and dissemination—is the real heart of the matter. That subject, however, is outside the scope of this book.

4.3   U.S. Wiretap Laws

For reasons that perhaps the FBI director knew—though never publicly shared—for decades, Hoover denied the existence of organized crime. He may have feared that investigating such a corrupting criminal group would inevitably result in some corruption of his own agency; he may have preferred to avoid the messy, long-term, high-risk investigations that might fail to net anything but low-level criminals; he may have simply preferred the cut-and-dried statistical summaries he could present to Congress each year of so-many-stolen-cars recovered, so-many-bank-robbers captured. Organized crime investigations rarely net clean statistics. Regardless of Hoover's lack of acknowledgment, organized crime was a problem from Prohibition onward.

Probes into organized crime present special problems. For one thing, organized crime embeds its tentacles into local law enforcement, corrupting both the police and the court system. For another, organized crime tends to focus on crimes where the victims are often unwilling to go to the police. This combination severely complicates investigations.

Once alcohol was legalized, organized crime turned to other "victimless crimes," including gambling, loan-sharking, and prostitution. In 1957 a New York state trooper uncovered a major meeting of organized crime bosses at an estate deep in the countryside; this discovery created headlines in newspapers across the country. Then in 1963, a minor member of the Genovese crime family, Joseph Valachi, testified in the Senate about the structure and system of bosses and soldiers within organized crime. The combination of these events provided public notice about criminal activities that were not supposed to exist.[46] The FBI belatedly aimed its sights on the syndicates. President Johnson created a commission on law enforcement and justice; the well-respected report, *The Challenge of Crime in a Free Society*, issued in 1967, recommended the use of wiretaps for investigating organized crime.

Wiretaps are a particularly intrusive form of search. Unlike other searches permitted under the Fourth Amendment, wiretapping occurs without the knowledge of the suspect.[47] The hidden nature of this practice threatens accountability[48]—something that members of Congress were well aware from their experiences with the FBI director. Surveillance is, after all, reminiscent of a police state. So the commission's proposal gave rise to significant concern that the wiretapping be carefully controlled and done only with sufficient oversight. The recommendation occurred during the midst of social upheaval resulting from the civil rights movement and the anti–Vietnam War protests, which was splitting the country and bringing great numbers of people to protest in the nation's capital. The period saw a number of political assassinations,[49] and in the middle of the decade there were race riots in Watts, Newark, Detroit, and elsewhere. It was a complicated time in U.S. history, and many Americans sought more "law and order."

In 1968 Congress passed the Omnibus Crime Control and Safe Streets Act,[50] Title III of which delineated the circumstances for obtaining a wiretap warrant for a criminal investigation. There needs to be probable cause that the suspect is committing, has committed, or is about to commit a serious offense (from a list of crimes enumerated in the law[51]), that the targeted communications device is being used in commission of the crime, that communications about the crime will be obtained as a result of the surveillance, and that the information sought cannot reasonably be obtained by normal investigative techniques.[52] Any state law authorizing wiretap warrants in criminal investigations had to be at least as restrictive as the federal law (approximately half of all wiretaps for criminal investigations in the United States are done under state wiretap warrants). There was also a provision for emergency access in which, for up to forty-eight hours, a wiretap can be placed without an intercept order.[53] Wiretap orders are good for at most thirty days, with extensions requiring judicial approval.

Surveillance must minimize interceptions unrelated to the crime—the teenage daughter on the phone, the call that is about buying milk (when "buying milk" is not code for something nefarious). This minimization requirement is privacy protective in two ways: directly and, by making law enforcement wiretapping expensive, preventing overuse of the tool. The average cost per Title III order in 2009 was over $52,000.[54] The cost is in agent time; in 2009 the average surveillance ran for fifty-seven days (an initial run of twenty-nine days, plus an extension of twenty-eight days for 94 percent of the wiretaps).[55]

Various kinds of wiretapping oversight were built in. Only a limited number of people may approve a wiretap application.[56] The target of a Title III order must be informed once surveillance has ended. To give wiretaps public oversight, each year the Administrative Office of the U.S. Courts publishes the *Wiretap Report*, which lists every Title III surveillance, which judge approved the intercept order, how long the wiretap ran, what crime was being investigated,[57] the length of the surveillance, how many interceptions and incriminating interceptions there were, how many arrests, and how many convictions. And, after the change in regulations permitting the export of products with strong cryptography,[58] the *Wiretap Report* now lists the number of times that encrypted communications is encountered in Title III wiretaps.

Even while Title III became law, not all law enforcement agents believed the law was necessary.[59] Various prosecutors had opposed federal laws permitting wiretapping,[60] and Attorney General Ramsey Clark testified to Congress that "I know of no Federal conviction based upon any wiretapping or electronic surveillance. . . . I also think that we make cases effectively without wiretapping or electronic surveillance. I think it may well be that with the commitment of the same manpower to other techniques, even more convictions could be secured, because in terms of manpower, wiretapping and electronic surveillance is very expensive."[61] President Johnson himself suggested that wiretapping be limited to national-security investigations and only be performed by federal officials.[62] Nonetheless the law passed and Johnson signed it.

Title III lays out requirements for wiretaps in law enforcement cases but left the issue of surveillance in national-security investigations open. In 1972, in the case of *United States v. United States District Court for the Eastern District of Michigan et al.*,[63] the need for new legislation became clear.

Three men were accused of bombing a CIA office in Ann Arbor, Michigan; one had been wiretapped without a warrant. He sought copies of the tapes to see if the government's case was tainted by wiretap evidence. The U.S. District Court had ordered the government to hand over the tapes. When the federal government refused, the case went to the Supreme Court, which ordered an end to warrantless wiretapping for "domestic national-security" cases.

Criminal investigations focus on solving a particular crime (or perhaps a set of crimes). There is a known actor—known not necessarily by name, but by action—and a (possibly partial) known set of activities. Criminal investigations should not be *fishing expeditions*: broad searches without clear evidence of a crime. Foreign-intelligence investigations are different. Their purpose is to obtain information on "the intentions, capabilities, and activities" of those countries and foreign groups "able to harm the United States"[64] and to gather information for foreign policy decisions. There may be no particular target and the set of issues may be unknown at the outset. As investigators pull together pieces of information,[65] patterns of behavior and a picture of a group, a leader, or a function may emerge. If an intelligence effort uncovers criminal behavior by a foreign agent (or anyone else) unrelated to foreign intelligence (say a bank robbery or cigarette smuggling), a crime report is sent to the Department of Justice. If an intelligence effort turns up foreign-power or foreign-agent activity related to foreign intelligence (say spying), then the counterintelligence side of the FBI would be informed instead. Because much intelligence work involves collecting information where no crime is being committed, such searches on U.S. citizens and permanent residents can easily run contrary to the Fourth Amendment. Thus the notion of "domestic national security" is at best confusing—and, at its worst, of highly questionable constitutionality.

Title III was already sufficient to cover spying and terrorism cases if the government's intent was obtaining evidence for a criminal prosecution;

what was lacking was a warrant procedure if the purpose of the surveillance was obtaining foreign intelligence.[66] Title III did not address such a situation and the Court recommended Congress attend to this gap. Instead Watergate intervened.

The Watergate affair was set in motion by a burglary of the Democratic National Committee (DNC) headquarters during the general election and culminated in the first resignation of a standing U.S. president two years later. The sequence of events began early on the morning of June 17, 1972, when a security guard discovered a taped lock in the Watergate Office Building in Washington. A group of burglars, paid by the Committee to Re-Elect the President, Nixon's campaign committee, had broken into the DNC offices to install a bug on the phone of Lawrence O'Brien, the Democratic Party chair. This was their second try. On their first effort, the burglars had placed a bug in O'Brien's secretary's phone, but received no interesting information on the party's political intentions—so the burglars had returned.

Discovery of the burglary led, over many months, to the uncovering of numerous illegal activities perpetrated by the Nixon administration. Within a week of the break-in, Nixon and his staff attempted to cover up the campaign's connection to the incident. That attempt was just one of many obstructions of justice that occurred during the Nixon presidency. It took two years, two enterprising reporters (and a strong-willed editor and publisher) at the *Washington Post*, a tough federal judge, a determined chair and counsel of the Senate Watergate Committee,[67] and many others before sufficient evidence surfaced to make a clear case for President Richard Nixon's impeachment. The president resigned, but if he had not, Richard Nixon would have faced four impeachment counts, including:

[Nixon] misused the Federal Bureau of Investigation, the Secret Service, and other Executive Personnel . . . by directing or authorizing such agencies or personnel to conduct or continue electronic surveillance or other investigations for purposes unrelated to national security, the enforcement of laws, or any other lawful function of his office; . . . and he did direct the concealment of certain records made by the Federal Bureau of Investigation of electronic surveillance (Article 2).

[Nixon] failed to take care that the laws were faithfully executed by failing to act when he knew or had reason to know that his close subordinates endeavored to impede and frustrate lawful inquiries . . . concerning the electronic surveillance of private citizens . . . (Article 2).

Investigations by journalists, Congress, and special prosecutors had revealed massive abuse of government investigatory powers. It was important to understand what allowed the "system" to fail; in January 1975 the Senate created a special committee to investigate government intelligence operations to determine the extent of "illegal, improper, or unethical activities" by government agencies.[68]

The committee—which became known as the Church Committee, after its chair, Senator Frank Church—started with the year 1936, a year marked by the reestablishment of U.S. domestic intelligence programs after a hiatus of about a decade. The Church committee uncovered a forty-year history of presidential, law enforcement, and national-security wiretaps of political opponents, journalists, members of congressional staff, Supreme Court justices, members of the administration, as well as law-abiding citizens engaged in peaceful political protest. The committee observed that the impact of such abuses was broad:

When Government infringes those rights instead of nurturing and protecting them, the injury spreads far beyond the particular citizens targeted to untold numbers of other Americans who may be intimidated.

Persons most intimidated may well not be those at the extremes of the political spectrum, but rather those nearer the middle. Yet voices of moderation are vital to balance public debate and avoid polarization of our society.[69]

The committee laid out a series of recommendations to control wiretapping for national-security purposes. Intended to prevent the abuses of the previous four decades from ever recurring, these were incorporated into the Foreign Intelligence Surveillance Act (FISA),[70] the 1978 law governing wiretapping for foreign-intelligence purposes.

Under FISA, decisions regarding wiretapping in national-security cases are made by the Foreign Intelligence Surveillance Court, a court of seven district court judges appointed from seven of the United States judicial circuits; amendments in the USA PATRIOT Act changed this to eleven judges. In contrast to the Title III requirement of probable cause that a serious crime is being committed or about to be committed, FISA requires that there be probable cause that the surveillance target is a foreign power, agent of a foreign power, or terrorist group,[71] probable cause that the communications device is being used by the foreign power or its agent, and probable cause that the purpose of the surveillance is to obtain foreign-intelligence information. As in Title III, it must be the case that other forms of investigation are unlikely to succeed.

FISA's purpose was to regulate foreign-intelligence surveillance carried out inside the United States against domestic communications as well as against international communications (communications with one component in the United States) carried by wire. FISA permitted warrantless wiretapping for up to one year if communications were exclusively between foreign powers.[72] The attorney general could authorize warrantless wiretapping for up to seventy-two hours in an emergency, so long as a surveillance order was obtained within that period[73] (if not, the intercepted communications may neither be used nor divulged). The law had a specific First Amendment protection: exercise of such rights by U.S. citizens and permanent residents *cannot* be the sole basis for concluding someone is an agent of a foreign power.[74] As with Title III, only high-level officials could certify a FISA application[75] and there were minimization requirements. The FISA Court hearings and decisions were secret. Unlike Title III, the target of a FISA wiretap would only be informed if indicted and then only if the government intended to use the wiretapped evidence in the case. There was no equivalent of the *Wiretap Report*; the only public information is an annual report to Congress on the number of surveillances approved, denied, and sent back for changes.[76]

The law did not apply to radio surveillance of satellite transmissions unless the government was targeting a known, particular citizen or permanent resident alien (known as a U.S. person) in the United States and did not in any way fetter the surveillance of cables that was carried out in other nations or in international waters.

Nothing precludes a FISA-based investigation from leading to a criminal prosecution. Because the law was written to enable intelligence collection, it was entirely reasonable that its probable-cause standard should be somewhat less stringent than the analogous requirement in Title III; it is nonetheless important that investigators not use FISA interceptions as a way to avoid the stiffer requirements of Title III wiretap warrants. Until the USA PATRIOT Act, the way this was handled was that foreign intelligence had to be the *primary* purpose of a FISA surveillance.[77]

Title III and FISA form the basis for U.S. wiretap law. They were written when electronic communication was the analog circuit-switched PSTN; digitally switched and packet-based networks provided new challenges to the government's surveillance efforts.

4.4 Modern Networks

In the early days of the telephone, an operator at the local switchboard connected callers, affording little privacy to the customers. As communications changed over to automated switches, privacy, or at least its appearance, returned. In fact, because in the United States even local phone numbers were retained by the local exchange for billing and business purposes, transactional information was never truly private. It was, however, physically stored within the phone company. Since it was not easy to obtain this information except by going through the telephone company, the data mostly stayed private. Things began to change as law enforcement realized the value of the data.

One such case occurred in March 1976, after a Baltimore woman who had been robbed began receiving calls from a man claiming to be the thief. When the robbery victim saw a car cruising her neighborhood that looked like one present during the robbery, she told the police. Sometime later the police discovered the same car and traced it to a "Michael Smith." Without first obtaining a court order, the police put a *pen register*, a device for real-time capture of all numbers called by a specific number, on Smith's phone line. Smith was indeed calling the woman. With that information, the police had sufficient evidence for a search warrant, which they obtained. They searched Smith's house and found evidence of the theft.

Now the 1970s already had seen a series of cases in which the Supreme Court considered the privacy status of information being held by a third party. In *United States v. Miller*,[78] the Court examined bank records subpoenaed after evidence surfaced that the suspect was illegally making alcohol. The Court wrote that "if we direct our attention to the original checks and deposit slips, rather than to the microfilm copies actually viewed and obtained through the subpoena, we perceive no legitimate 'expectation of privacy' in their contents."[79]

Thus, unlike in the *Katz* case, no search warrant was required for the bank data.

In the Baltimore theft case, *Smith v. Maryland*,[80] the Supreme Court noted that few people "entertain any actual expectation of privacy in the numbers they dial." Citing *Miller*, the Court observed, "This Court has held repeatedly that the Fourth Amendment does not prohibit the obtaining of information revealed to a third party and conveyed by him to Government authorities, even if the information is revealed on the assumption that it will be used only for a limited purpose and the confidence placed in the third party will not be betrayed."[81] Just as the depositor had assumed a certain risk of disclosure of his bank account information, so did the caller assume a risk of disclosure of his calling information. *Smith* had no expectation of privacy and no warrant was needed for the search. The *Smith* decision was not universally accepted. Some state courts used the privacy protections of their state constitutions to provide better protection for their constituents.[82]

In the 1980s new switching technology made it easy to capture calling data. Signaling System 7 passes the caller identification information down the switches of the call, changing the effort of determining the number initiating the call from a procedure taking minutes to one being instantly available as the call is made. The information used by the police in the *Smith* case became easier to access.

Congress responded and in 1986 enacted the Electronic Communications Privacy Act (ECPA)[83] to provide certain privacy protections in electronic communications. ECPA defined three types of communication: wire, consisting of human speech transmitted by wire, cable, or similar connections; oral, consisting of any spoken utterance "carried by sound waves through the air";[84] and electronic, consisting of any electronic communication that was not wire or oral.[85] This meant that wiretapping could include tapping of fax and data (e.g., email). ECPA added various privacy protections to communications depending on how they were being carried.

Under ECPA, cell phone communications were treated as wire communications and were fully protected even when the over-the-air portion was unencrypted. Other radio communications were electronic.[86] If a radio communication could be *easily* intercepted—for example, with store-bought equipment—then it would not be protected. If, however, such communications were difficult to intercept (e.g., encrypted), then they were protected under ECPA. This meant that intentional interception by private citizens was subject to criminal penalties, while such interception by government without an intercept order was subject to suppression in court.

ECPA added protections for stored electronic communications, an issue that had arisen as a result of ISPs providing such services. Here the law was surprisingly complicated. Interception by private citizens was prohibited. Interception by the government required a search warrant for access to unread mail that had been stored at an ISP for 180 days or less (a search warrant is easier to obtain than an intercept order). Contents stored for a longer period and contents stored after having being read were given less protection.

ECPA also regulated the use of pen registers and *trap* and *trace*, the real-time capture of all numbers calling a specific number. In contrast to wiretaps, only a court order was needed for the installation of pen registers and trap-and-trace devices; it could be applied for by *any* federal lawyer and granted by a federal district judge or magistrate. There was no probable-cause requirement; law enforcement simply had to state that the information sought was relevant to an ongoing investigation.

Though it had gained certain provisions, including the ability to do *roving wiretaps* (wiretaps where the address of the tap is not specified because it is believed that the suspect is changing locations to avoid electronic surveillance), law enforcement had opposed the bill. In the end, privacy protections for the citizenry won out. Part of the reason for this was lawmakers' belief that such protections were necessary if such technologies as cell phones and email were to be widely adopted.

Law enforcement pressed back. At issue was accommodating law enforcement wiretaps. In 1970 there had been a conflict between the FBI and a local telephone company about the amount of assistance the telephone company had to provide in arranging the wiretap. Congress's response was to add a small section to the wiretap law requiring that the provider of telephone services supply technical assistance to accomplish the wiretap and be compensated accordingly.[87] The issue of whether the telephone companies had to design their systems around law enforcement needs had not arisen previously.[88]

In 1982, a court-ordered breakup of the AT&T monopoly created a host of competing service providers, a climate of innovation, and the development of multiple new services. It also created problems for law enforcement. Instead of dealing with a single—and not rapidly innovating—supplier, the FBI and state law enforcement faced a bewildering array of telephone companies served by multiple suppliers. Wiretapping grew complicated and more difficult, and law enforcement sought legislative relief. In 1992 the FBI pressed for the Digital Telephony proposal, which would require that all digitally switched telephone equipment be built wiretap accessible. The proposed bill included requirements that all telecommunications providers, including private branch exchanges (the private switching centers used in large organizations), design their systems to accommodate government wiretapping; the private sector was to bear the cost. There were lots of objections to the bill—and no support. It went nowhere. Two years later, the FBI tried again.

The FBI claimed that wiretapping had resulted in over seven thousand convictions in a six-year period (1985–1991) in bureau-led investigations alone.[89] Officials of the first Bush administration cast doubts on these numbers.[90] The bureau also argued that "hundreds" of wiretap orders had been thwarted as a result of new communication technologies,[91] but these numbers could not be substantiated.[92] The U.S. General Accounting Office found that while the FBI had been unclear on its electronic surveillance needs,[93] the bureau was indeed encountering technical problems in tapping new services.[94] This included, for example, the fact that in call forwarding, the call never makes it onto the local loop of the communication and thus a wiretap misses any calls that have been forwarded. The government report also noted that the telephone companies lacked adequate wiretapping capacity for cellular systems.[95]

In a last-minute deal between the telephone companies and law enforcement, Congress passed the Communications Assistance for Law Enforcement Act (CALEA).[96] CALEA required telecommunication carriers to design their systems so that they could quickly isolate call content as well as originating and destination numbers of the communication. In addition, the companies provide this information to law enforcement in a format and to a site of law enforcement's choice; see figure 4.1.[97]

Implementation was to occur after appropriate consultation among law enforcement, the telephone companies, and representatives of the users.[98] The House of Representatives report on the legislative history[99] stated that "the telecommunications industry itself shall decide how to implement law enforcement's requirements."[100] It was expected that the standard-setting authority would devolve to the FBI, but the lack of consultation that followed was unexpected. Implementation was divisive and litigious, with the FBI consistently setting standards that the communication providers believed extended well beyond CALEA's requirements.

One controversy was over interception capacity. The first time the FBI did the calculation, the bureau developed a requirement that would have resulted in the telephone companies having a capability of providing thirty thousand simultaneous surveillances (where surveillances included wiretap, electronic, combination, pen register, and trap-and-trace devices). This was four times the *annual* number that had been conducted in 1993, the year used as a baseline.[101] When there were objections to this, the FBI tried a new way of calculating and arrived at a maximum simultaneous surveillance capability of 57 thousand simultaneous interceptions, or eight times the total number in 1993. The blurring of the line between wiretaps, which were considered an invasive search, and pen registers and trap-and-trace devices, which were not considered invasive, meant that the FBI could be requesting sufficient interception capability to perform 57 thousand simultaneous pen registers—or 57 thousand simultaneous wiretaps.[102]

The next controversy was over "post-cut-through dialed digits," the digits punched in after the call has been established by the carrier to a switch. These might be the actual number you are dialing after reaching your long-distance provider from a toll-free number, an extension, a bank account number and the pass code needed to access the account, or a prescription number to the druggist. Law enforcement agencies argued that the post-cut-through digits were call-identifying information and should be included in the transactional data delivered in a pen register;

Traditional Intercept Model

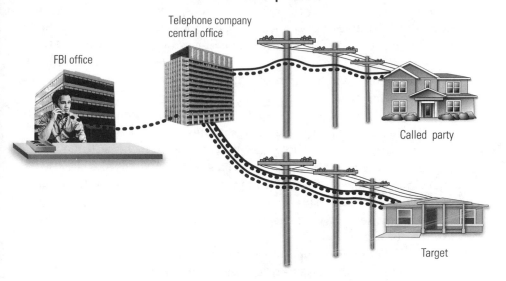

CALEA Intercept Model

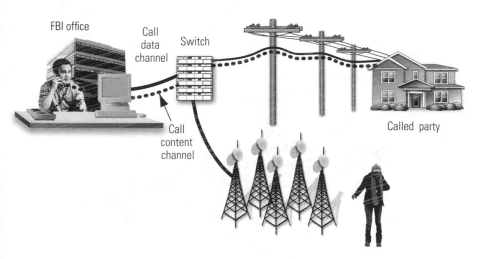

Figure 4.1
Traditional intercept versus CALEA intercept. Illustration by Nancy Snyder.

the telephone companies argued it could be content and should not. When the FCC accepted the FBI's interpretation, the case went to court,[103] which remanded it to the FCC, complaining about the lack of specificity in the FCC's ruling. The FCC determined that post-cut-through digits should be supplied with an "appropriate legal instrument," leaving open whether that meant a pen register for call-identifying information or a full-blown wiretap order for content.[104]

This case also included a dispute over location information. While CALEA stated that "such call-identifying information shall not include any information that may disclose the physical location of the subscriber (except to the extent that the location may be determined from the telephone number),"[105] the FBI pressed to have the information—in the form of the location of the closest antenna tower—included in the signaling information associated with cell phone communications. The court agreed to this.

As long as carriers complied with the CALEA standards, regardless of whether they could actually execute court-ordered wiretaps, the carriers fell under the "safe-harbor" provision of the law. But for each day that law enforcement was unable to execute a court-authorized wiretap on a non-compliant system, the telecommunications carrier was subject to a fine of $10,000. This was not inconsequential. Congress authorized $500 million to cover telephone-company costs to do the upgrades to CALEA—that was part of why the telephone companies had dropped their opposition to CALEA in 1994. As of 2008, only 10 percent of the funds remained,[106] while nearly 40 percent of U.S. switches remained noncompliant.[107]

CALEA marks a radical transformation of U.S. wiretap law. Title III, FISA, and ECPA delineated the circumstances under which a wiretap order could be authorized. Those laws left the customer-facing telephone companies in charge of determining how to satisfy the government's surveillance needs. By putting a law enforcement agency into the role of developing telephone switching standards, CALEA turned this model on its head. The FBI had little experience with telephone design, and even less with serving the privacy needs of the public. The process of implementing CALEA, supposed to be in place in 1998, has taken much longer.

There was also the issue of extending the law's reach. FBI Director Louis Freeh had testified in Congress that the FBI was not seeking to include voice communications over the Internet within the law's purview[108] and CALEA has a clear exemption for "information services."[109] In 1994 this meant the Internet.[110] Neither the legislative commitments nor the law prevented the FBI from notifying the FCC in 2003 that nascent VoIP services posed a threat to law enforcement wiretapping. The FBI asked that the FCC extend CALEA to VoIP. In the summer of 2005, mimicking its decision on how VoIP should handle E911, the FCC extended CALEA to broadband Internet access providers and providers of interconnected VoIP services, VoIP that could send and receive calls from the PSTN. In both instances, the VoIP user is connecting to the PSTN in a fixed, predetermined location, making the location of a tap easy to manage.

To no one's surprise, industry and civil liberties groups took the issue to court. To many people's surprise, the U.S. Court of Appeals concurred with the FCC. The dissenting judge told his colleagues to read the law,[111] section 1002 (b)(2)(A) of which explicitly states that assistance capability requirements "do not extend to information service providers."

Around the same time the FCC decided that VoIP providers connecting with the public telephone network would be required to give the location for any E911 calls.[112] This was a seemingly reasonable request on its face. In fact, IP-based networks do not automatically have such location information available, and this requirement is complex to satisfy.

Activities were proceeding on other fronts as well. In July 2000, the *Wall Street Journal* reported the FBI had developed a tool with the poorly chosen name of Carnivore for wiretapping at ISPs.[113] Carnivore was a packet sniffer designed to execute legally authorized wiretaps and pen-register orders at ISPs. The FBI argued that Carnivore was simply a natural application of wiretapping technology to the Internet, but the differing nature of the two networks suggested otherwise. There was concern over privacy of the users not targeted by the system, but nonetheless "seen" by it. Carnivore, later renamed DCS3000, had not been built with privacy in mind.[114] The ISPs were not pleased by the FBI solution, and, in at least one case, had gone to court over it.[115]

As the public and Congress raised questions about Carnivore, the Department of Justice seemed to be backing away from the tool. In the summer of 2001, the department agreed to a policy review of issues raised by the packet sniffer. But then September 11 occurred. With it, everything changed.

4.5 Wiretapping Post–September 11

The attacks of September 11, 2001, were an enormous shock to the United States. In one way, however, the Department of Justice was very prepared; just eight days after the planes flew into the buildings, Attorney General John Ashcroft provided Congress with a forty-page draft antiterrorism bill.[116]

There were any number of mistakes made by U.S. intelligence that allowed the events of September 11 to occur.[117] Nonetheless the immediate reaction after the events of that day was not to look at where government institutions had failed—indeed it took over a year before the September 11 commission was established—but instead to focus on giving the government additional tools to stop such an event from recurring.[118] Congress and the White House swung into action.

While initial administration and congressional efforts were bipartisan, within two weeks the White House began pressing hard for the adoption of its draft legislation. The discussion became partisan, and there was little room for public discussion of civil liberties issues.[119] Even focusing only on electronic surveillance—the legislation was much broader than that—the new law was quite expansive.

The most important change in the law was the transformation from foreign intelligence being the "primary" purpose to simply a "significant" purpose of the surveillance (§218). Other important interception aspects of the USA PATRIOT Act included: §203(b), permitting law enforcement officers to share wiretap information with other federal officials if the information contains foreign intelligence or counterintelligence; §206, which expanded FISA to roving wiretaps; §214, which weakened standards for FISA use of pen registers and trap-and-trace devices; §216, which stated that a pen register and trap-and-trace order applied nationally, not just in the jurisdiction in which it was issued;[120] §217, which eliminated the need for an interception order in cases where law enforcement sought to monitor activities of a computer trespasser.[121] In addition, the law added several crimes to the list of serious crimes for which an intercept order was warranted.

One section that was problematic was §216, which updated the law regarding pen registers and trap-and-trace orders to ensure they applied to the Internet. There was no definition of what "routing" and "addressing" meant in the context of pen registers and trap-and-trace devices,[122] an omission that the Department of Justice agreed left open the possibility that "reasonable minds may differ as to whether, and at what stage, URL information might be construed as content."[123] There was also initial concern that §217 might be used by law enforcement to monitor users simply with the consent of an ISP. However, the law was written to limit such interception to genuine trespassers and not to users of the system (whether paid subscribers, students on a university system, etc.).[124]

Several sections of the law were due to expire in 2005.[125] In the end, all but one—§203(b), which was modified—were renewed. It looked as though the United States, over a twenty-seven-year period from 1978 to 2005, had put together a robust legal regime for foreign-intelligence wiretapping. There was, however, a loophole.

4.6 Warrantless Wiretapping

When FISA was passed in 1978, it permitted the warrantless wiretapping of radio communications within the United States if at least one party on the communication was outside the country—as long as the government was not using the warrantless exemption as a way to target a known, particular U.S. person inside the United States. This exemption was intended to be temporary, with the expectation that Congress would provide legislation for radio surveillance later.[126] Congress never did. With time, the National Security Agency (NSA), the U.S. government's eavesdropping agency, grew to depend on this exception. And with time, the government came to believe that the exception could grow. Fiber-optic cables were replacing radio, and the decreasing percentage of overseas communications being sent by satellite was thwarting the warrantless exemption present in FISA.[127] The government argued for extending the old warrantless regime to a new communications technology. There was certainly a rationale for the U.S. government's warrantless surveillance.

The fiber-optic build-out that occurred in the last two decades of the twentieth century made the United States a communications transit point for the entire world. As is shown in figure 4.2, connections between Europe and Asia, between South America and Europe, and even between South America and South America, or Asia and Asia, went through the United States. There were any number of reasons for this geographic oddity. One was that U.S. providers underbid overpriced regional carriers, which explains why inter–South American traffic might travel via Miami. A second cause was politics: sometimes communications could not travel directly between two nations, but could go via a third party (for some time this was the case with Taiwan and China). A third reason was technology. The United States is home to many of the world's email servers (Yahoo Mail, Hotmail, Gmail).[128] Thus email between two people in Quetta and Kabul, for example, may travel via a server in Oregon. If any of those communications had gone by satellite, the NSA would have been able to simply pluck the signal out of the air. But modern technology meant that these communications were arriving in the United States by fiber-optic cable and that complicated the situation.

On December 16, 2005, the *New York Times* broke a story it had been holding for a year at the government's request, namely that since shortly

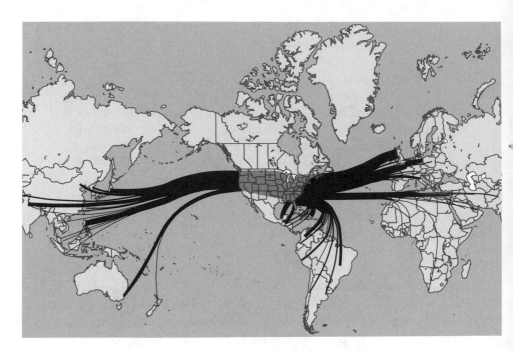

Figure 4.2
Traditional intercept model and CALEA intercept model. Illustration by Nancy Snyder.

after the attacks of September 11, 2001, the United States had been monitoring the international communications of hundreds, if not thousands, of people within the United States *without a warrant*. At any one time up to five hundred people were being monitored. The *Times* reported government claims that only international communications were targeted and no purely domestic calls had fallen into the intelligence agency net. The government also stated that the eavesdropping uncovered a number of plots, including that of Iyman Faris, a Kashmir-born truck driver who had plotted with Al-Qaeda to destroy the Brooklyn Bridge, and threats of fertilizer-based bombs at British pubs and train stations.[129] It was said that the program began "on the fly" in the panic-stricken days after the attacks and initially monitored calls between the United States and Afghanistan.[130]

A few months after the *Times* story appeared, *USA Today* exposed a new angle: the NSA was using the telephone companies' call databases to study calling patterns. This involved hundreds of millions of records from three of the four major long-distance providers: AT&T, BellSouth, and Verizon (Quest refused to participate).[131] This contradicted President Bush's claim that the surveillance was directed solely toward international calls.

Call Detail Records (CDRs) detail which number was calling, when, for how long, using which IP address (if an IP-based communication) and, sometimes, URL (if a Voice over IP communication). CDR had previously been purely internal telephone company records, used by the telecommunications companies for billing and business planning. Such records are, however, protected by §222 of the 1996 Telecommunications Act,[132] which says that the telephone companies should not disclose "information contained in the bills pertaining to telephone exchange service or telephone toll service received by a customer of a carrier" except as required by law. Yet the records were apparently given to the U.S. government without a court order—and used without any court oversight.

As any intelligence operative knows, communication patterns are full of information. From them one can discern organizational structure as well as behavioral patterns. Who do you call when there is a change in personnel at the company? Who do you let know when you discover your wife will be working late and you are suddenly free for the evening? Where do you call from after work—the office, a bar, a friend's apartment?[133] This information can be remarkably revealing. While law enforcement has long had access to the real-time transactional data of pen-register and trap-and-trace information, the CDRs provide a long view into history.

A third strand to the story now appeared. A technician at the AT&T switching office in San Francisco, Mark Klein, had come forward with a set of documents that showed the government had a system fully capable of performing massive spying on domestic communications.

After an NSA agent had visited the AT&T facility in 2002, the company constructed a secure room within its switching offices. According to Klein, only technicians cleared by NSA were allowed in this secured room.[134] The documents described a setup in which optical-fiber carrying communications was "split," with one signal going into this room. (Fiber is the communication medium of choice. The light pulses have low signal loss and the wires are immune to electromagnetic interference. They are also hard to tap.) There the signal was subject to analysis, with communications of interest then being shipped off to a monitoring facility. Because the AT&T office was a *peering point*—a place where administratively separate domains such as different ISPs or telephone companies interconnect—the information being scanned represented almost all the communications exchanged between AT&T and other major telecommunications providers in the San Francisco Bay Area.[135] There were similar collection points in other major U.S. cities, including Seattle, San Jose, Los Angeles, San Diego, and Atlanta.[136] It was not surprising that communications surveillance was occurring;

the location of the interception, at an internal peering point within the United States, was highly disturbing. Conducting eavesdropping at such a location meant that many purely domestic calls were likely to be caught in the snare.

The warrantless wiretapping and other forms of expanded surveillance, together known as the President's Surveillance Program (PSP),[137] occurred against a backdrop of other FISA activities. The 2001 PATRIOT Act had lowered the wall between FISA and Title III investigations, but the FISA Court, the eleven-member set of judges who make the decisions about foreign-intelligence surveillance, had grown increasingly dismayed over FBI errors in foreign-intelligence and criminal cases. Their concern was minimization, namely the reuse of information originally obtained through FISA. This law gives the government "a powerful engine for the collection of foreign intelligence information targeting U.S. persons," wrote the court.[138] The court noted that "the standard for retention of FISA-acquired information is weighted heavily in favor of the government"[139] and ruled the government's minimization efforts were not in accord with the law. The FISA Court ordered that the Department of Justice Office of Intelligence Policy and Review (OIPR) be invited to participate in meetings between the FBI and the criminal division discussing coordination of investigations.[140]

The Bush administration appealed the decision to the U.S. FISA Court of Review, the first time in the twenty-five year history of the FISA Court that a FISA review court had been convened. The review court agreed that the FISA Court had "misinterpreted and misapplied minimization procedures," and it removed the OIPR reviewing requirement.[141]

Yet things were not smooth sailing for the administration. Indeed, the administration itself was not fully agreed on the legality of the PSP. Memos supporting the program had been written by John Yoo, a deputy assistant attorney general and a relatively young member of the department. At the White House's insistence, the only DoJ officials "read into" the program were the attorney general and the counsel for intelligence policy, James Baker.[142] That situation changed in 2003, when Yoo was replaced by Patrick Philbin, and Yoo's boss was replaced by Jack Goldsmith. Both developed serious concerns about the program.

Yoo had argued that because the monitoring was part of a "military operation" the Fourth Amendment did not apply.[143] He had completely ignored the *Youngstown Sheet & Tube Co. v. Sawyer*[144] case, which limited presidential power, even during wartime. That omission, and the fact that FISA provided clear bounds on the process by which the U.S. government could wiretap for national-security purposes—a process that the President's Surveillance Program was disregarding—greatly worried Jack Goldsmith, who had become head of DoJ's Office of Legal Counsel in 2003. Goldsmith brought his concerns to the top: to Attorney General John Ashcroft and Deputy Attorney General James Comey.[145]

In March 2004 Ashcroft was incapacitated due to surgery. Comey, who was acting attorney general, was asked to sign off on a PSP recertification, a process that DoJ had been required to do every forty-five days. Comey refused. In a scene out of a Grade B movie, the president called Ashcroft's hospital room to say that White House counsel Alberto Gonzales and the president's chief of staff, Andrew Card, would be on their way. Ashcroft was gravely ill, and visitors had been banned. Ashcroft's wife informed Comey of this odd visit. The acting attorney general raced to the hospital, arriving before the president's staff. When Gonzales came to the room, he ignored Comey and asked Ashcroft to reauthorize the program. Though very ill, Ashcroft cogently expressed his doubts about the program's legality and then pointed out that Comey was acting attorney general. Comey again refused to sign. The White House was not deterred: the next day it continued the program even though PSP had not received the DoJ approval.[146]

Things grew worse for the administration. The FISA Court, which had had an almost 100 percent record on authorizing wiretap applications for a quarter century, now began asking for substantive changes in about 5 percent of the submissions.[147] This cost a substantial amount of time from NSA lawyers. After the appearance of the *New York Times* article reporting the warrantless wiretapping, one member of the FISA Court resigned in protest.[148]

Meanwhile the claims made about the PSP's effectiveness did not stand up. The Faris and fertilizer-bomb cases were already known from other sources. In another case, it appears that the targets of an FBI sting operation involving money laundering for terrorist purposes came to the attention of law-enforcement not through wiretaps (as had been originally believed) but through information from a notebook found in a terrorist camp in northern Iraq in 2003.[149] And many of the tips produced by the program had investigators spending time on chases that led nowhere.[150]

There was another problem. In the years after the PSP was established, some applications before the FISA Court had evidence that came from the program.[151] If a court case resulted from evidence from a FISA warrant that was based on information obtained from the PSP warrantless wiretapping, then the case itself would be tainted and inadmissible. James Baker was in charge of all FISA applications that were sent to the FISA Court, and he believed that FISA worked well.[152] He did not want to see the 1978 surveillance law irremediably undermined. So in 2002 Baker set up a program with the head of the FISA Court, Royce Lamberth, to ensure that any FISA wiretap application containing information that came from the PSP was flagged. Only Lamberth, and then later, his successor, Colleen Kollar-Kotelly, would see the FISA application. The judge would ensure that the application could stand on the non-PSP evidence. In 2004 this effort ran into difficulties: NSA was not telling Baker about all the people it was listening to. Consequently Baker was not properly flagging the FISA applications for Kollar-Kotelly, who had taken over as presiding judge.[153] Angry and concerned that the applications using PSP information would affect the integrity of the FISA Court rulings, the judge had DoJ suspend using information provided by NSA for FISA Court applications until the problem was resolved; this took a few weeks.[154]

Civil liberties groups and others filed suit against the government. The government lost round one: in August 2006 a federal judge in Michigan ruled that the PSP violated FISA and the Fourth Amendment.[155] Then the government won round two: in 2007 the Sixth Court of Appeals dismissed the case on lack of standing.[156] Naturally the plaintiffs could not prove they had been wiretapped by the government; the surveillance was secret.[157] The Supreme Court chose not to hear an appeal by the ACLU.

Another case caused particular worries for the government. An Oregon-based Islamic charity, al-Haramain, had been wiretapped under the PSP. This was revealed by the government, which had inadvertently sent classified documents describing the surveillance to al-Haramain's lawyers. The charity filed a lawsuit against the government, and the government sought dismissal, arguing that a trial would release "state secrets." (The state-secrets privilege permits halting a trial if public disclosures during the trial would endanger national security.[158]) While the classified documents were not accepted as evidence, the fact that the government was wiretapping the charity was discussed in a 2007 speech by FBI Deputy Director John Pistole; this gave al-Haramain legal standing to pursue the case.

The situation did not provide an all clear for the Bush administration. In conjunction with others, the Electronic Frontier Foundation (EFF) had filed suit[159] against AT&T over "illegal spying of telephone and Internet communications." AT&T acknowledged that the documents describing the layout and configuration for the secure room were genuine. This civil case, known as *Hepting*, was of great concern to the government. The phone company feared its liability, the risk resulting from the warrantless nature of the wiretaps, while the White House feared the release of details surrounding the program.

The administration argued that the PSP was legal under the Authorization for Use of Military Force (AUMF).[160] Passed a week after the September 11 attacks, the AUMF granted the president the right to "use all necessary and appropriate force against those nations, organizations, or persons he determines planned, authorized, committed, or aided the terrorist attacks that occurred on September 11, 2001, or harbored such organizations." Such a broad expansion of executive authority was a controversial claim, and Congress did not buy it. In the summer of 2006 the administration agreed to submit the PSP to FISA Court review.[161]

In 2007, after the furor created by the *Times* and *USA Today* revelations had somewhat died down, the White House argued that the legal procedures required by the FISA Court were unreasonably delaying necessary wiretaps and posing a threat to national security. The Bush administration pushed for legalizing the PSP. In July 2007, Congress did so, passing the *Protect America Act*.[162] The law provided that communications "reasonably believed to have a participant outside the U.S." could be intercepted without a warrant. Congress handled its unease about the statute by making the law valid for only a six-month period. In January 2008 Congress extended the law an additional two weeks, and then it lapsed. At issue was a Bush administration demand for protection of the telephone companies that had permitted the warrantless wiretapping.

In July 2008, Congress acceded, not only legalizing the warrantless wiretapping practices, but also, in what was a very controversial move, giving the telephone companies retroactive immunity.[163] Under the FISA Amendments Act,[164] the FISA Court would continue to review individual warrants for wiretapping communications that were purely domestic; the new law meant that certain classes of wiretaps—the ones in which one end was believed to be outside the United States—would not be reviewed individually but handled under procedures subject to periodic FISA Court review. A concession to privacy advocates was that FISA warrants would be required for wiretapping U.S. persons abroad. Prior to September 11, NSA practice had been to require a warrant when targeting U.S. persons overseas even though FISA did not require this. NSA changed its practice after the 2001 terrorist attacks. The FISA Amendments Act effectively ended the *Hepting* case and, with it, any chance for fully understanding the activities that had actually occurred. The FISA Amendments Act expires in 2012.

In March 2010, the government's warrantless wiretapping program suffered a non-fatal blow. Federal judge Vaughn Walker ruled that the warrantless wiretapping of al-Haramain had violated FISA.[165] Because FISA permits civil remedies to "aggrieved persons" whose rights have been violated, the government was liable for damages. But Walker's ruling was narrow. The government's defense had been limited to blocking the al-Haramain suit through the state-secrets privilege, and Walker's decision was similarly limited. He ruled that using state-secrets privilege to circumvent the warrant procedure for foreign-surveillance wiretapping violated FISA. Walker did not rule on whether the PSP itself was legal.[166]

Meanwhile similar activities were occurring elsewhere. Sweden passed a law[167] permitting its government to do warrantless wiretapping of all transit telecommunications. It was discovered that the German foreign intelligence agency, the Bundesnachrichtendienst (BND), was spying on communications between the Afghan foreign ministry and a German journalist,[168] the result of a Trojan-horse program placed on a computer in the Afghan Ministry of Commerce. This electronic eavesdropping violated Article 10 of the German constitution, which requires that "the privacy of letters, posts, and telecommunications shall be inviolable."[169] The BND has also searched through thousands of foreign PCs through installing software *key loggers*, which capture keystrokes and can thus reveal anything on a user's machine.[170]

The United States itself was also apparently wiretapping journalists. Russell Tice, a former intelligence analyst, claimed that U.S. news organizations and journalists were targeted by the NSA.[171] In the absence of a congressional investigation and sworn testimony, it is impossible to know what is true—the government has issued vehement denials—but there is supporting evidence to this claim. Lawrence Wright, a reporter for the *New Yorker* and author of *The Looming Tower: Al Qaeda and the Road to 9/11*, had reason to suspect he was one of them. Federal agents asked him about some of his phone calls to sources; it was clear from the conversation that he had been wiretapped.[172] *New York Times* reporter James Risen, who, with Eric Lichtblau, had broken the story of the PSP, found that Bush administration officials had copies of his phone records.[173] As of this writing, Risen and his lawyers have been unable to determine if the records had been obtained through a subpoena—the government was investigating the leaks that fed his 2006 book on the CIA—or through the Terrorist Surveillance Program that he and Lichtblau had revealed to the nation. In either case, the effect was chilling, not so much for Risen, who had the support of his newspaper, but for his government sources, who lacked such protection.[174]

Hoover's ghost did not die; to this day wiretaps enable political manipulation. In 2005 Representative Jane Harman, a member of the House Intelligence Committee, put pressure on the *New York Times* not to publish its story on the administration's warrantless wiretapping. In an odd shake of events, Harman was herself captured on a wiretap, this one a legally authorized one of two Israeli agents suspected of illegally distributing national-security documents.[175] Congressional leaders were to be informed of Harman's involvement, but Attorney General Alberto Gonzalez intervened and asked the CIA to delay briefing congressional leadership. Gonzalez's stated reason was concern that Harman would learn of the wiretaps before being interviewed by the FBI investigators. But government sources said the real reason for the delay was to "protect" Harman because she was a valuable ally in urging the *Times* not to publish anything on the President's Surveillance Program.[176] Harman was never interviewed by the bureau on this issue.[177]

During the period when the public was loudly decrying the warrantless wiretapping, the president authorized the Comprehensive National Cybersecurity Initiative, a little-noticed, but seemingly sweeping, project to install surveillance capabilities across the Internet in order to protect U.S. critical infrastructure against cyberattacks.[178] The surveillance being proposed was not only for government networks, but also for private ones. Because virtually all aspects of the project were classified, there was essentially no public discussion of the program. This was not the first time this had occurred for a Bush administration surveillance program.

I now turn to examining the effects of this surveillance.

5 The Effectiveness of Wiretapping

Immediately after the September 11 attacks, the United States embarked on a series of efforts to protect itself. Some measures, such as physical protection of critical infrastructure, were adopted without controversy (although these were not always implemented as well as they might have been). Others such as *data mining*, analyzing massive data sets for "interesting" patterns, and *behavioral surveillance*, monitoring peoples' involuntary reactions[1] to determine what they are actually thinking, were highly controversial. There were strong protests that these techniques abused civil rights, but generally the programs continued during the Bush administration.[2]

The critics had been asking the wrong question. In 2005, a panel formed by the National Research Council, the research arm of the U.S. National Academies of Science and Engineering and the Institute of Medicine, was tasked with examining privacy in light of government programs in data mining and behavioral surveillance. The group's most important conclusion: before a program is deployed, its effectiveness should be examined.[3] If a program is not effective, then there is no reason to deploy it, and no effort needs to be expended regarding its potential infringement of civil liberties.

The same criterion should, of course, apply to communications surveillance: how effective is wiretapping? There are problems with answering this question. There is little way to determine how a case would have turned out had there been no wiretapping and no way to see how a jury would have reacted with the wiretapping evidence—or without it. In national-security cases, the details of the investigation rarely come to light. Nonetheless, some information is available despite limitations on the answers.

Wiretapping is particularly useful in conspiracies such as organized crime and drug cases. Anecdotally we know, for example, that in 2007 wiretaps were used in a Tennessee narcotics investigation in which forty people were convicted, in a New York City investigation of a theft ring with thirty-three convictions, and in an Ohio drug investigation with thirty convictions.[4] Although details of the role wiretapping plays are rarely available, it is clear the tool is heavily used in national-security investigations. One example was the case of CIA counterintelligence officer Aldrich Ames, who was convicted of spying for the Soviet Union and Russia.[5] Transactional information, which lets investigators know who spoke with whom where and when, is particularly useful. Whether a group is a drug-trafficking ring or a terrorist cell, such data can reveal the organization's structure, which is of great value to investigators. Cell phones, typically tied to a person, reveal where a person is at a particular time.

Transactional information can be revealing even if no conversation takes place. In 2002, investigators began an almost two-year investigation tracking Al-Qaeda members through their use of prepaid phone cards, which had been anonymously purchased in bulk. The original tracked call had "lasted less than a minute and involved not a single word of conversation," but the agents exploited it to map out an Al-Qaeda network involving members in the United States, Pakistan, Saudi Arabia, Germany, Britain, and Italy. Calling it "one of the most effective tools" they'd had, a law enforcement official said, "The perception of anonymity may have lulled [the Al-Qaeda members] into a false sense of security." A number of cell members were arrested. One person whose location was discovered through this was Khalid Sheikh Mohammed, said to be the architect of the September 11 attacks.[6]

The ability to track makes electronic surveillance quite useful to intelligence and law-enforcement agencies—and particularly threatening to those who might be the subject of such investigations. This risk has kept Osama bin Laden off electronic communications since the late 1990s.[7] Preventing criminals and terrorists from using modern forms of communication is a strong benefit of electronic surveillance.

Clearly wiretapping can be remarkably effective in criminal, foreign-intelligence, and terrorism cases. Yet since full data are not publicly available, evaluation is difficult. Consider an analogous situation. In 1996, a National Research Council report on cryptography concluded that it was possible to have a reasonable public debate on cryptography on an unclassified basis.[8] I conjecture that the same is true here: there is sufficient public data on wiretapping to have an informed public discussion on wiretap effectiveness, even while omitting discussion of specific cases. That is the intent of this chapter.

5.1   New Gold: Transactional Data

The biggest use of wiretapping tools is not actually the capture of conversation but something that is not really wiretapping at all: the capture of transactional information. The last decade has seen a huge investigatory use of communications location information. This is through both the use of pen registers and trap and traces, which provide real-time access to location information, and access to CDRs—the customer call-detail records amassed by the telephone companies that are a treasure trove of peoples' activities.

Under the Smith ruling, little privacy protection is afforded to transactional information. ECPA established that subpoenas, which are easier to obtain than warrants, would be required for installation of pen-register and trap-and-trace devices. That level of legal protection seemed appropriate, because transactional information is information shared with the telephone company—a third party—and therefore is not subject to stringent Fourth Amendment protections. But then things changed.

Cell phones and, more recently, mobile computing, including smart phones such as the iPhone, have entered the scene. Behavior with cell phones is very different than with landlines. Users broadcast their location whenever their phone is turned on—and the phones can be manipulated to do such broadcasting even when the phone is off. People use their communications devices frequently, often for very brief conversations. This has proved to be a major boon for law enforcement.

In criminal investigations, if law enforcement wants the past history of a suspect's calls, it will seek a court order for access to the CDRs; if, instead, prospective information is the object, then law enforcement will seek an order for a pen register. Minimal court oversight exists in both instances. In contrast, in intelligence investigations, the FBI may use a National Security Letter (NSL), which is served directly on the communications provider.

Originally created in 1978 to give FBI investigators in foreign intelligence cases an exception to the privacy protections already in the law,[9] NSLs were limited to use against foreign powers and people believed to be their agents.[10] Because providing such proof was difficult, NSLs were rarely used. The PATRIOT Act greatly expanded the FBI's authority to use NSLs, permitting field offices to issue them and changing the requirement that the information sought must pertain to a foreign power, or agent of one, to the requirement that the information sought must be relevant to protecting against "international terrorism or clandestine intelligence activities."[11]

The new law also allowed the bureau to require the recipient of an NSL to keep it secret, not informing the subject—or anyone else—about the request.[12]

Use of NSLs vastly increased after the PATRIOT Act; between 2003 and 2006, the FBI issued 192,000 NSLs,[13] the overwhelming majority for telephone records.[14] The FBI increasingly relies on NSLs as the primary investigative tool in terrorism and espionage investigations,[15] often using the records to support FISA applications.[16] One knowledgeable government source called NSLs "a real game changer." In 1995, the bureau wanted spoken content, because that "was the most important information we could get." But listening in turned out to be far less valuable than link analysis: connecting who was talking with whom. The fact that many people were using cell phones made such information even more valuable, for the devices reveal their owners' location.

The U.S. Marshals Service, responsible for tracking fugitives, seeks pen-register information with the location of the first and last daily cell sites of the target's phone. These data combined with information about the fugitive's background has allowed the Marshals Service to cut its average investigation time from forty-two days to two. The principle is simple: if the suspect's cell phone registers at the same cell tower each night at 11:00 and again the following morning at 10:00, and this happens to be the tower serving a friend or relative of the suspect, there is a good chance the fugitive is sleeping at that friend's or relative's home. Law enforcement's ability to track is not just to a cell site, but to "phones hidden in an office building."[17] Such tracking enabled the arrest of one of the men later convicted in the attempted bombings of the London transit system on July 21, 2005: Hamdi Isaac Adus fled to Rome, but he was tracked to his brother's apartment through the movements of his cell phone.[18]

Real-time access to location information can sometimes enable breaking the case in a matter of hours. In kidnappings where the child has been taken by a noncustodial parent, there is a known person with a known cell number. Investigating such cases is a matter of tracking the location of the parent's phone (or sometimes the child's phone). Cell phone location has also been used to break other kidnapping cases, most often those when the abduction is unplanned and the victim still has the phone even if it is off.

Sometimes law enforcement uses pen registers to develop sufficient information to then apply for a Title III warrant. In such cases the investigation focuses on these questions: Are these two phones in contact? How often? Is this new person part of the conspiracy? Law enforcement investigators request various types of location information searches, such as the following:

• All phones at the sites at the time and location of the Washington sniper.[19]
• All phones in the vicinity of the Westin Copley Place Boston on the evening of April 10, 2009, and all phones in the vicinity of the Boston Marriott Copley Place on the evening of April 14, 2009.[20]
• All phones registered at a particular tower between 10:00 and 10:30 p.m.

The first search combines both pen-register—real-time—with retrospective data, while the second and third are retrospective. Such searches may be used directly to net the criminal—unsuccessful in the first case, successful in the second—or indirectly, such as in finding witnesses.[21] Police map out the conspiracy based on the accumulated data. This is where things get complicated for the telephone companies.

While the average time for a Marshals Service pen-register investigation is at most ten days, the FBI uses the orders for their full period of sixty days—and even longer. Investigations by the Drug Enforcement Agency can last up to half a year.[22] Law enforcement first seeks the records on targets, then broadens the search to their associates, then to the associates' associates, and so on. A pen-register order can be used to apply for information about the calls of one suspect. Then it can be used to return a day—or a week or a month later—for calls of someone whom the original suspect called, and so on. The clock starts anew each time the order is served for a new user, and the list can grow to thousands of people. According to Al Gidari, privacy partner at the law firm of Perkins Coie LLP, a single pen-register order can effectively be "a daisy chain that never expires as it is used with successive service providers."[23]

In France, if police are tracking a suspect, they will scan all cell phones in a given location.[24] If the suspect is a credit-card thief, the police will correlate those appearances in places where the card is being used.[25] Suspects who think they are being clever by using pay phones are fooling themselves. The French police track the appearance of cell phones—on or off makes no difference[26]—in the vicinity of the pay phones, destroying the anonymity the criminals thought they were achieving.[27]

Although the Department of Justice is required to report to Congress annually on its use of pen registers and trap-and trace-devices[28] including what type of crime was involved, the district in which the surveillance occurred, and so on, the department has fallen far short of doing so. In 2004 the department filed an aggregate report for 1999–2004[29] with

Congress. From this we learn that in 1999 there were 4,949 federal pen-register applications and 1,553 applications for trap and trace; in 2000, the numbers were 4,210 and 1,869; in 2001, 4,172 and 1,511; in 2002, 4,103 and 1,208; and in 2003, 5,932, and 1,336. The number of investigations, extensions, and persons whose telephones were affected in each of these years is also reported.[30]

The data are missing required information, such as crime involved and district in which the interception occurred. This makes it impossible to connect a surveillance to a particular crime and leaves no way to determine the effectiveness of the pen registers and trap and traces that the DoJ has been increasingly performing. The incomplete data prevents oversight. Even worse, the numbers appear incorrect. While historical data from the 1990s shows that the total of pen registers and trap-and-trace orders was somewhere between ten and fifty times the number of Title III warrants,[31] the recent numbers released to Congress show a sharp break from that pattern with much lower numbers of pen registers and trap and traces than expected. In addition to pure pen register and trap and trace, law enforcement has also been using "hybrid" orders combining past and future user locations in a single request.[32] In 2009, the four major wireless carriers have been receiving roughly twenty thousand orders annually for such hybrid data.[33] Thus it is likely that underreporting has been occurring.

In fact there is already clear evidence of this. An email released under a Freedom of Information request reveals one of the FBI agents commenting as follows:

We deal mostly with the Fugitive squad here and, like in many other offices, these guys have a reputation for cutting corners (I'm not bashing them; it's the way they do business). Getting a court order is absolutely the last step, if they have to. Before I had a blow-up with a particular Agent almost exactly one year ago, we were constantly asked to call our contacts at service providers to see if we could get various information without having to get a court order. . . . Doing this once or twice to help turns into SOP [Standard Operating Procedure]. . . . I also had a problem with the Fugitive guys calling the service providers and telling them it was I who was calling. . . . We also had an Agent try to knowingly pass a bad court order to us.[34]

It is clear why law enforcement would choose this way to conduct an investigation if possible. Use of the telephone company's location information, both real time and in the CDRs, represents a major cost savings for police. One former investigator observed that subpoenaed phone records provide the same information as thirty days of covering a suspect with a five-person surveillance team—at a fraction of the cost (at least to law enforcement). But accessing this information is not free; ultimately someone pays. The burden on the carriers in the longer investigations "can be enormous," according to Gidari. The search for cell phone records for the Washington sniper was expensive in other ways as well: the AT&T wireless system crashed, while Verizon ran into problems.

There has been concern that NSLs were being overused, and in 2009, eight senators introduced a bill to place safeguards on the use of National Security Letters,[35] namely, that NSLs were to be issued for phone records only when they "pertained to a suspected agent of a foreign power, an individual who is the subject of an ongoing and authorized national security investigation"[36] and related instances.[37] The lack of oversight has led to abuses. It may also create security risks when the wrong people illegally use the system.

It is not always necessary to access the phone company's records in order to track users. The FBI uses technology developed by the Harris Corporation: Triggerfish, which employs the target's phone, an antenna, and a laptop to determine a cell phone user's location. Whenever a cell phone is on, the phone registers with the nearest cell tower. The Triggerfish antenna intercepts the signals,[38] and by analyzing direction and signal strength from the targeted phone, Triggerfish determines the cell phone's location.[39] Although the telephone company is out of the loop, a court order (pen register or trap-and-trace order) must still be obtained by law enforcement before the system can be employed.[40] The system is expensive, running upward of $50 thousand, which keeps use limited.

The near ubiquitous use of cell phones means that the ability to track users is available to others than law enforcement. Google, of course, offers such tracking as an opt-in service (Latitude). A U.K. company, Path Intelligence Ltd., has gone one step further and markets such services to third parties. Path Intelligence offers tracking to within a couple of meters of a person's location, which means that the system knows not only which store the individual is in, but where the person is within the store—which counter—and whether they are looking at Prada handbags or something much cheaper.[41] Path Intelligence does this through devices planted throughout the mall that monitor the user's phone signal. Currently the company advertises the ability to collect aggregate statistics: how much traffic passed a store, how much traffic is in the mall at a particular time of day or in response to a special event, but the company proposes following individuals. The imagination shudders at the highly targeted advertising that is likely to result: "Buying Merlot again? Why not a good Scotch instead?" In the United States such tracking by a private entity would not be permitted. It would violate the pen-register statute, which permits tracking only by law enforcement, and only with a court order.

5.2 How Effective Is Wiretapping in Criminal Cases?

Effective police work rests on acquiring information. In preventive police work, such as community policing, the information might be innocuous: which shopkeeper is off on vacation, whose daughter is getting married. Or it might be of a more interesting variety: which young people are spending time with the more unsavory characters in the neighborhood, who seems to have a lot of cash lately. Central to police work, of course, is information about criminals' plans.

Sometimes this can be obtained through the observations of others, but the most useful acquisition of information occurs if law enforcement can overhear criminals discussing their plans. If police listen in through bugs or wiretaps when criminals talk among themselves, the eavesdropping requires a warrant. Sometimes, however, a criminal will talk with someone who might share information with the police. This could be an informant, including one who is wired.[42] Such taping of conversations does not need a wiretap warrant.

In some cases, evidence may not be as easy to produce. This is especially true in cases where the victims may find it difficult to testify (as in a 2001 investigation into telemarketing fraud that targeted older victims,[43] or in a "victimless" crime such as gambling and prostitution). Wiretap evidence can be particularly valuable in such situations. Wiretapping is also extremely useful in investigating corruption cases, where penetrating into the conspiracy, whether it is a case of bribery, insider trading, price fixing, and so on, is difficult.

The 1967 commission on crime recommended the use of wiretaps because of their value in cracking conspiracy cases. Wiretaps may have the subject himself saying what he is doing, when, how, and where he is doing it, sometimes even why the act is occurring. A Schenectady County, New York, district attorney observed of a 1998 gambling investigation, "When the targets heard their own voices on the tapes, the impact [was] obvious."[44] That case resulted in eight arrests and five convictions. With such cases, it is no wonder that government agents have fought so hard to keep this surveillance tool alive in the face of changing communication technologies. The reality of the tool is, however, a little different.

The *Wiretap Report* tells how many arrests and convictions there are in each Title III wiretap case, but the real issue is whether the wiretap played a significant role in the conviction. In some sense, that is impossible to tell, for the *Wiretap Report* does not include the court hearings and what swayed the jury or judge. This lack of hard evidence on the efficacy of wiretaps has been a concern since at least the passage of Title III; in 1972 Schwartz looked at four-and-a-half years' of Title III wiretaps. He found:

In *United States versus Poeta*, the US Court of Appeals opened its opinion by observing that the tap-derived evidence was unnecessary to the conviction; in another case, *Uniformed Sanitation Men versus Commission of Sanitation*, the Court made the same observation. In a 1971 report, a Nevada prosecutor reported two indictments in a kidnapping case in which wiretapping was used . . . but candidly added that the indictments were "not as a result of the interception."[45]

In 1975 in testimony to a federal commission examining wiretapping, Schwartz noted:

There is an assumption which the Administrative Office [of the U.S. Courts] does not sufficiently dispel, that the arrests and convictions that are reported are a result of the installations involved. I think that should be dispelled.

Indeed, I found, curiously once, a prosecutor from Arizona wrote in, "We got one conviction, but it had nothing to do with the tap."[46] . . .

The picture as to convictions purportedly resulting from electronic eavesdropping in those jurisdictions which do wiretap is still not complete. . . . Moreover, there is a very difficult question of causality: even where wiretapping was used in a case, how closely related was it to whatever results were achieved? In more than a few cases, courts and prosecutors have commented on the irrelevance of the wiretap evidence. . . . In many cases involving the disclosure of illegal taps, federal prosecutors have argued that whatever wiretapping was done did not produce any of the evidence used at the trial.[47]

Senator Arlen Specter, then in private practice after a stint as Philadelphia district attorney, also testified to the commission:

I am opposed to wiretapping because I believe its harm as a serious invasion of privacy far outweighs its value to law enforcement. At the outset, I put aside cases involving national security since my experience does not extend to that area. Based on eight years as a District Attorney . . . and six more years in other prosecutorial and investigative work, I have not seen any cases where wiretapping would have been of assistance on any major felony, such as murder, robbery, rape, arson, or burglary.

After reviewing the data compiled by the Administrative Office of the U.S. Courts on orders authorizing wiretapping, it is my conclusion that wiretapping has not been a major weapon against the most serious forms of criminal conduct.[48]

During the 1990s fight over the right to use strong encryption, Whitfield Diffie and I studied the use of wiretaps in the three decades since the passage of Title III. Using the government's *Wiretap Report*, we found:

• Initially the main crime targeted by wiretaps was gambling. At the time Title III was passed, gambling was a major source of income for organized crime, and thus a major focus of wiretaps. For the first five years after the law's passage, 64 percent of wiretaps were used in gambling investigations.[49]

Despite this, organized crime was not particularly damaged. As states began using legalized gambling (largely state lotteries and off-track betting) as a new source of revenue, organized crime turned instead to other activities, including drug dealing.

• Wiretapping's main domestic use then shifted to the war on drugs. By 1997, drug cases were the vast majority of Title III cases.

• During the Crypto Wars, FBI Director Louis Freeh often cited the need for wiretaps in kidnapping cases. Not surprisingly this issue resonated with every member of Congress.

In fact, wiretaps are rarely used in kidnapping cases. In the twenty-five-year period between 1969 and 1994, wiretaps and microphone bugs were used eighty times in kidnapping cases, or less than 1 percent of the time.[50] The reason is clear: in a classic kidnapping case (which does not mean a case of kidnapping by a noncustodial parent), law enforcement rarely knows who to wiretap. If police eavesdropping occurs at the home of the victim's family, then it is a consensual overhear, not a wiretap. The average of under three cases a year is an alarmingly small number on which to base a national telecommunications policy.

• Hearing the plotting of a crime does not necessarily prevent its occurrence. As Patrick Fitzgerald, U.S. Attorney for the Northern District of Illinois, testified, "People talk cryptically, they harrumph, they refer to this guy, they refer to that guy, that place over there."[51] It is often very difficult to determine intent. From law enforcement not able to understand the language being spoken,[52] to not understanding the "street slang and police jargon,"[53] crimes have occurred even when the plotting was captured on a law enforcement wiretap.

• Conviction in a case where wiretapping played a role does not mean that wiretapping helped solve the crime or resulted in a conviction. Only a careful study of the court proceedings—and sometimes an interview with the jury or judge—can indicate that.

Little has changed. There were no instances of Title III wiretap investigations used in terrorism cases.[54] Drug cases accounted for an increasing percentage of wiretap investigations during the period, starting at 72 percent in 1998 and rising to 86 percent by 2009. The number of Title III wiretap orders has increased, rising to 1764 in 2009.[55] Over the twelve-year period from 1998 through 2009, wiretaps were used sixty-three times in kidnapping investigations, for an average of 5.3 kidnapping cases annually. Encryption appeared to be a nonissue for law enforcement interceptions. As of 2000 the Wiretap Report includes all instances of encryption encountered while wiretapping.[56] At first, state and local law enforcement agencies were running into a number of cases a year,[57] but only one of the cases was reported impossible to decrypt. One change worked very much to law enforcement's advantage: the shift to cell phones. As cell phone use became ubiquitous in society, law enforcement tapped suspects' conversations while they were on the move. By 2009, 96 percent of Title III wiretap orders were for cell phones and digital pagers.[58]

Thus in the first decade of the new millennium, rather than being impeded, police found wiretaps had become an even more powerful tool in investigations of criminal activity.

5.3   How Effective Is Wiretapping in National-Security Cases?

The head of the Japanese Navy, Admiral Isoroku Yamamoto, was known to be exceedingly punctual. Electronic surveillance and code-breaking during World War II enabled the U.S. military to discover Yamamoto's plans to conduct an inspection tour of Japanese bases in the upper Solomon Islands in April 1943.[59] Army Air Corps pilots intercepted Yamamoto's entourage and shot down his plane. This well-planned effort was a surprise to the Japanese, who believed the attack had been simply a lucky break for the Americans.

In November 2002 electronic surveillance and voice recognition enabled the United States to target an Al-Qaeda operative traveling in a remote part of Yemen.[60] The Al-Qaeda agent, Qaed Senyan al-Harthi, was using a standard commercial satellite phone. An NSA agent, listening in, recognized al-Harthi's voice while the satellite phone revealed his location. The car in which he was riding was then targeted by a Predator drone, which launched a missile and blew the car up.

There is no question that electronic surveillance has enabled remarkable successes in U.S. national-security cases. Yet the issue to consider here is a much narrower one: the effectiveness of domestic communications interception in national-security cases. The record in this regard is difficult to analyze.

While there have been a number of trumpeted public announcements of arrests and domestic terrorism incidents averted, many cases turned out to be less of a threat than they originally appeared. These include the arrest of three Detroit men whose house contained "airport-employee identification badges and a date book with hand-drawn diagrams of aircraft and runways,"[61] the claim that a Brooklyn mosque had "helped funnel millions of dollars to al Qaeda,"[62] and a plot by seven Miami men to blow up the Sears Tower in Chicago.[63] The U.S. government itself petitioned the courts to have the Detroit case thrown out, while the charges regarding the Brooklyn mosque turned out to be groundless. After two mistrials, the Miami case ended up with one acquittal and five convictions, but a number of legal scholars argued that the evidence was weak; one former prosecutor commented that this was not a case involving terrorism but rather "an overcharged gang case."[64]

There are numerous reasons for the hype surrounding the arrests, ranging from the desire of the Bush administration to be seen to be doing a good job on combating terrorism to the FBI's own interest in appearing on top of the situation. The problem was made worse by the multiple definitions of terrorism used by the United States. The investigative agencies (including the FBI, Secret Service, Immigration and Customs Enforcement, and Bureau of Alcohol, Tobacco, Firearms and Explosives) have one definition for terrorist activities; the federal prosecutors have a different definition, and the Department of Justice's National Security Division, which coordinates national-security efforts within DoJ, has a third.[65] These differing definitions greatly complicate the situation.

As the Syracuse University Transactional Records Clearinghouse (TRAC) recent study on terrorism investigations observed, "To the extent that investigators waste their time targeting the wrong suspects, the chances increase that they will fail to identify the real terrorists who right now may be seeking to plant bombs, spread poisons, or otherwise harm a much larger number of innocent people."[66] As TRAC notes, though, investigations that do not result in prosecutions or convictions are not necessarily wasted efforts; they may provide useful insights into terrorist activities.[67]

Large, sustained terrorist actions cannot occur without logistical support. In the absence of being able to prove terrorism—and there is little value in proving a case against the September 11 hijackers or the July 7 bombers after the fact—law enforcement has used a strategy of prosecuting for a lesser offense, say an immigration violation or cigarette smuggling (trafficking cigarettes from low-tax states to high-tax ones without paying the required tax has been used by groups as a way to fund terrorist activities[68]). A conviction that removes the criminal from action for a time may be sufficient.

TRAC found that in the period 2004–2008, investigators referred 1,730 "terrorism" cases for prosecution (this is under the federal court definition of terrorism[69]). But only one-seventh of these were prosecuted.[70] Even then the charge of terrorism in a court case can be a red herring. The TRAC study notes that "prosecutors sometimes chose to file a specific terrorism charge against an individual even in situations where that person does not appear to have any connection to terrorism."[71] By inducing plea bargaining, the heavy penalties applied to terrorist convictions may be a strong motivator for the terrorism designation.

TRAC followed the 1,730 cases defined by federal prosecutors as terrorism investigations. Of the 235 cases that went to trial during the period, there were some very serious cases. These included prosecutions for

• Providing material support for terrorism, including fundraising:
The Texas-based Holy Land Foundation (HLF) sent more than $12 million to Hamas, a terrorist organization, and affiliated groups. Five leaders of HLF were convicted and given sentences of from fifteen to sixty-five years in prison.[72]

Naji Antoine Abi Khalil and Tomer Grinberg tried to export military night-vision equipment—controlled equipment that cannot leave the country without an export license—to Hezbollah, a terrorist organization.[73]

• Providing logistical support to terrorist organizations:
Uzair Paracha, a twenty-one-year-old Pakistani in New York, posed as Majid Khan to the U.S. Immigration and Naturalization Service and other U.S. institutions; Khan was an Al-Qaeda member who sought reentry to the United States. Paracha's subterfuge was to make it appear that Khan had been out of the United States only briefly (this was done to simplify Khan's return).

• Providing terrorist training both in the United States and abroad:
Christopher Paul pleaded guilty to providing explosives training in Ohio and Germany.[74]

Oussama Kassir was sentenced to life in prison for helping establish a jihad training camp in Bly, Oregon, in 1999.[75]

• Passing classified information regarding the movements of a U.S. Navy battle group to a group alleged to have terrorist connections:[76]
U.S.S. *Benfold* signalman Hassan Abu-Jihaad (formerly Paul Hall) was convicted of passing classified information about Navy ship movement to a terrorist organization.

• Plotting to bomb a shopping mall:
Derrick Shareef planned to set off grenades at a Rockford, Illinois, shopping mall.[77]
• Attempting to smuggle illegal aliens into the United States:
Al-Qaeda is not the only organization seeking to bring illegals into the country. Many terrorist groups view the United States as an excellent place for money laundering and other illegal activities.

Jose Tito Libio Ulloa Melo and Jorge de los Reyes Bautista Martinez pleaded guilty to attempts to smuggle aliens into the United States from Colombia (the aliens were posing as members of the Revolutionary Armed Forces of Colombia—better known as FARC, a terrorist organization).
• Attempting to purchase arms, including surface-to-air missiles:
This was by members of the Sri Lankan terrorist group Tamil Tigers.[78]

TRAC data shows that almost half the time U.S. attorneys turned down cases because of weak or insufficient admissible evidence or lack of criminal intent.[79] The 235 prosecutions resulted in 187 convictions, 77 of which had sentences of five years or more, 23 of twenty years or more, and 6, life sentences.[80] The low number of long sentences gives an impression that there are few serious cases of terrorism.

The conflicting interpretations that the cases and the numbers give of important successes and few serious cases are both correct. Because thinking about a terrorist act is not a crime, terrorism investigations present great complexity. It is critically important that terrorists be stopped before they commit an act of terrorism. Thus criminal planning can proceed only so far before police intervention. Khalil and Grinberg were arrested moments after they sold the night-vision goggles to an undercover FBI agent, while Shareef was arrested when he met with a federal agent to exchange stereo speakers for grenades. Intervention too early can prevent gathering sufficient evidence for conviction of a serious crime, and the timing of an arrest is a difficult issue for law enforcement.

With few exceptions, in the United States radical Islamic terrorism efforts have focused on recruitment and fundraising (right-wing terrorism in the United States has not followed the same pattern). Thus while wiretapping has been used in a number of successful terrorist investigations including the Holy Land Foundation case and the cases of Jose Padilla, accused of plotting to set off a "dirty bomb" but eventually sentenced on lesser charges, and Derrick Shareef, it has rarely been the crucial tool that prevented terrorist activities from occurring within the United States. (Much of the wiretapping done in the United States has been to aid investigations abroad, particularly in the United Kingdom.) A recent case was different.

In the summer of 2009 officials became concerned about an Afghan-born, Pakistani-raised resident of Aurora, Colorado, Najibullah Zazi. Zazi and others were purchasing large quantities of beauty products containing acetone and hydrogen peroxide, two of the three ingredients in triacetone triperoxide (TATP), the explosive used in the London transit bombings.[81] Zazi had done web searches for locations selling muriatic acid, a diluted version of hydrochloric acid, the third component of TATP.[82] On August 28 and September 6 and 7, he rented a hotel room in Aurora. It was after his second stay, when he "attempted to communicate on multiple occasions—each communication more urgent in tone than the last—seeking to correct mixtures of ingredients to make explosives"[83] that the FBI tested the oven vent for explosives and chemical residue and found the presence of acetone. Bomb making required that the chemicals be highly concentrated, and one way to accomplish this is through heating them.

Zazi rented a car and left for New York on September 9; he was stopped the next day while crossing the George Washington Bridge into Manhattan. He became suspicious that he was being investigated, a fact later confirmed by an acquaintance,[84] and he returned to Colorado. He was arrested several days later. Evidence against him included bomb-making instructions on his laptop (searched while Zazi had been in New York), the chemical purchases, the communications about the mixture balance, and the acetone found on the Aurora hotel stove vent. In February 2010 Zazi pled guilty to conspiracy to conduct terrorist activities and to providing support for Al-Qaeda.[85] His intent was to blow up New York subway cars using TATP. Others have also been charged in the case. The government has not said how it came to home in on Zazi, but there are clear indications that wiretaps provided the crucial initial evidence that something nefarious was afoot.[86]

Zazi was not the only U.S. case in which such electronic surveillance played a role. Abu-Jihaad was investigated by the FBI after a computer disk found during a search of a London apartment revealed classified information about Abu-Jihaad's naval convoy.[87] The subsequent investigation led government agents to Derrick Shareef. Many terrorism cases proceed using such a set of links. It is often the case that intermediate points lead to more significant targets.

When considering the efficacy of wiretapping in national-security investigations, it is important to keep in mind that a number of other tools have been brought to bear in domestic terrorism. One is to "follow the money." In 2001 under the Bush administration, counterterrorism officials began examining financial records from a large international database, SWIFT, which runs an international financial messaging service;[88] this program, which had not undergone any public scrutiny prior to being implemented, netted some useful information.[89] In the United States, Uzair Paracha, who sought to aid an Al-Qaeda member's entry into the United States, was identified through U.S. surveillance of banking transactions.[90] The tool has also been useful outside the country: Riduan Isamuddin,[91] accused of helping to plan the bombings in Bali in 2000 that killed 202 people as well as numerous other terrorist attacks, was located and captured in Thailand as a result of studying a money trail. Given that radical Islamic terrorist efforts within the U.S have focused on recruitment and funding, tracking money may be a particularly useful investigative strategy.

The government's read of the value of the President's Surveillance Program (PSP) was decidedly mixed. While FBI management—including FBI Director Robert Mueller—called the program "of value," the DoJ's Office of Inspector General's report described the tool as "one of many" and concluded it played a limited role in the FBI's counterterrorism efforts.[92] The CIA and personnel in the Office of the Director of National Intelligence[93] called the PSP one tool of many. The strongest statement about the value of this highly controversial program was that "there are several cases identified by IC [intelligence community] officials . . . where PSP may have contributed to a counterterrorism success."[94] One investigator said that information garnered from the PSP did not result in much new information, but what it did provide in some cases was that there was no reason to be concerned about certain people who were under suspicion. Being able to focus investigations on the serious suspects is, of course, of great value.

The DoJ characterization of the PSP as "one of many" is not surprising; intelligence investigations are a matter of filling in a confusing picture and each tool clarifies only a small part. The full picture may be understood even while there is some fog obscuring the whole, and if a tool such as wiretapping clears up even one aspect, that may be crucial in developing a true understanding of the situation. Nonetheless, the less-than-ringing endorsement by field investigators of the necessity of the PSP is worth noting. There was strong political pressure in a highly politicized administration to conclude otherwise; the investigators did not.

5.4   A History Lesson

Effectiveness needs to be measured in terms of costs. An ambulance that races to a hospital causing accidents along the way is not effective. Similarly, communications interception decisions that end up compromising communications security may provide more cost than benefit. What happens if, in designing for communications intelligence, what results is communications insecurity? It is worth looking at the Crypto Wars of the 1980s and 1990s to discover what lessons can be learned in hindsight. In particular, it is worth examining fielded communications products and their security characteristics.

In 1982 Europe began work on a cell phone system. The Europeans wanted a mobile network that could be used across the continent. They wanted the system security to be at least as good as the security of the wired-line network. So those developing the standards had to solve two problems: protecting the privacy of the communications between the handset and the radio tower and protecting the privacy of the phone so that it could not be identified, except by the cell tower (the latter is really about providing anonymity for the user). This called for cryptography, which created complications.

Cryptography is, of course, a dual-use technology with both civilian and military applications. During the Cold War, the United States and its allies controlled the export of equipment that could be used for military purposes through the Coordinating Committee on Multilateral Export Controls (CoCOM), an organization whose membership included the United States, Canada, Australia, New Zealand, Japan, and most western European countries. Export between CoCOM countries was also regulated, which meant that the development of the European cell phone system, GSM (originally standing for Groupe Spécial Mobile, and now for Global System for Mobile Communications), fell under the CoCOM regulations.

This was challenging. "It was the first time that [telephone engineers] had actually developed a universal cryptographic product that went into the hands of the users," recalled Charles Brookson, who had been chair of the GSM Algorithmic Experts Group. There were justifiable concerns about the cryptography, which, because of CoCOM rules, had not been made public and was of limited strength.

The cryptographic algorithm leaked, and in a series of papers between 1999 and 2003, academic cryptographers found ways to break the GSM system. These did not appear to result in actual attacks. The bigger security gap in GSM, however, was a known flaw that no one had expected to be much of a problem. To simplify the authentication of the user to the system, the GSM protocol did not require the cell tower to authenticate itself to the cell phone. This allowed fake towers to be set up and spoof phones in the network. These problems were corrected in the next-generation system, 3G, which is rapidly replacing GSM.

The U.S. government did not stop controlling export of military-grade equipment with the end of the Cold War. Cryptography's dual-use status meant that export from the United States of products containing cryptographic algorithms was determined by the Office of Munitions Control with the advice of the NSA.[95] In the 1990s the U.S. government constrained deployment within the country of strong cryptography by controlling the export of products containing that type of cryptography.[96] In 1992 the NSA and an industry association reached an agreement that "mass-market" software using 40-bit keys could be freely exported. Even at that time, 40 bits was not very impressive; 2^{40} is about a trillion operations. In 1992, a workstation could do a brute-force search of the entire key space in about an hour.

Still, this was a first step in loosening export controls, an important issue to the computer industry. U.S. companies were loath to produce two types of products: one with strong cryptography for domestic markets and one with weaker cryptography (shorter key lengths) for export. Thus export controls constrained the domestic market as well.

One effect was on secure telephones. In the fall of 1992 AT&T was poised to change telephony. The company announced a mass-market device for secure telephones: the Telephone Security Device Model 3600 (TSD 3600). The idea was not new. Other companies, including Gretag and Crypto AG in Switzerland, and Cylink, Datotek, and TCC in the United States, had sold voice-encryption systems. AT&T had figured out how to do this using a single processor for the digital signal processing. Planning on selling the devices for an initial price of $1295, AT&T envisioned a vast market of businesspeople who would want secure communications as they traveled.

Then the U.S. government stepped in. The proposal sounded benign: the NSA expressed interest in using the TSD 3600 for certain government applications but there was an export problem. What if AT&T made two sets of phones, one with their own encryption chip, which used 56-bit DES, and one with a new cryptographic algorithm developed by the agency? The latter would not have export-control issues and AT&T could market them abroad.

The NSA's new algorithm, Skipjack, was embedded within a key-management scheme in which the 80-bit key was split into two components, each of which was to be stored at a secure facility operated by an executive-branch federal agency. Keys would not be released except under "proper legal authorization."[97] The program was officially known as the Escrowed Encryption Standard (EES) and unofficially as "Clipper," after the tamper-resistant chip implementing the 80-bit encryption algorithm. The system was stronger than 56-bit DES, which in 1993 was finally coming to the end of its lifetime. But storing the keys indefinitely meant that a communication was never actually safe; there is always the danger that stored keys may be revealed.

As a group of security experts observed, "The ability to recover traffic continues to exist long after the original communication has occurred. . . . The relevant keys [are] stored instead of destroyed, so that later government requests for the plaintext can succeed. If the keys are stored, they can be compromised; if they are destroyed, the threat of compromise ceases at that moment."[98] Who would ensure that the communications traffic would not be read by a rogue insider? There were objections to the idea of a storage facility that held everyone's keys; that was simply too big a target. The system's complexity would create too high a risk of compromise. Users and governments abroad were not impressed with the idea of U.S. government storage of keys. Despite strong government inducements for industry to develop products using escrowed encryption, there was no interest in Clipper or Clipper-type efforts, and the U.S. government was unable to interest other nations in multilateral key-sharing agreements.

AT&T built multiple models of its TSD 3600 device, some of which ran Clipper and some of which ran algorithms developed by Datotek and by Gretag AG. Some of the phones were interoperable, some were not. The large market that AT&T envisioned did not happen, and the program was not a success. Instead of the TSDs jumping off the shelves at Radio Shack, a chain of electronic retail shops found at U.S. shopping malls, after two years, sales of the device were about seventeen thousand.[99] A majority of those went to the FBI, which was attempting to get a market rolling. Clipper not only killed off AT&T's effort at a mass-market telephone security device, but other efforts as well.

The export controls had exceptions, most notably for the use of cryptography for authentication (determining that the sender is who he claims to be) and integrity checking (protecting a communication so it is received in untampered form). Export of cryptography for use for confidentiality was generally not permitted. This was not a clear-cut line; many of the technologies used for authenticity purposes and integrity checking could also be used for ensuring confidentiality of communications. The result was a confusing government process that delayed the deployment of computer security that network architects, security researchers, industry, and the government agreed was essential for the safe operating of the network. One such instance occurred with DNSSEC.

In 1997 Hugh Daniel submitted a classification request to the U.S. Bureau of Export Administration (BXA) for a DNSSEC implementation. This implementation, Integrated DNSSEC, used an encryption toolkit, RSAREF, for performing the authentication; Daniel's export application clearly stated this (as well as observing that the encryption software was used only for authentication).[100] BXA determined that because Integrated DNSSEC was "publicly available," the product did not require an export license for distribution outside the United States and Canada.

Several months later, a problem arose. Philip Karn, an engineer, wanted BXA to classify the export status of a computer disk that included RSAREF for confidentiality purposes. Karn was informed that to ship the disk outside the United States and Canada he would need an export license. Karn wrote BXA, pointing out that Daniel's DNSSEC product had not needed an export license even though it used the same software.[101] BXA's response was to reclassify Daniel's DNSSEC product so that a license was required for distribution of the product outside the United States and Canada.[102] Lee Tien, Daniel's lawyer, objected, observing that "authentication programs are reviewed on the basis of what they do as published, rather than on what they might do if someone rewrites them."[103] Of course. But the BXA's reclassification of the DNSSEC implementation as an export-controlled item lasted until the U.S. government loosened cryptographic export-control regulations several years later.

In the world of Web 2.0 and cloud collaboration software, it is easy to forget that such tools are relatively new. Online collaboration was far more difficult in the 1980s and 1990s when the desktop was king and the sharing was essentially email, net news, and file transfer. Lotus Notes was a set of software applications for coordinating business processes (e.g., tracking a bug, a help-desk request) and included a discussion tool, email, and a document database. The working model was personal computers connected via a local-area network with one of the PCs acting as a dedicated server. That server would be set up to communicate with servers of other local-area networks; concurrency control that they managed enabled everything to stay synchronized. In so doing, Lotus Notes put branch offices on par with the home office, and it was enormously successful software. It was also software that demanded encryption; collaboration across networks simply could not be secure without it.

Lotus Notes worked hard to make that happen. The first version of Lotus Notes used 64-bit cryptography—sort of. The software had two implementations for communications: 64-bit for U.S. communications, 32-bit for international ones.[104] This was in 1989, when a message encoded with a

32-bit key would take about two days—and four billion computations—on a supercomputer to break. It was a time when few customers were thinking about security, and so no one queried Lotus's decision regarding the weaker international algorithm.[105]

A few years later, this weak security solution no longer pleased Lotus's international customers. Lotus went to 40-bit cryptography in the international version (it continued using 64-bit cryptography for U.S. customers). This solution pleased no one but the NSA; by the mid-1990s, the 40-bit cryptography was too easy to break.

Then Lotus built a product with exportable 64-bit cryptography. This was a neat trick given that export rules at the time limited mass-market cryptography to 40 bits. Ray Ozzie, the Lotus Notes developer, had worked out a deal with NSA: systems using 64-bit cryptography that could be exported, because NSA knew 24 bits of the key.[106] Although Ozzie had explained this key-escrow solution quite publicly in 1996, not everyone had heard of or understood its import. In particular, members of the Swedish ministry of defense were quite disturbed when they learned that the security of their communications was 40 bits—one billionth of the 64-bit cryptographic strength they had thought they were getting.[107]

The effect of these cases (and many others) was much larger than the disapproval of the individual export licenses. The cases were like the ripples after a stone has been dropped into a pond. An export license denial creates fear, uncertainty, and doubt[108] in other developers, engineers, and companies, and creates a strong hesitancy to spend time and money on a project that might not be able to be marketed (in the 1990s half of U.S. hardware and software sales were abroad). The upshot of a single export license denial was not a single product stopped but rather a large set of products neither built nor sold. The effectiveness of wiretapping, which was the reason for preventing the widespread deployment of strong cryptography, must be measured against the set of problems that resulted from deploying insecure systems.

5.5   Export Control Changes

After years of slowing the deployment of products containing strong cryptography, in 2000 the U.S. government abruptly changed policy. Key length would no longer determine exportability; instead the determination would be made on the basis of what the product did. If it was for *retail* purposes, meaning a high-volume, noncustomized item that was widely sold *and* not for use in communications infrastructure, then the product would largely be free of export controls. Depending on the customer, nonretail items remained under export controls, with more stringent controls applying if the customer was a government.[109] While these new controls had limitations and some lack of clarity, for the most part the difficulties that industry had been facing for the preceding two decades went away.

The FBI was not pleased for the previous policy had worked well for the bureau. By preventing the export of U.S. products containing strong cryptography, the U.S. government had slowed the deployment of strong cryptography within the United States. The NSA, however, supported the changes (otherwise they would not have occurred). There were several reasons underlying the NSA's policy change.

The primary one was that the NSA was already losing the cryptography wars. The computer industry had been extremely unhappy with the controls, and over a period of several years, their allies in Congress had introduced bills to liberalize cryptographic export controls. By the summer of 1999 the Security and Freedom through Encryption Act had passed the five committees with jurisdiction and was moving to the House floor when the change in export regulations were announced.[110] From the NSA's perspective, it was safer to have the White House control the change in regulations than to allow Congress to do so.

The shift in NSA policy also allowed the agency to strike a bargain with Congress. The agency was beginning a program in exploiting enemy networks and information systems for information. In loosening cryptographic export controls, the agency was giving something up, and it could gain something in return. Funding was low for NSA's new project in network exploitation,[111] and the agency received a substantial appropriation for the new effort.

There was another, very important, issue for the agency. This new effort would be crucial in the changing communications world of the twenty-first century and the agency needed to understand the new communications products it was facing. As always, such products were easiest to examine if they were manufactured in the United States, but export controls were driving manufacture of secure systems overseas. Loosening export controls would give NSA better insight into network exploitation possibilities.

Since about 1996, the U.S. government's effort to press key escrow (a necessary component of the export controls on strong cryptography) had been counterproductive for the NSA. The agency was becoming the enemy of the computer industry while gaining very little. Export controls hampered use of strong cryptography by criminals, which advantaged the FBI, but these efforts had little effect on most collection of foreign intelligence, the NSA's focus.

There was also an issue that was a whisper in 2000 and has become much more important in the years since. The U.S. Department of Defense was unable to obtain the sufficient communications security in commercial-off-the-shelf (COTS) equipment. After the second Iraq War, that need was critical. The U.S. military had to communicate securely with Iraqi forces, but the high-grade government off-the-shelf[112] equipment would take years to develop. So the soldiers turned to commercial VPNs and IPSec implementations and, using interoperable COTS equipment, were able to communicate securely.

CALEA added a different set of problems. Telecommunications and computer companies expressed concern over the threat to innovation posed by the expansion of CALEA.[113] Both these risks are important and real, although in fact, it is difficult to point to specific products that were not developed. That is unsurprising when one carefully considers innovation in this arena. Two phenomena are at play here. The first is that because CALEA adds cost, deployment of new products is slowed; such product delay occurs in multiple ways and is unlikely to explicitly appear as "slowed by CALEA." The second issue is more subtle. Telephone companies traditionally have a history of incremental innovation, with more radical change coming from outside the industry. It is no surprise, for example, that the Internet or, to pick a more recent example, Skype was developed from outside the telephone industry. CALEA's real effect is to prevent innovation from being proposed in the first place. Neither of these effects is easy to delineate.

What we do know is that the controversy over CALEA's standards contributed to a long delay[114] in the law's implementation.[115] Disagreements over interception capacity, the necessity of capturing post-cut-through digits, and location information contributed to fear, uncertainty, and doubt as to what was actually required. One reaction, naturally enough, has been that some companies have created greater surveillance capabilities than the law requires.[116]

5.6 NSA Scrutinizes Traffic on Public Networks

In September 2007, a *Baltimore Sun* reporter, Siobhan Gorman, reported that the NSA was planning to monitor government and private civilian networks to prevent unauthorized intrusion and protect the networks from attacks by hackers and terrorists.[117] The spy agency had always played a role in protecting government communications, but giving the NSA a major role in securing unclassified networks represented a significant change. How do you protect civilian networks without observing the traffic on them? The government was not forthcoming, not even after President Bush signed National Security Presidential Directive 54[118] in January 2008. NSPD54 called for the formation of the Comprehensive National Cybersecurity Initiative (CNCI), whose purpose was to secure U.S. government networks and keep the U.S. government's sensitive information safe.

Details were sparse, but a few aspects of the CNCI were made public. These, however, turned out to be cybersecurity programs that had already begun a few years earlier:

• *Trusted Internet Connect*   A 2007 Office of Management and Budget program to limit the number of federal government connections to the Internet to under 100
• *Einstein*   A 2004 Department of Homeland Security program to examine, collect, correlate, and analyze electronic traffic into and out of civilian federal agencies[119]

The original Einstein project collected, correlated, and analyzed the electronic traffic in and out of federal agencies, seeking to understand the nature of the threats. Data collected included the source and destination IP address, packet length, source and destination port, time stamp, and underlying protocol.[120] Agency participation was voluntary.

A new version of Einstein, Einstein 2, appeared in 2008, and participation by federal agencies was now required. Deployment has been slow. This version of Einstein was active, protecting federal systems through an intrusion-detection system that recognized potential threats through comparing the characteristics of the incoming traffic with known malware and known malicious actions (e.g., a DDoS attack). Monitoring was done at each participating agency's Internet access point (per the Trusted Internet Connect program).

Einstein was located on the federal network, and was monitoring traffic intended for federal systems. In that sense it was not a privacy threat, since users knew they were connecting to a federal system. Yet for some users— for example, people accessing their records at the Veterans Administration or sensitive information at a public website at the Department of Health and Human Services—the idea that some personally identifiable data, such as IP addresses, were being retained, was highly disturbing. The Department of Homeland Security (DHS) concluded there was no privacy threat in the government's use of Einstein 2.[121] DoJ's legal analysis found that so long as there was a banner warning users that their traffic was being monitored, private citizens had no expectation of privacy in accessing government sites.[122, 123]

Government workers had no legitimate expectation of privacy while on a government network, even if their actions involved conducting private business on a private site—for example, reading email on their private Gmail or Yahoo account.[124]

In this, government employees were no different than an employee elsewhere. In the United States, employers are allowed to monitor their employee's communications if the workers are using the employer's communications system and they have been warned that such monitoring may occur. What is new to the situation, however, is that the person with whom the employee is communicating is unlikely to be aware that such monitoring is occurring. They are communicating with their friend or colleague via a private account but the government may be scanning the communication because the government employee is accessing the communication through a government-owned system. (As this book went to press, the Supreme Court ruled in the 2010 case *City of Ontario v. Quon*,[125] that auditing text messages sent by a policeman on a department-supplied pager did not violate the policeman's expectation of privacy. But the court's ruling was narrow. The auditing had been ordered because monthly text limits were being greatly exceeded; the Ontario Police Department wanted to know whether this was due to professional use of the pager. Given the circumstances, the Court viewed the search as "reasonable," making clear that the decision was based on the specifics of the case and that a generalization was inappropriate.[126])

Einstein 3 represented a major change. Einstein 2 monitors communications at the federal network access points. In Einstein 3, agency-bound traffic is diverted to an intrusion-prevention system. The communications are searched using NSA tools and hardware.[127] Traffic matching known or suspected malware will be blocked.[128] As of 2009, the effort is in experimental stages, being tested on the AT&T network, which sought Department of Justice written approval before it agreed to participate.[129]

Einstein 3 differs from its predecessors in that it is designed to check packet content in addition to transactional information.[130] That creates one type of privacy risk. Another is that the system might pick up purely private communications. At least one DHS lawyer did not see this as a problem. Stewart Baker, who had once been the NSA chief counsel and who was in 2008 the DHS assistant secretary for policy, dismissed concerns, saying, "If, by mistake, some private communication is directed through this system, the result will be that the malware . . . won't be delivered, to which the right response is, 'Thank you very much,' not 'You've violated my rights'."[131]

With Einstein 2, the federal government made clear that users accessing government sites and government workers have no privacy rights with respect to their Internet communications. Einstein 3 is potentially more intrusive, and the program leaves more questions open than answered. Einstein 3 will collect personally identifiable information. What are the rules governing the use of this information? How long will the data collected by Einstein 3 be retained? What type of auditing will be employed in Einstein 3? Under what circumstances would information gained from Einstein 3 be shared with law enforcement or national security?

There are fundamental questions to be asking here: What privacy and security risks are created by the Einstein program? Is there a more effective way to be pursuing the same strategic goals? That conversation, like many about surveillance technologies, has not been raised in the public sphere.

Note added in proof: In a recent development, the Administrative Office of the U.S. Courts changed its methods of data collection on encryption information. Encryption information had been included only in the yearly summary reports submitted to the office. In August 2009, the Administrative Office revised its forms so that data on encryption would be in the reports submitted at the conclusion of each wiretap. This new data collection method should result in more accurate reporting—and quite possibly an increase in the encryption numbers.

6 Evolving Communications Technologies

In the nineteenth century, the invention of the telephone, telegraph, and telex changed the practice of business and government. The process was gradual, but when it was done, it had fundamentally transformed the way work was done. Although written letters and signed documents still had their place, the world was now one in which important communications took place electronically. That transformation took decades.

A second communications revolution began in the mid-1990s. The opening up of the Internet to commercial traffic, the massive laying down of fiber-optic cable around the globe, and the worldwide adoption of cellular phones occurred at a rate many times faster than the original communications revolution. Its consequences, which are taking place in under a generation, will have a much more profound effect than the original transformation. Interactions between people and businesses, between citizens and their government, between corporations and other corporations, were revolutionized. Major new businesses were created (including, of course, the usual suspects of Amazon, eBay, and Google), and others, including ones one might not have expected (e.g., newspapers), were completely changed. Major new modes of production, including open source,[1] began, or were greatly expanded.

The question is what next. While this book is not a study on the future of the Internet, security risks of communications surveillance change as communications technologies do. In this chapter I discuss nascent communications technologies likely to soon have an impact on business, government, and people.

6.1 The Networked World

One of DARPA's motivations in sponsoring the research that led to the Internet was that data and programs at one site did not need to be replicated, but instead could be accessed as needed. By the late 1980s the connectivity provided by the Internet and the high number of unused cycles on many users' machines enabled a new paradigm: farm computation out. At the time, Internet communication was largely limited to email, net news, and file transfer. So the methods used to parcel out data for the computation were fairly primitive—at least by current standards.

The first such project was factoring the ninth Fermat integer,[2] $F_9 = 2^{512} + 1$, an integer of 155 digits, into primes (a prime is an integer whose factors are only itself and one). Fast algorithms for factorization were important for cryptanalysis, and Fermat numbers were interesting numbers with which to test the factoring algorithms. People interested in helping the Fermat number project contacted one of the project members by email or phone and were shipped a portion of the computation to do on their machine.[3] In under half the time that it would have taken to solve the problem had it been done by a single supercomputer, F_9 was factored.

These days a number of problems are done in such a distributed fashion, but there is nothing ad hoc about the process. Consider SETI@home, the Search for Extraterrestrial Intelligence, which is run out of University of California at Berkeley. SETI@home sorts through radio signals from space. Because narrow-bandwidth radio signals—signals confined to a small part of the spectrum—are not known to occur naturally, their appearance would be an indication of extraterrestrial intelligence. The problem is that radio telescope signals are extremely noisy because of a combination of noise from the radio telescope itself and celestial background noise. So separating out the narrow-band signals is computationally expensive. But it is easy to divide up the radio signals by the segments of the sky from which they come. By farming out these segments to users, searching for narrow-bandwidth signals is a perfect candidate for a distributed calculation. With five million participants in the project—who can resist the glamour of participating in a search for extraterrestrial life—SETI certainly distributes the computation. The project calls itself the "world's largest supercomputer."

The same "world's largest supercomputer" is also being used for calculations at the microscopic level. Folding@home is a Stanford University distributed computing project to determine the shape of proteins. Strings of amino acids folded in complex ways, proteins are the building blocks of our bodies. Folded correctly, proteins digest food, coordinate biological action, attack viruses and bacteria, and enable life. Folded incorrectly, proteins are culprits in Alzheimer's, "mad cow" disease, and a host of other ailments. Thus understanding protein folding is part of determining potential treatments of these illnesses. Protein folding obeys Newton's laws of motion applied to *each atom* in the system, and is thus hard to study. Mimicking those laws, and the slight changes that can cause an error, for the thousands and thousands of atoms in a single protein is computationally intensive, perfect for a distributed computation project.

Folding@home has users produce hundreds of thousands of simulations, each with its own trajectory starting at an initial position and with a random velocity. This enables the Folding@home researchers to estimate the rate of folding in the protein[4] and has already resulted in numerous advances.[5]

SETI@home and Folding@home are projects in which users actively join in solving a complex computation. A joint computation of a very different sort is one in which users' questions are put to work. This is Google Trends,[6] an aggregate compilation of the Google searches people make. Just as the Centers for Disease Control and Prevention (CDC) can track outbreaks of diseases by compiling data from hospitals, individual healthcare providers, and labs, so can Google track issues of interest by combining search data to spot trends. Google Trends studies aggregate user data to determine what users are interested in at the moment. Tracking economic data, such as peoples' searches for "unemployment insurance" or "foreclosure," means that Google Trends may be a potential predictor of an economic crisis before the U.S. government collects sufficient data to make a more definitive prediction. Similarly, by studying queries on influenza-like illnesses, Google Flu Trends has been able to spot flu outbreaks two weeks ahead of the CDC, a rather impressive difference.[7]

The *network effect*, describing the rise in value of a network as more people use it, is far larger than anyone might have anticipated as packet-switching protocols were being designed, or even when search engines were being developed. This effect has expanded in highly unexpected ways—and is likely to continue to do so for quite some time.

6.2 Cloud Computing

Another form of distributing computation is cloud computing, where computing is done not locally, but within the Internet cloud.[8] This is computing as a utility, much like electricity or water. While the notion may seem surprising to those who are accustomed to having an IT department in their midst, this is not so odd an idea. It has happened for other services. In the nineteenth century each factory had its own power source and generated its own electricity. Alternating current enables low-cost transmission of electricity over a long distance. Once that scientific understanding took hold, the advantage to centralizing the production of electricity was clear, and electric power companies were born. The economies of scale they provide in producing electricity far outweigh the costs of transporting the electricity. Computing is similar. With high bandwidth and ubiquitous connectivity increasingly available across the United States and the world, outsourcing of computing is possible. It carries all sorts of advantages: economies of scale, better predictability and use of resources, and better ability to adjust the amount of computing used to the instantaneous demand.

No longer would each business or individual user need to provide sufficient computation power for all their needs; users would pay only for the capacity they actually used. No longer would each business need to maintain their own data center; they could use a cloud service like Amazon's Elastic Compute Cloud (EC2) to supply it. Even individuals could benefit. A cloud service such as Google Calendar, in which multiple people could post and read entries, and available anywhere with access to the network, is infinitely useful for scheduling anything involving more than one person. Similarly, no longer would a user need to maintain copies of a document on their laptop; they could use Google Docs storage. (Such remote storage is particularly useful for group projects, since the revised document would not need to be shipped back and forth between users.) Rather than have local servers or personal computers do the work, the work is done in the "cloud," and accessed when needed.

Google Calendar and Google Docs are manifestations of Software as a Service (SaaS) in which functionality moves from the desktop to the cloud. Amazon's EC2 is an example of Infrastructure as a Service (IaaS); the service provided is raw computing and storage. IaaS is especially useful to start-ups, which can avoid initial capital costs by purchasing computing power only when it is needed in a pay-as-you-go model. IaaS allows businesses to scale up quickly.

SaaS and IaaS are two ends of the cloud computing spectrum; in between lies Platform as a Service (PaaS), which provides support for user-created services. Thus while SaaS is a single service or suite of services, PaaS provides a computing platform for the user to create her own applications. PaaS provides such underpinnings as concurrency management and security, and such mechanisms as visualization tools for the user to see how customers are using the company's services, or database tools to help track user behavior. SaaS, IaaS, and PaaS are not so much fundamentally different computing structures as they are different levels of software support offered on what may be a common network of computers.

By moving where the data are stored, cloud computing changes many playing fields at once. It makes computing and data storage much cheaper. It consolidates the industry. And it changes risk. Data on a laptop, desktop, or company's server is only as secure as the protections provided by the user or company's system administrator. Data in the cloud is likely to be better secured—a cloud provider that cannot protect the data it is storing is a cloud provider that will not be in business very long—but the data-protection equation is fundamentally changed. Cloud computing means that a company's proprietary and private information is exposed on a public network. If the network is wiretapped, it is a novel source of risk to cloud customers.

Cloud computing shifts control from the laptop and desktop to the compute farm. From the point of view of law, cloud computing changes who has the data (and how accessible it is). Recall the *Miller*[9] decision: the Supreme Court ruled that "the Fourth Amendment does not prohibit the obtaining of information revealed to a third party . . . even if the information is revealed on the assumption that it will be used only for a limited purpose."[10] Data on a laptop or desktop is subject to the stringent Fourth Amendment protections against "unreasonable search and seizure;" data in the cloud currently has lesser protections.

6.3   The Network of Things

Today's Internet connects millions of IP-enabled devices: servers, desktop computers, laptops, notebooks, BlackBerrys, iPhones, routers, NAT boxes,[11] and more. This network is unimaginably huge by the standards of the DARPA pioneers, but is a fraction of the size the network is likely to be within a decade. Billions and billions of small, low-powered devices will soon be connected to the network. These devices will do everything from noting the passage of a car through a tollbooth to monitoring the movement of rare species. The devices are of two types: RFID (radio-frequency ID) tags, microchips intended for wireless data transmission; and sensors, inexpensive devices for measuring physical attributes (such as temperature, humidity, vibration) with limited computing power and energy supply.

RFID tags have a computer chip and an antenna; they receive and respond to radio-frequency queries from a transmitter. Tags are often the size of a barcode (which they are in the process of replacing). They are able to hold much more data than a barcode, to the point of being able to identify a single item instead of a class of items (e.g., a particular can of Coke and not all cans of Coke manufactured at a particular plant on a particular day), and they do not need a direct line of sight between reader and device.

Active RFID tags have a power source and can initiate communication with an RFID reader; passive tags are cheaper and derive power from a reader's querying signal. Car fobs that unlock a car from a distance are examples of active RFID tags, while subway cards are examples of passive ones. Today's tags are used for access to a building or room, for payment (e.g., such as are used by various gas stations), for inventory tracking and supply-chain management (following a pallet of lobster tails from a Jacksonville fish supplier to a Wal-Mart freezer[12]), or even for knowing how long a plate of sushi has been circulating on a restaurant conveyor belt.[13] Anticipated uses include smart appliances, such as washing machines that can read the RFID tags on clothes and adjust water temperature and agitation according to fabric type, terminals in stores that can read the prices of full shopping carts and charge the customer's account, and cell phones that can read an RFID tag on a movie poster and discover showtimes at the nearest movie theater.[14]

Neither RFID tags nor sensors are new. The latter, for example, were used during the Cold War to monitor the movement of Soviet submarines.[15] Two things change the situation: the decreasing cost of the technologies and the ability to easily access the data through the Internet. Much RFID data are accessed locally and does not use the Internet for transport. Other information, including data that is constantly changing and frequently updated, will traverse the Internet. Given the nature of their functionality, in measuring anything from the temperature and humidity of the soil to bridge movement[16] to monitoring activity or heart rate in an older person, much sensor data are likely to transit the network.

6.4 The Convergence of Telephones and Computers

A telephone was once a fixed object using the PSTN to connect with similar devices. A computer was also once a large, fixed electromechanical processor that performed complex calculations and used an Ethernet cable to communicate with other computers (and perhaps a printer). Increasingly cell phones are digital, with some moving even one step further to an IP-based architecture. Early on the Internet was thought to be too unreliable for voice,[17] but "the explosion of VoIP service in the last four years has put that myth to rest," as the FCC observed in 2008.[18] Telephones and computers are converging in the type of applications they support.

Yet while computers and telephones have, in many ways, become inter-changeable, the networks that support them most definitely have not. The circuit-based PSTN uses a separate signaling channel to communicate transactional information, while Internet signaling information is con-veyed within the same packet as the content. Thus the device conver-gence—for example, with IP-based telephones—creates complications, at least for a PSTN system that inherently assumes "phone number equals location." One is the emergency call system—in the United States this would be the E911 system—the enhanced 911, or emergency service, that automatically associates a location with each phone number.[19] It is worth a brief digression into the E911 system to see what these problems are.

Public Safety Answering Points (PSAPs), facilities that receive E911 calls and refer them to the appropriate emergency services, are spread through-out the nation. Determining the location of the caller can be sticky; such information is not normally conveyed as part of the call signaling data. But because the location is needed by the phone company for billing pur-poses, enough information is transmitted with each call to determine caller location. The question was how to put things together for E911 services.

For callers using traditional wireline phones, the PSAPs use data trans-mitted with the call to query a location database.[20] This is done automati-cally, set up so that as the call is being answered at a PSAP, the caller's location appears on the E911 operator's screen. Cell phones, of course, present a problem. There is no location database for the phone number. The phone moves. So cell phone companies provided a workaround.

At the point at which a cell phone call connects to the PSTN, it goes though a switch (the Mobile Switching Center). If the call is to 911, the call is assigned a pseudo-number that corresponds to a phone number within the same sector of the cell site[21] (the area covered by a cell tower is split into sectors). That pseudo–phone number is transmitted to the PSAP. When the PSAP queries the location database for the call location, it uses the pseudo-number to do so. Complex workarounds as these solutions may be, they are at least solutions. The situation for interconnected VoIP was more confounding. This was as much for business reasons as for technical ones.

Like cell phones, VoIP is nomadic, and there were numerous instances where callers used VoIP to reach E911 only to discover that the emergency service had no idea of the caller's location.[22] But while cell phones could make use of telephone-company facilities to handle changing locations, VoIP is owned by competitors to the telephone companies, which saw a way to disrupt VoIP. Congress intervened. Under a law passed in 2008, the telephone companies are required to offer VoIP providers the same rights to interconnect with E911 services that they do for providers of cell service.[23]

6.5 Bugging Everywhere

Cell phones can act not only as location beacons but also as wiretaps—and have been used that way. In an investigation of the Genovese organized crime family, law enforcement interception of conversations in sixteen restaurants, cars, an auto store, an insurance office, a jewelry store, a boat, and even on public streets occurred through a cell phone that had been modified to intercept and transmit conversations within its range *regardless of whether it had been turned on.*[24]

Our cell phones are not the only modern tools that can be used to wiretap us: our cars can be programmed to do the same thing. Want to know the nearest pizza place or fancy French restaurant? Want alternate directions because there is a traffic jam? Through a combination of GPS and cellular technology, some automobile manufacturers offer a high-end in-car communications service giving 24/7 access for navigation, roadside assistance, and emergencies. In addition, if the car is reported stolen, the automobile company can, at the car owner's request, activate the "stolen recovery mode." The car's communication system will be turned into a roving bug, transmitting all sounds made within the car. This will continue until the car engine is shut off or cellular reception ends.

The FBI wanted this on-board system to be used as a wiretap; the automobile company claimed that doing the FBI's surveillance would disrupt the car's communication system. This was indeed correct, because the only function that would still work would be the emergency button, and even that would not function as advertised. The court ruled for the car manufacturer.[25]

The ruling turned on the thinnest of threads: the wiretapping, as proposed by the FBI, would disrupt the car's communication channel, and federal wiretap law says that wiretaps should function with a "minimum of interference."[26] If the car's communication system had been designed in a way in which such surveillance would not disrupt it, it could have been used as a wiretap.

Cell phones and cars can now wiretap us; what will be next?

6.6 Deep Packet Inspection

Our ISPs are also well prepared to wiretap us. To keep traffic flowing, a user's ISP has to know with whom, at least in terms of IP address, the user is communicating, but rather suddenly the intrusiveness jumped several levels. The technique is called deep packet inspection (DPI), and it involves studying not just IP headers, but actual packet content. DPI is just packet filtering by a firewall, but much more intrusive packet filtering than existed when firewalls were introduced. Traditionally firewalls simply examined packet headers, which have a fixed format and always appear in the same location in a packet. Despite the fact that the firewall filtering must be done in real time, the task is relatively easy to accomplish: the checks are simply whether the source or destination address matches particular addresses and/or which IP ports are being accessed. (A port number identifies which service on a system a packet is being directed to. For example, port 80 means this is an http request and port 25 is for email using the SMTP protocol.) The work for DPI is harder: the format and location of content in the packet payload are more variable. That makes DPI more difficult and more costly in time taken to accomplish. That is much of the reason why DPI was not possible until recently. Two uses made it come to public attention.

In 2008 Charter Communications, the fourth largest cable company in the United States, wanted to use DPI to provide users with targeted ads. An online advertising company, Nebuad, would place hardware doing deep packet inspection on Charter's ISP servers, then use that information to analyze where the customer was browsing, then target ads to Charter's customers (so if the sites were about Barcelona and Seville, and the originating address was in Texas, the ads might include flights from Dallas to Madrid). Public outcry, including some objections by Congress, canceled this plan,[27] but in the United Kingdom the ad company Phorm (www.phorm.com) forged a deal with British Telecom (BT), which serves millions of users, to serve up targeted advertising. As with Charter Communications, once this arrangement became known, public response scuttled the effort.

Meanwhile DPI can help manage traffic flow over the network. This is of great interest to ISPs. If all Internet traffic were text, the network has grown sufficiently that there is bandwidth for everything to hum along quite nicely. But Internet traffic has increasingly involved such data-rich applications as voice and streaming video. Not only are these quite demanding of bandwidth, these types of communications do not function well if subject to delays. One way carriers seek to solve the problem is by examining packets and determining traffic priorities; DPI would allow the carriers to do so.

Reality is actually both more complex and simpler. The more complex part is that this situation has already arisen. It occurred with an application that a cable company did not want to support on its system. Comcast objected to customers running BitTorrent, the peer-to-peer file-sharing program. After some curious problems that Comcast customers had with running the program, the Associated Press found that Comcast was interfering with customer use of peer-to-peer applications.[28] Subsequently three researchers at the Electronic Frontier Foundation discovered that Comcast was inspecting customer packets. Every time a Comcast customer and a BitTorrent host were about to initialize a TCP connection, Comcast would send a forged packet appearing to be from the BitTorrent host resetting the connection.[29] The TCP handshake could not occur and the connection could not happen. This prevented BitTorrent from working on the Comcast network and broke the Internet end-to-end delivery model in which systems in the center of the network are supposed to transfer packets without reading, modifying, or in any way touching the packet content. The company's behavior also demonstrated that there was no privacy or freedom of communication for Comcast users.

It is difficult to imagine the analogous situation occurring in the PSTN, where this type of intrusion is eavesdropping. While the telephone companies do occasionally listen in to calls for quality-control purposes, they do not discriminate depending on whether one is sending a fax or talking over the phone line.[30] That AT&T or Verizon might provide differential service on such a basis is not only not credible; it is illegal. It is not illegal, however, to discriminate on the basis of content of SMS messages and in 2007, Verizon Wireless did exactly that, blocking Naral Pro-Choice America from using a five-digit "short code" for its supporters to receive text messages from the organization; the company later changed its stance.[31] The FCC concluded that Comcast's actions were not "reasonable network management"[32] and ordered the company to halt such behavior.[33]

There is no need to do deep packet inspection to determine traffic priority. The simple solution to the traffic congestion problem consists of IPv6, the long-delayed IP protocol, and Internet usage pricing. IPv6 has two fields, one for type of service (VoIP, web browsing using http, SMTP for email, etc.), and one for the quality of service designated by the user (e.g., email can go slowly, VoIP must have priority, etc.). Instead of the ISP determining the traffic shaping, the customer can do so, and can pay for the privilege of employing the faster service. That is common for all forms of package transfer, from the U.S. Post Office to FedEx. Doing this would require that ISPs move from a model of all-you-can-eat data consumption to one of paying by the gigabit. This change is probably overdue now that video streaming and other data-rich applications are surging across the network. Such a change would leave the customer in charge of what type of service they receive, removing any incentive for the networks to block legal applications on the Internet. It would be a win for all involved.

DPI also has another use: censorship. Both China and Iran are reported to be using DPI tools for censorship and surveillance.

6.7 Legally Authorized Spyware

Not content with eavesdropping capabilities already in place, the FBI has also been building its own spyware. The first hint of this came in 1999, when the bureau placed a hardware keystroke logger on a computer belonging to Nicodemo S. Scarfo. Scarfo was the son of a former crime boss in south Jersey and was suspected of running a gambling ring. The FBI had been unable to decrypt records secured on Scarfo's computer. Armed with a search warrant, in a black-bag job, agents placed a keystroke logger (a small device placed between the keyboard and the computer to log all keyboard activity) on Scarfo's machine.[34] Shortly afterward the logger sent out the needed information over radio waves,[35] and the FBI was able to decrypt Scarfo's files. With the evidence, the bureau won a conviction.[36] Implanting the physical keylogger was a complicated solution; within several years, it became known that the FBI was working on delivering keystroke loggers the same way the hackers delivered viruses: through the network. The FBI program, "Magic Lantern," was written to be downloaded by unwitting users. Of course, it was to be used subject to a search warrant.[37]

Over the years, FBI online eavesdropping efforts have grown in sophistication. In an affidavit filed in an Olympia, Washington, courtroom in June 2007, the FBI revealed it was using an online pen register, Computer and Internet Protocol Address Verifier (CIPAV), to acquire user IP address, list of open TCP and UDP ports, list of running programs, operating-system type, including the version, the default browser, the currently logged-on user (which may or may not be the actual user), and the last website visited. The FBI would then monitor all outgoing communications, transmitting the IP address of each, along with the time and date.[38] This tool has been in use since at least 2005 and utilized in cases involving extortion, identity theft, and harassment.[39]

6.8 Mobility

Aside from the convenience, it would seem that mobility would not create any fundamental changes in Internet usage. After all, mobility has long been part of the Internet; for well over a decade, laptops, BlackBerrys, and other IP-enabled devices have been moving on and off the network, requiring IP addresses for anything from just a few minutes to several hours.

Mobility does change things. Just consider the phone systems and the differences in usage between cell phones and wireline devices. Both phones are used for brief calls—"Pick up milk on your way home"—but wireline phones are also used for long conversations, including business conference calls, while cell phone calls exhibit a pattern of short, frequent calls.[40]

Because full-size web pages will not fit on phones or handheld computers, web design, and thus web usage,[41] will be different to accommodate the smaller devices.[42] Communications will be brief and timely—think Twitter rather than email—and not necessarily meant to be kept until the "end of recorded time." So while Internet protocol needs may not be any different depending on whether one is connecting via an iPhone or a laptop, usage will be. And that will in turn change Internet functionality and protocols.

6.9 Traffic Analysis

Backing down from its previous stance, the U.S. government acknowledged in 2000 that strong encryption was needed to protect civilian communications and that export controls would be loosened. The expectation was that content would become protected, and so NSA expected to amplify its focus on traffic analysis, the study of who is talking to whom, when, and for how long.

Traffic analysis, part of signals intelligence, has long been an important military tool. Patterns of communication can show the chain of command, where activity is about to occur, and often what type of activity is likely to occur.

Traffic analysis started with the advent of radio, which gave admirals and generals great ability to command from a distance. At the same time, it gave the enemy unprecedented capability to listen in, not only for content, but also for the existence of the communications. Within two weeks of the outbreak of World War I, for example, using the volume of the signal as a measure of its strength, the French mapped the likely locations of senders and receivers on the German front (later the French used direction finders to help with this). The French recorded call signs (identifiers from transmitting stations), traffic volume, and correspondents from all the German stations. From this information they had a detailed picture of the German forces they were facing, a picture that was largely correct.[43] Historian David Kahn calls this the "first radio traffic analysis;"[44] it was a highly successful one at that.

During World War II, the Americans had decoded the Japanese crypto-system and enjoyed a tremendous advantage over the Japanese as a result (the Japanese military had not accomplished the reverse). But many of the U.S. successes had nothing to do with understanding the actual communication. The radio operators learned, for example, that messages on a particular frequency meant that an evening air raid was in the offing. Such deduction was faster and simpler than decryption. Analysts could often determine the target simply from a study of the call signs used in the Japanese message.[45]

For much of the Cold War, NSA analysts were unable to listen in to the Soviet leadership's telephone calls. One problem was accessing the signal, which no longer traveled by radio but by buried landlines and microwave relays.[46] By the late 1960s the United States had solved this problem through satellites, which provided the ability to acquire microwave-relay communications traffic. The other difficulty was decrypting this traffic: on October 29, 1948, "Black Friday," the Soviets deployed new encryption systems that the United States was unable to break for the next three decades. This changed in the late 1970s, but success was brief because spies in NSA and GCHQ,[47] the British equivalent, revealed the breaks to the Soviets, and the systems closed off again.

The NSA used other means to determine what was happening in the Soviet Union. One method involved eavesdropping on unprotected modes of Soviet communications; the "Gamma Guppy" intercepts of Soviet leaders chatting via their mobile phones while in their cars were particularly useful in this regard.[48] The other valuable source of Soviet intentions was traffic analysis. Such was the case during the invasion of Czechoslovakia in 1968. Although the NSA could hear what Soviet leaders were saying through the Gamma Guppy intercepts, the members of the Politburo were speaking in code, and the intelligence analysts had no idea what the words meant regarding an invasion; instead, intercepted traffic indicating troop movements was a more accurate predictor of Soviet behavior.[49] Traffic analysis was also heavily used by the NSA to correctly predict the Soviet invasion of Afghanistan in December 1979.[50]

Traffic analysis is useful not just in determining enemy plans; the United States uses it to find out about the plans of its friends. Increased diplomatic traffic between Israel and France on the eve of what turned out to be the 1956 Suez War led the CIA to correctly conclude that France might be joining Israel in the effort.[51]

During the Vietnam War the NSA was unable to decrypt well-protected communications used by the North Vietnamese and the Viet Cong leadership. Instead the agency had to use other techniques to discover enemy plans, including exploiting low-level communications in the field, unencrypted communications, and traffic analysis.[52] The last was particularly useful. For example, NSA SIGINT (signals intelligence) analysts realized that before a big attack, traffic volumes would substantially increase. North Vietnamese and Viet Cong radio operators would also take precautionary measures, changing radio frequencies and encryption systems. By 1966 the NSA was using traffic analysis to predict not only when and where an attack was to occur but even which enemy units would be involved.[53] Traffic analysis could even determine whether North Vietnamese forces or the Viet Cong would be using the Ho Chi Minh Trail to South Vietnam.[54]

In civilian life, traffic analysis can similarly discover the existence of personal relationships,[55] organization within a corporation, even whether a merger discussion is occurring. Thus, governments, both U.S. and European, have became quite interested in using CDRs as a possible tool to find *communities of interest* (COIs) for a specific phone number. (A community of interest is a small group of users whose communications are almost entirely within the group.) Communities of interest may be as innocuous as knitters in the upper Midwest or as potentially dangerous as the September 11 hijackers. Governments are typically not interested in knitters in the Midwest or elsewhere. But the idea that applying data-mining techniques to CDRs to uncover terrorist cells has proved irresistible to policymakers. In the United States the NSA began accessing CDRs in secret rooms in telephone switching offices across the country.[56] As it happens, the telephone companies were also interested in finding COIs, for it helped them uncover fraudulent activity. They had developed tools to discover such groups.[57]

In 2002 Europol—a European Union agency consisting mainly of police from member states and concerned with counterterrorism—proposed a European Union law requiring that telephone companies retain call data information for law enforcement. This proposal was not greeted with delight. Even with the dropping costs of storage (essentially by half every eighteen months), keeping such voluminous records would add substantial costs for telephone companies and ISPs.[58] And, unlike wiretapping, for which court orders delineated wiretapping specific suspects, the Europol proposal was that the communications providers keep records on every transaction of *every* person, not just suspects. Civil libertarians argued that this collection was disproportionate to the security needs of the state and thus violated Article 8 of the European Convention on Human Rights. These protectors of privacy contended there was no proof that there was any security gain whatsoever. In 2005 the European Parliament rejected the initiative, but in 2006 the Parliament passed it.[59]

The European data-retention directive has a wide scope. Under it, all data necessary to trace and identify the source and destination of a phone, email, and VoIP communications are to be retained.[60] Time, date, and duration of a completed communication, all the information needed to identify the communication itself, as well as type of communication device and its location at the start of and for the duration of the conversation are also to be kept.[61] Because the law applies to Internet communications, every web search and access is subject to retention. Not surprisingly, implementation has been slow. While the directive obliged every member state to pass a national law supporting data retention by September 2007,[62] many member states took advantage of a loophole that allowed delaying implementation for another eighteen months.

The temptation that traffic analysis will yield valuable results impossible or too expensive to discover in other ways has proved great and the research technique has become a business. In the United States, unless you are the phone company or have an order for a pen register or trap and trace, mapping who is talking to whom is illegal; in much of the rest of the world, it is not. ThorpeGlen, a British firm, is one of several companies that offer commercial traffic analysis.

ThorpeGlen sells systems that analyze vast amounts of communications data in order to discover the people worth investigating. Well-connected people with many links to others are not of interest. It is the isolated groups, the pairs and small groups who only connect with a few others, that draw suspicion. Indonesia is one government that uses ThorpeGlen products,[63] but it is far from the only one. The company won a 2009 U.K. government award for having grown substantially in international trade. ThorpeGlen grew out of 1990s British Telecom work in fraud detection. The company has a business because computer storage and search have become inexpensive and because law enforcement believes that searching out the people who have odd communications patterns can uncover the bad guys.

Certainly drug dealers exhibit such patterns. Throughout the "working day," the dealer repeatedly gets a page and responds by making a telephone call. But unlike plumbers, doctors, and other salespeople, the dealer never calls family, friends, or the office. And while a drug dealer's calling patterns may form a recognizable pattern, many other bad guys do not fall into such types. Nonetheless, studying calling records to find unnatural communications patterns *appears* to offer great benefit to law enforcement at relatively low cost. Instead of uniformed men and women walking the beat and developing relationships that enable them to search out anomalous behavior, computers working behind locked doors, coolly sifting calling patterns, can do the same. Researchers at MIT, Northeastern University, and the Santa Fe Institute report, for example, that it is easy to infer friendship networks simply based on contextualized proximity and communications transactional data,[64] while a research group from Cambridge University has observed that knowing even a limited amount of personal information—eight "friends" of a person's Facebook friends—can enable a full mapping of someone's social network.[65]

This is not to say that terrorist groups or drug dealers will actually advertise their "friends" on a Facebook page. What this result actually shows is that exposing limited amounts of personal data can turn out to be quite revealing. A Cambridge University researcher, Shishir Nagaraja, who looked at the email traffic data from 1,700 university users (researchers, graduate students, and staff), studied how many nodes have to be fully surveilled in order to infer the behavior of a large segment of the network. Confirming earlier, related research, Nagaraja showed that if 8 percent of the nodes in a network were spied on, investigators could determine the communications "circle" of 45 percent of the users, while if the traffic of 28 percent of the users was known, then investigators could determine the behavior of fully 95 percent of the users.[66]

What these results *do not mean* is that searching for unusual communications networks can be used to readily reveal terrorist groups in our midst. The reason is simple. In the military, patterns of communications disclose levels of activity (activity increases before battle) and organizational structure. In the civilian world, a small group of people communicating only among themselves could be a terrorist cell or a drug dealer's crew. Or they could easily be a group of people planning a new business venture or rock band. Probability tells us that they are much more likely to be the latter.

On the other hand, following the communications connections of a person of interest to other possible suspects can help crack cases. On July 7, 2005, three London Underground trains and one London bus were bombed, resulting in fifty-six deaths and hundreds of injuries. There were other attempted bombings on July 21; those attacks did not succeed. Retained data helped police track one of the suspects. Using a false passport, the suspect, Hussain Osman, quickly fled to Rome. From earlier investigations, police knew the number of one of his friends and monitored communications on that line. Italian police discovered that the phone was being used by Osman himself, who was captured shortly afterward.[67]

This success story was not a case of data retention: at the time of the failed bombings, Osman was already a person of interest to the police. He was in police files because in 2004 he had taken part in a camping trip that had attracted police attention.[68] The friend's number was known previously to law enforcement. This was also not a case where the criminal was uncovered because his communications patterns "looked interesting." In the absence of other information—for example, presence at a camping trip with military exercises—an unusual communications pattern is far more likely to be a red herring than an indicator of nefarious activity. What is true is that link analysis is extremely useful. This is no surprise; pursuing such connections has been the approach followed by detectives and law enforcement since the beginning of such professions. The ability to do so quickly and easily, a result of legal changes and the ease of accessing customer calling records, explains why use of NSLs for obtaining these records has exploded in recent years.

6.10 Tools for Anonymization

The famous 1993 *New Yorker* cartoon "On the Internet, no one knows you're a dog" may be true, but the network makes it easy to trace your online behavior.[69] Actions that are anonymous (at least if transactions are done in cash) in the offline world—purchasing a book on Osama bin Laden, viewing materials on sexually transmitted diseases—leave traces when done in the online world. As one corporate executive said in 1999, "You have zero privacy anyway. Get over it."[70] In the 1980s David Chaum proposed several systems for providing anonymity to users, including anonymous digital cash systems and anonymizing communications systems. The latter has the contradictory property that messages transit from sender to receiver but eavesdropping intermediaries are unable to determine who is communicating with whom. The technology behind this combines public-key encryption, go-between "mix" servers that permute the order of messages, and batching the communications. The ensuing confusion means that an eavesdropper is perplexed as to which message is going where.[71] This technology has been used in various anonymous remailer systems.

In the 1990s a different approach to anonymous communication emerged. Tor (which stands for "The onion routing")[72] is focused on making it hard to determine who is communicating with whom unless you can watch all endpoints of the network at once. There are two parts to Tor technology: a "proxy" Tor client that determines a route for the communication and a large set of Tor nodes in the network through which the communication travels. When an application (a web browser, Instant Messaging, Internet Relay Chat) connects using the Tor network, the first thing that occurs is that a path is built using a subset of the Tor nodes chosen by the Tor client over which the application's messages travel. Then the communication is encrypted using the keys created for that path.

Each Tor node decrypts the message using its key for that path and then passes the communication to the next Tor node in that communication's Tor path. Paths are torn down once the application using it is done.[73] Each node knows where a communication has immediately come from and where it is immediately going, but no node sees both source and destination. Only the client proxy that determined the route knows these. Such decentralized control is appropriate; it protects privacy.

Work on onion routing started in the Naval Research Laboratory in 1995. It may seem odd that this was a DoD effort. On reflection, this makes perfect sense. Members of the military are often stationed overseas in situations where it is better that their affiliation not be known. When they need to hide who they are communicating with—for example, with Norfolk or another Navy post—using Tor is a way to do so. This is not a theoretical argument. A group in the U.S. Navy periodically based in the Mideast over the last decade needed to make their Internet communications anonymous; otherwise they risked giving away their cover if it was noticed that they were communicating with a .gov or .mil site (this could be noticed by an eavesdropping local ISP). Using Tor, there would be no way for an eavesdropper to tell where the communications were going, *not even to which country.*

The military is not the only set of government users of this anonymizing software; law-enforcement investigators have found Tor useful for surveilling certain chat rooms and websites. This can be done without leaving IP addresses traceable back to government offices. For good reason, the law enforcement and military units that use Tor do not publicize it. In the early years of its distribution, that made Tor usage a bit dicey: was it simply a way to hide the distribution of pornography? There was some of that, but there was much more, as evidenced by the fact that a number of different agencies in DoD have helped support the tool's development.

That leads to the natural question of why DoD might release a general-purpose anonymizer for Internet communications rather than limit usage of the tool to military personnel. That answer is simple: "anonymity loves company."[74] The more diversity of users an anonymizing system has, the more anonymous its users become. Thus opening up Tor to the general public helps the military protect the anonymity of *its* communications. The network has been in public use since October 2003. In February 2010 it had 1,500 servers, with the number having steadily increased over the previous five years.[75] The network's users include reporters,[76] whistleblowers, labor organizers, bloggers whose companies might not appreciate their employees' writings, military and law enforcement personnel, businesses (to enable them to find out information they might not want the competition to discover they are seeking), and IT professionals troubleshooting their system[77]—in short, Tor is a tool employed by people who want to communicate without revealing to potential eavesdroppers with whom their conversation is occurring. As for the number of Tor users, that information is not easy to estimate, not even for its developers.

Tor is essentially the only widely used general-purpose tool for anonymizing Internet communications. Open proxy servers, servers that act as intermediary access points to the Internet and effectively hide network addresses, provide some circumvention capabilities. These do not, however, provide anonymity in the rigorous way that Tor does.

At the beginning of the millennium Tor appeared to be a tool for privacy aficionados, Chinese dissidents, and CIA agents. A decade later, anonymizing engines have become more widely deployed across a much greater swath of society.

6.11   It's Not a U.S. Network Anymore

In 1965 packet networks were a twinkle in the eye of some engineers. In 1975 they were a DARPA project. In 1985 the NSF began its own Internet connecting supercomputing sites; within four years, hosts in Australia, Germany, Israel, Japan, Mexico, New Zealand, and the United Kingdom had joined the network. In 1995 the Internet was a public network, open to commercial enterprises.

In 1985 most of the network expertise was in the United States; the breakthrough of easy hypertext linking and a browser, though, was due to a British physicist, Tim Berners-Lee, and came from a nuclear laboratory on the French-Swiss border. In 1995 the World Wide Web Consortium (W3C) was formed, with offices in the United States, France, and Japan. The Internet had become an international effort.

Governance was slowly shifting that way too. Despite the name, the Internet, of course, is not a thing; it is a collection of interconnected autonomous networks without a central governing authority. For many years the Internet Engineering Task Force (IETF), a group of government-funded researchers, developed the Internet standards. In the early 1990s, the IETF became part of a newly formed organization, the *Internet Society*, an international nonprofit guiding the network's development. With the Internet being a collection of self-governing networks, naming is an important issue and much control of the network resides in determining who the name registrars might be. Here the U.S. government appeared, at least at first, to be less willing to cede decision-making power.

In 1998 the U.S. National Telecommunications and Information Administration proposed private administration of the Internet name space and created a nonprofit organization, the Internet Corporation for Assigned Names and Numbers (ICANN), which existed under an agreement with the U.S. Department of Commerce. The fact that ICANN was not independent of the U.S. government raised concerns. With the exception of objections to a top-level domain of *.xxx* for adult sites,[78] the United States has largely kept a hands-off attitude toward ICANN; worries about excessive U.S. authority dissipated. Yet as the power and importance of the network have become apparent, other governments have sought greater control of the network and, in particular, of the root zone (recall the issues of DNSSEC and signing the root zone). There has also been pressure for control of the network by other international organizations, including the International Telecommunications Union, a United Nations agency that develops telecommunication standards, including the interface between the Interment and the PSTN.

As of 2009, the eight most popular websites on the Internet are American—Google, Facebook, Yahoo!, YouTube, Windows Live, Wikipedia, Blogger, and Microsoft Network—but Baidu.com, the leading Chinese search engine, is ninth, and Yahoo.co.jp, the Japanese version of Yahoo, is tenth.[79] Yet the U.S. hegemony of the network, remarkable in its exclusivity in 1993, is ebbing. English remains the most popular language for web pages, with 338 million people online,[80] but China leads the world in terms of actual users. While the Internet of 1985 was an American engineers' network, the Internet of today is not really either anymore. The governance of the network will undoubtedly change to reflect this new reality.

6.12   Coda: Changes in Law Enforcement Practice

Though it was working hard to keep surveillance techniques concurrent with changing communications technologies, internally FBI communications infrastructure was way behind. Unbelievable as it may sound, in 2003 the FBI could not perform fundamental searches of their own files,[81] and experience with wireless communications in the work environment was still limited to senior staff.[82] In 2004 FBI agents and intelligence analysts still did not have routine access to the Internet.[83] The reasons for such backwardness ranged from a culture that promoted secrecy to technology that "air gapped" computer systems between the different U.S. intelligence agencies, often making it impossible for analysts at the different agencies to communicate by any means other than phone and hand courier.[84]

In 2005 the director of national intelligence, John Negroponte, tackled the problem. Air Force Major General Dale Meyrrose was made chief information officer for the director of national intelligence, a newly created position. He took an important step: from then on, the agencies would buy off-the-shelf interoperable software instead of customized systems.[85] This small change enabled the different agencies to communicate electronically. Meanwhile, on the suggestion of a CIA chief technology officer, the agencies started *Intellipedia*, an intelligence-community information-sharing site modeled on *Wikipedia*. Any agent with a classified clearance could read or contribute information to the site; the idea was to enable analysts with disparate information to be in a position to "connect the dots" (something that was sorely missed for the September 11 hijackers). The FBI joined the online world, using tools that everyone else had been taking for granted: databases, the DNS WhoIs, VoIP, encryption, and Google. This was a seismic shift from a few years earlier.[86] While the U.S. intelligence agencies may not have moved Quantico and Langley (these are respectively the FBI research and training center and CIA headquarters) to Silicon Valley, they appear to have substantially improved the agencies' ability to use network tools and capabilities to their advantage—even though the dots were certainly not connected in the 2009 case of Umar Farouk Abdulmutallab, who tried to blow up a plane on Christmas Day 2009 using explosives he brought on board.[87]

7 Who Are the Intruders? What Are They Targeting?

The Morris worm made the front page of the *New York Times* in November 1988. As computers and connections to the Internet have become widespread, so have attacks on computer systems, and these now only rarely make the news. Two other aspects of cyberattacks have changed as well. Such exploits once carried a certain prank status and occasionally even an outlaw romantic air. That is long gone in the wake of the serious disruption caused. The other change has been in the nature of the attackers.

Originally computer-system vulnerabilities were exploited by those seemingly curious to test their ability to raise havoc. That role has been taken over by "script kiddies," people who download preconfigured tools that they then use to launch assaults. This group is not without ability to cause economic harm, but because these prefabricated attacks are already well known, appropriate defense is frequently in place. Exploits by script kiddies tend to be less disruptive than other attacks.

New technologies are usually taken up by criminals, and the Internet has been no exception. Spam, offering bargains in drugs or stocks too good to be true—and they are too good to be true—is quite common. A study of stock spam, which urges people to buy penny stocks, shows that there is a small bump in the stock price shortly after the mail is sent. Because these bumps occur on a predictable timetable, spammers are able to sell at the right moment and make a small profit.[1]

Spammers often use compromised machines, or *bots*.[2] These bots may have been compromised through malware from an infected web page, or perhaps through a virus or worm received in an email; the bots form a network controlled by a single entity, a *botnet*, and in at least one instance, a botnet included infected PCs from U.S. defense agencies.[3] The varied IP addresses of the botnet participants provide a way of disguising the initial phases of an assault, and this complicates defenses.

Botnets distribute a task over thousands of hosts across the Internet, and range in size from several thousand to well over a hundred thousand endhosts, or computers.[4] Bots regularly check in with a server that provides new software to download, gives instructions on a site to attack, and so on. Spammers can rent a botnet for about $1,000 an attack.[5] The use of spam for the penny stocks showed that renting botnets is "on average a profitable business model (for spammers)."[6]

In 2007 the nation of Estonia was subjected to a major DDoS attack. First the Estonian foreign minister's website was bombarded with packets, but soon the attack was extended to other government agencies as well as Estonian businesses.[7] In the initial two weeks, there were 128 separate DDoS attacks on Estonian websites. Most of the incidents were short, but seven lasted at least ten hours.[8] The cost to mount the attacks was estimated at under $100,000;[9] the cost to Estonia, in terms of lost business and disruption, was far greater. A more serious DDoS attack was made against Georgian government and media websites during the Russian invasion of Georgia in August 2008, effectively shutting these information sources down. Because Georgia was not particularly dependent on the Internet for critical functions, the effect of the cyberattack was limited to silencing the Georgian government's voice.[10] Although this was the first instance of cyberattacks coordinated with a physical one, the 2007 attack on Estonia, which is a more cyber-dependent society, was, in fact, more disruptive.

Cyberattacks and cyberexploitation share a number of characteristics: existence of a vulnerability, access to exploit the vulnerability, and software to perform the exploitation.[11] The payload may be a virus, a Trojan horse, or a *rootkit*, a program with access to the computer's functions that can remain hidden from the host computer's operating system. It may arrive accidentally downloaded from a website, it may be in an email attachment, or it may be rogue software on a USB flash drive. Where cyberattacks and cyberexploitation differ is in execution: cyberattacks are about disrupting or destroying the host, while cyberexploitation's purpose is gaining information. Espionage is most effective if the host is unaware that such exploitation has occurred, for then the spying may continue indefinitely. Vulnerabilities created by building surveillance into communications infrastructure enable cyberexploitation. They may or may not enable direct attacks. Thus I will mostly concentrate on cyberexploitation rather than cyberattacks.

7.1   Is Anyone Spying?

The best way to find out about a nation's military capabilities and intentions is to spy on its government and military, but there are other valuable sources of information as well. Whether in fictional accounts regarding the German army's purchases of wool in 1940—a signal that could indicate that Germany was intending to attack the Soviet Union—or apocryphal accounts concerning late-night purchases of pizza near the Pentagon toward the end of 1990—indicating that planning for an attack on Iraq was occurring—eavesdropping on business communications is a well-known espionage technique. Such sources help agents flesh out the target's plans. So while at first the Soviet Union focused on U.S. government communications, by the early 1970s Soviet attention had shifted to include defense contractors. In 1971, a KGB directive ordered agents to target scientific and technical work, and specified such U.S. companies as Grumman, Fairchild, GE, IBM, Sperry Rand, and General Dynamics.[12] An NSA history reported that the Soviets were believed to have "obtained information on the most sophisticated new weapons systems, including the F-14 fighter, B-1 bomber, Trident submarine, and advanced nuclear weapons developments."[13]

Protecting civilian sites was more difficult than protecting government targets. Contractors are more widely spread across society and are softer targets than military ones. If Soviet spies were listening in on defense-industry communications, then their communications would need to be secured. This necessitated a change in the U.S. defense posture.

The first concern was microwave transmissions. Such transmissions spread out, with the signal larger than the antenna dish. This allows nearby receivers, say on the tops of buildings close by, to access the signal. A large number of defense contractors are located around the Washington Beltway, and the Soviet embassy is located in a relatively high part of Washington, its roof bristling with antennas. With the realization that the Soviets were listening to business communications, National Security Advisor Henry Kissinger issued a "highly sensitive" national-security memorandum directing that "Washington area microwave communications be buried to the extent possible."[14] Defense-related communications turned out to be one part of an increasingly complex problem.

Domestic communications about even mundane things had national-security implications. In 1972, the same year that the United States was enjoying a bumper wheat crop, the Soviet crop failed. The Soviets had been monitoring transmissions between wheat traders and the Department of Agriculture and had a better picture of prices and crop status than the U.S. government and its farmers did. In a matter of a few weeks, the Soviet Union purchased 1.5 million tons of wheat from the United States. This was five times as much as it had previously purchased; it occurred at a time when the wheat-crop failure extended to much of the world. The Soviet purchase was shrewdly done. It was expensive for the United States. Domestic wheat prices increased by several hundred percent between June 1972 and February 1974.[15]

Soviet monitoring was not limited to Washington. The Soviets had purchased a country home in Glen Cove, a suburb of New York. The Long Island dacha happened to be perfectly situated so as to eavesdrop on microwave communications along the Eastern Seaboard. IBM headquarters and corporate offices were located in Westchester County, not far from Glen Cove as the crow or microwave signal flies. The NSA discovered that Soviet agents were listening to calls of IBM executives on the company's private microwave network and warned the U.S. company.[16] In the late 1980s a similar incident occurred with a different U.S. corporation;[17] IBM changed its communication policies.

Another Soviet eavesdropping station was in Lourdes, Cuba, strategically located a hundred miles from Key West. This site consisted of twenty-eight square miles bristling with antennas monitoring satellite communications between the United States and Europe. Lourdes became active in 1962.[18] For many decades the site listened in on unencrypted commercial communications traffic between the United States and its trading partners.

The ease of microwave eavesdropping was a two-way street, for the United States benefited from the insecurity of transmissions in Cuba, which used microwave relay systems rather than landlines (these had been built by RCA International in 1957). These unprotected links provided an easy way for the NSA to listen to all telecommunications between Havana and the rest of the island.[19]

After a 1970s government study, the United States became quite concerned about the extent of Soviet electronic espionage of defense contractors.[20] The CEOs participating in the study were "shocked" by the extent of the eavesdropping. While burying microwave communications would solve part of the problem, a more complete solution was needed. The government embarked on a program to deliver secure phones to a large portion of the defense industry.[21]

That was solving only a piece of an increasingly large problem. While during the Cold War U.S. intelligence focused its attention on the Soviet Union, some U.S. allies were also targeting U.S. industry. Some made no bones about it. The former director of the French intelligence agency, Direction Générale de la Sécurité Extérieure (DGSE), Pierre Marion, who initiated a program of spying on U.S. business, explained, "It would not be normal that we spy on the United States in political matters or in military matters, but in the economic and technical spheres, we are competitors; we are not allies."[22] Spy they did.

The French government passed along product information to French competitors of U.S. companies. Intelligence agents were reported to have taken "unusually sensitive technical information for a struggling [French] company."[23] Seeking to support France's defense sector, French intelligence agents were said to have focused on U.S. companies working on missile and satellite espionage technologies.[24] France targeted Boeing, General Dynamics, Hughes Aircraft, Lockheed, McDonnell Douglas, Martin Marietta, and the Office of the U.S. Trade Representative (responsible for negotiating U.S. trade agreements)[25] and placed spies in Corning, IBM, and Texas Instruments.[26] In one instance Cie. des Machines Bull sued Texas Instruments (TI) for patent infringement only to have the U.S. company discover that the patent in question had been stolen by a French mole working at TI years earlier.[27]

Israel, another close ally of the United States, was described in a 1996 U.S. government report[28] as having stolen technologies for numerous military systems; some of these were shared with Israeli companies.[29] One documented case occurred at the Illinois company Recon Optical.

Recon was building state-of-the-art airborne surveillance systems capable of peering seventy miles. The company signed a $45 million contract with the Israeli government to develop a system to be able to see twice as far, and three Israeli Air Force officers went to work at the Illinois company. The contract between Recon and Israel specified that all intellectual property rights belonged to the U.S. company. A few months into the effort, the Israeli officers were caught stealing proprietary material, which they were sending to Israel. The officers were dismissed, the contract abrogated. After a four-year trial, a panel of arbitrators ordered Israel to pay Recon $3 million for the theft of secrets.[30]

Asia is another part of the economic espionage picture. Japan, with a small military and virtually no defense-based industries, focuses on consumer-oriented technologies. Much of the Japanese industrial spying is done by private companies, but Japan's Ministry of Economy, Trade and Industry (METI)[31] and the Japanese External Trade Organization have aided the efforts. Corporate espionage by Japanese firms runs across multiple U.S. industries. Hitachi, having purchased a partial set of stolen guides of product specifications for future IBM systems, attempted to obtain the full set; the conspirators were arrested and the out-of-court settlement was reputed to be $3 million.[32] Fifteen Japanese firms targeted Honeywell for its single lens reflex autofocusing technology, while Fuji attempted to illegally obtain Kodak's disposable 35 mm camera.[33] When Mitsubishi was unable to buy Celanese's formula for a high-quality industrial film the company had developed, it turned to illegal means to obtain it.[34]

Japan's focus on consumer technologies has not stopped it from spying on U.S. military technologies. Three Japanese companies, Nissan, Mitsubishi, and Ishikawajima-Harima Heavy Industries, bought stolen software that had been developed for the Department of Defense's Strategic Defense Initiative ("Star Wars"), hoping to employ it in civilian applications.[35]

As nations expanded their industrial bases and new industries developed, new targets for industrial espionage emerged. Currently, biotechnology and energy technologies are of particular interest. Research and development of biologically tailored drugs may cost millions, but successful drugs can reap billions in profit. Taxol, a drug used to treat breast and ovarian cancer, is one example.

Taxol originally came from the bark of a yew tree, but the tree is an endangered species, and Bristol-Myers Squibb spent $15 million finding an alternative process for culturing the drug. Profits from Taxol are now estimated to be a billion dollars a year for Bristol-Myers Squibb. In 1995–1996 the formula for producing Taxol was the target of theft by three employees of Taiwan's Yuen Foong Paper Company.

During the 1980s and 1990s, France, Germany, Israel, Japan, and South Korea were the main players in economic espionage against U.S. industry among the U.S. allies.[36] More recently, India, Indonesia, and Taiwan have joined the action. But the most serious threats come from China and Russia. China targets U.S. industrial, scientific, and technical work, while Russia is more focused on military technology and energy technologies (specifically gas and oil).[37]

In 1996 the FBI reported that "biotechnology, aerospace, telecommunications (including technology to build the Internet), computer software and hardware, advanced transportation and engine technology, advanced materials and coatings, including 'stealth' technologies, energy research, defense and armaments technology, manufacturing processes, and semiconductors" are the targets of industrial espionage. In addition, information about business plans—including bidding, contracts, and strategy—is targeted.[38] In the United States, acquiring intelligence on competitors is legal. Economic espionage is not. Even if actions are committed abroad, U.S. companies attempting the same type of espionage on competitors as was being done to them would be violating U.S. law. Meanwhile each piece of technology stolen, each trade secret lifted, each marketing plan discovered, is costly to U.S. business, weakening the economy and U.S. industry, and ultimately U.S. national security.

In 2003 the FBI estimated the cost to the U.S. economy of industrial espionage at $200 billion.[39] In point of fact, pinning down actual damages is quite difficult. Many times the espionage occurs without being noticed. Even when it is discovered, it is difficult to put a dollar figure on the lost sales and increased costs incurred by a company that has to compete differently as a result of the theft.[40] Nonetheless there is no question that the damage done to U.S. competitiveness as a result of economic espionage is substantial.

Much of the industrial spying comes in the form of HUMINT, human intelligence—corporate or government spies who visit U.S. plants and laboratories posing as potential customers or partners, foreign graduate students placed in specific U.S. university laboratories,[41] and industry funding for U.S. academic researchers that is tied to a commitment that the research will be shared with the foreign funders first.[42] Other forms of penetration include the time-honored methods of spycraft:[43] bribing insiders for information, attending industrial meetings and chatting with company employees, even going through trash.[44] Then there is electronic eavesdropping employed by U.S. allies; faxes are particularly fruitful sources of information.

German intelligence shared the information gained with German industry,[45] while French intelligence did so for French industry. The French not only tapped phone lines, but were even alleged to have bugged first-class airline seats and hotels in order to eavesdrop on U.S. business visitors.[46] The Japanese government was believed to monitor all telecommunications traffic from the Japan offices of U.S. corporations for the benefit of Japanese corporations.[47]

The U.S. government response has generally been to stay above the fray and press for level playing fields. In the process of targeting the Soviet Union during the Cold War, information including proprietary data from foreign companies fell into the hands of U.S. intelligence, but it appears that the government did not use this information. With the end of the Cold War, the gloves partially came off. U.S. intelligence, which had previously confined its interest to military and diplomatic affairs, now sought, in the words of former CIA Director Stansfield Turner, to "redefine 'national security' by assigning economic strength greater importance."[48] The CIA embarked on economic espionage.[49]

This turned out to be a heavy-handed effort. It was not a perfect fit for an agency more accustomed to narrowly defined missions than the open-ended ways of economic investigations. CIA agents doing industrial spying in Germany and France were discovered and quite publicly expelled.[50] Explicit economic targeting died a quiet death, although indirect targeting continued.

Intelligence was sometimes gleaned through ECHELON, a collection and analysis system jointly run by the United States, the United Kingdom, Canada, Australia, and New Zealand. Although in use for many decades, ECHELON seems to have come into public view in the late 1990s, first with the 1996 publication of Nicky Hager's *Secret Power: New Zealand's Role in the International Spy Network*, and then as a result of a 1999 European Union report by investigative journalist Duncan Campbell.[51] The report noted that ECHELON targeted commercial communication channels; this fact caught Europe's attention in a major way. With the Americans listening in, the Europeans wanted to protect their proprietary business information, and European governments relaxed their cryptographic export controls. (In turn, six months later the United States relaxed *its* cryptographic export controls.) But it appears that the United States was not using the proprietary information it acquired in the same way the Europeans anticipated.

A close read of the Campbell report showed only two examples where U.S. intelligence had actually shared business information outside the U.S. government. Both were bribery cases: Thomson-CSF, a U.K. electronics and defense contractor,[52] which was alleged to have bribed members of a Brazilian government selection panel in order to sell a $1.3 billion surveillance system for the Amazon rainforest, and Airbus, which had offered bribes to Saudi officials. In the latter case, the information was passed to a U.S. trade negotiator who had been pressing the Saudis to "buy American." The Saudis bought their planes from Boeing and McDonnell Douglas.

While spy agencies of foreign nations stole trade secrets and proprietary information and gave it to their nation's industries, it seems that U.S. agencies did not. The intelligence garnered by U.S. agents went to U.S. trade negotiators. Even then, only a particular type of information was used. Former CIA Director James Woolsey told the Europeans, "We have spied on you because you bribe . . . you bribe a lot. . . . When we have caught you at it, you might be interested, we haven't said a word to the U.S. companies in the competition. Instead we go to the government you're bribing and tell its officials that we don't take kindly to such corruption. They often respond by giving the most meritorious bid (sometimes American, sometimes not) all or part of the contract."[53]

The U.S. government policy of limiting the sharing of economic intelligence to information on unfair trade practices of other nations,[54] but not sharing the fruits of intelligence with private companies, is unusual. In our cynical age, many find it hard to believe that the U.S. government really behaves this way. It is, of course, difficult to prove a negative, but there is evidence to buttress this. Primary, of course, is the lack of any evidence to the contrary. Further evidence takes the form of the 1996 Economic Espionage Act,[55] which criminalizes theft of a trade secret if there is intent to benefit a foreign government or related agency (§1831).[56] It is notable that few, if any, other nations criminalize economic espionage.[57] Nine years after the Woolsey statement, a 2009 National Research Council report observed,

The United States has a long-standing policy not to use cyberattack or cyberexploitation to obtain economic advantage for private companies . . . the economic domain is one in which the operational policies of adversaries are markedly different from those of the United States. That is, adversaries of the United States are widely believed to conduct cyber-espionage for economic advantage—stealing trade secrets and other information that might help them to gain competitive advantage in the world marketplace and/or over U.S. firms . . . the intelligence services of at least one major nation-state were explicitly tasked with gathering intelligence for its potential economic benefits. This asymmetry between U.S. and foreign policies regarding cyberexploitation is notable.[58]

Meanwhile, according to the FBI, almost a hundred nations are targeting U.S. technologies, with China accounting for almost half the investigations into export violations.[59] Targets of foreign espionage are not so much the "crown jewels"—the newest computer virtualization technology, the best night-vision goggles—as dual-use and dated military technologies. The techniques used in the last century, front companies, approaches by foreign intelligence at industry conferences, foreign research labs located near U.S. universities, spies within visiting delegations, remain the same, but espionage has become much simpler to arrange.

Instead of a foreign scientist having to visit a U.S. R&D facility, or placing a foreign graduate student in a U.S. lab, the "visit" comes via the network. This can happen in ways that are completely unnoticed. Such espionage is cheaper and safer than traditional forms of snooping. It should be no surprise that the Internet has become a major tool for economic espionage. The U.S. Department of Defense reported in 2008 that the number of foreign contacts evaluated as suspicious was growing exponentially. A large cause was the ease of conducting such efforts via the Internet.[60] This form of spying is happening at a time when the Internet is increasingly embedded in the production process. It is to that role of the network that we now turn our attention.

7.2 Supply Chains in the Information-Based Economy

Supply chain is a fancy term to describe the systematic way of moving products from the maker to the consumer. As such, supply chains are part of human history and are older than the Silk Route and trading across the Mediterranean in ancient times. A supply chain can be as simple as a farmer bringing fruit to market and as complex as an automobile being designed in Germany, with components produced in Japan, Taiwan, and Singapore, assembled in Korea, and sold in the United States.[61]

Many pieces have to be in place for complex supply chains to function. At each level of the chain there must be enough suppliers to deliver products to the next. Products at each level must be sufficiently customizable. And delivery must be reliable. For a farmer delivering produce to the local market, this is easy to manage; for a manufacturer building a car or a computer, the links are more complicated.

The 451 different parts in the Apple iPod, for example, come from China, Japan, Korea, the Philippines, and Taiwan.[62] The hard drive is manufactured by the Japanese firm Toshiba, which produces most of its hard drives in the Philippines and China. The display module and panels are made by the Korean company Samsung; the video/multiprocessor chip comes from the U.S. firm Broadcom; the controller chip is from another U.S. firm, PortalPlayer; and memory is provided by Samsung.[63] Final assembly is done in Chinese factories operated by Taiwanese firms.[64] The overall concept and design of the iPod, as well as organization of the supply chain, are handled by Apple in the United States.[65] As such things go, the iPod is a relatively simple device.

Modern supply-chain management requires information technology (IT). While supply-chain complexity increased after World War II, in the 1950s it still relied on people, paper, and phones. The first customized inventory management systems were introduced in the 1960s. By the 1980s, IT's ability to quickly aggregate and analyze massive amounts of data made much accurate forecasting of business needs possible.

Wal-Mart was one of the first companies to tap into this. Every sale in a Wal-Mart store is linked through a satellite-based communications system to company headquarters. Sales information is fed into a database that Wal-Mart's suppliers use to adjust their production.[66] Wal-Mart has discovered, for example, that before hurricanes people stock up on beer and afterward on easy-to-store, nonperishables like Pop-Tarts. The chain modifies store stocks according to storm forecasts.[67] Other companies manage stocks even more directly. The Italian clothing company Benetton does its own production. By tracking daily sales in the company stores, Benetton nimbly adjusts manufacturing. Are pink turtlenecks selling, but not yellow? Make more pink.[68] Communication technologies allow a complex model of production,[69] with an ability to respond to customer demand almost instantaneously.

Outsourcing is not limited to production. For example, U.S. clothing retailers The Limited and The Gap not only outsource the manufacture of the clothes they sell, they outsource the business processes behind the manufacturing. Both companies use Li and Fung,[70] a Hong Kong company that exports goods and services, to manage the supply chains of their dispersed manufacturing base.[71] Li and Fung manage schedules, including inventory and just-in-time flow, through the supply chain. Modern communications technologies enable small clothing companies to compete profitably with large firms.

Such collaborations carry many intellectual property risks and require various forms of information security, from laws protecting intellectual property, to contracts protecting collaborating partners, to cryptographic algorithms protecting the data transiting between them. Each aspect of security is crucial if this globalized system of production is to function. It is not news that data must be protected, but there are two new aspects to the equation: the increasing complexity of the supply chain and the role information plays as a commodity. It is worth looking at this particular aspect in more detail. I have chosen to examine the collaborations that Sun Microsystems, a computer manufacturer, has with its partners.[72]

Sun Microsystems, a subsidiary of Oracle, is a computer company that produces workstations, servers, storage, software, and services. Most software is developed in house, and virtually all the rest of Sun's technology offerings are designed by Sun—and built and assembled elsewhere.

Outsourcing is simply moving production outside the company, subcontracting as a way to lower production costs, access cheaper resources, including labor, and focus on core business functions. In many ways outsourcing is a natural progression from the division-of-labor model that began over two centuries ago. Thus, for example, a computer manufacturer has no need to be its own travel agency, for example. Instead of staffing a corporate department responsible for booking travel, it is far more cost effective for the manufacturer to outsource that function to a travel agency, which naturally has much greater expertise in making hotel, car rental, and flight reservations.

Sun's first decision was to outsource certain aspects of manufacturing that had become too expensive to do in house. Sun engineers would design the chips, boards, and modules, but these would be fabricated elsewhere (though Sun would still be hands on in testing). As Sun's product line grew, there were increasing numbers of partners. Pieces were manufactured by different suppliers and assembled by partners—a process not unlike the manufacture of the iPod.

From chips to servers, Sun designed the system while partners built individual pieces. The product was ultimately a Sun server, a Sun storage device, and so on. As with the iPod, Sun's role is creating the technology and managing the supply chain. Sun developed "one-touch" outsourcing: each customer order—and keep in mind that such high-end systems are highly customized—requires Sun to configure the supply chain a single time and then pieces would be shipped, configured, combined, perhaps multiple times, without any additional hands-on management from Sun.

In 2001 Sun's model changed to partnering with other companies to provide services.[73] This complicated security. It is one thing to outsource production, where the intellectual property being shared, although potentially voluminous, is a fixed amount. It is quite another thing to outsource where the ability to provide the services may require constant connection into the heart of Sun's own systems.

Consider customer support, for example; at Sun such support is provided not by the company itself but by outside partners with which it has contracted. Sun sells high-end systems to large financial customers. Customer support does not consist of answering simple questions like "Why can't I print?"[74] but instead resolving complex issues where the documentation to answer the questions may be available only within internal Sun systems. Performing customer support for these customers means Sun's partners have access to large swaths of Sun internal information. The image of what is "inside" the company and what is "outside" changes when such outsourcing occurs. The outside partner is inside the company. The security challenge is clear. Sun's contractual arrangements with suppliers carry numerous requirements, from physical security to personnel security to process security, and Sun conducts periodic security audits to ensure these are met.

On the communications side, Sun's original solution was dedicated digital T1 and T3 lines (respectively carrying 1.5 and 44 million bits per second) for communicating with suppliers. Later the company switched to using virtual private networks. Both solutions secure communications between outside suppliers and Sun internal networks. What Sun does not—and cannot—do is secure the communications systems of the outside suppliers. If these are penetrated, then so are Sun's. This is part of the business risk that arises when suppliers are in nations where electronic eavesdropping is a matter of course rather than a matter of probable cause.

In its reliance on outsourcing, Sun is far from unique. The fiber-optic cable connecting the United States and Europe to parts of the world where educated labor is much cheaper means that outsourcing is a permanent part of the economic landscape.[75]

7.3   Critical Infrastructure Risks

In recent years, the need to protect critical infrastructure has become a mantra. We hear that risks to critical infrastructure are great and we are in much danger. Yet there appear to have been no attacks. For a topic so much in the public eye, critical infrastructure risks remain remarkably obscured by fog (not to mention sturm and drang). Confusion begins with the definition of critical infrastructure, which the PATRIOT Act calls the "systems and assets, whether physical or virtual, so vital to the United States that the incapacity or destruction of such systems and assets would have a debilitating impact on security, national economic security, national public health or safety, or any combination of those matters."[76] The definition in a U.S. 2006 National Infrastructure Protection Plan is even more expansive, listing the following as key infrastructure resources:

agriculture and food, defense industrial base, energy, public health and healthcare, banking and finance, drinking water and water treatment systems, chemical facilities, commercial facilities, dams, emergency services, commercial nuclear reactors, materials and waste, information technology, telecommunications, postal and shipping, transportation systems, and government facilities.[77] The list also includes national monuments and icons, which are surely not critical infrastructure by anyone's definition.

The first known IT threat to critical infrastructure was an incident that might have escaped notice had it not happened to shut down an airport. In 1997 a teenage hacker accessed a NYNEX switch in central Massachusetts—one that did not require authentication—and corrupted information in the switch, disabling access to the Worcester Airport. The main radio transmitter was unable to communicate with the control tower, and incoming planes could not activate the runway lights. The airport was closed for six hours.[78] The problem arose from a convergence of an old-style switching network—the PSTN—with new-style control. The Worcester situation illustrates the generic problem that results when closed proprietary control networks are connected with the open Internet. New vulnerabilities are created. Nowhere is this more apparent than in the supervisory control and data acquisition systems (SCADA systems) that control industrial processes, including the electric power grid, water and sewage systems, oil and gas pipelines—in short, much critical infrastructure.

Such industrial systems require constant monitoring of temperature, pressure, power, and other variables. Depending on the application, they must be controlled on a minute-by-minute, second-by-second, even millisecond-by-millisecond basis. Consider electric power. The generation of power is due to the need, which can change from minute to minute as people wake up in the morning, turn on their coffeemakers, run their hair dryers, check their email, and so on. Power must be available when the customer wants it. Generating systems must respond to rapid changes in demand. In recent years, deregulation has engendered competition, and power companies do short-term sales of power to each other depending on who is generating power most cheaply. Contracts are of very short duration—minutes, not hours. The cost of power is determined through measurements made by the SCADA systems.

There were no networks at the time SCADA was developed, and the systems were designed with the expectation that they would work independently. SCADA systems send messages in the clear, without encryption and without requiring authentication.[79] Yet where once SCADA systems used proprietary protocols to communicate and were designed with the expectation that they would be operating in an isolated network, now these are IP-based systems connecting to networks outside the plant. Matters were not helped by the fact that vulnerabilities in critical infrastructure became known as a result of efforts to handle the Y2K problem in the late 1990s.[80] While much information was removed from public view in the wake of September 11, knowledge of the vulnerabilities is not so easy to take away from potential attackers.

One might think that security could simply be added ex post facto to SCADA systems, but security is never easy to add on. Because SCADA systems operate on millisecond accuracy, it is particularly difficult to build security into this environment. Security will slow processes down, resulting in performance degradation, something the plant operators find unacceptable. Despite the lack of security there are many reasons, from ease of use (control the systems remotely) to efficiency requirements, why control systems end up connected to outside networks. Connections happen in myriad ways: through direct and indirect connections to the Internet, through communicating via other channels, such as radio signals, through mobile devices, like an infected USB stick.[81]

Energy, information and communications technology (ICT), government services, and financial systems are the four enabling critical infrastructures whose disruption would cause an immediate crisis.[82] My concern is how IT-related critical infrastructures of telecommunications, the Internet, and embedded control systems may imperil the critical infrastructures of power grid, water, telecommunication, and the financial sector. Vulnerabilities have already been exploited to do so.

In 2000 in Australia, for example, a disgruntled ex-employee of the company that had installed a sewage plant's control system remotely accessed the control system of the plant using radio transmissions and his computer. He caused a failure at the pumping station, resulting in the release of hundreds of thousands of gallons of sewage onto a tourist resort.[83] In 2003, a contractor at the Davis-Besse nuclear power plant bypassed the plant's firewall and connected to the network, accidentally unleashing the Slammer worm and infecting the plant, disabling a safety monitoring system. Fortunately the plant was shut down at the time and no harm was done.

As these things go, the attacks did not cause huge amounts of damage. This does not mean that such an attack could not do so. In 2007 researchers at the Department of Energy's Idaho National Laboratory demonstrated they could access a power plant's control system through the Internet. They ran the experiment on the lab's emulator, which is used by utilities to check out their new software. (The emulator is connected to the Internet, but not to the actual power grid.) Included in the test were twenty-two lines of code that power-cycled a 27-ton generator at quite short intervals. The generator began to rock, then to smoke, and finally it exploded.[84]

This potential for exposure to attack, code-named "Aurora," drew immediate concern. It demonstrated serious vulnerabilities in the control system for the power grid, a concern that had been raised multiple times by the computer security community, but that had been denied by executives of the electric companies, who claimed that the systems were secure.[85] An attack that requires insider access or the ability to skirt a corporate or government firewall is easier to defend against than one that can be mounted by anyone with Internet access. "Anyone" is a misnomer here; the Aurora attack was not easy to mount, and a script kiddie or simple hacker would not be able to do it. But the situation gives rise to the question that if critical U.S. infrastructure is at risk through connectivity to IT infrastructure, why hasn't the nation experienced devastating attacks against its critical infrastructure? The answer is that some players lack capability, while others lack incentive.

Some networks are highly protected. While banking and the financial infrastructure rely heavily on electronic communications, that the SWIFT network runs on a separate communications network makes an intrusion more difficult to achieve and would most likely need the help of insiders. This is not to say network-based attacks on financial institutions have not occurred; there were two, for example, in 2008, with large financial repercussions.

A group of criminals from St. Petersburg, Russia, and Estonia broke into a server at the Atlanta-based RBS WorldPay card-processing company. They took information on customer accounts: card numbers and encrypted PINs. They were then able to decrypt the PINs, and they crafted counterfeit debit cards for accounts on which they had raised the withdrawal limits. "Cashiers" working for the group lifted $9 million from 21,000 ATMs in 49 cities from around the globe in a matter of hours.[86] Another attack occurred against Heartland Payment Services, a major processer of credit-card and debit-card transactions. Heartland's internal systems were penetrated and a packet sniffer placed to read records traveling between the merchant point-of-sale devices and Heartland systems authorizing the sale. At the time—Heartland has since changed its systems—these records were unencrypted while in transit. Over 130 million account numbers were compromised.[87] The data was sent to servers in California, Illinois, Latvia, the Netherlands, and the Ukraine and used to create cloned cards.[88]

The theft of $9 million and the theft of records from 130 million credit and debit cards is no small potatoes. There have surely been many more such attacks that have not been publicly reported, some of which may have had higher losses. Financial institutions are particularly loath to be public about such intrusions. Citibank's 1995 example shows why. It was the victim of such a theft, with numbers that seem small today: all but $400,000 of the $10 million taken was recovered.[89] But when news of the theft became public, Citibank's competitors tried to win the bank's largest accounts, claiming they would provide better security.

Despite the seriousness of such financial crimes, the effects have been limited in scope. The attacks have been against single systems, not against the financial network. The latter would have had devastating consequences, the former, much less so.

Because of its vulnerability to cascading failures, the power grid faces greater risk than the financial system. Cascading failures have nothing to do with network communication and are simply a way to protect electrical equipment. When loads suddenly surge around the power grid, generators and transmission equipment drop off to prevent overloading. Thus it can happen that a small overload in one part of the network can lead to a cascading series of failures. This is what occurred during the 2003 blackout in parts of the Northeast and upper Midwest in the United States and in almost all of Ontario, Canada.

The problem started with a generator shutdown at First Energy in central Ohio, followed by the failure of an alarm and logging system in the First Energy control room. As transmission lines heated up during the day and came in contact with overgrown trees, they shut down; at this point, First Energy could have averted a blackout by dropping service around Cleveland and Akron. It did not do so and so more transmission lines failed, causing a major transmission line to fail. It was a hot summer day with high power demands, and the sudden failure of the main transmission lines led to "unsustainable burdens" on nearby lines. The failure followed.[90] At least some of the cause was due to a failure of monitoring systems.[91]

A set of simultaneous attacks against multiple sites could lead to a very serious situation. Currently the capability for mounting such an attack is probably only within nation-states and not with nonstate actors. There is evidence that other nations are, at a minimum, exploring the possibilities. According to a 2009 *Wall Street Journal* article, the control systems of the U.S. power grid have already been penetrated by cyberspies. These attackers are believed to have left behind software that could presumably be activated at a later date.[92] The lack of an attack is thus due, not to lack of capability, but to lack of incentive. Any attack of this sort on the United States would be counterproductive to the nation-state that mounted it.

Therein lies the key to understanding the threats to critical U.S. infrastructure that arise from the vulnerabilities in communications networks. Attackers fall into four types: hackers; nonstate actors, including terrorists and criminals; insiders; and nation-states. Hackers and terrorists are capable of mounting disruptive DDoS attacks.[93] There has certainly been interest since at least 2001 by members of Al-Qaeda in using the Internet to attack the dams and water supply in the United States,[94] but neither the hackers nor the terrorists currently have the skill to use the IT network to mount a sustained attack against critical infrastructure. The CIA believes that in the short term, terrorists will focus on traditional methods of creating havoc, though the agency anticipates growing cyberthreats in the future.[95] Both insiders and nation-states, however, have the capability to inflict major damage to critical infrastructure through exploiting the vulnerabilities in communications networks. It is to these two groups that I now turn.

7.4   Insider Attacks

In the late 1980s, Soviet intelligence officers who were secretly supplying the CIA with information began disappearing. The first hint of a problem occurred in May 1985, when a CIA source was abruptly recalled to Moscow; then in June 1985, a meeting between a source and a CIA officer was thwarted by the KGB, the Soviet secret police.[96] The CIA began investigating and thought the source of information might be CIA agent Edward Lee Howard, who had indeed been supplying the USSR with information since early 1985. When KGB colonel Vitaly Yurchenko defected to the United States, Howard was in danger of being exposed, and he fled[97] the United States. But U.S. "assets" continued to vanish.

One Moscow source was arrested for espionage.[98] Another, based in London, was called to Moscow and arrested. A third, arrested in Budapest, was forcibly taken to the KGB's Moscow headquarters.[99] Two more were recalled from Washington and were arrested, tried, and executed. Agent after agent disappeared. Over twenty operations were compromised,[100] but only some of these could be laid to Howard.[101] It took the CIA and the FBI, which was brought into the case much later, six years before they began seriously looking at Aldrich Ames, a CIA counterintelligence officer. Ames, with access to information identifying essentially every U.S.-controlled double-agent operation,[102] was the consummate insider. He was in a position to completely compromise the CIA's Soviet efforts, which is exactly what he did.

Insiders are trusted individuals with access to sensitive information within an organization. Even outsiders who gain insider access do not have the same role as insiders, for they lack the trust relationship with the organization that genuine insiders have. That gives insiders the ability to seriously disrupt an organization:

• The master insider spy was Kim Philby, who rose to a high position within British intelligence while actually being a Soviet agent. He was part of a group called the "Cambridge Five"[103] who were recruited while students at Cambridge University in the 1930s. A few years later Philby claimed to have changed his allegiance and said he was no longer a member of the Communist Party; he was hired as a British intelligence officer in 1940. In 1944 Philby was made responsible for combating Soviet subversion in Western Europe. In that capacity he knew the identities of British intelligence agents and had access to hundreds of classified documents. In his role as double agent, Philby betrayed many Western agents to the Soviets. He was later appointed British intelligence liaison officer to the CIA and FBI, a highly sensitive post giving him access to vast amounts of information about U.S. intelligence. It was through this that he was able to warn his fellow Soviet spies, Guy Burgess and Donald Maclean, of official suspicions about them. Both men fled the United Kingdom in 1951 and defected to the USSR. Philby followed a little over a decade later when his activities were finally uncovered.

• Beginning in 1979, FBI agent Robert Hanssen spied for the Soviets for twenty-two years. Like Ames, he exposed U.S. moles to the Soviets. He revealed the existence of a rather expensive NSA/FBI tunnel built underneath the Soviet embassy in Washington for surveillance purposes, which became worthless after Hanssen's revelation. Hanssen gave the Soviets information on U.S. plans for continuity of operations after a nuclear attack as well as extensive information on U.S. MASINT (Measurement and Signals Intelligence), specifying the technical means for determining source, emitter, and sender of signals. Because Hanssen served in the FBI's counterintelligence unit, he was able to check the FBI automated systems to make sure that he remained undetected.[104]

• Between 1977 and 1986, an unknown researcher at Fairchild Semiconductor supplied huge amounts of data covering corporate research and business plans—as much as 160,000 pages—to the Japanese consulate in San Francisco. Fairchild was badly weakened as a result, needing U.S. government help to fight a 1986 attempted takeover by Fujitsu.[105]

• Research chemist Gary Min began working at DuPont in 1995. In late 2005, he gave notice that he was leaving to work for a competitor. DuPont discovered that in the previous four months, Min had downloaded tens of thousands of abstracts and documents from the company database, fifteen times more than anyone else in the company. This covered DuPont's products as well as emerging research. Almost all of the downloaded material was unrelated to Min's research at DuPont. Much of it was found on computer disks, a laptop, and various papers at Min's home during a search by FBI and Department of Commerce agents. The Department of Justice estimated the fair market value of the work Min had taken at $400 million.[106]

As these cases begin to illustrate, insider attacks can be exceedingly difficult to counter. Insiders know your system: they know where the important data lies, what the auditing procedures are. As a National Research Council report observed, insider attacks are "particularly pernicious."[107]

Motivation for insider attack varies. Insiders may turn against their organization for ideological reasons. Ames's motivation was pure greed: he received much of a promised $2 million for his efforts before he was arrested. Personal grievance, revenge, and ego are among the main reasons that insiders in the financial sector have betrayed their organizations.[108] Finally, some insiders are just lured in. First they hand over relatively innocuous material. Then they go farther in order not to have the initial leak revealed.[109]

Arranging to get inside information out is much easier to arrange than it used to be. Once one had to plan ahead, sneaking documents out, surreptitiously photocopying papers at night and on weekends, bringing cameras to do the work. But the Internet allows one to accomplish virtually what had been difficult to do physically. Techniques for information transmittal encompass employee email (including the use of steganography to hide the data within other data, especially photographs); portable storage devices, especially USB sticks, but also disks and smart phones; and the use of personal webmail at work. Insider abuse appears to account for slightly under half of all types of security problems.[110]

The increased ability of insiders to accrete and surreptitiously release information has not escaped organized crime's notice.[111] For many years insider attacks on banks were one-off operations, and the insider operated on his own or with a few accomplices.[112] Now such robbery can be done from afar. An increasingly common tactic has been for the criminal group to use an insider to transfer sensitive data. Meanwhile the criminal group is itself in a location where prosecution is difficult. Financial institutions report that the temptation for employees to steal sensitive personal information has sharply increased.[113]

Insider attacks on IT infrastructure are particularly threatening to society. In a world in which electronic communications has replaced face-to-face meetings, to electronically eavesdrop is to know all that is occurring: every political intrigue, every love scandal, every newspaper scoop, every plan of every sports coach and business leader. It is unclear if the unauthorized 2004–2005 wiretapping of senior members of the Greek government involved insiders, but it appears insiders were involved in the wiretapping scandal at Telecom Italia, in which six thousand people were targeted over a period of ten years (1996–2006). Dossiers on the personal, financial, and business dealings of politicians, financiers, businesspeople, bankers, journalists, and even judges were amassed, in part through massive wiretapping at Telecom Italia.[114] Collection on such a vast scale is astounding; it means that at least one in a thousand Italians was wiretapped[115] and that no business arrangement or political deal was truly private. As of this writing, the case is still in trial. It seems that money, including the use of the information for blackmail, was at least part of the motivation here.

Protecting against insider attacks has become more difficult with the shifting boundaries of inside and outside. Outsourcing extends the traditional corporate boundaries, making company resources and information accessible to third-party processors, company partners, and vendors. This process lowers company loyalty, further increasing the risk of insider attack.[116]

One might expect a different situation when boundaries are strikingly clear, but the cases of Ames, Hanssen, and various others show that even U.S. law enforcement and national-security agencies are not immune to insider attack. A review ordered in the wake of Hanssen's espionage found "a pervasive inattention to security."[117] Five years later, another government review concluded that ongoing FBI information-security weaknesses still left the bureau "vulnerable to insider threats."[118] Protecting against insider threats is simply not easy to do.

Criminal groups are not the only type of large organizations that might exploit insiders for gain; terrorist groups and nation-states also have the resources and capabilities to do so. While there is no evidence that terrorist groups have successfully used insiders, we know that nation-states have employed insiders in their cyberexploits against the United States. They have used a host of other tools as well.

7.5   Attacks by Nation-States

In 1981 a senior KGB officer, Vladimir Vetrov, handed to French intelligence a veritable treasure trove of documents detailing Soviet strategy for acquiring Western scientific and technical information.[119] While much material the Soviets acquired came from publicly available documents, the most useful information was stolen. It was estimated the USSR was acquiring technical expertise at about 1 percent of the cost it took the West to develop the work.[120] The technology transfer in radar, computers, machine tools, and semiconductors was so complete, it was as if "the Pentagon had been in an arms race with itself."[121] Much of the spying was done by capitalizing on scientific exchanges between Soviet and Western scientists. There were hundreds of Soviet case officers and agents involved in this effort, which used joint Soviet-U.S. collaborative working groups in agriculture, civil aviation, nuclear energy, oceanography, computers, and the environment to aid the Soviet espionage.[122] Another major source for Western scientific and technical information was the Soviet Union's Eastern European allies.[123]

As the West learned about the Soviet espionage effort, the Soviet spies were removed, but not before the United States played a deeper game of sabotage. One example that has since become public involved a trans-Siberian gas pipeline being built by the Soviets, who sought Western computer systems to manage the complex control systems needed by the pipeline. While the Soviets were permitted to buy the hardware, they were not allowed to purchase the required software from the United States. Finding a Canadian company producing what they sought, Soviet spies lifted it. Unbeknownst to them, the software had been "improved."

For a time, the pipeline control system worked fine. However, after an appropriate interval, a Trojan horse that had been embedded in the stolen software began to reset pump speeds and valve settings. This created pressures that burst pipeline joints and welds, and the result was the "most monumental non-nuclear explosion . . . ever seen from space."[124] At that point, the Soviets realized they had been had. Their problem went very deep: they had no idea which systems they had stolen were compromised and which stolen systems they could trust.[125]

The pipeline burst in 1982, but Soviet economic espionage against the West did not end. The spying let up briefly when the Soviet Union broke up in 1991, but several years later the number of Russian intelligence agents targeting U.S. technology had increased again.[126] Meanwhile another nation-state appeared to be entering economic espionage in a big way. And this one's efforts began in earnest just at a time when the Internet became particularly useful as a way to conduct economic and military espionage.

In 1997 the number of Internet users in China was reported to be under a million.[127] The nation of over a billion people quickly came up to speed, at least in certain aspects of using the network. One night in October 2004, someone scanned various U.S. military computers to determine which ones were using particular unpatched software. On November 1, at 10:23 p.m. PST, these vulnerabilities were exploited. Outsiders entered. With great skill, they probed computer systems at the U.S. Army Information Systems Engineering Command at Fort Huachuca, Arizona. Less than three hours later, the attackers used the same unpatched software to enter the military's Defense Information Systems Agency in Arlington, Virginia; two hours after that, they attacked the Naval Ocean Systems Center, a Defense Department installation in San Diego, California. At 4:46 a.m. PST, they hit their last target: the United States Army Space and Strategic Defense installation in Huntsville, Alabama.[128] Large amounts of sensitive material, including army helicopter and flight-planning software used by the U.S. Army and Air Force, were downloaded.[129] The files were shipped first to Taiwan and Korea, and then to southern China (Guangdong province).

This series of digital surveillances and thefts were among hundreds of coordinated intrusions into government systems between 2003 and 2005[130] (the set of intrusions was dubbed "Titan Rain"). They raised many questions, first and foremost being who was responsible. Was it the People's Liberation Army (PLA)? From the tracks left in the network, it was not entirely clear. It is unlikely that a download of this size into China could not have been accomplished without government awareness of the incident. More instances of attempts at such espionage followed.

Members of the U.K. Parliament were targets of well-crafted attempts at email espionage. Personally tailored emails were sent to the MPs and their secretaries and staffs. If the email attachments were opened, it would download spying software that searched through the users' machines and sent files of interest to a server in the Chinese province of Guangdong; the theft was obstructed by the Parliament's computer security system.[131] Oak Ridge National Laboratory experienced a similar cyberespionage attempt in 2007, but in this case, the cyberspies were successful.[132] In 2007 and 2008 a number of governments reported cyberexploitation efforts, although the nations did not want to name China as the culprit.[133] This included New Zealand, Australia, India, Belgium, and Germany.

Another incident involved espionage against the Tibetan community. As with the attempts with the U.K. Parliament and Oak Ridge National Laboratory, Trojan horse programs were inserted into host machines after being downloaded from carefully socially engineered email that looked as if it came from legitimate sources. By enabling the operation of attached devices, including microphones and cameras, the Trojans allowed remote control of real-time surveillance. In addition, files were downloaded and communications were monitored. University of Toronto researchers[134] studying the network found that a total of 1,295 computers in 103 countries were infected,[135] including those in ministries of foreign affairs,[136] embassies,[137] the Asian Development Bank, and a computer handling unclassified material at NATO headquarters.[138] The servers controlling the network were located mostly in China (Hainan Island, Guangdong and Sichuan provinces, Jiangsu), though one was in the United States and one in Hong Kong.[139]

As with the other cases, it is unknown who was responsible for this particular espionage. The Toronto researchers noted that targets centered on foreign policy concerns especially vexing to the Chinese government—Tibet and Taiwan—and in at least two instances information available from the targeted machines was used by the Chinese government. In one case, an activist was arrested on her return to Tibet and "full transcripts of her

Internet chats" were shown to her.[140] In another, a foreign diplomat who had been invited via email to a meeting with the Dalai Lama was called by the Chinese government and warned not to participate.[141] But because the organization for which the activist worked used communications devices known to be insecure,[142] this is not definitive proof of Chinese government involvement in the "Ghostnet" surveillance. It is entirely possible that this effort was a do-it-yourself spyware system by a particularly fervent Chinese patriot.

The last decade of the twentieth century and the first of the twenty-first saw the extraordinary rise of China as an economic power. This development has been accompanied by an equally extraordinary modernization of China's military. Only a decade ago China was dependent on Western high technology, but that is rapidly changing. Struck by the U.S. use of information technology in the first Iraq War and realizing what a force multiplier such technology can be, the Chinese military has become increasingly networked. The nation is in the midst of a C4I (command, control, communications, computers, and intelligence) revolution,[143] a revolution enabled by the "digital triangle" of booming Chinese IT companies, Chinese government investment in research-and-development infrastructure, and major military innovation (the military is also funding research).[144] It is worth noting that the world's second largest maker of mobile telecommunications equipment is Huawei, a privately held Chinese company.[145]

One can trace Chinese military interest in electronic reconnaissance to at least 1999, when two Chinese experts on information warfare wrote, "We can use computer information networks set up in peacetime and enter networks as different users to do the surveillance in an area broader than the battlefield. We can borrow the power of computer experts, especially hackers, to finish computer surveillance tasks."[146] China's industrial espionage is part of its larger cyberwarfare efforts, which begin with probing the enemy to gain intelligence.[147] Since 1999 there has been increasing Chinese attention to electronic warfare. In 2000 Dai Qingmin, a general, wrote that an active offense was needed; by 2003 Dai had written *Deciphering Information Security*, a book with a description of an information-security university teaching such skills as hacker attacks and virus design.[148] That same year PLA announced that it would start high-tech units capable of conducting information warfare.[149] Since 2005 the intrusions have mounted and there is a great deal of circumstantial evidence that the PLA is behind these efforts.[150]

As China has become more of a world power, it has moved away from disruptive hacker attacks, which are now a serious, though not always prosecuted, crime in China. The nation has embarked on cyberexploitation of a more damaging nature.[151] China is interested in economic espionage and is quite willing to engage in long-term groundwork to get what it wants. Moles placed in useful situations may take years before they begin providing useful information. An example is Chi Mak, an engineer who immigrated to the United States from China in 1978 and began passing information to the Chinese government in 1983.[152] Mak's focus was military technologies, a frequent target.

NASA, the U.S. space agency, has had plans stolen for rocket-engine designs, for the design and testing of satellite command-and-control software, for the shuttle-engine design, and for rockets for intercontinental missiles. Some of the theft appears to have been by criminal groups operating in Moscow, but vast amounts of data appear to have been exfiltrated to Taiwan—and from there almost certainly to China. This has included operational information about the space shuttle, and information about *all* of NASA's research projects. Boeing and Lockheed Martin had been managing the networks from which the shuttle information was lifted. In total, at least 20 gigabytes of data were taken.[153] One U.S. government official characterized NASA as "completely open" to the Chinese.[154]

"China has downloaded 10 to 20 terabytes of data from the NIPRNet, DoD's non-classified IP Router Network," according to Major General William Lord, the air force's chief information officer.[155] A 2009 U.S. National Research Council report remarked that U.S. "DoD systems have been subjected to foreign cyberexploitation" for sensitive business and personal information,[156] but did not disclose the nation or nations involved. Lord's statement that the Chinese posed a nation-state threat regarding cyberexploitation was a rare public admission by a member of the U.S. government.

Another incident, covered in detail in a report prepared by Northrop Grumman, describes intrusion and data exfiltration through—or originating from—China. This set of intrusions, which targeted a number of large U.S. firms, were worked with the same precision and speed as the Titan Rain ones.

The intruders accessed the system through previously stolen usernames and passwords, and were sophisticated in their choice of user accounts. There are indications that reconnaissance done earlier allowed the intruders to develop a full understanding of the target's file structure and where data of interest was kept. Once the intruders were in the host machine, they immediately navigated to particular files, not stopping to look at other files along the way. Prior to downloading and removing the targeted files, the intruders checked that particular company internal servers were available as intermediate transfer points. Once the targeted files were moved to these intermediate servers, the files were renamed, making their movement outside the system less liable to arouse suspicion. The intruders tested the downloading capability of channels using a video file before they began moving the targeted files. This was a highly professional operation. The intruders were able to move significant amounts of data before the company's IT staff observed the problem and stopped the operation. It is unknown how much information the intruders intended to move.[157]

The initial cause of Titan Rain was unpatched software, but these other intrusions have not just been lucky hits. Given the tight timing of the exfiltrations, careful scouting work had clearly occurred earlier; the exploit was characteristic of a professional, well-trained organization. The incident described in the Northrop Grumman report shows high professionalism as well. The targeting done of the U.K. Parliament and Oak Ridge National Laboratory demonstrated further technical capabilities. The type of highly technical information being taken and the fact that it is unlikely that criminals could monetize these thefts give clues as to who the cyber-intruders might be; the general conclusion is that the thefts are state sponsored.[158]

The attacks on Google that were widely publicized in January 2010 also followed this pattern. Intruders gained access using a Trojan horse downloaded through an Internet Explorer browser that had an unpatched—and previously unknown[159]—vulnerability. The intruders were able to access certain Gmail accounts (they were interested in human rights activists), although they only found out account information[160] and engaged in the theft of intellectual property.[161] There appeared to have been reconnaissance of Google beginning the previous April; these intrusions fit earlier patterns seen by other American and European companies and government agencies.[162]

In 2007, the British counterintelligence and security agency MI5 took the unprecedented step of writing 300 business leaders, warning them of state-sponsored economic espionage efforts by China. The letter did not recommend stopping doing business with China but noted that the espionage was highly sophisticated and "designed to defeat best-practice IT security systems." The United Kingdom's critical infrastructure, including telecommunications companies, financial firms, and water and power companies, were all warned of the potential dangers.[163]

Other nations continue to spy on U.S. industry. Recent federal reports on foreign economic and industrial espionage show, for example, Iranian,

Iraqi, Russian, and Israeli activity, and so it might seem that China does not pose a more serious threat than other nations. One must keep in mind that China's approach to industrial espionage involves the collection of lots of pieces of information, "an inefficient, but not ineffective" system according to the U.S. government.[164] The Chinese system of enlisting civilians in industrial spying efforts[165] means that China's ability to perform economic espionage runs on a scale different from other nation-state players.

A decade ago cyberwar was a subject beloved by science fiction writers; it has now become an area of intense interest on the part of defense agencies around the world. The reason is asymmetric warfare. Not only is a computer with a network connection all that is needed to launch a cyberattack, but the U.S. heavy reliance on the network has made the nation particularly vulnerable to cyberattacks. In cyberwar the asymmetry tilts very much in favor of the attacker. This fact has escaped neither other powers nor terrorist groups.

Although many believe that the Russia government was behind the attacks on Estonia and Georgia, there is not only no "smoking gun" evidence;[166] since 1998 Russia has been warning that information warfare may be as destructive as nuclear weapons and appears to be seeking a prohibition on the development of cyberwarfare tools.[167] The Russians are nonetheless believed to be developing cyberattack capabilities.[168] China, on the other hand, sees a great advantage to using its citizenry in a cyberwar.[169] It is actively training members of the PLA, as well as private citizens, to engage in cyberwar activities.

The United States would appear to have much more to lose than win in an outright cyberwar (an undeclared action, such as occurred with the trans Siberian pipeline, could well be a different story). The nation is more heavily dependent on cybersystems to run critical infrastructure than its adversaries are, and there is evidence that the systems controlling the power grid have been penetrated by intruders who have left code in for future use.[170] It is impossible to know what DoD cyberattack capabilities are, and whether the United States could inflict more damage on its enemies than attackers could.

What is clear is that the United States is losing on the civilian side of the equation. With many poorly secured systems, highly professional attackers, and a legal system that makes economic espionage illegal—while its adversaries have very different laws—the United States is being weakened by the very information technologies that brought the nation such wealth in the last decades of the twentieth century.

7.6   Who's Winning?

The race between criminals and law enforcement has always been a game of leapfrog. The bad guys used telephones to conduct their activities, and the police learned to wiretap. The crooks thwarted that by using pay phones; in turn, law enforcement gained the use of *roving wiretaps*, in which they did not have to spell out ahead of time the phone number they would be tapping. Drug dealers moved to cell phones and pagers and the police learned to exploit calling patterns.

The FBI believes that it is making some progress on organized-crime efforts in cybercrime. The 2004 Council of Europe treaty, to which the United States is a signatory, addresses extradition for certain types of computer-related offenses and helps in this regard. But even more importantly, "Simply the negotiations on the treaty showed the need for international cooperation," explained Steve Chabinsky, deputy assistant director of the FBI. The bureau has been witnessing increasing global cooperation on cyber-crime. Fighting cybercrime, which means catching the bad guys even when they attack people outside your country, is being seen as both "defending [your] own interests and being a good global citizen." In recent years the FBI has seen cooperation not just from European nations ranging from the United Kingdom to the Ukraine, but from authorities in "Hong Kong, Egypt and Turkey, really from across the globe," Chabinsky said.[171] Where the FBI is less sanguine is about risks within the U.S. supply chain. Here the bureau has good reason to be concerned. Two examples show the range of problems.

Organized crime groups in Pakistan and China modified credit-card readers *while still in the factory*. The readers were used to authenticating chip-and-pin credit cards. In a chip-and-pin system, an embedded microchip is used instead of the magnetic strip on the back of the credit card; the card reader uses this to check that the card is genuine. Then the customer types in a four-digit PIN, which is checked against the PIN encoded on the card (the reader has decoded the PIN). If they match, the customer is legitimate.

The card readers had been modified at the factory so that, by first hopping via a wireless connection to a local network, they transmitted the secret details of the card to Pakistan.[172] These data were used to clone credit cards; the criminal gang then used the cards to siphon funds from cus-tomer accounts. The only visible difference between the corrupted readers and legitimate ones was a few ounces in weight[173] (this had MasterCard investigators traveling around Europe weighing card readers to find cor-rupted ones). The tampered smartcard readers had been exported to Britain, Ireland, the Netherlands, Denmark, and Belgium. It took investigators months to determine the cause of the problem. An extra chip had been installed behind the card reader's motherboard. Its function: to transmit customer card information to Lahore once the card data had been decrypted by the smartcard reader.

Supply chains can be corrupted in many ways. In 2008 the FBI uncovered a major flow of counterfeit Cisco equipment into the United States;[174] the fake material included routers, switches, and other networking equipment.[175] Counterfeit equipment had been sold to the U.S. Naval Academy, the U.S. Naval Warfare Center, the U.S. Undersea Warfare Center, a U.S. airbase in Spangdahlem, Germany, the General Services Administration, and Raytheon, a defense contractor, as well as various universities and financial firms, among other institutions. Depending on what they did or didn't do, the fakes could have wreaked serious havoc. All the problems in fact seemed relatively minor[176]—a user's network was shut off when using the equipment, a network upgrade failed, and there was a fire caused by a faulty power supply.[177] The situation could have been a great deal worse. Confidential communications could have been dropped or delayed, or copied and transmitted elsewhere.[178]

The Cisco incident raises a serious concern: Who is building U.S. information and communications technologies? Often it is not U.S. companies. In early 2010, for example, there were three contenders to sell AT&T equipment for radio access in fourth-generation mobile phone technologies:[179] the French supplier Alcatel-Lucent, the Swedish provider Ericsson, and the Chinese company Huawei. Even if there had been a U.S. provider of the technology, with globalized supply chains, having a U.S. manufacturer does not actually mean that the product is made in the United States. (Recall that the iPod, the product of a quintessential American company, has parts from China, Japan, Korea, the Philippines, and Taiwan.) If one is buying Huawei technology—or Alcatel-Lucent or Ericsson[180]—risk mitigation is required. You study the source code carefully. What is in there and why is it doing what it is doing? You study the updates. This is complicated, because updates can be frequent, especially at first. Where and when is data exfiltrated? Is the system calling home simply to report a malfunction? When it does so, exactly what data are being sent back? And you ask the experts. In deciding which radio access technology to purchase, AT&T had conversations with the NSA, which told the company "the kinds of things we should be looking for." This is due diligence, and it is necessary irrespective of whether the vendor is based in Shanghai or San Francisco. It points to the complexities of securing our electronic communications.

8 Security Risks Arising from Wiretapping Technology

From the 1940s to the 1970s the U.S. government received copies of most international telegrams sent from the United States.[1] In 1969 NSA began monitoring communications containing information "on U.S. organizations or individuals who were engaged in activities which may result in civil disturbances."[2] In a decade that saw hundreds of thousands of Americans marching to support civil rights and later to oppose U.S. involvement in the Vietnam War, such surveillance involved wiretapping thousands of U.S. citizens whose protests should have been legally protected under the First Amendment to the U.S. Constitution.[3]

Instead, "ordinary citizens involved in protests against their government" and organizations that were "nonviolent and peaceful in nature" were placed on NSA watchlists.[4] Their electronic communications were intercepted,[5] and the government kept files on their political activities. NSA was not the only U.S. intelligence agency surveilling the public. The FBI had been wiretapping since at least the 1930s. Because a Supreme Court decision had decreed there be no "interception and divulgence" of wired communications, FBI electronic eavesdropping was conducted in secret without warrants.

The hidden history of government communications interception of law-abiding citizens became public as a result of Watergate, the 1972 break-in at the Democratic Party headquarters at the Watergate complex and the investigations that ensued. These uncovered widespread intelligence-agency surveillance of political and private activities conducted under the guise of "national security." Recommendations proposed by the Church Committee, the Senate investigating committee studying these transgressions, were put into law in the Foreign Intelligence Surveillance Act, which made clear delineations between national-security investigations and law enforcement ones. It looked as if warrantless surveillance of domestic communications might be a thing of the past. That turned out not to be the case.

Indeed, despite strong opposition to intelligence-agency shadowing of citizens engaged in protected First Amendment activities, such surveillance continued. It continued in the investigations of a student group, the Committee in Solidarity with the People of El Salvador (CISPES), where the government developed files on 2,300 individuals and 1,300 groups, including Oxfam America, the ACLU, and Amnesty International.[6] It continued with a ten-year investigation of the General Union of Palestinian Students, a peaceful student group,[7] and a twenty-year investigation, prosecution, and ultimate dismissal[8] of a case against seven Palestinians and a Kenyan in Los Angeles who in 1986 organized a public fundraiser for a Palestinian organization.[9] There were multiple such cases, but though Call Detail Records were used in the CISPES investigations, it appears that warrantless electronic surveillance was no longer being used. Then in late 2005 and early 2006 the *New York Times* and *USA Today* revealed that the U.S. government was surreptitiously wiretapping Americans.

The papers released by Mark Klein, the technician who had worked in AT&T's San Francisco switching facility, gave strong hints on how the surveillance effort might be being carried out. According to the AT&T documents, the secure room contained Narus Semantic Traffic Analyzers and Logic Servers.[10] Such analyzers are capable of examining traffic content as well as headers. An experienced network designer, Scott Marcus, served as an expert witness in the *Hepting* case; he concluded the Narus machines were likely performing high-speed screening identifying potential data of interest.[11] Parameters were most likely determined by the NSA, with screening accomplished at carrier speeds of 10 gigabits/second. The selected communications were sent to a central monitoring facility, presumably an NSA site (this has never been acknowledged by the government). The level of surveillance in this and other facilities seemed well beyond the Bush administration's claims of limited surveillance in the NSA warrantless wiretapping program.

Although the secret room was supposed to be secret, there was no reasonable chance it could be. It is one thing to wiretap a single line or set of lines (investigating a conspiracy might lead to tapping multiple lines within a single frame), but inherent in the problem of eavesdropping on a wide swath of public communications is the wiretap architecture to enable such surveillance. Optical fiber carrying the inter-ISP traffic had to go through a splitter before part of it could end up in the secret room. There was no way to hide the existence of the splitter from AT&T technicians working the floor. In fact, the technicians had to install and service the splitting cabinet. That means that even though the documents about the cabinet were marked "AT&T proprietary," the fact that wiretapping was occurring on so public a scale could not be expected to stay secret. Klein reported that "it was known by the technicians [that the NSA was doing this] within a few weeks" of setting up the room."[12] That, in itself, was a significant security violation for the surveillance program.

Wiretaps are a risky business: they are an architected security breach[13] that can be subverted and put to nefarious use. No one knows this better than the Greek government, the subject of that ten months of wiretapping in 2004–2005.

The "Athens Affair" tapping occurred around the time of the 2004 Athens Olympics. Vodafone Greece had purchased telephone switches from Ericsson, and an Ericsson update of the switch had included CALEA-like wiretapping software. Because Vodafone had not paid for such surveillance capabilities, the wiretapping system was not enabled in the update. Neither was a system designed to audit the wiretapping. Someone—the parties remain unknown as of this writing—surreptitiously entered the cell phone network and turned on the wiretapping technology in four of the Vodafone switches. Every time a call was made to or from one of the targeted lines, the wiretapping technology simply sent a duplicate stream of digitized voice to a network of fourteen cell phones, prepaid and thus suitably anonymous. The harmful software hid the tapped numbers in memory that was isolated from the rest of the switch's software, and the intruders installed a rootkit that enabled them to return and update the surveillance software as needed. For ten months the system wiretapped communications from selected phones. The system was only uncovered when some SMS messages went awry. But the tappers got away.[14]

The ability to illegally wiretap the Greek government stemmed from vulnerabilities deliberately built into telephone switches. These were a direct effect of complying with CALEA-like requirements.

Wiretapping creates two types of risks: risks to communications security and threats to the society's social fabric. These can be described as technical risks and policy risks. In this chapter, I will examine the technical vulnerabilities that arise from building wiretapping into communications infrastructure; in the next, the policy risks.

8.1 The Insecurity of Communications

While wiretapping in the United States is illegal without a court order, it is often not hard to find ways to listen in or to discover revealing transactional information.[15] But that does not necessarily mean that it is easy to track all communications by a particular party. To law enforcement that distinction is important, but for someone whose communications or communications patterns are revealed, the distinction between *all* communications being tapped and *sometimes* being listened to may be academic.

If someone is talking over the PSTN from a fixed location, then, as has already been described in chapter 4, a wiretap can be placed anywhere from the phone itself to the switch at the central office, although the latter typically requires insider help if it is not to be discovered. The fact that the phone location is known makes surveillance simple. It is well within the capability of anyone with a bit of training.[16]

If someone is talking 1990s fashion over a cell phone, radio scanners in the area can easily pick up the conversation. Both the sale and use of such scanners are illegal in the United States, but there are numerous examples of scanners picking up such conversations. One well-known one was of Speaker of the House Newt Gingrich discussing how to spin the ethics charges against him, picked up by a Florida couple in 1996.[17] The example demonstrates why communications security matters. The couple was not targeting Gingrich, but simply scanning the airwaves and found an interesting conversation, which they recorded.

Three things improve the security of cell phones: that communications are digital rather than analog, that the scanner must be in the right cell to pick up the conversation, and that digital cellular systems are encrypted in the "air interface" between the handset and the cell tower. However, the first is minimal protection: equipment to decode the digital signal is not hard to find. The second provides somewhat more protection: it means that in order to obtain all your communications your adversary must be following you.

SMS messages are essentially broadcasts between the cell tower and a cell phone. As such they are easy to intercept. The messages are encrypted. However, the type of encryption, which varies with the type of network, is not considered very secure.[18]

Communications over the Internet are easier to intercept than communications over the PSTN or cellular networks. The underlying reason is that the packet-switched network allows many parameters to be set dynamically in response to demand. This flexibility gives attackers many potential openings.[19] Eavesdroppers can attach a packet sniffer or a mirroring technology that sends copies of Internet communications by exploiting such vulnerabilities as improperly secured communications switches (e.g., with easily guessed passwords or default logins), or improperly secured control interfaces for the switches, routers, and so on.[20] The fact that calls in the

PSTN or cellular networks rarely pass through more than two carriers, while communications in the Internet are likely to travel through a number of domains controlled by different network operators,[21] increases the opportunity for interception. This is compounded by the fact that packet-sniffing tools are more widely available than the equivalent interception equipment for telephone networks.[22]

If someone is using the Internet to communicate, their communications security is entirely dependent on the application's security. Unless email and IM are encrypted or secured through a VPN, these communications can be eavesdropped on. Confidentiality of VoIP depends entirely on the security of the particular VoIP protocol. Skype, for example, encrypts conversations end to end. A 2005 analysis of Skype conducted by cryptographer Tom Berson concluded that "the confidentiality of a Skype session is far greater than that offered by a wired or wireless telephone call or by email and email attachments."[23] The same level of communications security, however, was not present for Tom-Skype, Skype software for use in China. In 2008 a University of Toronto researcher discovered that Tom-Skype scanned text chat messages between Tom-Skype and Skype users for words deemed sensitive by the Chinese government and stored these, along with IP addresses, usernames, and time and date of messages from Tom-Skype calls made from cybercafés (transactional information was also collected from Skype users interacting with Tom-Skype users). This information was kept on "insecure, publicly-accessible web servers."[24]

The Tom-Skype vulnerabilities were two: an architecture designed to allow eavesdropping on Internet communications and poor securing of the collected communications. The former highlights the problems of VoIP security. As a National Institute of Standards and Technology report on securing VoIP concluded, "VoIP can be done securely, but the path is not smooth."[25]

Even encrypted communications can leak serious amounts of information. Work by Johns Hopkins researchers showed that through knowledge of phonemes within a language, it is not hard to determine particular words and phrases spoken over an encrypted VoIP channel.[26]

This ease of interception combined with the wealth of information traveling communication networks puts us at greater risk than when the Soviets cornered the U.S. wheat market in 1972. It is not just email that can be read, but VoIP conversations listened to, browsing sessions observed and so on.[27] What if a foreign power were eavesdropping on the network and was able to read queries posted to Google? What if the adversary aggregated the data and performed the same computations as Google Flu

Trends? Cornering the wheat market is one thing but cornering the market for a flu vaccine just as a pandemic were about to hit the United States would be quite another.

8.2 Network Convergence Creates Security Risks

When two disparate systems are combined, security problems may arise as a result of the two systems unwittingly violating each other's security expectations. Such is the case with network convergence, the interconnection between the PSTN, cellular networks, Internet, sensor and RFID networks, and control systems.

Recall that SMS messages use the SS7 signaling channel. Unlike voice communications, SMSs are *store and forward:* data are held in an intermediate machine until the next device in the network is available to receive it (this also differs from the Internet best-effort protocols). When phone circuits are busy, voice calls do not make it through, but SMS messages are queued until there is system availability. This allows SMSs to saturate the SS7 signaling channel and could permit a DoS attack on the PSTN. Such situations have already occurred accidentally. In 2002 SMS traffic sent in response to questions asked in the Indian version of "Who Wants to Be a Millionaire?" choked up *all* Indian GSM networks for an hour;[28] there have been multiple such incidents.[29]

Patrick Traynor, Patrick McDaniel, and Thomas La Porta have modeled the number of SMS messages needed to saturate cellular networks, and the number is surprisingly low.[30] (Note the use of the word *model*; it is illegal to actually test this.) No solution appears readily extant for the problem, but the federal Government Emergency Telecommunications Service (GETS) program enables emergency personnel to connect through cell phones and landlines even when these are congested.

Convergence breaks the security model of physical separation that the networks had used as one aspect of security. Previously each network used the form of authentication that provided appropriate security for the network. For the PSTN, that was the phone number (of course the authentication was only of a physical address, not of a person). For cellular networks, authentication was also found in the phone number, and here there was a higher chance than in the PSTN that the number designated a particular individual. For local area networks, including SCADA systems, authentication was provided by physical access. Commands could be entered only by a trusted employee in an access-restricted control room on-site. Once the networks were no longer "air-gapped" from one another, that aspect of security disappeared. Through VoIP the Internet links to the PSTN, while RFID and sensor nets as well as control system networks are directly connected to the Internet.

Sometimes linkages happen without full knowledge of those who run the system; often the connection is made without a sufficient replacement in hand for the old form of authentication. (Nowhere is that more clear than in the recent appearance of commercial mobile devices—BlackBerrys— marketed to remotely manage SCADA systems: "Whenever the Internet is available, so is your information."[31]) That creates serious and major vulnerabilities.

Other risks arise from network interconnection. In order for VoIP calls to connect to the PSTN, there has to be a software interface between the PSTN and the Internet. The PSTN was not designed with the idea that random software could access a switch. This gateway, if not properly configured, can provide a way for malware to enter the PSTN. Consider the 1990 AT&T outage resulting from a software update of its 4ESS switches. A single switch signaled its neighbors that it was out of commission. A few seconds later, the switch announced it was back in service. That update caused neighboring switches to fail, and they sent out their own signals to their neighbors that they were out of service; they followed this with an update that they were back. Unfortunately their neighboring switches had the same software. The cascading process shut down AT&T's long-distance service.[32]

AT&T was performing its own update; technicians were able to quickly pinpoint the source of the problem and halt the failure. What if someone nefarious had targeted the switches with flawed software? In order for such an attack to work, the attacker has to be able to access the switch, possible because the 1996 Telecommunications Act[33] requires that telephone companies permit connection to the SS7 infrastructure for a small fee,[34] which, in 2009, was under $2,000 a year for AT&T (the fee varies by phone company and location).[35] This is well within the budget of a terrorist or criminal organization. The attacker would have to be able to download software to the switch. The ability to do so depends on AT&T's authentication model. Finally, the software would have to include a cascading fault much like the one just described. We already have experience that such software is possible to design.

Denial of service due to lack of bandwidth is already a concern in cellular networks. In 2009, even as AT&T embarked on a high-profile campaign urging customers to talk and use the Internet at the same time,[36] the company was seeking to cut customer bandwidth use.[37] This is a harbinger of another vulnerability of network convergence: denial of service because of conflicting demand between voice, SMS, and data on cellular networks. All services want the bandwidth at once.

Cell phones are now both phones and computers. That means that the malware that plagues personal computers has a chance to spread to cellular networks. Currently few major attacks against cell phones exist. That is an artifact of the multiple operating systems powering the devices as well as a result of the fact that, in the United States and Europe, cell phones are rarely used for financial transactions. That situation is changing.[38] Once it does, attacks on cell phones will undoubtedly proliferate.

Mobility creates a set of new risks. Cell phones check in with their networks periodically. In GSM networks, for example, this is typically every thirty minutes, but it can be longer if the network is congested; BlackBerrys connect more frequently. Location information is given even when the phone is not being used to communicate. An eavesdropper could use this information. Recall ThorpeGlen, the British company that sells tools for commercial traffic analysis. There are other ways of tracking as well, including companies that sell services to track individuals.[39]

Cellular networks now create temporary identifiers for cell phone users; this effectively hides the user's identity to an idle scanner listening in on all transmissions. But a more sophisticated system with some knowledge of a user's traffic patterns—or the triangle of home, office, and a stop at the neighborhood bar after work—may be used to track the user despite the encryption. Malware installed on a user's cell phone may also leak location information. Finally, as long as the battery remains in the phone, in some circumstances it is possible to turn a cell phone on remotely, enabling the phone to act as a beacon without the user's knowledge. So while the cellular network itself now provides some location privacy for users, true location privacy is possible only if the cell phone being carried is without its battery and is simply a dead piece of metal or plastic.

8.3 Wiretapping Mobile Communications Creates Security Risks

Eavesdropping on conversations made over the PSTN includes placing a tap at the central office. Wiretapping cell phones is more complicated. If the cell phone is in use in a cell within its home system, the wiretapping process is essentially the same as for the PSTN: the tap is placed at the switch and is activated whenever the phone is in use. Complexity arises when the cell phone roams.

A roaming cell phone sends a signal to the HLR once it is turned on and periodically after that. Since calls to the phone naturally go through the Mobile Switching Center (MSC) while routed to the roaming phone's cell, the tap can be turned on at the MSC. Tapping outgoing calls is different. Once the roaming cell phone "registers" with the home switch, outgoing calls made from the phone do not consult the HLR, and thus do not necessarily activate the wiretap. There are ways to circumvent this problem (including routing the call to the target's home system and back again), but doing so may cause the cell phone to behave anomalously. This could alert a suspicious target. If that aspect of cell phones is a problem in investigations, society's ubiquitous use of mobile phones has given law enforcement more than it has taken away. Recall, for example, the criminal investigator who noted that phone records give the same information as thirty days of covering a suspect with a five-person surveillance team. The massive amount of transactional information available has greatly simplified law enforcement's work. Criminals now advertise both their whereabouts and their network of associates.

Voice over IP is a different matter for law enforcement wiretapping.[40] Some forms of VoIP present no particular challenge for legally authorized wiretaps. Intercepting a VoIP call made from a fixed location with a fixed Internet address that connects directly to a large ISP's switch[41] (e.g., a home computer with a direct network connection) is the equivalent of tapping a normal phone call, and presents no technical problems. The VoIP call connects to the PSTN at a predetermined gateway switch; the wiretap is placed at that switch. If the call is peer-to-peer VoIP, however, establishing the wiretap is significantly more complicated. To understand why, we need to consider how the VoIP connection is established.

Suppose VoIP subscriber Alice wants to make a VoIP call to Bob. As in figure 8.1, Alice is in an airport lounge and has Internet service through a local provider, FlyISP. Alice starts up a VoIP session and types in Bob's identifier, bob@packetalk.com. FlyISP connects to Alice's VoIP service provider, IPVoice, which starts a call setup process with Bob's VoIP service provider, PackeTalk. PackeTalk checks whether Bob is online. If so, PackeTalk passes on Bob's current IP address, obtained from his local ISP, SipsISP, to IPVoice, Alice's VoIP service provider. This is the VoIP call setup step, or *rendezvous*. IPVoice passes Bob's current IP address to FlyISP, Alice's local ISP, and PackeTalk passes Alice's current IP address to SipsISP. Then the two VoIP service providers, PackeTalk and IPVoice, exit the picture.

The problem for law enforcement is the wiretap location; the VoIP communication, which is just a data connection, travels peer to peer through

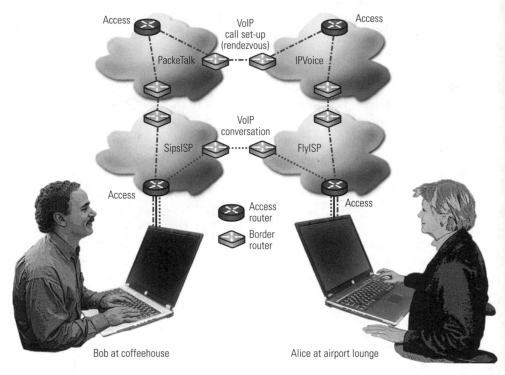

Figure 8.1
Telecommunication flows. Illustration by Nancy Snyder.

the Internet "cloud." One could have the VoIP provider guide the target to a rendezvous point controlled by law enforcement and a tap could be installed there. This solution, however, does not solve the problem of wiretapping highly mobile, widely traveling communicators, whether road warriors, drug dealers, terrorists, or spies engaged in their tradecraft.

Consider the scenario in which law enforcement has a court order to wiretap Alice's calls. A wiretap can readily be installed at Alice VoIP service provider. Alice's VoIP calls are unlikely to traverse this router. Instead the wiretap should be installed at FlyISP, the Internet analogy of the telephone central office. But how does law enforcement do this in real time to capture Alice's calls to Bob? Unless law enforcement shares the wiretap order with all possible Internet service providers—clearly not viable—the local ISP is unlikely to be aware of Alice's wiretap order in advance. In order for the tap to work, the local access routers need instructions from Alice's VoIP provider to wiretap her—and these instructions need to arrive and be implemented instantaneously.

The complexity of the situation is clear. Alice's VoIP service provider may be anywhere on the network. It may or may not have a relationship with the ISP that is providing Alice with local service. (If Alice's VoIP provider were owned by her ISP—or vice versa—the situation would be simpler, but there is no reason to expect this.) The order must be responded to without necessarily having sufficient time to determine its legitimacy. Much of the time when a wiretap order arrives at the central office, the paperwork arrives sometime after the law enforcement official has asked the phone company technicians to start the tap, an arrangement that works because law enforcement and the phone company technicians know each other (a variant on all wiretapping is local). For VoIP wiretapping to succeed, the wiretapping order will be at one location, but the actual wiretapping must be done somewhere else completely.

A further complicating factor is that like many Internet communications and unlike the PSTN, VoIP is identity agile, with users easily able to have multiple identities: Bob in Paris April09, Bob_in_Madrid_April09, Bob_in_Vancouver_May09. To track Bob, the first issue is to recognize that these multiple identities are a single user, and this is difficult unless one has access to content and not just call-identifying information.

The installation of a wiretap at Alice's current ISP raises issues of trust. How can Alice's local ISP know that the wiretap request is legitimate? The order will be authenticated, but that is not sufficient. Furthermore, how can law enforcement trust the local ISP to properly wiretap Alice (and not, for example, tip off Alice that her communications are being surveilled)? The request to wiretap can cross borders and this complicates matters even more. Alice and Bob might be in the United States but using a VoIP provider elsewhere. Or Alice might be anywhere in the world but using a U.S.-based VoIP provider.

For wiretapping to work in such a dynamic system, not only must wiretapping software be available at all ISPs, it must be real-time configurable. As the example from Vodafone Greece demonstrates, the ability to do so remotely and on the fly creates security risks.

Consider what needs to be done to secure the wiretapping facility. That involves securing the physical setup of the switching and routing equipment—and how plausible a scenario is this when the ISP is the local coffee shop or a free wireless network in a town or neighborhood?—and securing the logic of the switches and routers. As of late 2009, the United States had almost 1,500 domestic ISPs with fewer than 100 employees. These are highly unlikely to have the expertise to secure wiretapping configurations, or even adequate physical security to prevent tampering.

PSTN wiretapping is built on the model that the wiretap can be placed on the line to the user's house or at the telephone company central office to which the user connects. But Internet users have no such facility. Internet users move frequently. They have one IP address in the morning, another for lunch, a third in the afternoon at the coffeehouse, and a fourth once they return to their table after ordering another latte. This mobility complicates activating the wiretap at the local access provider.

It is worth noting that the worldwide GSM network, which despite its insecurities was relatively secure for its time, required twenty years of development. There were meetings with participants from all the European Postal, Telegraph and Telecommunications services—at that time, most European communications providers were state owned, not private—and it cost billions of dollars. The network continues to have trouble with CALEA-type interceptions. Wiretapping VoIP is much harder.

Requiring that collection be limited to the target of court orders and, within that framework, to communications pertaining to the court authorization, is an important aspect of the U.S. wiretapping approach. The mobility of VoIP communications makes isolating and tapping the proper VoIP communication exceedingly difficult. A court could approve acquisition of an entire packet stream with the target communications isolated afterward. There is precedent for this type of approach. For example, when a private-branch exchange (the private switching centers used by large institutions) is connected to the PSTN, the target's phone number is not visible. In this case, a trunk-side wiretap is permitted, with the appropriate call sifted out later.

This would not, however, solve the problem of securing the wiretapping technology, which must be available at each and every possible local access provider. This would mean securing the physical facilities of each of these ISP's routers and switches as well as the logic of those same switches and routers. Getting the security right is confoundingly hard. Many ISPs are small and lack the ability to do so. Not only are Internet communications insecure, attempting to architect them for real-time law enforcement wiretapping may make them even more so.

The underlying problem is that the PSTN-type model of wiretapping does not extend to the Internet. The PSTN is a large "bricks-and-mortar" business, requiring large investments in capital to build and run the wires, radio towers, and networks for signal transmission for modern telephony. The ISPs, by contrast, are built from commodity hardware, inexpensive to purchase and run. So while some ISPs have millions of customers, there are thousands of smaller firms servicing dozens of users. The archetype of wiretapping at a "Ma Bell" facility falls apart when the ISP is a VoIP provider with four employees.

The illegal wiretapping that occurred in Greece was very skillfully done, but not all wiretapping needs to be so skillful in order to be successful. The information that might be sought by a criminal or spy—specifications for a new computer chip, the draft of a judge's opinion, a company's bid for new sites for drilling for oil—might require wiretapping only for a brief period, instead of the months of eavesdropping that occurred in Greece. Thus tampering with the local ISP's wiretapping software to achieve illegal eavesdropping might not need the same level of expertise. Extending CALEA to VoIP may well result in decreasing the security of VoIP communications.

8.4 Remote Delivery Creates Security Risks

It has become the norm for modern communication systems to remotely deliver wiretap signals. CALEA expects it. It was done in the warrantless wiretapping at the AT&T switching office in San Francisco. Norm or not, such delivery creates risks.

A wiretap is a silent third party on a conference call, something that is easy to implement in digital telephone switches. In opening up communications to an unacknowledged third party, wiretapping is a security transgression. It increases the possibility that communications security can be violated with minimal risk of discovery.[42]

What is needed to prevent such unauthorized eavesdropping is unimpeachable auditing systems for the surveillance. While such systems may not prevent all cases of illegal wiretapping, their existence and ability to aid prosecution provides a deterrence effect. The lack of auditing capabilities is part of what went wrong in Athens. This makes the auditing problems in the FBI's DCS system all the more inexplicable.

DCS3000 (formerly Carnivore) was developed for remote delivery of wiretaps and pen registers at ISPs. This system is supposed to provide both investigative and prosecuting tools, which require that the chain of evidence be unimpeachable. But FBI documents showed that DCS3000 had numerous problems that could lead to major insecurities. The system used an auditing scheme with shared user logins, which could easily be spoofed. Auditing of who used the system depended on a manual log sheet.[43] The system was highly vulnerable to insider attacks. The same type of poor auditing schemes Robert Hanssen used to check FBI's systems to see if the bureau was onto him were still being put into FBI wiretapping systems being built in the mid-2000s.

Remote delivery means that not only can information be exfiltrated from an electronic surveillance; rogue software may be introduced. There is increased risk of introducing a vulnerability into the communications system. This could be the installation of a general wiretap capability or one targeting a specific person.[44]

8.5   New Wiretapping Requirement Creates Threats to Innovation

The Internet has flourished because of its design that minimizes the constraints a new application must satisfy; innovation is cheap and easy. Or it was until CALEA reared its head. One of the major advantages of VoIP is cost savings,[45] but CALEA compliance can be expensive.

In 2006 the DoJ Inspector General examined CALEA compliance and noted that "a VoIP provider contracted to pay approximately $100,000 to a trusted third party (TTP) to develop its CALEA solution. In addition, the TTP will charge a monthly fee of $14,000 to $15,000 and $2,000 for each intercept."[46] Such a price is not a serious problem for an established communications provider, but it is prohibitive for a start-up. It can prevent the development of new VoIP products. It can ensure that communications providers do not add new features; the DoJ Inspector General reported that "[telephone company] officials were concerned that the government would mandate that every new feature would have to be CALEA-compliant prior to being offered to the public."[47]

Nor are such threats the only problem. In 2006 the FBI prepared a bill for Congress that would have required CALEA compliance for every possible communications service and application: Instant Messaging, massively multiplayer online role-playing games (MMORPGs), any online application with real-time communication.[48] This was highly problematic. As Bellovin et al. note, "The Internet architecture is rich and flexible, and VoIP is not the only real-time communication in which Internet users indulge."[49]

Or consider Second Life, the virtual world launched in 2003. It was a beginning of online games that were immersive experiences rather than games with dragons to slay and pots of gold to find. In such worlds, participants create their own environments and build things (Second Life allows users to create objects using the game's software and sell them in the real world, and this has become a rather large business in itself). But another aspect of Second Life is as an outlet for conducting real-world efforts virtually. The site is used for news conferences, and many manufacturers have launched new products on Second Life, while politicians have held press conferences. Musicians release new music and universities use the platform for education, and so on. Because Second Life was built without any ability for privacy within the space, various companies, including Sun and IBM, have been developing "secure" virtual worlds for use by businesses, creating virtual worlds where employees can meet, collaborate, and chat over coffee.

Had CALEA compliance been required for Second Life, its development in the United States would have been greatly impeded. The slow speed of its standards development process[50] and the fact that other nations— specifically Japan and Korea, which have great interest and thriving industries in MMORPGs—lack CALEA-compliance requirements, might well have caused the application to be developed elsewhere.[51]

The low barriers to entry for Internet products mean that many of the network's most useful applications began experimentally, released to the public in a "beta" version without charge or guarantees.[52] The Internet's high bandwidth and ability to support smart endpoints allow a richness in applications, enabling diverse communication models within a single application (e.g., combined with whiteboards for sharing documents, voice, and the immersive environments of virtual worlds).[53] Applying CALEA-compliance requirements to any application with communications would have extremely negative impacts on innovation and the U.S. economy.

8.6 New Forms of Surveillance Create Risks of Excessive Collection

The Bill of Rights serves to protect the people from potential excesses of the government, and the Fourth Amendment is present to protect against potential excesses of the state's police power. That philosophy underlies the tight restrictions on state wiretapping in Title III and FISA. The state is very powerful; its right to enter people's homes and businesses would constitute trespass were it done by anyone else.

One does not need too many examples of corrupt or totalitarian states to understand the dangers of an unconstrained police force. Yale law professor Jed Rubenfeld has observed that the Fourth Amendment quite deliberately states that "the right of the people *to be secure* in their persons, houses, papers, and effects, against unreasonable searches and seizures, shall not be violated" (emphasis added).[54] Security is the point of the Fourth Amendment, security of the people against excessive searches by the state. In the decades before the American Revolution, the British used writs of assistance to conduct searches, general warrants that were nonspecific as to person, place, or item to be searched and that could be arbitrarily extended wherever and however the British officers—or their appointees—wanted them to be. Objections against excessive taxation fueled the American Revolution, but it was the "wanton exercise"[55] of the writs that raised the ire of the colonists.

Anger against the writs of assistance began to rise in 1761. James Otis Jr. was at the time advocate general of the Boston Vice-Admiralty Court, but he resigned his position when the British asked him to defend the writs. Instead he argued in Boston's Old State House, "A man's house is his castle; and whilst he is quiet, he is as well guarded as a prince in his castle. This writ, if it should be declared legal, would totally annihilate this privilege. Custom-house officers may enter our houses when they please; we are commanded to permit their entry. Their menial servants may enter, may break locks, bars, and everything in their way; and whether they break through malice or revenge, no man, no court can inquire."[56] Otis's speech reverberated over the next quarter century, greatly influencing the Fourth Amendment. As the ideas that became the Bill of Rights coalesced, the standard for search moved from a mere suspicion standard to the probable-cause one present in the Fourth Amendment. As Rubenfeld points out, that stipulation provides the security ensured by the amendment.[57]

Consider how the notion of security translates to the modern era. In a world where many of the most valuable pieces of property are bits, wiretapping is not simply a violation of privacy, it is a violation of security.[58] When collection is excessive, it creates a greater security violation.

One way excessive collection can occur is through a lack of clarity on what data are being requested. With all its drawbacks, one value of CALEA was that it required a standardized format for the output to law enforcement. This meant that the hard questions were answered in a—somewhat—public discussion. What data was law enforcement requiring and how should it be received? In contrast, the pen-register statute does not define or standardize what network information constitutes dialing, signaling, addressing, or routing information. The result, according to Al Gidari, "is like a fire hose for the application. Manufacturers and carriers decided what was included when CALEA was standardized—and the result was still a lack of clarity in the various implementations. One manufacturer's solution did not realize that the data channel used to deliver pen register data would also capture and deliver SMS messages, a clear error because such messages are content, not pen register data."[59]

Even when just pen-register information is supplied, there are risks. Transactional information is remarkably revelatory. It can be so at a personal level; one systems administrator, for example, read-protected his email logs because of a love triangle within his user community, which led one person to monitor the email traffic of the other two.[60] Transactional information can also reveal economic information. Anyone studying the communication patterns between the management of Sun Microsystems and Oracle during the week of April 13, 2009, could have easily discerned that an acquisition discussion was underway,[61] a discovery that would have been worth millions on the stock market—illegally obtained millions—had such a purchase been known in advance of the public announcement.

Since the September 11 attacks, the U.S. government has been highly enamored of the idea that the terrorists can be easily found by simply "connecting the dots" if sufficient data are collected and mined. It is unlikely that groups of terrorists can be determined solely on the basis of their communication patterns; such efforts are more likely to waste both time and investigative resources, as well as creating a source of risk. Recall that when Shishir Nagaraja examined seventeen hundred users[62] on an email network, he concluded: "Since close to 80% of the population must be monitored to detect all the communities, it means that in the short run, government surveillance budgets are more likely to cause harm to privacy than to uncover hardened terrorist cells."[63]

Anonymization, perturbing the data sufficiently to prevent identification of the parties involved yet leaving the property in question able to be determined,[64] has been proposed for protecting privacy in data-mining work. It turns out that the anonymization tools do not work as advertised. Arvind Narayanan and Vitaly Shmatikov have shown that if a small amount of "seed" data is known, reidentifying nodes on an anonymized network is not only possible, but relatively simply done.[65] Such seed information is, unfortunately, easily available. In recent years social networks, networks of users who frequently connect with one other and whose connections are made relatively public (e.g., if Alice is a Facebook friend of Bob's, then Alice knows who Bob's Facebook friends are[66]), have become increasingly popular. This can function as seed data. Narayanan and Shmatikov showed that it is possible to use seed data, even seed data with inaccuracies, and reidentify the anonymized network. The short message: in social networks, including calling networks, anonymization does not provide protection. Thus Nagaraja's conclusion regarding privacy is likely to be correct.

The combination of automating collection and removing the telephone companies from a direct role in the implementation of wiretaps—situations brought about through technology and law—creates risks of excessive collection. One of the values of the specificities required in wiretap warrants is that the act of preparing and executing Title III and FISA wiretaps brings several organizations into the loop: the law-enforcement or national-security investigator who prepares the warrant, the judge who approves it, and the carrier who actually implements eavesdropping. The NSA's warrant-less wiretapping, legalized under the FISA Amendments Act (FAA) and apparently realized in the architecture of various switching offices, removes the oversight provided by communications carriers.[67] Such safeguards provide more than legal window dressing. By furnishing a check on govern-ment investigators' work, oversight systems ensure the system works correctly.

Less than a year after the passage of the FAA, in a practice described by intelligence officials as "significant and systemic," NSA was overcollecting domestic communications of Americans;[68] these included personal emails of former President Bill Clinton.[69]

A similar overcollection problem occurred with phone records. In 2002 the FBI created a Communication Analysis Unit (CAU) in which telephone-company personnel worked in the FBI offices supplying telephone record information to bureau agents. The idea behind this was that collocation would provide timely dissemination of information found in the calling activity.[70] Of course, the records were to be provided only with proper legal authorization. Because a glimpse into a subscriber's history has the poten-tial to be remarkably invasive, the Electronic Communications Privacy Act (ECPA) requires that service providers keep subscriber records private unless the records are "relevant to an authorized investigation to protect against international terrorism or clandestine intelligence activities, provided that such an investigation of a United States person is not conducted solely upon the basis of activities protected by the first amendment to the Constitution of the United States."[71]

There are two tools that law enforcement can use to access the CDRs: grand jury subpoenas and NSLs. The latter can be used only for interna-tional terrorism and espionage investigation. Under FBI guidelines, NSLs are authorized "only upon the written request of an FBI Special Agent in Charge (SAC) or other specially delegated senior FBI official."[72] This process means that an agent cannot simply open such an investigation. Rather the agent has to show that the information sought by the NSL is relevant to *an already open investigation* against "international terrorism or clandestine intelligence activities."[73] In addition, there are four steps in the NSL approval process: the agent's supervisor, the chief division counsel, an assistant special agent in charge, and the special agent in charge.[74]

In the aftermath of September 11, the FBI signed contracts with three telephone companies, arranging that each would supply employees for the FBI's Communications Analysis Unit (CAU) (these employees were also on call outside business hours).[75] The point was to give bureau agents easy, real-time access to phone records during investigations. As one might expect, the tight integration between the phone companies and the bureau agents[76] brought down the barriers on this information sharing. This was to have serious consequences.

The FBI New York field office, involved in investigating the September 11 terrorism attacks, had begun using *exigent letters*, letters requesting immediate access to telephone records stating that appropriate subpoenas had already been submitted to the U.S. Attorney's Office.[77] The process was adopted by the CAU when one of the telephone-company employees working at the New York field office moved to the CAU.[78] But the situation in the CAU was different from the New York field office. The CAU was mostly working with NSLs, and nothing in ECPA permits exigent letters with "legal process to follow."[79] In fact, the situation in the CAU was much worse than that because often the legal process follow-on did not occur. There were many problems in the FBI access of CDRs:

• Many of the exigent letters never received required legal follow-up with an NSL. Such a process would not have been followed in any case, since ECPA does not provide for after-the-fact NSLs.[80] The process on preparing the exigent letters was so lax that the telephone-company employees often prepared the letters themselves.[81] FBI requesters frequently did not determine if there was an open NSL at the time the exigent letter was issued. As a result, "records for hundreds of telephone numbers" need to be purged since there was no legal basis for requesting the information.[82]
• In a number of cases, private subscriber data was supplied without a written request by FBI agents. Written requests followed weeks and months later. In some cases, written requests were never submitted.[83]
• Only 11 percent of the exigent letters were appropriately specific on what data was being requested. In particular, date ranges were often missing. The result was that often telephone-company personnel supplied far more data than the FBI was legally authorized to receive.[84]
• FBI agents frequently used one company's community-of-interest search tool without determining whether the additional information supplied by the tool was relevant to the investigation.[85] The automatic supply of additional information was done without the relevance determination required by ECPA[86] and thus this information was inappropriately collected.[87]

• Many of the exigent letters were not related to genuine emergencies. In one case, exigent letters were used to obtain records for "hundreds of telephone numbers associated with a dead terrorist" when there was no apparent emergency;[88] exigent letters were also used for investigating media leaks, fugitives, and other non-life-threatening cases.[89] Such searches severely impede reporters' ability to uncover issues, especially those concerning the government (this is discussed further in chapter 9).

• FBI agents routinely used "sneak peeks"—verbal, email, or telephone requests to see CDRs—to determine if there was data of interest. The agents would either describe what they were interested in or, in some cases, simply sit with the phone company analyst and view phone company records without any legal process in place first. If the agents found data of interest, then they would issue an exigent letter or start a legal process to officially obtain the data.[90] This aberration occurred quite often; one company reported that half of the FBI requests were for sneak peeks.[91] The data requested included "whether the telephone number belonged to a particular subscriber, the number of calls to and from the telephone number within certain date parameters, the area codes [redacted] called, and call duration."[92] According to DoJ's Office of Legal Counsel, this violated ECPA.[93]

• A similar situation arose with "hot numbers," numbers agents sought to investigate. Prior to starting any legal process, FBI agents would inform the telephone companies that a number was hot; if the number belonged to one of the company's subscribers, the company would respond to the FBI and inform the agent whether the number was active (e.g., there was calling activity).[94] Sometimes the companies would provide more information, including call origination and termination information.[95] In 2006, the National Security Law Branch deputy general counsel who reviewed the FBI contracts with the telephone companies concluded that a pen register was required for obtaining this type of information.[96]

• Finally, in multiple cases, information submitted as part of FISA Court applications was described as having been obtained through NSLs even though the NSLs were obtained weeks after the FBI had acquired the information—through the use of exigent letters.[97]

It seems that this activity occurred without the knowledge of the senior levels of FBI management, a serious procedural error.[98] After the 2007 Inspector General report detailing problems with FBI access of CDRs, employees of the three telephone companies moved from the FBI offices.[99] While the physical proximity was not illegal, breaking down the wall between law enforcement and telephone-company personnel let the phone employees lose sight of where their responsibilities lay. In addition, the

FBI purged records for 18 percent of the phone numbers on which records were collected through the exigent-letter system (739 telephone numbers out of 4,091).[100]

If wiretapping modern communication systems leads to large-scale tapping of nontargets, the legal basis for wiretapping is undermined. In addition, public support for wiretapping will fade.[101]

8.7   Never Underestimate Murphy's Law

Architects start with an image of a beautiful building and many designs look appealing on paper. Building codes, which affect the design, are there to ensure that the buildings withstand hurricanes, earthquakes, and other potentially structurally damaging threats.[102] Computer scientists design networks. Engineers build them. It is from experience in the nitty-gritty of the real world that Murphy's law—"Anything that can go wrong will go wrong"—comes. That knowledge should also inform the thinking about communications interception systems.

Sometimes it does. In 2000, the IETF's Network Working Group considered including wiretapping requirements as part of the design process for IETF standards. The IETF is an open, public standards-setting organization responsible for establishing the Internet's communication standards. These ensure that computers around the world can communicate over the network. IETF standards work because they are based on sound engineering practice (in engineering understatement, this is described as "technical competence").

The Network Working Group decided that wiretapping did not fit into the communication protocols that the IETF develops. One problem was scope: IETF is an international technical standards body, while wiretapping is a part of a legal process that varies from jurisdiction to jurisdiction. The main issue, however, was technical. Adding wiretapping requirements to a protocol increases complexity, creating a security risk (wiretapping is an intentional security breach). The Network Working Group said that Internet protocols should not include wiretapping capabilities.[103]

The group further observed that many network features "if deployed intelligently" already provided the ability to wiretap, the exception being when end-to-end encryption was in place.[104] As the events in Greece and Italy, and the overcollection in the United States, showed, experience bore the working group's conclusions out. So did other evidence.

In 1993 the U.S. government announced the Clipper chip, the federal encryption standard with 80-bit keys for protecting voice, fax, and computer information transmitted over a telephone system. The plan was a failure; there were strong public objections to the system, and very few Clipper phones were ever made or sold.[105] Clipper was a failure in another way as well. An AT&T researcher, Matt Blaze, discovered a way to spoof the system so that communications were encrypted without the government having access to the keys.[106]

A decade later a group of researchers, including Blaze, found flaws in wiretapping technologies that allowed the tapped party to manipulate the wiretapping, disabling pen registers and disrupting wiretaps. The techniques were similar in style to the 1960s blue-box attacks in which the hacker would spoof the phone system by sending a false signal of the correct frequency down the line. The flaws used the fact that analog decoders for dialed digit signals have different built-in tolerances for reading the dialed signal based on manufacturer. Law enforcement wiretap equipment was not sensitive to all the different tones, and the wiretapping equipment made mistakes when received signals were at the end of the tolerance limits. The researchers were able to deceive law enforcement pen registers into believing the number dialed was 215-898-5000 (Matt Blaze) rather than 987-654-3210 (Tony Soprano).[107] This means that criminals could manipulate pen-register information to finger innocent parties and/or clear themselves. In these systems, law enforcement equipment used a single in-band channel to carry signaling information rather than having separate call content and call data channels. Thus the wiretapping system could be fooled through a target's false use of a signal of the right frequency to signal the call was "idle."[108]

Nor was this the only problem in implementing CALEA. As has already been discussed earlier in this chapter, there are also problems in the auditing systems the FBI developed for remote delivery of wiretaps and pen registers in DCS3000, resulting in weak cryptographic systems for securing auditing data[109] permissions, auditing formats that could easily be spoofed, and so on.

In 2010 an IBM researcher, Tom Cross, described major security holes he had found in a Cisco wiretapping architecture for IP networks;[110] the architecture was designed based on standards published by the European Telecommunications Standards Institute (ETSI) for law enforcement telecommunications interception. Systems based on the Cisco architecture were already being used by service providers throughout the world.

Cross showed that it was easy to spoof the system to allow unauthorized parties to receive intercepted communications. With relatively little effort, a criminal could produce a request for interception that had a valid username and password, thus enabling him to get the fruits of a wiretap.[111] To make matters worse, audit mechanisms for detecting unauthorized use of the interception mechanism were inadequate and easily bypassed.[112] As the IETF Network Working Group had both predicted and feared, wiretapping systems create security risks.

Aside from two people walking into a field out of the range of potential eavesdroppers and parabolic microphones, there is no communications security. As the NSA once put it, "*No* deliberate transmission is free from the possibility of hostile interception," for if a communication were really uninterceptible, then "the *intended* recipient, your own distant receiver, could not pick it up."[113] Clearly interception of some transmissions is easier than others. Whether communications are targeted is a combination of the ease of targeting and the value of the information gained.

Just as every electronic communication runs the risk of being intercepted, so does every interception capability run the risk of being exploited. The lessons from the ways interception systems can be fooled should teach us about the risks of fielding them. A critical lesson to be learned is that the efficacy of interception systems must be weighed against the increased risk that one's own communications may be exploited.

The internationalization of the supply chain adds risks.[114] A problem that recently came to light concerned corrupted Seagate hard drives manufactured in China. They came equipped with a virus that searched for passwords to online games, sending them to a server in China.[115] What if these hard drives, rather than sending passwords for online games, had been sending bank or email account passwords instead? The quantity of data leaked was small, and unless it is looked specifically for, unlikely to be uncovered.

A generation ago the telephone company was AT&T, and interception was done by placing a "friendly" line between the telephone switch and the subscriber (recall that a friendly line is one used for monitoring; it feeds directly into a secure location). The risks from corrupted software and corrupted suppliers were essentially nonexistent. (This was not true outside the United States, however.) That is no longer true today. Foreign-manufactured switches are often less expensive than U.S.-manufactured ones. Federal purchasing rules require that government agencies buy from the lowest bidder, so intelligence agents take apart the systems to check for bugs before deploying them.[116] But do the small phone companies and ISPs do this? Large corporations have security offices that perform due diligence on the security of their communications infrastructure. Small companies do not have the resources and are not likely to check whether their communication providers, often low bidders, have secured their networks. That is simply not an issue that businesses are accustomed to raising.

Another risk comes from outsourcing interception. While the large carriers such as Verizon and AT&T can easily manage the law's surveillance requirements, there are 3,400 wireless carriers in the United States. Many of them are too small to develop a system for secure delivery of wiretapped signals to law enforcement, so they outsource. Largely they outsource to major suppliers such as Ericsson, but a security risk exists anytime a new party is introduced into the wiretapping equation. The bottom line is that the business of wiretapping has grown more complex. In so doing, it has introduced new potential for error.

8.8 Security Has to Be Built into the System

Nowhere is communications security more important than for the military during wartime. The surprise attack on Pearl Harbor succeeded because the Japanese strike force of aircraft carriers, destroyers, and battleships maintained radio silence during their thirteen-day trip across the Pacific.[117] Yet even the military has trouble in having troops follow through on communications security. An NSA history of military communications during the Vietnam War observed that "no matter how dramatic the evidence of threat, if we simply go out and say, 'Stop using your black telephone,' it's likely to be effective for two weeks."[118] Old habits reasserted themselves.

It was clear that the enemy could eavesdrop on tactical communications of U.S. soldiers in the field, but service members did not believe that the North Vietnamese Army or the Viet Cong would actually monitor these communications. When it was shown that the enemy was doing so, the U.S. soldiers argued that "[the enemy] couldn't understand us, especially given our arcane tactical communications jargon." Or that if the Vietnamese could comprehend the import of the eavesdrops, they were not in a position to exploit the information. Even when U.S. forces captured an entire Vietnamese unit devoted to communications interception, with radios, intercept operators, and linguists filled with "transcriptions of thousands of US tactical voice communications with evidence that their operators were able to break our troops' home-made point-origin, thrust line, and shackle codes *in real time*," the communications security situation of the U.S. forces did not improve. The American combatants simply did not like the NSA-supplied secure communications equipment but since they had to communicate, they did so—insecurely.[119]

It makes no difference if communications occur in wartime in the rice paddies of the Mekong Delta or during peacetime in the building canyons of Manhattan. It does not help to tell people to be secure. In order for their communications to be secure, security must be built into their communications systems. It must be ubiquitous, from the phone to the central office and from the transmission of a cell phone to its base station to the communications infrastructure itself.

If the integrity of the wire between a subscriber and the central office is violated, the communications of a single line is at risk. If messages between cell phones and base stations are not encrypted, the communications of every user within the area of that base station is at risk. If the integrity of a communication switch is violated, then every communication traveling through that switch is at risk.

Wiretapping on a massive scale creates its own set of risks. The surveillance at the AT&T San Francisco switching facility demonstrated the obvious: it is difficult to hide the existence of widespread wiretapping. Extensive and pervasive surveillance of customer communications changes worker attitudes toward customer privacy.

Telecommunications companies that adhere to customer privacy are unlikely to suffer problems such as Telecom Italia has. U.S. telephone companies highly respected customer privacy and telecommunications security and required their employees to do the same. Matt Blaze, who once worked for AT&T, recalled, "There was no faster way to be fired (or worse) than to snoop into call records or facilitate illegal wiretap."[120]

In a system that is itself architected insecurely—for example, with the potential for packet sniffers at routers throughout the infrastructure—two actions can substantially improve communications security. End-to-end encryption will ensure security of the message content.[121] As for security of transactional information, it is worth recalling NSA's thoughts on the matter: if the message were "really uninterceptible" then "the intended recipient, your own distant receiver, could not pick it up."[122] In order for the message to be delivered, transactional information must be easily and widely available along the nodes of its route. (Yes, as noted, Tor and other systems allow anonymized communication. These have high overhead and are not expected to be used by the vast majority of users.) But the most important way to secure transactional information is through company policies that follow practices such as the following: "Secrecy of communications is a basic requirement and important company policy. It includes divulging neither the conversation nor the fact that a call was made between two telephones."[123] Although secrecy of transactional information can never be fully guaranteed, it can be protected significantly better than it is at present.

8.9 Creating Long-Term Risk

Over the last decade, the combination of CALEA and CDR usage in the President's Surveillance Program has led to a situation in which both communications content and transactional information are more easily accessible than in times past. The CDR data, in particular, has moved from the telephone companies to the government. In Europe more records are kept long term, a result of recent data-retention laws. There has been some movement by the U.S. government to develop similar laws. There is "bugging everywhere," including cars that enable remote tapping without the placement of a bug and some new products such as VoIP that leave records of content (in contrast to voice calls, which were far more ephemeral). It is appropriate to step back and think about the responsibilities of the U.S. government to its people.

The foundation of U.S. law is the Constitution; the Preamble lays out what type of nation the United States is to be:

We the People of the United States, in Order to form a more perfect Union, establish Justice, insure domestic Tranquility, provide for the common defence [sic], promote the general Welfare, and secure the Blessings of Liberty to ourselves and our Posterity, do ordain and establish this Constitution for the United States of America.

Because the Preamble is not a source of authority for government nor a provider of specific powers, constitutional scholars have by and large ignored it.[124] The Preamble does, however, set a stage for the role of government. As a result, the Supreme Court has occasionally relied on it in decisions determining limits on the power of the government. In *Kansas v. Colorado*,[125] for example, the Supreme Court focused on the phrasing "We the people of the United States," pointing out that it was not the people of one state, but the people of *all* states[126] who framed the Constitution. The Court concluded that the Tenth Amendment did not give rights not reserved to the federal government to the states, but rather to the people. In *U.S. Term Limits, Inc. v. Thornton*,[127] the Court ruled that Arkansas could not put term limits on congressional service because allowing a state to do so would be a "fundamental change in the constitutional framework," enabling "individual States to craft their own qualifications for Congress . . . thus [eroding] the structure envisioned by the Framers, a structure that was designed, in the words of the Preamble to our Constitution, to form a "more perfect Union."[128] Again the Court turned to the Preamble in forming the basis for its opinion.

With these examples in mind, consider the values the Preamble deems important. The context for the Preamble and the U.S. Constitution is the failed Articles of Confederation, which too loosely bound the states to be effective. In its early years, the United States faced a certain amount of internal turmoil (e.g., Shay's Rebellion[129]) that threatened domestic tranquility. The U.S. Constitution, creating a stronger federal government, was the response.

In the Preamble to the Constitution, justice and tranquility precede defense, general welfare, and liberty. While this may seem odd—surely it is not the case that justice and domestic tranquility are more important than security[130]—it is understandable in the context of the internal problems that existed in the early years of the republic. This ordering indicates that external security without justice and domestic tranquility is of little value; justice and domestic tranquility are sufficiently important that security should not trump them.

Along with preserving justice and domestic tranquility is the government's responsibility for the preservation of liberty. Here the Preamble employs a very interesting construction: liberty should be protected not only for the present *but for our posterity*. This clearly states that the U.S. government has a paramount responsibility to preserve the liberty of its citizens. Richard Posner has argued strongly that civil liberty curtailments taken in times of crisis—the Civil War, World War II, and the Cold War[131] were "fully restored" once the crisis ended.[132] The crucial aspect of the issue is the length of the loss of civil liberties. As Supreme Court Justice Robert Jackson has observed,

No one will question that [the war] power is the most dangerous one to free government in the whole catalogue of powers. It usually is invoked in haste and excitement, when calm legislative consideration of constitutional limitation is difficult. It is executed in a time of patriotic fervor that makes moderation unpopular. And, worst of all, it is interpreted by judges under the influence of the same passions and pressures. Always, as in this case, the Government urges hasty decision to forestall some emergency or serve some purpose, and pleads that paralysis will result if its claims to power are denied or their confirmation delayed. Particularly when the war power is invoked to do things to the liberties of people, or to their property or economy that only indirectly affect conduct of the war, and do not relate to the management of the war itself, the constitutional basis should be scrutinized with care.[133]

That last point is critical: the constitutional basis should be scrutinized with care. The case in front of Justice Jackson concerned federal rent controls,

controls that were imposed after World War II because of a shortage of housing that resulted from the war. Jackson supported the controls, but wrote, "I cannot accept the argument that war powers last as long as the effects and consequences of war, for, if so, they are permanent—as permanent as the war debts."[134]

For a moment, suppose that we grant that under emergency circumstances, justice and domestic tranquility can take a second place to security. Under the U.S. constitutional system, such periods should be brief. The absence of liberties should be measured in days and weeks, not months and years. It should never be decades. That is where the problem of changing technological standards to accommodate wiretapping becomes very important. Even if we were to grant that liberty can briefly take a second place to security, changing technological standards to accommodate wiretapping fails the test, because it becomes a change of decades, a change that is far greater than is permissible under the Constitution.

When a law is rescinded, either legislatively or as a result of a court ruling, new instances operate under the previous law. But technological "law"[135] does not work this way. Technology cannot simply be rescinded. Indeed, because technology must often be "backward compatible"—that is, capable of interoperating with older devices—technological standards often endure long after new ones have replaced them. Thus, for example, Microsoft was forced to keep support of the old operating system DOS (Windows 3.1) in its Windows system for fifteen years.[136] Only with VISTA was Microsoft able to jettison the old system—and the security risks included in it.[137] Another example is QWERTY, the layout of letters on a keyboard,[138] which has lasted over a century.

In the case of large, complex infrastructure, standards last for decades (the PSTN must recognize the 1950s telephone that sits on my desk). We have seen many instances of security vulnerabilities in interception systems. The longevity of technology infrastructure increases the risk that the eavesdropping capabilities might be used against the United States, destroying those very "blessings of liberty for our posterity."

9 Policy Risks Arising from Wiretapping

The United States has led the world not only through technology and innovation, but also as a moral leader. For decades the Statue of Liberty has stood as a beacon of hope, offering economic and political freedoms. This freedom has played an important role in keeping the United States secure from homegrown terrorism, while European democracies have come under attack from their own citizenry. But the technological and policy changes enacted beginning in 1994 with the passage of the Communications Assistance for Law Enforcement Act, and continuing with the USA PATRIOT Act and the warrantless wiretapping of the Bush presidency, threaten those freedoms.

In chapter 5 I examined the effectiveness of electronic surveillance in the "war on terror." Here I look at the other side of the coin, examining the policy risks inherent in communications surveillance since the mid-1990s. The "security" protections that have arisen in the first decade of the twenty-first century have costs. As Georgetown law professor Laura Donohue has observed, "The damage caused to the United States and the United Kingdom by antiterror legislation is significantly greater than it appears."[1] Much of that occurs on the policy side of the equation.

What is the right approach in securing the nation's communications as we face the competing—and contradictory—demands of a mobile society, critical infrastructure that is increasingly reliant on an IP-based network, and a dangerous, nihilistic foe? How should we structure communications surveillance? Any resolution of these questions must adhere to the fundamental principles espoused in the U.S. Constitution, principles very similar to those espoused in the Universal Declaration of Human Rights and the European Convention on Human Rights.[2] These will be my compass as I examine the policy risks emanating from wiretapping.

9.1   Wiretapping the Press

A fundamental aspect of U.S. democracy is the First Amendment:

"Congress shall make no law respecting an establishment of religion, or prohibiting the free exercise thereof; or abridging the freedom of speech, or of the press; or the right of the people peaceably to assemble, and to petition the government for a redress of grievances."

The amendment occupies a hallowed position in U.S. law; its importance cannot be overemphasized. The freedom to publish cannot be restricted by the government. For the press to fully function, however, more is needed than the freedom to publish. The press must also be able to gather information.

Of course the government may restrict access to information, and the consequences of publishing restricted information remain a contested issue. Without the ability to do such investigative reporting, there would be no information on abuses by government—corruption in the New York City Police Department,[3] Watergate, Abu Ghraib, the warrantless wiretapping of the Bush administration, the torture memos—and no ability to right these wrongs. Yet the rights that investigative reporters have to protect their sources remains murky.

In the 1972 *Brazenburg v. Hayes* decision,[4] the Supreme Court found that First Amendment protections did not excuse a reporter from testifying before a state or federal grand jury. The court ruled that a reporter can be subpoenaed by grand juries for information about criminal activities: the identity of a source, notes from an interview, or other data that may be useful to law enforcement. Yet, the Court noted that "news gathering is not without its First Amendment protections."[5] Recognizing the lack of clarity in its response, it suggested that a situation in which the courts would be "embroiled in preliminary factual and legal determinations" as to whether a reporter should be subpoenaed would put the courts in the position of making law, which would be inappropriate.[6] The Court suggested that working within the confines of the First Amendment, state legislatures could craft laws regarding reporters' privilege; Congress could as well.[7] As of this writing, thirty-five states and the District of Columbia have done so; Congress has periodically discussed the issue but has not passed legislation.

Because of concerns that the prosecutorial power of the government not prevent a reporter from broadly covering controversial public issues, the Code of Federal Regulations restricts the government's ability to investigate journalists. In particular, before law enforcement attempts to acquire telephone toll records of any member of the media, all reasonable alternative investigative approaches must first be tried.[8] The chilling effect that government investigations might have on journalists' ability to gather information is viewed as sufficiently reprehensible that no one less than the attorney general can approve the issuing of a subpoena for telephone records.

This makes the actions of the FBI in obtaining phone records of *New York Times* and *Washington Post* reporters outside the rule of law inexplicable. According to the 2010 DoJ Inspector General report, an assistant U.S. attorney assigned to a leak investigation discussed the possibility of acquiring subpoenas for the reporters' phone records with the FBI agent assigned to the case. Although both DoJ employees knew that attorney general approval was required to obtain the records, they thought it was reasonable to find out if the information would be available from the communications service providers at the Communications Analysis Unit (CAU). An FBI special agent, who was a liaison to the CAU, was asked to inquire about this.

Shortly afterward, *without further prompting by the liaison agent*, the FBI agent in the CAU issued an exigent letter asking for records on nine telephone numbers, seven of which belonged to reporters at the *New York Times* and the *Washington Post* (the other two were described as belonging to the suspected leakers). Although the original request was for a seven-month period, the exigent letter to the telephone company had no such date limitations. The analyst duly searched and supplied records on twenty-two months worth of phone calls and returned transactional data on sixteen hundred phone calls. These were put into a database available for searching by authorized FBI personnel.[9] This was *not* the only incident in which the telephone-company employees in the CAU supplied information about reporters' calls absent a subpoena.[10]

Such actions have a chilling effect on the press by making it harder for reporters to ensure anonymity for their sources. As Jed Rubenfeld has observed,

The Fourth Amendment is not violated by searches and seizures that make criminals insecure. It is violated by searches and seizures that rob the law-abiding of their security. . . . The Fourth Amendment exists not to increase marginal criminality, but to give people the security they need to exercise the freedoms that the state's prohibitory laws leave open to them (including but not limited to their constitutional freedoms of speech, of religion, and so on).[11]

The reporters had not broken the law, but the FBI's actions intruded upon society's ability to have a free press. The FBI has a sworn responsibility to uphold the Constitution; in this case, it failed that responsibility. In so doing, it damaged the ability of reporters to do their job, the ability of the American public to have access to information, and the belief that the U.S. government obeys the rule of law.

9.2   The Value of the Rule of Law

Rule of law matters. Consider, as an example, Northern Ireland. Ireland was partitioned in 1920 over the objections of the Catholic minority in the north. The Catholics sought a single nation, while the Protestants—who were a majority in the north—preferred partition and rule under the British Crown.[12] In the late 1960s, thousands of British troops came to Northern Ireland in response to civil unrest. Originally they were welcomed by the beleaguered Catholic minority; the situation rapidly changed.

Beginning in the summer of 1971, British troops began to exercise the Special Powers Act, a 1922 law that allowed them to indefinitely intern anyone suspected of attempting to damage the public peace. This included the Irish Republican Army (IRA), which supported a single, all-Ireland, state and who had initiated much of the violence. Applying the Special Powers Act to suspected IRA members, the British interned almost three thousand people in two days alone.[13] This was a tremendous number in a nation of 1.5 million; if the same ratio had been applied in the United States after September 11, this would have meant arresting and indefinitely jailing over half a million people. As one might expect, this action turned public opinion against the British and in favor of the opposition.[14]

Bloody Sunday, a 1972 protest in which British troops fired on unarmed citizens at the end of a civil protest, killing thirteen and wounding fifteen, was a singular turning point for the Catholic population. Despite strong evidence to the contrary, the government inquiry that followed stated the troops had fired only when fired on and cleared the soldiers of blame. The government whitewash strongly contributed to a public sense of its illegitimacy in Northern Ireland.[15] The law had not protected the people on Bloody Sunday, and there was no legal redress afterward.

After a quarter century of violence, the political scene began to shift; in the 1990s peace agreements came into place. Significantly, in 1999, the British government opened a new inquiry into the events of Bloody Sunday; this took over a decade to complete and was made public in June 2010. The new report put clear blame on the British soldiers for what Prime Minister David Cameron called "unjustified and unjustifiable" shootings, a remarkably strong response from the British government. "What happened should never, ever have happened," the prime minister told the House of Commons.[16]

By 2007 the Republic of Ireland had removed unification from its constitution, and the IRA had decommissioned its military branch and rid itself of weapons. In a power-sharing arrangement between Protestants and Catholics, Northern Ireland became self-governing.

Rule of law buys trust. The new inquiry into the events of Bloody Sunday was an important factor in making the British government a credible partner in the peace process. The same need for rule of law has been evidenced in many nations at many times—for example, by the Truth and Reconciliation Commission in South Africa, which bore witness to crimes committed under apartheid, and by the Gacaca Courts in Rwanda, which did the same for the 1994 Rwandan genocide.

In Northern Ireland, British unwillingness to obey the rule of law in the early years of the "Troubles" enhanced the IRA's ability to recruit followers. Such coercive and counterterrorist behaviors by the government may alienate important ethnic and religious groups.[17] The suspension of the rule of law is often, in the long run, entirely counterproductive.

This may well be the case with the warrantless wiretapping promulgated under the Bush administration. This tapping, predicted to result in overcollection,[18] did so.[19] Expressing concern that the Protect America Act would cause collection of legitimate communications, Congressman Rush Holt observed that his Arab-American and Muslim constituents would think they were the law's targets.[20] What problems might ensue from such estrangement? People who are already somewhat disenfranchised can be pushed over the edge by activities that appear to violate their rights. This is an inherent danger of government's warrantless wiretapping.

The insidious leak of terrorist investigative techniques to ordinary criminal cases worsens this situation. Counterterrorism laws are typically passed during times of heightened tension, yet often their extraordinary powers are subsequently applied to run-of-the-mill cases.[21] For example, "sneak-and-peek" warrants, search warrants permitting a search to proceed without first notifying the owner or occupier of the premises, were authorized under the USA PATRIOT Act, but in 2008 were used 65 percent of the time in drug cases. Only 1 percent of the sneak-and-peek warrants were employed in terrorism cases.[22]

In multiple cases the FBI used exigent letter requests for CDRs without any justification. Some information obtained through these then made their way into FISA Court applications. The FBI deemed this "nonmaterial" from the point of view of the FISA Court's Rules of Procedure.[23] Such actions undermine the public's faith in the government. James Baker, the DoJ counsel for intelligence policy during the Bush administration, has asserted that "[FISA] worked in the 20th century; it works today."[24] The faith of Americans in their government underlies civil society, and the distrust created by going outside FISA creates risks. Undermining the trust with marginalized groups within society may well attenuate the very security surveillance seeks to protect.

This has certainly happened on the international side. Few have arguments against tapping to find terrorists, but tapping communications of the UN Secretary General in order to manage a Security Council vote in favor of an invasion of Iraq in 2003[25] is quite another story. By violating international norms and putting the United States in a poor light, the action is likely to have been counterproductive to long-term U.S. interests. As Harvard Kennedy School professor and journalist Samantha Power has observed, "meeting [unconventional] threats [such as Al-Qaeda] will sometimes entail using military force, but it will almost always require mustering global cooperation. . . . [There are] security consequences to the loss of respect for the United States around the world: the US requires the assistance of others to aid in combating terrorism, halting nuclear proliferation, and reversing global warming."[26]

Cybersecurity is one place where international cooperation is very important. A 2009 National Research Council report on cyberwar stated that "a predominantly military approach to national security is too narrow, and . . . the United States would be well served by a much broader strategy that puts hearts, minds, and ideas at its center."[27] Rule of law is as important internationally as it is domestically.

With those concerns in mind, I turn to domestic terrorism.

9.3 Who Are the Terrorists?

Domestic terrorism is not new to the United States. The country suffered racial terrorism under the Ku Klux Klan (founded in 1866); faced terrorism by German saboteurs, who were seeking to disable military production prior to the U.S. entry into World War I[28] and who caused far greater destruction than the actions of September 11; and underwent the violence of the urban riots in Los Angeles, Detroit, Newark, Washington, DC, and other cities in the 1960s. U.S. domestic terrorism has been spawned by multiple groups. Since the late 1970s, abortion clinics have been the site of arson, bombings, and other violent attacks. Violent right-wing antigovernment groups have been active since the early 1990s and helped fuel

Timothy McVeigh's bombing of the Murrah Building in Oklahoma City. Until the September 11 attacks, this was the most destructive terrorist act to occur in the United States. For present purposes, I will focus on violent Islamic fundamentalists.

For several years after September 11 it seemed as if the United States was immune to the homegrown terror besetting Europe. Yet while the U.S. experience of greater economic and social integration occurring for second- and third-generation immigrants contrasts with the European one, Muslims in the United States are still susceptible to the radical message of the jihadists. A New York City Police report analyzing the homegrown threat concluded that "Muslims in the U.S. are more resistant, but not immune to the radical message."[29]

New York City, the financial, cultural, and immigrant center of the United States, is often the target. As Mayor Michael Bloomberg put it, "When we catch somebody, a bad guy, around the world, they have a map of New York City in their pockets. They don't have a map of other places."[30] So shortly after September 11 the New York City Police Department (NYPD) hired an ex-CIA deputy director of operations to help broaden their work from fighting crime to protecting against terrorist activities.[31]

Studying both European- and U.S.-based terrorist groups, including those behind the March 2004 attacks on the Madrid train station and the July 2005 attacks on the London transit system, as well as those whose attacks were thwarted like groups in Amsterdam, Melbourne and Sydney, and Toronto, the NYPD saw the process of jihadist revolution[32] as a funnel,[33] with four clear stages on the way to radicalization:

Preradicalization The individual is relatively "ordinary"; nothing untoward has occurred. The individual may be living in an ethnically isolated community.

Self-identification The individual begins to explore the jihadist ideology. There may be a personal crisis, a death in the family, a job loss, that prompts this search for identity. He—and almost all members of violent Islamic fundamentalist groups are male—begins to associate with others with the same increasingly fervent interest.

Indoctrination The individual intensifies his beliefs. He fully adopts the jihadist philosophy and moves to a situation in which militant jihad is the only appropriate response. At this point, he removes himself from the mosque, which no longer offers what he needs.

Jihadization This is the stage of operational planning, and can be as brief as a matter of months—or even just weeks.[34]

According to this analysis, radicalization does not appear to stem from the expected triggers of "oppression, suffering, revenge, or desperation," but rather from an "individual looking for an identity and a cause."[35] Finding potential terrorists in the initial stages of this four-stage process is not easy. Preventing their activities requires discovering intent of serious criminal activity—doctored passports and lapsed visas do not count—where often the act of terrorism is the only criminal action.[36]

Disrupting a plot requires figuring out what is happening when the initial actions occur almost silently. The first step, often carried out through the Internet (but also through videotapes, books, and other sources), is likely to be invisible. The next step, which involves joining with other people of like nature, is a point where the trajectory may be stopped, but doing so requires knowing who might be at that point. Here is where connections to the community matter. Because the last stages of radical jihadization can occur quickly, it is important to catch plotters at the self-identification stage.

9.4   What Works in Terrorist Investigations?

David Cohen, who runs the New York Police Department's counterintelligence division, classified the world of attacks by violent Islamic fundamentalists into three sets: (1) "Al-Qaeda Central" attacks, such as those on September 11, where the plotters work or train with Al-Qaeda; (2) "franchise operations" allied but not operated by Al-Qaeda (in business parlance, one would say with a "dotted-line" connection to the terrorist group); and (3) those with no international linkage at all.[37] The third group is much more difficult to uncover than the other two. Because it is homegrown, the members hide in plain sight and do not show up on intelligence radar.

Yet such extremists are not invisible. We know now that the four bombers of the London transit system had spent months working with the peroxide blend that fueled their bombs. They used commercial-grade refrigerators to keep the explosive stable[38] and kept their apartment windows open but covered up; nearby plants wilted from the fumes.[39] In short, there were visible signs that their neighbors might have noticed and reported on. No one had done so.

Open communication with immigrant communities is key to successful prevention of homegrown terrorism. Being a city with a 40 percent foreign-born population, New York relies on its immigrants. They have proved to be core to the city's defense.[40] In Europe the police worry about the immigrant populations. "Do Moroccans from the third generation join the Dutch police? Or the Dutch military?", a deputy inspector of the NYPD counterterrorism unit asked rhetorically, and then answered the unasked question, "But in the States, they do join the police."[41]

Even those who do not join the police department can be beneficial to the city's security. Members of the community provide additional eyes and ears for law enforcement. That was how a serious attack planned for the New York City subway was averted in 1997. A newly arrived immigrant from Egypt, Abdel Rahman Mosabbah, happened upon his Palestinian roommates in the process of building explosive devices they intended to set off at a crowded Brooklyn subway stop. Mosabbah, who had been in the country two weeks and could barely speak English, found police, who raided the apartment and prevented the bombing.[42]

In both Europe and the United States, sleeper cells are a serious threat. We should recall the lessons that harsh investigative techniques in Northern Ireland—massive searches and surveillance, abuses of prisoners under detention, ill-treatment in jail—often backfired. We should remember that cooperation of people within the community is crucial to discovering those on the path to jihadization. We know that such warnings from members of the community have already helped prevent attacks.

In July 2005 several people in Walthamstow, a working-class neighborhood in London, tipped off police about a small group of angry young men. Surveillance began, and it was discovered that one of the men had paid $260,000 in cash for an apartment. Wiretapping and other surveillance revealed a plot to blow up transatlantic flights using HTMD, a highly volatile liquid explosive.[43] "The whole deal here is to engender the trust that one afternoon may allow one of those Islamic leaders to say to the sergeant, 'You know, I am worried about young so-and-so,'" explained Ian Blair, commissioner of the London Metropolitan Police.[44]

In 2009, Umar Farouk Abdulmutallab attempted to blow up a plane as it was landing in Detroit on Christmas Day. This attack could have been prevented, because Abdulmutallab's father had warned the U.S. Embassy in Nigeria about his son's apparent radicalization. And when five young men from Washington, D.C., suburbs disappeared from home, the Council of Islamic-American Relations put the families in contact with the FBI;[45] as of this writing, it appears that the men were seeking jihadist training in Pakistan. Warnings provided to the government by the families were—or should have been—invaluable.

Many Muslim immigrants to the United States come from repressive regimes, and they seek many types of freedom, including political as well as economic. Wiretapping may yield useful information in a terrorist investigation. Excessive wiretapping, especially if it appears to be targeted at Muslims, will not engender trust in communities whose very help may be crucial.[46] In discussing the case of Umar Farouk Abdulmutallab, who had tried to blow up a plane over Detroit, Attorney General Eric Holder asked, "Would that father have gone to American authorities if he knew his son might be whisked away to a black site [a secret prison set up in a foreign country] and subjected to enhanced interrogation techniques? You are much more likely to get people cooperating with us if their belief is that we are acting in a way that is consistent with American values."[47] But while warrantless wiretapping in immigrant communities and whisking someone away to a black site are very different actions, the issue of engendering the trust by the communities is not.

9.5   Value of Network to Economic Growth

Excessive surveillance has other impacts as well. One of the strengths of the U.S. economy has been its communications networks. From the beginning, the United States saw good communications as essential to supporting not only the new country but democracy. By extending postal service to rural areas, having cheap rates for newspaper delivery, and incorporating privacy protection in the postal service, the postal system fostered political discussion, strengthening the fledgling democracy. Indeed, in a nation that eschewed a strong central government, the U.S. Postal Service was one of the few strong federal institutions in the early days of the republic.[48]

In contrast, European postal systems functioned as a form of state control and surveillance. As new types of communication systems emerged over the next century, these national distinctions remained and were, in some ways, magnified. The United States took the private route in developing the telegraph, and multiple competing systems emerged. In Europe the telegraph was state owned and afforded a form of government surveillance and control. For a time the use of ciphers was even banned.[49]

Adoption of the telegraph was faster in the United States, where, instead of many different governments, different languages, and competing regulatory systems, there was a single nation spanning the continent. The deep-seated belief that the spread of knowledge would aid the nation's democratic values helped the telegraph's expansion in the United States.[50] But a bedrock reason for the growth of telecommunications in the United States was privacy. The privacy afforded to communications spawned trust in using the systems. With that use came a growing dependence on them.[51]

In considering the role of communications networks in economic growth, I look briefly at Russia, China, and India. In 2009 the three nations had, respectively, populations of 140 million, 1.33 billion, and 1.17 billion people, and per capita incomes of $15,630, $6,020, and $2,940 (these incomes are viewed in terms of purchasing power). Of these, only one nation has a vibrant high-technology sector—India. Consider the factors that enabled this to happen.

At the beginning of the twentieth century none of the three were industrialized. Indeed the lack of industrialization and the things that come with it—roads, telegraphs and telephones, trains—contributed to the shock World War I created in Russia. Historian David Fromkin has written:

Of all the principal belligerents in the First World War, Czarist Russia proved the least able to cope with these challenges [violent and rapid social change, displacements in morals, politics, employment patterns, investment patterns, family structure, personal habits] for it was weak in the elements of infrastructure—transportation systems, communication systems, engineering industries, and capital markets—that make a modern economy resilient and adaptable.[52]

The Soviet Union industrialized after World War I. Although it developed a large cadre of extremely well trained scientists and engineers during the Cold War, this expertise did not help the country match the explosion of software that accompanied the development of the personal computer. In the 1960s and 1970s the Soviet software industry was not unlike that of the United States, focusing on business and government projects. The introduction of the PC in the United States in the 1980s changed the U.S. software industry but had essentially no effect on the Soviet Union. After the country's collapse, concerns about the long-term viability of Russia's institutional reforms, which made outside investment quite problematic, and the lack of a developed venture capital industry in Russia have hampered the development of a Russian software industry.[53]

China industrialized more recently. Yet despite the fact that over the last two decades China has become the world's manufacturing hub, the country has not become a leading manufacturer of information technology. This is not for lack of education or technical skills. Columbia University economics professor Jagdish Bhagwati has written that "from 1981 to 1995 China had 537 scientists and engineers doing research and development per million people while India had only 151, and China had three times personal computers as India and a 4-to-1 lead in Internet usage."[54] Rather the problem stems from a political system that tightly controls information.

China's economic explosion and seeming embrace of capitalism might make it seem as if the Communist Party has greatly loosened control of the country's daily activities. This is not the case. President Hu Jintao has said that the party "takes a dominant role and coordinates all sectors."[55] The 2010 incident that resulted in Google deciding it would no longer censor its search queries in China—even if that meant the company could no longer operate there—reminded the world of China's control over information. The censorship is not just over activities of Falun Gung and Tibetan activists, but is also over tainted milk, corruption in the National People's Congress, and the collapse of school buildings during the May 2008 earthquake. Relentless, daily control of information is an inescapable aspect of life in modern China. It is censorship with many costs. While political and social freedom are the obvious ones, among the less obvious ones is economic innovation. Bhagwati explained that "because China has an authoritarian regime, it cannot fully profit from the information revolution, thus inhibiting the technology that is at the heart of growth today. The PC (personal computer) is incompatible with the C.P. (Communist Party)."[56]

The Internet model of bottom-up collaboration, available to anyone with a computer and an IP connection, allows people disconnected in time and space to build and create together. Such a model is anathema in China. At times, the government is willing to go to extreme measures to prevent communication. Imagine running a world-class business without an Internet connection. That is how Xinjiang province operated in 2009–2010. After uprisings in the province by Uighur nationalists, China shut down Internet communications there for ten months.[57] The network silence prevented activists from connecting; it also negatively affected scientific research, disrupting drug trials and scientific collaboration.[58]

Chinese engineers do not work on the innovative projects that their colleagues in the rest of the world attempt. Bhagwati has written, "So India, with its robust and chaotic democracy—what V.S. Naipaul has called a 'million mutinies'—has moved dramatically ahead of China in computer technology," and noted that by 2001, "India was producing one-fourth more software [than China], and exporting most of it."[59] The gap has only increased since then.

Open networks enabling private and secure communications benefit economic development. As Secretary of State Hillary Clinton said in a speech on Internet freedom in January 2010, "There is no distinction between censoring political speech and commercial speech. . . . Countries that restrict free access to information or violate the basic rights of Internet users risk walling themselves off from the progress of the next century." Crypto Wars aside, the United States has been a strong supporter of privacy and security of communications. And while its competitors pursued other paths, that support has enhanced U.S. economic competitiveness.

9.6   The Value of Communications Security to Civil Society

In chapter 7 I examined national-security risks to the economy if U.S. business communications were insecure, but communications security plays a far broader role for national security than simply protecting business communications. Somewhat paradoxically, the widespread availability of communication security is also important for U.S. national security. One reason is that the U.S. intelligence community now solves mysteries, unraveling "issues that cannot be discovered even in principle,"[60] rather than finding out secrets. This is a new role for the agencies.

Some examples explain the distinction. During the Cold War the United States faced an enemy with military capability roughly on par with its own. Though under Mutually Assured Destruction the situation was quite dangerous, the Cold War nonetheless provided a certain stability. It was clear who the enemy was, who its proxies were (though the 1956 Suez War put the United States in the odd position of siding with the Soviet Union over its natural allies, France and Britain), and what information the United States needed to know. Intelligence focused almost exclusively, and sometimes perhaps mistakenly, on finding out answers to concrete questions. How many SS-18 missiles did the Soviets have? What was the size of their nuclear warheads?[61]

The 1991 dissolution of the Soviet Union abruptly changed the situation. Instead of a well-known enemy with secrets, the United States now faced rogue states such as North Korea and Burma, nonstate actors with international intentions, and the fruits of a long-term transformation of nation-states to market states. National intelligence, which had had a primary focus on the Soviet Union and its proxies, went from being "predictable and incremental"[62] to handling diffuse and unclear foes in a rapidly changing world. The shift went from finding out secrets to solving mysteries.[63]

Iran is one example. In the late 1970s the country was a mystery to the United States, although the U.S. government did not realize this at the time. Because the United States had a strong ally in the shah of Iran, U.S. intelligence agencies paid little attention to Iran's internal politics, and the U.S. government was in the dark as to the real political situation in Iran. Indeed President Carter called Iran an "island of stability" just as the Islamic revolution began to take hold. After the shah fell, Iran, which had been a strong ally of the United States when the shah ruled, became unremittingly hostile. The misread of the Iranian political situation by U.S. intelligence was to have long-term repercussions.

Solving mysteries requires deep, often unconventional, thinking and a full picture of the world around the mystery. In late 1977, Iran was a society where public protest did not occur. The revolution came through activities in the mosques. There was little understanding in the United States of the role of religion in Iran. Iran appeared both modernized and secular, but no one asked what would happen if religion became the impetus for political activity in the country. If such a transformation were to occur, how might religious leaders communicate with the people? How would the people rebel against the government? What would be the organizing force? Knowing what to ask requires information. Often answering questions is simpler than framing them. The answers can be hiding in plain sight; it takes understanding the situation in order to be able to ask the right questions.

The tools to solve mysteries are different from the tools that uncover secrets. The United States can photograph an Indian nuclear testing site to determine whether there has been increased activity at the site, but it cannot discover the intent of the government that way. Determining the intentions of the Hindu nationalist government means solving a mystery (the government had campaigned on the issue of nuclear weapons, so its support of tests was not exactly a secret[64]). In mysteries often what is needed is tools on the ground, finding out what the people are thinking. In 1996 former NSA Director Bobby Inman explained,

I find . . . what you need are observers with language ability, with understanding of the religions, cultures of the countries where they're observing, where one does not need the cost of the processing tied to the denied collection.

The challenge in this new era, as it was in 1946, is how do you absorb, how do you collect that vast array of openly available information, . . .

We have to rethink how we go about assembling the vast array of information that is openly available to observers who have the competence to understand what they're doing.[65]

In the time since Inman's testimony, many of the world's trouble spots have become considerably less safe for U.S. government personnel. Embassies are tightly locked and guarded places, Foreign Service members, circumspect in their travels. Where the Foreign Service once worked, nongovernmental organizations (NGOs) and businesses have now become the people in place. RAND researcher Gregory Treverton has observed that in a "world that is not fully open everywhere but that is not very closed anywhere, humanitarian NGOs will know more about many African countries than does the CIA, and oil companies will be experts on Indonesia."[66]

The United States Pacific Command discovered that NGOs provide an excellent on-the-ground understanding of the local culture and politics, as well as an understanding of the local infrastructure.[67] Indeed, the National Intelligence Council has included briefings by such NGOs as CARE when determining strategy in humanitarian crises.[68] Had such briefings been part of the standard in 1993, the debacle in Mogadishu (in which U.S. Rangers sent to participate in a UN humanitarian mission to aid Somalia became embroiled in local infighting) might have been avoided.

The U.S. government needs to know what the people in the street are thinking, what the dissidents are saying. Here is where civilian communications security becomes so very important to U.S. national security. NGOs often operate in countries where freedom of communication is not a given. This is especially the case for human rights organizations, which often operate against the local government's wishes. Human rights groups have used encryption to protect their communications and anonymizing technologies to protect their identities.[69] In 1999, anonymizing services enabled ethnic Albanians to provide firsthand accounts of Serbian atrocities in Kosovo without fear of retribution.[70] Receiving this information during the time the atrocities were occurring, rather than months or years later, was important in enabling international response.

Empowering NGOs to communicate securely and privately is important to UN efforts; privacy-enhancing technologies such as Tor play crucial roles. Widely available, easily used, ubiquitous tools providing privacy and anonymity are critical for operating in dangerous places or in countries with repressive governments. Note that such security is needed not just by NGOs.

One such tool is Martus, secure, information management software that lets users create a searchable, encrypted database on their computer and then back these data up remotely to their choice of publicly available servers (Martus is the Greek word for "witness"). Martus is used by human rights organizations, journalists, government officials, and others who need to secure sensitive human rights information from eavesdropping, theft, or equipment failure. Designed for users in very insecure environments, Martus features a "panic button" that erases data from their computer (but not the remote server) in the event of a security emergency. Martus is an open-source application available in English, French, Spanish,

Russian, Arabic, Nepali, Farsi/Dari, Burmese, and Thai. It has been used in many countries around the world, including Colombia, Egypt, Guatemala, Hungary, India, Iraq, Kenya, Lebanon, Mexico, Nepal, Peru, the Philippines, Russia, Sierra Leone, Somalia, Sri Lanka, Thailand (both in-country and for Burma), the United States, and Zimbabwe.

New communications technologies have breached the walls of some repressive regimes. Shirin Ebadi, Iranian human rights lawyer and Nobel Peace Prize Laureate, observed, "The difference between today and the Iran of 1979 is that information technology and the Internet have made blackout censorship impossible."[71] And indeed, the video of a young woman dying, shot by a sniper as she exited a car near an antigovernment demonstration in Tehran, was a video that circled Iran and the world. As of 2010, 2.7 percent of Google's users are from Iran.[72] In Iran, the cost of hiding information from the people is untethering the nation from the world's communication infrastructure, impossible except for brief periods of time.

The U.S. Department of State strongly supports an uncensored Internet. In 2006 DoS established the Global Internet Freedom Task Force (GIFT) to monitor Internet freedom around the world, reporting on the free flow of information on the Internet, protesting abuses to freedom of expression, working to enable the international free flow of information, and empowering users.[73] In other words, the Internet should extend the First Amendment wherever it was technologically feasible. In 2010, Secretary of State Hillary Clinton reiterated that commitment: "We stand for a single internet where all of humanity has equal access to knowledge and ideas." Clinton said that Internet users should have five freedoms: freedom of expression, freedom of worship, freedom from want, freedom from fear, and freedom to connect.

In recognizing the contradictory aspects of secrecy afforded to Internet communications, Clinton said, "Those who use the internet to recruit terrorists or distribute stolen intellectual property cannot divorce their online actions from their real world identities. But these challenges must not become an excuse for governments to systematically violate the rights and privacy of those who use the internet for peaceful political purposes." Clinton committed the U.S. government to "the development of new tools that enable citizens to exercise their right of free expression by circumventing politically motivated censorship. . . . We are working globally to make sure that those tools get to the people who need them, in local languages, and with the training they need to access the internet safely."

The U.S. government may find privacy-enhancing communication tools problematic when doing law enforcement and national-security work, but

just as a 1996 National Research Council report on cryptography concluded that on balance the United States was better off with more
widespread use of cryptography,[74] I would argue that for the United States
the more widespread use of privacy-enhancing technologies outweighs the
disadvantages. The government agencies that have funded the development of Tor would appear to agree.

9.7   DPI: Creating a Security Threat

Recall deep packet inspection (DPI), in which intermediate nodes in the
network examine not just IP headers, but actual packet content. The rationale behind the DPI is that its use can improve service and protect endpoints. In recent years, ISPs have begun offering to do packet inspection
for larger customers. By checking packet content, an ISP can prevent
known malware from reaching the endpoint hosts and infecting them.

DPI underlies the Einstein 3 program, designed to protect the computer
systems of federal civilian agencies against attacks. Traffic bound for the
federal civilian agencies is to be pulled off and run through a DPI monitoring system, Tutelage. According to a *Washington Post* article, Tutelage will
either "block [attacks] or watch them closely to better assess the threat."
As of 2009, the system was being used for protecting military networks,[75]
but in 2010 news came of an effort to expand the program to certain
industries in the private sector, including critical infrastructure.[76] AT&T is
to be the first carrier to participate in a test of Einstein 3.

The impetus for ISPs to use DPI came from CALEA (there was also pressure from movie studios, which wanted the ISPs to prevent users from
sharing copyrighted materials illegally).[77] A 2006 FCC ruling extending
CALEA to certain cases of VoIP meant that when facilities-based broadband
access providers were served with a pen-register order, they were responsible for providing the FBI with the equivalent of post-cut-through dialed
digits, those numbers punched in after the initial call has been connected
by a carrier to a switch. In the IP-based world, in order for providers to
supply the equivalent of the post-cut-through dialed-digit information, the
access providers would need to inspect the packets. DPI was the solution.
The ISPs' next issue was to find a way to make money with the DPI equipment they had bought for implementing CALEA.

University of Colorado law professor Paul Ohm has written that ISPs
had a serious case of "Google envy." They sought to mimic the company's
success in monetizing the information it gains from a person's searches,
and DPI gives them a tool to do so.[78] In capitalizing on this tool to conduct

real-time surveillance of their subscribers, the ISPs would be in a position to offer a host of new services, from ads targeted to the user to more efficient versions of the services the user was seeking. The providers could do so based on what the subscriber was viewing *right then* as well as over the last day, last week, last month, last decade. For the service providers, who are under a great deal of financial pressure in a commoditized market, the use of DPI for their business purposes could provide a potential goldmine.

It might seem that network use of DPI would simply be an extension of the telephone companies' traditional use of the CDRs to guide the development of future business services, but this view would be incorrect. DPI has often been analogized as the mailman not only reading the address on the envelope before he delivers your mail, but also opening the envelope and reading the letter. That analogy rather misses the point. DPI is a letter carrier who reads all your mail, listens to all your calls, follows you as you browse downtown and in the mall, notes your purchases, listens in as you ask questions of the research librarian, and watches over your shoulder as you read the daily paper—and then correlates all that information in real time.

Such knowledge about your habits would be exceptionally useful to the ISPs. Currently when you use a search engine to look up "heartburn remedies" on Google, ads appear for medications, diets, and doctors. The ads are supplied by Google. But if your ISP were to search the packets as it transmits the content, there would be no need for the ads to all come from Google. The service provider could supply some of the ads itself. This scenario is not imaginary; in some cases, such hijacking has already occurred.[79]

The potential for abuse is enormous, and the risks to privacy cannot be overstated. As Ohm says, "The *New York Times* [may] track which articles we read on its site but has no way of knowing what we do when we visit the *Washington Post*."[80] Google may track your searches, your travel (Google Maps), and your appointments (Google Calendar), but the company's ability to do so is limited by the number of different Google services of which you avail yourself. If you object to Google's privacy policies, you can choose to use other services. By contrast, your ISP knows everything you do online. Because most people lack access to multiple ISPs,[81] the ability to hide your activities among different service providers is minimal. (And, of course, it may be that none of them offer privacy.) A single ISP will know what you are browsing, what your email says, VoIP, and so on. In a matter of days, possibly even hours, an ISP using DPI can develop a remarkably detailed dossier on a person. It has already been said about the ability to amass this amount of information that "the Stasi could only dream of such data."[82]

Currently wiretap law would appear to make such collection illegal. As Ohm has noted, there are sections of the law that permit carriers to examine communications content if that is being done to protect "the rights and property of the service."[83] That exception has so far been narrowly construed. However, the dynamics surrounding the protection of communications content have been changing. Service providers currently seek to provide the added service—and added charge—of protecting customers from malware; from there it is a small step to monitoring content in order to do so.

Despite the enormous risks posed by such activity, the FBI continues to press for such quotidian packet surveillance. In 2008, FBI Director Robert Mueller testified that

legislation has to be developed that balances, on the one hand, the privacy rights of the individuals who are receiving the information but, on the other hand, given the technology, the necessity of having some omnibus search capability utilizing filters that would identify the illegal activity as it comes through and give us the ability to preempt that illegal activity where it comes through a choke point, as opposed to the point where it is diffused on the Internet.[84]

That is, after all, what Einstein 3 does for communications destined for federal systems (including private communications sent to private email addresses if those communications are accessed via a federal system). Once the idea is accepted that communications carriers have the right to examine communications content for malware, it is not hard to imagine, as Ohm does, that the next step could be for "providers [to] argue that the service provided is 'ad-subsidized web surfing.'"[85]

The risks to privacy would be enormous. These are dwarfed by the risks to security. Were an ISP to collect this information it would zealously seek to protect it, for such data are an extremely valuable business asset. Consider the value of these data for the Washington metropolitan area, which includes thousands of employees of the CIA and FBI, not to mention members of Congress and their staff, Pentagon employees, and the military contractors surrounding the city. Or consider the value of such data for employees of the high-technology firms of Silicon Valley, or for members of the media. The incentive to misuse the information will be great, the ability to protect it, poor. How will ISPs guard against insider threats, or sophisticated attacks from the outside? Recall that 1,500 ISPs in the United States have fewer than one hundred employees. It is impossible to imagine that such data can be secured.

The only way for a user to avoid the risks from ubiquitous use of DPI by the carriers would be to encrypt *everything*: every web browsing session, every email communication, every touch to another endpoint. That is not done now, but it is not unreasonable to expect that email, VoIP, IM, and other forms of personal communication be routinely encrypted. Indeed, in the wake of the attacks that occurred in late 2009 and early 2010, Google started routinely encrypting all Gmail. Skype has always used end-to-end encryption for its VoIP service. Because the endpoints would have to encrypt and decrypt, transmission would be slower (more precisely, transmission time within the network would be unaffected but transmission time to the human user would be slower). A communications network in which all communications were encrypted would impede the work of law enforcement and intelligence agencies. Yet in the same way that one locks one's car and one's house, encryption would become a daily part of Internet communication.

The real issue about ubiquitous DPI would be a necessary reliance on anonymization tools such as Tor to hide transactional information. Anyone not using these privacy-preserving, security-protecting tools in the face of omnipresent DPI usage by communications providers would be endangering themselves, their companies, and anyone with whom they communicated. Looking purely from the vantage point of security, it is difficult to understand law enforcement's push for the ubiquitous use of DPI. This is a short-term solution to enable wiretapping with severe long-term negative consequences for communications security.

9.8   Putting Terrorism in Context

It is important to keep in mind that domestic terrorism is not a new phenomenon. In 1916 a munitions storage depot in New York Harbor was blown up by German saboteurs, destroying windows in nearby Jersey City, Manhattan, and Brooklyn. A total of over two million pounds of explosives were destroyed.[86] A half year later, a shell-assembling plant was completely destroyed through arson.[87] In 1995 explosives tore apart the Murrah building in Oklahoma City. The attacks on September 11 were physical attacks, but in some sense, their largest impact was on the American psyche (which was, of course, the intent). It was made clear that the oceans on either side of the United States no longer provided security.

With the anthrax attacks occurring on the heels of the attacks on the World Trade Center and on the Pentagon, it was easy to imagine the world had suddenly changed. In one sense, it had. The United States discovered it was facing terrorists who would exult in killing thousands, if not millions. In another sense, nothing changed. Tony Judt put the attacks in context:

Terrorists are nothing new. Even if we exclude assassinations or attempted assassinations of presidents and monarchs and confine ourselves to men and women who kill random unarmed civilians in pursuit of a political objective, terrorists have been with us for well over a century.

There have been anarchist terrorists, Russian terrorists, Indian terrorists, Arab terrorists, Basque terrorists, Malay terrorists, Tamil terrorists, and dozens of others besides. There have been and still are Christian terrorists, Jewish terrorists, and Muslim terrorists. There were Yugoslav ("partisan") terrorists settling scores in World War II; Zionist terrorists blowing up Arab marketplaces in Palestine before 1948; American-financed Irish terrorists in Margaret Thatcher's London; US-armed mujahideen terrorists in 1980s Afghanistan; and so on. . . .

The only thing that has changed in recent years is the unleashing in September 2001 of homicidal terrorism within the United States.[88]

The response to the attacks was immediate, and in many ways the United States of September 10 disappeared. The USA PATRIOT Act was passed. The warrantless wiretapping program started within weeks of the September 11 attacks. CALEA was extended to cases of VoIP. What did not occur was a serious public discussion on the types of threats the United States faced, and whether the changes in law enforcement and national security were appropriate for the most important ones.

An issue rarely mentioned in the terrorism discussion is the frequency with which natural disasters unfold. In the first decade of the twenty-first century, the Indian Ocean earthquake tsunami left 283,000 dead, and the Haitian earthquake, 230,000. Such numbers are not unusual—and dwarf the numbers of September 11. In 1839, the Indian cyclone was estimated to leave 300,000 dead, the 1887 Yellow River Flood, 1–2 million, the 1931 Yellow River Flood and the 1970 Bhola cyclone, both with a half million to a million dead. In considering the security risks of building surveillance into communications infrastructures, it is time to consider another facet of the issue: the need for secure communication during times of crisis. I now turn to that subject.

10 Communication during Crises

Four years after the attacks of September 11, Hurricane Katrina made landfall in southeastern Louisiana. A category 5 storm in the Gulf of Mexico
and category 3 by the time it reached the Louisiana coast, Katrina was one
of the strongest hurricanes ever recorded in the Atlantic. The storm was
followed a month later by Rita, another hurricane of surprising strength.
Thousands of deaths and huge financial losses resulted. While the aftermath of the storm caused a major political fallout, the storm had surprisingly little impact on the general public's conception of crises, which
continued to focus on terrorist attacks. Yet historically, natural disasters—
hurricanes, cyclones, earthquakes, and tsunamis—have had far more catastrophic effects than terrorist acts.

They are likely to continue to do so. In the fifteen-year period before
Katrina and Rita, the United States had suffered through a series of highly
damaging hurricanes,[1] massive flooding in the Midwest in 1993, the North-
ridge earthquake, which measured 6.7, in 1994, major ice storms in the
Southeast United States in 1994 and in the Northeast United States and
Quebec in 1998,[2] and a series of devastating tornadoes and floods in the
south-central and upper Midwest in 1995 and 1997.[3] Some of these events
arrived with a warning, if only a partial one (though hurricanes may be
tracked for days, their strength on landfall is not always easy to predict[4]).
Others, such as earthquakes and tornadoes, may occur with no advance
notice. The United States is, of course, far from unique in suffering from
natural disasters. Many nations have a higher risk from severe earthquakes,
volcanic eruptions, and tropical cyclones.

During natural disasters buildings may be destroyed, roads may be made
impassable, power may be down. From government services to financial
systems to distribution of food and fuel, much critical infrastructure may
be severely disrupted. This is when communications become critical.
Despite the disruption of infrastructure—indeed, because of it—government

communication systems need to function during a crisis, and first responders must be able to communicate with one another.

10.1   What Types of Communications Function in Crises?

It is instructive to look at two recent U.S. disasters: the attacks of September 11 and Hurricane Katrina[5] and see how communications functioned. In the case of the terrorist attacks, I consider only the attacks on the World Trade Center, since communications were not particularly affected by the other two hijacked planes.

As New York City Mayor Bloomberg said, "[Every bad guy has] a map of New York City in their pockets." The city is a center for art, theater, finance, fashion; it is also a major communications hub. When the planes crashed into the Twin Towers on September 11, they destroyed communications capability. How much functioned despite the destruction varied by type of network.

The North Tower of the World Trade Center—the first tower to be hit—held many transmission antennas, including those for nearly all of New York City's television stations and for several radio stations. The South Tower had several ISP Points-of-Presence (POP); this is where ISP customers dial in to connect to the network. These ISPs lost their POP connections to the Internet when the South Tower fell. In addition, some major fiber-optic channels were destroyed as a result of the fires and general destruction in the area.[6] A major switching office, Verizon's West Street building, was badly damaged during the collapse of World Trade Center Building 7; the office served three hundred thousand of Manhattan's two million voice lines.[7] A nearby Broad Street central office serving the New York Stock Exchange was also affected, although not as severely as the West Street office.

The telephone network began experiencing trouble shortly after the first plane hit. Overloaded switches in northern New Jersey hindered the national toll-free calling system just as government officials began using the GETS system to give their calls priority. Meanwhile within a half hour of when the first plane hit the North Tower it had become extremely difficult to make calls into or out of New York City, a situation that continued for some time.[8]

Cellular networks also experienced problems. While only five sites were lost when the towers fell, by later in the day damaged phone lines and power outages caused an additional 155 sites to fail. This constituted 5 percent of Manhattan's capacity.[9] Meanwhile phone usage was up because of the attacks, and the problems with landline phones caused people to turn to their cell phones. New York City had a 400 percent increase in the number of calls that day. The networks could not easily handle this, and a high percentage of calls did not get through.[10]

ISPs also suffered major damage. Although there was the POP loss, and customers who directly connected to equipment in the Verizon office lost service,[11] with minor exceptions,[12] whatever was not destroyed, functioned. The Internet routed around trouble just as it had been designed to do.

There was fast response by the service providers to the physical destruction. By the time the New York Stock Exchange opened six days after the attack, Verizon had rerouted fourteen thousand circuits; all of these had a working dial tone on that Monday morning. Ten million gallons of water had flooded into Verizon's Broad Street building, so fiber-optic cables were routed from the street along the outside of the building and then through fifth- and eighth-floor windows to connect with the switching fabric. By mid-October service had been restored to 90 percent of switched voice circuits served by the West Street building.[13]

Other responses were even faster. Except where there was physical damage to the network, the Internet was up and functioning relatively normally on September 11.[14] Its flexibility of design meant that other systems could patch into it. This happened repeatedly, and through a variety of different protocols, including VoIP (still a nascent service at that time), Instant Messaging to replace voice calls,[15] and wireless links to working connections.[16]

The situation with Hurricane Katrina was somewhat different. Katrina devastated a hundred-mile swath along the Gulf coast of Louisiana, Mississippi, and Alabama, decimating telephone switching offices, transmission lines, and cellular towers. A U.S. House of Representatives report put it in striking terms: "The entire communications infrastructure on the Mississippi Gulf coast was destroyed."[17]

Repairing such devastation did not occur as quickly as repairing the systems in lower Manhattan. The geographic area was large, and the destroyed communications systems were not clustered in one location. In late September 2005, five weeks after the disaster, the director of the FCC's Office of Homeland Security testified,

More than 250,000 customer lines remain out of service. More than 500 DS-3 equivalent interoffice facilities [standard "low bandwidth" interoffice trunks, typically provisioned between two central offices] remain down. Three public safety answering points remain out of service. Although many cell sites have been restored, more than 300 cell sites are still not operational in New Orleans.[18]

Given the importance of communications in coordinating the relief efforts, these lingering problems exacerbated an already extremely difficult situation.

While the BellSouth phone hub in New Orleans remained working during the storm, most landlines were out, and a backup generator powering the city's emergency-communications radio system broke down after being punctured by a piece of flying glass. Two forms of communication worked: the Internet and satellite phones. Even while the phone system was out, the broadband connection was functioning in the Hyatt Hotel where New Orleans Mayor Ray Nagin and his staff were lodged. They realized they could use VoIP, and one aide's Vonage account became their connection to the outside world.[19]

Satellite phones—mobile phones that connect via satellite instead of through cellular towers—also functioned during the Katrina crisis. In multiple instances these were the only communication devices working. Satellite systems work when landlines and cell towers—terrestrial systems—are damaged or destroyed, and satellites cover the world's surface, providing connectivity in the mountains of Peru and the deserts of Afghanistan. After the 2010 earthquake in Haiti, the International Telecommunications Union donated a hundred satellite phones and set up a hundred Wi-Fi hotspots.[20]

Satellite communications, however, are not a perfect answer. For one thing, they are expensive. That often precludes their use, even if local governments receive some aid to offset costs; a Congressional report noted that, "In Louisiana, most of the parishes did not have satellite phones because they chose to discontinue the service after the state stopped paying the monthly fees."[21] In addition, satellite phones do not work without a line of sight between the phone and the satellite, a problem when there are clouds, mountains, or buildings in the way.

That is what worked, and did not work, for the general public on September 11 and during Hurricane Katrina. The situation was somewhat different for first responders: firefighters, police, and emergency medical technicians (EMTs). One of the most disturbing lessons from September 11 was the lack of interoperable communications systems. The systems used by the firefighters and police could not communicate. As the *New York Times* reported,

Minutes after the south tower collapsed at the World Trade Center, police helicopters hovered near the remaining tower to check its condition. "About 15 floors down from the top, it looks like it's glowing red," the pilot of one helicopter, Aviation 14, radioed at 10:07 a.m. "It's inevitable."

Seconds later, another pilot reported: "I don't think this has too much longer to go. I would evacuate all people within the area of that second building."[22]

The warnings were clear, and police evacuated; firefighters did not. Partially the issue was cultural: firefighters were "not going to take an evacuation order from a cop that morning."[23] Partially the issue was "fog of war": the confusion, or uncertainty, surrounding adversary capability that makes all the incoming data foggy. And partially the problem was technical.

The firefighters' radio channel was congested. Many communications overlapped and were impossible to understand.[24] After the South Tower fell, the Fire Department (FDNY) did issue an evacuation order for the North Tower. Some FDNY radios did not pick it up because radio communications were impeded in the high-rise building. In other cases, the channel was sufficiently noisy to drown out the order.[25] The *Times* concluded, "No other agency lost communications on Sept. 11 as broadly, or to such devastating effect, as the Fire Department."[26]

The issue of interoperability is not new. New York City first responders—police and firefighters—could not communicate with each other during the 1993 bombing of the World Trade Center. Afterward the two departments discussed establishing a common radio channel, but nothing came of it.[27] The result of the lack of interoperability was that hundreds of firefighters died when they might have been able to evacuate the building instead.

In both the World Trade Center attacks and Hurricane Katrina, physical infrastructure—cables, cell sites, switching offices—was destroyed, but of course the logical underpinnings remained. Anywhere there was a connection to a network (e.g., the New Orleans Hyatt), it was possible to communicate via the Internet. The other discovery—very well known to countries without extensive wired networks—is that it was easier to establish wireless infrastructure than wired.[28]

That, of course, was all true in the aftermath. What first responders use during crises is radio.

10.2 What Is Needed?

First responders rely on Land Mobile Radio (LMR) systems consisting of handheld radios, antennas, and a dispatch system. The radios use FCC assigned dedicated frequencies; the particular technology is trunked mobile radios, which use channels in a highly efficient manner to enable private group communication. How communications travel varies with the situation:

it may be through the nearest tower, through a repeater, from central dispatch, or directly radio to radio. "Push-to-talk" functionality is necessary, whether for the firefighter in a burning building or for a SWAT team.[29]

Achieving interoperability for first-responder communications has been remarkably slow. This may seem odd since civilian communications already interoperate (a caller using an Apple iPhone on AT&T's network can connect with someone using a Motorola Droid on Verizon's network). Interoperability is more complicated for first responders, whose communication needs are quite different from the general public's.

Some first-responder communication patterns are highly unpredictable: periods of minimal use punctuated by periods of high traffic. For first responders, response is time-critical: a busy signal is not an option. Thus first-responder communications have their own spectrum. This immediately adds one complexity, for it means that first responders are buying special systems.

Additional complexity comes from the fact that 90 percent of first responders are in state and local jurisdictions, and it is the individual jurisdictions that decide what systems to buy. (To further complicate matters, even within a single jurisdiction, police, firefighters, and emergency medical services may all use different, noninteroperable systems.) For interoperability to exist, fifty thousand local, tribal, and state governments, and the federal system making the decisions,[30] have to be convinced that they receive value for doing so. Right now different agencies use different frequency bands and technologies, and often they cannot communicate with one another.

Interoperability is complicated, for interoperable means widely so. Consider, as an example, firefighters, who to do their job day to day, need to share information in a dozen different ways. When the unit chief says, "Evacuate NOW," everyone needs to hear it. Firefighters communicate up and down their chain of command (the incident commander, the unit chiefs, the individual firefighters); those systems need to be interoperable. Fire departments provide mutual aid across communities; a large fire in one district draws firefighters from nearby ones, whose areas in turn are covered by departments from neighboring localities. In addition, firefighters communicate with police, EMTs, hazardous-material teams, and so on. All the communications systems need to be interoperable.

Interoperability does not mean that every firefighter should be able to communicate with every police officer or every EMT on the scene via radio; there would be too much chatter.[31] First responders work within hierarchical teams. LMR systems have multiple channels and these may be dedicated in various ways: one channel per fire company, one "fire" channel for command and control for the different fire chiefs to communicate, one channel for EMTs, and so forth.[32] That is the solution if the system has been engineered to be interoperable.

Making change happen is not easy. Currently interoperability may consist of the police at the scene having a single radio to communicate with another agency's network.[33] Or interoperability may consist of the firefighters' unit commander standing with the police commander and the two share information they are garnering from their radios.[34] "The biggest barrier [to interoperability] is the human barrier," Chris Essid, director of emergency communications at DHS, explained. "It's the coordination aspect."[35] Cost is also a factor; while there are federal grants to help local communities update their systems to interoperable ones, funds to do so are limited.[36]

Following a general pattern, these communications systems are moving to IP-based devices because of the robustness, flexibility, and lower cost of packet-based communications. Furthermore, IP-based systems allow the sharing of data as well as voice.[37] There is real value in a firefighter being able to download the building plans as the fire truck speeds to the site.

The focus on interoperability and functionality is not surprising, but it might seem as if communications security is not on the list. In fact, it is—as well it should be. In the federal push for interoperable systems, the government included encryption in the standards, and most federal first-responder systems use encryption (AES) to secure their communications. But while law enforcement naturally embraced secured communications, other first responders have been less sure of the need. Sometimes when federal agents operate with state or local first responders, the federal agents have to shut off the encryption, because the state and local systems are unencrypted and the systems cannot interoperate. DHS is pressing to have all first responders use encrypted communications systems.

NSA has been a strong supporter of this effort. In 2005 NSA instituted Suite B, a full set of public algorithms for the transmission of both unclassified and classified communications (see chapter 3 for a fuller explanation of Suite B). NSA's Information Assurance Directorate is responsible for securing national-security communications; Dickie George, IAD's technology director, wants to see secure communications on the civilian side too. He explained, "We've got Type 1 Suite B product that we can use at the highest level of communications"—meaning in communications with the president—"and we've got to have straight commercial Suite B systems that are available [for purchase] at the mall, at Radio Shack, for first responders. Everyone buys into the concept," George said.[38]

If communications systems with end-to-end encryption can be bought at the mall by first responders, they are also available at the mall for anyone else. End-to-end encryption may not be in standard use in wired or cellular phone systems, but it is part of Skype and Gmail, and the Information Assurance Directorate wants to see it in wireless radio systems available for sale at the mall. This policy suggests that at least a piece of NSA approves securing communications within the United States through the use of end-to-end encryption.

11 Getting Communications Security Right

When the Internet was a DARPA effort, what little security there was focused on protecting network communications. As the Internet became a public system in the mid-1990s, the computer-security conversation moved to the risks posed by and to networked systems. A new word, *cyber-security*, emerged to describe such perceived dangers. Cybersecurity posited new types of threats: threats to the reliability and availability of the network itself; threats created by use of the network by criminals for communication, theft, and child pornography, and by terrorists for operational planning and recruitment; and threats created by the use of the network to support much societal infrastructure.[1] This is the distinction between traditional computer security, which protects machines through reducing vulnerabilities and providing defense in depth, and cybersecurity, which checks the road to see who is out there, what they are doing, and why are they doing it.[2]

The distinction is useful, for it helps put into perspective the conflict over the intrusive communication surveillance regime that has developed since the mid-1990s. As NYU professor Helen Nissenbaum has observed, controversial surveillance laws and technologies—proposed expansion of CALEA to IP-based communications, Einstein 3,[3] deep packet inspection— are of the cybersecurity flavor. Public objection stems from the way that everyone, and not just potential suspects, is caught within the "net of suspicion."[4]

These technologies are a response to the ubiquitous networking that has radically altered the boundaries of organizations. Is an employee's home laptop connected via a VPN inside the corporate network or outside? If it is inside, and then later connects to a family network, what happens when it connects back to the corporate network? The machine has traveled far outside the confines of the corporation. Firewalls are insufficient, since there are many ways to access a network that bypass such protection (recall this was how the Slammer worm was released in the Davis-Besse nuclear plant).

The cybersecurity model developed with the idea of preventing bad activity by stopping malware from ever reaching the end hosts. This would prevent machines from infecting other machines, thwart the installation of hidden code for later use, and halt the exfiltration of data. Surveilling the Information Superhighway is immensely attractive, and the idea found natural takers in law enforcement, who always want more data to help solve crimes; intelligence agencies, which have never turned down an extra bit of information if they could have it; and service providers, who want more data in order to better protect their networks (and if they can also create new business opportunities in the process, so much the better).

The problem is that this viewpoint is flawed. This protection model conflates widely disparate problems. Attacks on end hosts, either by planting code and compromising the host for later use in a botnet, or for identity theft, are criminal activities of a very different nature than exfiltration of large amounts of data from industry and military sites. The latter are typically highly targeted and cleverly crafted efforts, unlikely to be uncovered in a broad surveillance effort. Successful attacks against critical infrastructure can be expected to be similarly subtle and custom tailored. These custom attacks are unlikely to be discovered by a network surveillance system programmed to look for the Internet equivalent of shoplifters.

This surveillance solution poses a serious security threat. Along with energy, finance, and government services, information and communications technology (ICT) is an enabling critical infrastructure. ICT can be viewed as the most fundamental critical infrastructure, for its role is to support all the others. Wiretapping integrated into a communication network is an architected security breach. An exploitable weakness in a wiretapping system puts society broadly at risk.

When unknown outsiders broke into NASA systems, they were able to remove a large number of plans.[5] If these intruders had instead broken into a service provider's switch, then unless communications transiting the switch were encrypted, the intruders would be able to eavesdrop on *all* communications traveling through the switch—which was what was done at Vodafone Greece in 2004. If intruders instead were able to access DPI equipment at the switch, unless Tor or other anonymizing technologies were used for routing communications, these intruders would be able to build full dossiers on the activities of anyone whose communications transited the switch. Or if the intruders were able to access databases at the provider of the DPI equipment (perhaps a company doing DPI to provide advertisements for the service provider), they would access full dossiers on anyone whose communications transited the switch and who did not use anonymizing technologies for communication.

Given the difficulty of getting the technology right (consider the wiretapping at Vodafone Greece and the exploits possible in the Cisco surveillance architecture) and the threat of attacks by insiders or nation-states, the decision to build surveillance capabilities deeply within network infrastructure appears poorly considered. The context is providing communication for a highly mobile society grown dependent on instant, always available, communication. Threats will come from both friends and enemies of the United States. (That "friends" are a threat may be surprising, but economic competition is global, and much of the world does not view the theft of industrial secrets as criminal.[6]) In the middle of this maelstrom lies the Internet, an overwhelmingly successful experiment that has been a remarkable driver of worldwide economic growth since the mid-1990s. Can we possibly get communications security right?

Although the fact that there are frequent attacks on the network is well known, the details and scope of the problem are less well understood. There has been a tendency to focus on hacking and DDoS attacks. The genuinely serious threats are, however, intrusions into industrial and military systems. These may leave code embedded for later use, or may exfiltrate data—or both. These national-security threats are the backdrop to the issue of whether building surveillance into communication infrastructures is a security benefit.

Many governments, including the U.S. government[7], are developing capabilities to alter and disrupt, deceive and degrade, and even destroy their enemy's information systems.[8] Some of these cyberattack systems are apparently already being tested against the United States. Effects can be devastating. The power and force with which a government can attack a computer system can be overwhelming. It is one thing when an Israeli competitor spies on Recon Optical, and quite another when the spy is the Israeli government.

Israel is not the main threat, however. It is a small country with only seven and a half million people. As noted earlier, beginning in 2007 U.S. industry and government computers, along with those of New Zealand, Australia, India, Belgium, Germany, and the United Kingdom, were penetrated, with information exfiltrated and perhaps code infiltrated.[9] The perpetrators appear to be hackers in China unofficially working for the government.[10] China's People Liberation Army is roughly three million people. Cyberwar, the use of such cyberexploitation and cyberattack for military gain, is of strong interest, and the problem of surveillance of U.S. information systems and exfiltration of data is unlikely to disappear soon. In coming years the network will change. The dominant form of computing is likely to be not computers, nor even cell phones or PDAs, but billions and billions of small, embedded processors acting as sensors or actuators.[11] This, then, is the confusing context for future communication networks that should, among many other requirements, support secure communications and legally authorized wiretapping.

11.1   Envisioning the Future

After the initial euphoria over the resounding success of the Internet in the 1990s, it became clear that there are also problems with the network, the first and foremost being security. Across the globe there are projects on a clean-slate network architecture: What would we do if we could design Internet protocols anew? How would we do it?

What do we want from the current and future network? We know that the packet-based model and the end-to-end principle—that the application knows best how to implement the function in question[12]—work. The Internet architecture enables the innovation and running of applications sufficiently rich to accomplish what end users need and seek.

We want to share rich content—movies, music, voice communication— in real time. We want to enable smart grid technology (the ability to control electricity usage to maximize efficiency). We want to deliver complex services, such as emedicine, over the network (this might include long-distance consultation with specialists, for example). We want to be able to measure much more—the temperature and humidity of cropland and the activity of an older person living on their own—and to use the data to respond in real time to the needs that are indicated. These are just some applications, but they give a flavor of the varying types of communications we expect to be supported. A future Internet should enable all these things. It should be

• A network for people to connect through voice communications, data, and video
• A tool for corporations to operate in an environment where outsourcing and global supply chains are common aspects of business
• A system for sensors and actuators to transmit data ranging from measurement of natural phenomena (soil temperature to carbon emissions) to personal data (movement of a housebound individual)

- A communications system for the transmittal of nonclassified government information
- A communications system for the transmittal of classified government information
- A medium for control of critical infrastructure

These communications will, of course, have differing needs for confidentiality, authenticity, integrity, anonymity, and availability. The question is how to have a secure network that supports these needs. In fact, there are already ways available to accomplish much of what is required.

A National Research Council study recommended that information technology systems develop a defensive strategy of encrypting communications between system elements, keeping Internet exposure minimal for systems that do not need the exposure, using strong authentication mechanisms when appropriate, and robustly configuring the systems (that is, making sure all the security knobs were set appropriately).[13] That was in 2002. These changes did not happen.

Consider the security flaws that Tom Cross found in 2010 in deployed wiretapping systems for IP communication.[14] There were a number of reasons for the problems. Among the most important were design flaws allowing implementers more flexibility than necessary.[15] While the system design recommended encryption, some implementations omitted it.[16] The architecture recommended throwing out interception-request hashes shorter than 12 bytes, but many implementations failed to do so. These errors left them open to an easy-to-mount brute-force attack that enabled guessing a valid password.[17] Because there was no effort to validate implementations, there was no cost to companies that did not follow the suggested implementation. Security solutions cannot solely rely on technical means. It is clear that there are at least two different sets of issues to getting security "right": technical concerns and economic ones.

11.2 The Right Technical Stance

In designing for a future Internet, we need to incorporate protections where they are most needed. We also need to acknowledge that the communications system will not work perfectly. A system as flexible and open to innovation as the Internet will necessarily also be open to problems. That is a compromise one makes. There was little petty crime in the German Democratic Republic,[18] but few would argue that the trade-off of loss of freedom was worth the absence of shoplifting and minor theft.

The Internet is not simply a piece of technology; it is a piece of technology embedded with human values. David Clark was chief protocol architect for the Internet Activities Board in the 1980s; now he is working with the U.S. National Science Foundation on a next-generation project, Future Internet Design. In considering what a future Internet might look like, Clark wrote:

It is not realistic to imagine that a set of technical solutions will produce a network that is free of all vulnerabilities or attacks. The Internet is a technical artifact deeply embedded in a social, economic and human context. Attacks involve all those modalities. Our goal for the network technology should be to narrow the range of attacks, simplify the problem of detection and response, degrade certain forms of attack to the point that they are not useful to an attacker, and to allow the design of operational procedures for security to be positioned in the context of a clear model of what the network can and cannot do.[19]

With fifteen years of experience with a public Internet, we have experience that the DARPA engineers did not.[20] NSF's Future Internet Design, a program consisting of a variety of research projects, is focusing on everything from the underlying infrastructure of the network to architectures for the applications. It is examining social issues, seeking to address economic trade-offs, privacy, and security concerns up front in system design. Some researchers are also considering what an Internet for the "next three billion" might look like, examining access, literacy, and diversity for those not connected to the network.

Testing some of the new ideas may be difficult. It is possible to use an experimental test bed, but then one lacks real data. Using a real system to test experimental protocols is problematic, since network administrators are loath to disrupt their systems.

One piece of research is an innovative platform, OpenFlow. Modern switches and routers have flow tables, tables with rules as to where traffic should be routed, for implementing firewalls, NATs, and so on. OpenFlow virtualizes this, allowing the possibility of running multiple switching systems over a single physical switch. A network administrator can partition traffic going through flow tables into production and research traffic (by default, traffic is production unless otherwise noted). By using the experimental rules, the research traffic enables new routing techniques to be tested. For example, this might be routes that minimize the number of hops or that control traffic coming to or going from a particular node.[21]

One early application of OpenFlow, Ethane, allowed the establishment of a "controller" that approves the communication flow and picks the path. Ethane provided security through enforcing rules such as "VoIP phones are not allowed to communicate with laptops."[22] Ethane was not intended for the general Internet, but rather for enterprise networks, where such control is quite appropriate. Experimental work indicated that Ethane could be successful in controlling networks with ten thousand machines, the size of a small enterprise.[23]

Researchers moved on to networks with software-defined rules controlling routing, access control, energy management, and other features. The idea behind this is that packet forwarders should be simple, commoditized pieces of hardware controlled by software. These Software Defined Networks (SDNs) have already been deployed in data centers; the owners appreciate the reduced costs (SDNs enable the use of less expensive hardware) and the flexibility afforded by implementing features in software. The intent is to employ SDNs everywhere: data centers, enterprises, college campuses—even homes.

That different portions of the network should enforce differing security rules is not a change from the current Internet. What is new is the clarity of the proposed security model. This simplicity makes it easier to implement than the ad hoc security protections that have grown up for the public Internet. Underlying SDN is a security model that private networks should connect with public networks at very clear junctures. By segregating insecure end hosts—a problem that is unlikely to disappear[24]—within the private network, the security model isolates problems, a very useful outcome. SDN, which does enforcement from the switch level, is one of many possible security models; there is also work looking at controls at the information-dissemination level.

The original Internet communication model let any device communicate with any other. But in a world in which SCADA and DoD systems are connected to the network, that makes no sense. Some webservers like Amazon .com or whitehouse.gov should be fully accessible to the public Internet. These will be open to attack, since anyone can connect to them. As David Clark has pointed out, "They should not be used for any task (such as hosting confidential information) that makes them valuable as a platform (e.g., for exfiltration) if they are infiltrated. Machines that host valuable information should not also be used for any roles where they need to connect to unknown persons. Any machine used for this sort of task should be embedded in a strong identity/authentication/authorization architecture."[25]

The idea that the sensitivity of the data on a device should be coupled to the broadness of who may access that device is certainly not new (it is, for example, common practice for members of the national-security community). Such a model of communication requires a clear partitioning of the "internetwork": some portion will carefully screen all packets in and out of their piece, requiring attribution and strong authentication, while other portions of the network will be open and broadly available, and others will be somewhere in the middle on a sliding scale. To achieve such a model requires many changes to the way we design systems.[26] It means applying identity mechanisms and attribution more broadly than has been done heretofore. What it does not mean is deploying identity and attribution across the network. For the same reason that websites such as Amazon.com and whitehouse.gov should be open to anyone, there is no reason for such sites to seek identity or attribution information from those who access them.

Partitioning the network—a situation that already exists with corporate and government firewalls that allow some types of access but not others—interposes intermediaries in a communication path, either to ensure identity, authentication, or authorization or to examine the communication itself to ensure it is not carrying damaging malware. Interposing such intermediaries may itself create problems. The presence of such intermediaries may simplify attacking the communications themselves.[27] As we saw with DPI originally implemented for CALEA compliance, the same DPI technology can be used for purposes other than originally intended. While it will not be simple to implement such partitioning and doing so will create problems, it is possible to have a future Internet that preserves the ability to innovate and communicate broadly while nonetheless enabling the network to function more securely.

Technical solutions to the wiretapping conundrum are less clear. We have learned some lessons that it would be useful to apply. After the passage of the Protect America Act, a number of researchers warned that the warrantless collection at the AT&T San Francisco switching office risked exploitation by opponents as well as overcollection, and that new vulnerabilities would be created by the collection of the CDR information.[28] These predictions came to pass—though not necessarily there and then. The Greek wiretapping case showed that wiretapping capabilities built into communications infrastructures can and will be exploited by opponents. The United States warrantless wiretapping program resulted in overcollection.[29] When communications service personnel were placed at an FBI location, the lack of genuine two-organization control on surveillance resulted in the service-provider personnel giving the FBI customer data without legal oversight.[30] In short, making wiretapping easy from a technical point of view makes wiretapping without proper legal authorization easy. We know, from the efforts carriers are making to use DPI for business purposes, that security services, such as examining packets, should be doing those services for *the purpose of security only*. Finally, we have learned through the case of Vodafone Greece and the problems with the Cisco architecture that it is easy for wiretapping systems to be subverted, leading to exploitation by unauthorized parties.[31]

As security researchers have understood for over a hundred years, security mechanisms need public vetting. This may seem odd to nonprofessionals, but trusted insiders and other nation-states will be in positions to find the flaws in interception systems. Public protection means that the interception system must be as well vetted as possible and that means public visibility of the system. Cisco should be lauded for having allowed their system to be open to public view.[32] One suggestion for improving the situation is that the sale of legally authorized interception systems for domestic use should be predicated on the systems being made public to enable examination. Note that such a requirement will have no effect on the NSA, which fields its own systems.

The combination of the increasing use of mobile communications, the increasing complexity of communications infrastructure, and the difficulty of correctly building complex systems makes it very hard to get communications interception 100 percent right. But getting these systems right is crucial. Theft of U.S. corporate and manufacturing secrets as a result of an interception system subverted by a foreign nation is too high a price to pay for catching one more drug dealer or even for stopping a terrorist intent on setting off bombs at a shopping mall.[33] This is not a business argument; this is a national-security issue. For this reason, communications interception systems should not be deployed domestically unless they have been shown to be secure.

11.3 Economics: A Necessary Part of the Solution

Economic costs, or the lack of them, play an important role in cyber insecurity. In computer systems, network effect—the fact that the value of a system increases as more people use the system[34]—and software compatibility issues means being first to market is remarkably important. Since economic losses due to poor security often accrue not to the system vendor or operator, but elsewhere, this puts security on the back burner. In this sense, security is a system externality; those who develop and purchase the system are not affected by the security weaknesses. Rather it is a third party that has not been involved in the economic transaction for the system that suffers from any problems.

That creates an apparent pressure point for cybersecurity. Whoever bears the risk strongly affects whether the system is configured securely. Ross Anderson provides a compelling example of this concerning ATM fraud:

In the United States, the first "phantom withdrawal" case was decided in favor of the customer, leading to Regulation E and its limits on customer liability for unauthorized transactions. In the United Kingdom, initial cases went the other way; banks got away for years with claiming "our systems are secure so if your PIN was used it's your fault." This created the obvious moral hazard, leading banks to be careless about ATM security, and ultimately [there was] an avalanche of ATM fraud in 1992–1994.[35]

When risk is placed appropriately, it provides incentive to improve security. As University of California economics professor Hal Varian has written, "Liability should be assigned to the parties best able to manage the risk."[36]

However, the liability "solution" to the security problem is, in fact, quite difficult to implement. To hold vendors and operators responsible for inflicted harms, one has to show that security breaches came from product design or system implementation and that the system departed from an appropriate standard of care.[37] As one might expect, the notion of imposing liability for security breaches is controversial. Many worry that it would harm innovation. A difficult issue to resolve is determining metrics by which to measure whether a system design and implementation has been appropriately secured. These battles have been raging for a number of years now without resolution.[38]

In the case at hand, the issue is not of securing a general-purpose operating system, but of securing a significantly simpler system designed to legally intercept interception. Thus the arguments against liability—threats to innovation, inability to develop metrics for security—are not really at issue.

Currently wiretap law provides both criminal and civil liability against interception. (There are exemptions for legally authorized interceptions in criminal and foreign-intelligence investigations, if the interception is being performed by the service provider for quality control, if one of the parties to the call permits the interception,[39] or in the case of trespass, if the owner of the computer being used in the trespass authorizes the interceptions of the trespasser's communications being made to, through, or from the owner's machine.[40]) It would be appropriate to make communications providers liable if due care has not been exercised in the development or implementation of an interception system that has been misused and allowed eavesdropping on a user. This could force more rigorous security evaluations of proposed systems for communications interception. It could help keep badly designed systems out of use. The DCS3000 architecture that still included MD5, a hash function with known insecurities, would presumably not pass muster. A rigorous public vetting might have uncovered the security flaws in the 2004 Cisco architectural design before its deployment.

Under current practice, it is the purchasers and developers of interception systems who make the decisions about security. When an interception system is subverted, the person who has been wiretapped on pays the price for the system's problems. There are problems with this liability proposal, the greatest of which is how someone would know that their communications had been intercepted as a result of a faulty implementation of a legal system. The point, however, is that transferring liability to those in a position to manage the risk helps incentivize securing interception systems.

Such transfer of risk would not stop all types of warrantless wiretapping. In particular, the PSP ran at the request of the U.S. government. It is likely that the wiretapping done under the program would not fall under an "unsecured" interception category. However, a transfer of risk that would put communications providers under legal responsibility for ensuring that interception systems are secure seems a rather obvious and necessary requirement for the communications systems on which society relies.

11.4 The Right Policy Stance

At the present time, there appears to be close to a complete absence of a government role in ensuring that domestic communications surveillance is done securely. That sounds hard to believe—and yet it is true. Consider the agencies involved in telecommunications and surveillance issues: the FBI, the NSA, the National Institute of Standards and Technology (NIST), and the FCC.

The NSA has always had a dual role with respect to communications: its job is to secure government communications and to conduct foreign signals intelligence. These two responsibilities feed off one another in a very useful way. The communications-security side of the agency and the signals intelligence side constantly test each other's products to ensure that these are doing the job they are supposed to do. While communications security and signals intelligence are on opposite sides, the NSA has no conflict in doing both: the agency's role is to secure *U.S. government* communications and conduct surveillance of *foreign* communications.[41] The

NSA has no official role in ensuring nongovernmental communication systems are secure.

Under the 1987 Computer Security Act,[42] NIST[43] was to be responsible for the development of standards for protecting the security and privacy of sensitive information within civilian federal systems (the official term is "nonnational security systems"). As one might expect, this was turf that the NSA had viewed as its own, and there were battles over the passage of the act as well as over its implementation.[44] By the late 1990s, the NSA had ceded to NIST the role of developing cryptography standards for the nonnational security side of the federal government. NIST ran a highly successful competition for an Advanced Encryption Standard to replace the aging DES.

NIST's Computer Security Division (CSD) has various responsibilities for communications security. CSD develops new cryptographic standards and is currently at work on a new hash algorithm to replace SHA-1. In conjunction with Canada's NSA equivalent, the Communications Security Establishment, CSD runs the Cryptographic Module Validation Program for testing commercial cryptography products. NIST's reputation as an honest broker means that CSD participation in international standards efforts is highly regarded, and helps to further security standards. CSD develops numerous guidelines for secure use of IT systems, including VoIP, IPv6, and DNSSEC, which aid both the public and private sector in their implementation.

What CSD does not do is evaluate the security of the nation's communications infrastructure. It does not even evaluate the security of the federal government's nonnational security communications infrastructure. CSD has traditionally been quite underfunded and is a poor cousin to NSA;[45] it simply lacks the resources to do the type of testing and evaluations needed to ensure that fielded communications systems are appropriately secure. In addition, NIST does not have the authority to require that government agencies implement the security guidelines that CSD prepares; the Office of Management and Budget has that role. Without a doubt, the broader issue of securing private-sector communications systems is well outside NIST's bailiwick.

The Federal Communications Commission and the Department of Homeland Security have programs to ensure that emergency communications work in times of national crisis; programs include GETS, which enables first responders to have priority on communications networks during emergencies, and SAFECOM, which focuses on ensuring interoperability for the communications systems used by emergency response agencies. But neither the FCC nor DHS has programs for securing the nation's private communications networks.

As a result of CALEA, the FBI was given the role of developing standards for interception in digitally switched networks, standards that have since been extended to cover broadband Internet access providers and providers of interconnected VoIP services. The FBI is concerned with communications interception; security of communications infrastructure is not an FBI issue.

While the FBI has been involved in some programs to protect business computer systems,[46] the bureau does not examine the long-term issues of national competitiveness and global strength. That is not a law enforcement issue, but a national-security one, and the bureau is a crime-fighting agency. In that guise, the FBI appropriately seeks to use communications interception during investigations and wants interception capabilities such as CALEA, Carnivore, and CIPAV. It is not in the FBI's investigative interest to publicize weaknesses in communications infrastructure that allow the bureau to deploy its various investigative tools. Or as a senior intelligence agency official once remarked, "If there is a hole in your fence, counterintelligence doesn't want to fix it the right way."

The problem is that providing such communications-security protection is not an NSA responsibility either. It would be a confusing role for an agency whose responsibilities are for protecting national-security systems and gathering foreign intelligence. Yet if the FBI is using CIPAV, the U.S. government should be concerned as to who else might be doing so. Currently there is no agency in the U.S. government chartered with securing private-sector communications infrastructure.

There have been occasions when the NSA has informed U.S. companies that they were being spied on and suggested appropriate changes to secure their communications. However, the NSA has no statutory responsibility for securing the nation's private communications infrastructure. The intelligence agency can help secure a particular company's systems only under very narrow circumstances. There is no problem securing communication systems if the products are for use in the DoD. If the product is for use by the nonnational security side of the government, the NSA can be involved in securing the system *only if* aid has been requested by a federal agency (e.g., Department of the Treasury) and then only if the help is of a narrow and specific nature. Such a request must pass legal review before the NSA is permitted to participate.

Few are comfortable with the idea that the NSA should aid communications providers in securing their systems. It is the U.S. government agency with the most expertise in communications security, but its role in communications intelligence presents serious problems. The fact that the NSA was involved in warrantless wiretapping not just from the 1940s to the 1970s but within the last decade creates serious problems for the agency playing a role in civilian communications security. Some in the intelligence community understand this problem well. One official remarked that while he would be perfectly comfortable with *his* agency working with service providers to secure their networks, for civil liberties reasons he would feel very queasy if a different three-letter agency was involved in doing so.

We communicate via increasingly insecure systems. While it is possible to secure communications using end-to-end encryption, few people do.[47] No government agency is responsible for ensuring the security of the communications infrastructure, though one is responsible for designing interception systems to be placed in the system. Even knowing the history, it is difficult to understand how the United States might have ended up with such a policy. It is not a solution designed for securing the nation.

11.5 CALEA's Use in Packet-Based Networks Should Be Narrowly Limited

When the Communications Assistance for Law Enforcement Act was passed in 1994, almost all communications were circuit switched. Packet-based communications existed, but the Internet had not yet made a serious dent in public-switched networks. CALEA had a clear exemption for "information services." The FBI was pressing for a law for wiretapping digitized circuit-switched networks and at the time did not see the Internet as a serious concern.

Packet-based communications are rapidly replacing circuit-switched ones, and in 2003 the FBI sought to extend CALEA to some instances of VoIP. It was successful in doing so. In 2006 the bureau sought further extensions and floated a bill in Congress. An Internet CALEA would have very negative effects on innovation[48] and on security[49] and ultimately the bill did not move forward. The attempt to extend CALEA to a completely new model of communications—packet-based networks—brings serious problems.

We live in a very different communications and security environment than the period in which CALEA was passed. It is worth recapping the salient features of interception in the context of CALEA, the Internet's growth, the rise of terrorism, and increasing globalization:

• Wiretaps can be extremely useful in certain types of law enforcement and national-security investigations. Content may be less important than the knowledge that two parties have been communicating. In particular, it is very important to be able to capture the fact that communications between suspected terrorists outside the United States and people inside the country have occurred. The essential aspect of such cases is discovering with whom inside the United States the communication is happening; details of the actual communication may be much less important.

• We are rapidly moving from a circuit-switched to a packet-based communications system. Packet-based networks are significantly harder to secure than centralized circuit-based networks. Our communications are highly mobile. Surveilling mobile communications provides more challenges than wiretapping communications to a fixed line. Wiretapping packet-based, mobile communications can be even more difficult; how difficult depends on the type of technology employed. It is not packet-based communications that make interception hard, and it is not mobility that does so, but the combination. Depending on how and where the surveillance mechanisms are configured, wiretapping may create serious risks that put the security of the underlying communications network in jeopardy.[50]

• Economic espionage threatens both the nation's economy and its national security. Because of increasing reliance on electronic communications for everything from managing supply chains to managing remote workers, the need for secure communications for U.S. business is a national-security concern. Sophisticated adversaries are able to take advantage of security weaknesses in U.S. systems to exfiltrate data and to install code for exploitation at a later date.

• Weaknesses in an enterprise's communication system expose that enterprise to risk; weaknesses in a service provider's network expose *all* users in the system to risk.

The ability of the government to wiretap under legal authorization is an important tool for law enforcement and national security—*but the ability of the government to wiretap under legal authorization is quite different from the government requiring that the network be architected to accommodate legally authorized wiretaps*. The latter should not be done if interception jeopardizes communications security.

Law enforcement and national-security investigations against the few should not require reducing security for the many. Tapping mobile packet-based communications may be more difficult than law enforcement or national security would like. So be it. We need laws and technologies that provide secure communications, not laws and technologies that undermine the security of communication networks. Extending CALEA functionality to packet-based networks is to create unwarranted risk.

11.6   Wiretapping without CALEA-type Systems

In arguing against the expansion of CALEA to packet-based communication systems, the argument is not against the use of legally authorized wiretaps but against designing interception capabilities into communications infrastructures. That does not prevent law enforcement and national security from conducting communications surveillance in other ways.

The inundation of new communications technologies means that government investigations proceed in ways unimagined even a decade ago. With location data, pen registers, and CDRs easily available in real time, law enforcement has far more investigative capability than ever before. Transactional data enables the mapping of an individual's social network and an organization's chain of command. Following the metadata has become an important investigative tool for law enforcement and national security.

Tasks that once took days of an investigator's time can be accomplished in seconds. Cell phone location data enabled the U.S. Marshal service to cut the average time to find fugitives from forty-two days to two. Such data similarly enabled the rapid arrest in Rome of one of the men convicted in the 2005 attempted bombings of the London underground. Browsing history stored on Najibullah Zazi's laptop quickly revealed his interest in obtaining bombing materials, which led to his arrest and indictment days before he intended to detonate explosives in the New York City subway. This information would have been far slower to obtain if done the old-fashioned way through following Zazi and interviewing shopkeepers.

Despite the plethora of new communications technologies, wiretapping voice remains quite useful, and some of the old wiretapping technologies are still employed. So while alligator clips and placing taps at the central office are considerably less useful than they once were, these techniques are occasionally used. Cell phones are often what matters; by 2009, 96 percent of Title III wiretaps were for mobile devices (cell phones and pagers).[51] Wiretapping cell phones is more complex than wiretapping landlines; it is accomplished through a tap at the target's Mobile Switching Center or through the use of more expensive tracking technologies such as Triggerfish. But by supplying location information, tapped cell phones and other mobile communications provide richer investigative data than tapped landlines ever had done.

Electronic bugging tools, from employing microphones placed in an adjacent dwelling to bugs placed within a telephone receiver (this was the technique involved in the famous Watergate taps), can also be used to capture voice communications. Other techniques that do the same thing from a greater distance include parabolic microphones (parabolic reflectors[52] and laser microphones[53]).

The continuing vulnerability of end hosts leaves open the use of compromising tools such as CIPAV to tap communications. Such forms of wiretapping will be available until such time as communications equipment is built error free. Because cell phones, smart phones, laptops, and other communications devices are reliant on complex software and hardware systems, that day is a long way off. Police and spies can be assured that there will continue to be many ways to collect electronic communications. It is also worth noting that nothing precludes the development of end-to-end encryption techniques that give the government easier ways to decrypt than brute force (recall the techniques that Lotus Notes employed in the mid-1990s).

CALEA changed the model of who bore responsibility for government's access to communications. Instead of wiretapping being a law-enforcement concern, it became a communications providers' problem: design the networks so that there was an "easy button" for government to push when it needed to tap a suspect. CALEA means that, subject to legal authorization, at virtually no cost and with very little pain, the FBI and other law enforcement agencies have access to what they want. Yet as the solutions above demonstrate, CALEA is not the only solution. There are many ways law-enforcement agencies can obtain the information they need. Virtually everything law-enforcement investigators need can be acquired without embedding interception capabilities into communications networks.

Missing from law-enforcement's equation is the fact that CALEA is not free. Government investigating agencies do not bear the cost of CALEA— society does. CALEA's cost resides in the building of the switches, whose cost is passed on to consumers. CALEA compliance means innovative telecommunications systems are delayed or not deployed. Money spent on CALEA is money diverted from investment in system infrastructure and in developing new products.

CALEA's biggest cost, however, is in the potential vulnerabilities it creates. Compliance creates risks to communications security by those capable of exploiting those vulnerabilities (insiders and other nation-states). Threats to privacy are posed by the telecommunications providers themselves, who seek to recoup their CALEA investments for their own business purposes. Is providing law enforcement with a "free and easy" wiretap button worth the potential cost to network integrity and commercial telecommunications innovation when safer wiretapping alternatives are available?

Without CALEA-type systems, investigators might need other routes, developing individualized tools in order to successfully wiretap. Although developing and implementing such solutions may be complicated for law-enforcement agencies, such an approach is plausible. After all, such technologies form the basis for foreign-intelligence collection. Government investigators would need to innovate, finding new electronic surveillance solutions as old ones cease to be effective. Surely that is not too big a trade-off in exchange for not introducing vulnerabilities into U.S. communications infrastructures.

11.7   What It Means to "Get Communications Security Right"

The conflict created between communications security and communications surveillance may appear technical. Its resolution is not. The resolution will occur not in some abstract nation of the future, but in the United States of the twenty-first century. The present conundrum of national security and communications surveillance needs to be resolved within the framework established by the U.S. Constitution. U.S. wiretap policy should be governed by the following principles:

Secure communications is necessary for freedom, security, human dignity, and consent of the governed. Such security is necessary for democracy. The preamble to the Constitution says the responsibility of the government is to "secure the Blessings of Liberty to ourselves and our Posterity." The Fourth Amendment states that "the right of the people to be secure in their persons, houses, papers, and effects, against unreasonable searches and seizures, shall not be violated." As Jed Rubenfeld convincingly argues, "A search or seizure would be *unreasonable if and only if it violated the people's right to security.*"[54]

This does not mean that under proper legal authorization, the government cannot wiretap. Indeed the preamble does state that providing for the common defense is one of the responsibilities of government. Wiretapping is an important tool in many types of criminal and foreign-intelligence cases. However, in providing for a common defense, the government should not be obstructing the people's right to be secure. Private and secure communication is necessary for businesses to function, for personal relationships to flourish, and for political activity to occur. Proposed laws and technologies for wiretapping should not substantively impede the peoples' communications security.[55] Any wiretapping law or technology should be measured against the threats it poses to the security of the communication. It should not be implemented if it poses a substantive threat to the freedom, security, human dignity, or consent of the governed.

Interception technologies intended for use in public networks must be peer reviewed.[56] They must also have regular security reviews to ensure that they have not fallen prey to new forms of attack.[57]

The U.S. government should "secure the Blessings of Freedom . . . for our Posterity." Communications surveillance must be designed with this principle fully in mind. Technologies change with remarkable rapidity. Laws come and go. Installed infrastructure, however, has great longevity. Changing an installed base is complicated and expensive. As a result, infrastructure tends to last for decades. Thus there is a very high cost if insecure eavesdropping capabilities are built into communications infrastructure such as network switches and routers. Securing the blessings of freedom for posterity means that the government must ensure that wiretapping technologies do not create such risks. Interception systems are not built insecure by design; rather, flaws creep in as they do with any complex system. That is why the IETF Network Working Group chose not to include wiretapping capabilities within its standards track functionality.[58]

To ensure the blessings of freedom for our posterity, certain principles must be adhered to during the development and implementation of surveillance systems for use in communications infrastructures, as well as afterward, during actual usage. First and foremost, interception technologies must be designed so that auditing is automatically on. The design system must not allow auditing to be turned off. Unlike many computer technologies, design of interception access should minimize flexibility; this will minimize risks that the eavesdropping system can be subverted.[59] The interception system should be designed to have genuine two-organization control. Finally, the design should be subject to open public review before implementation in any communications network. Technologies that cannot meet these criteria should not be used for interception in any public communications system.

These rules cannot guarantee that an interception system will work correctly, but they are important safeguards. Or as a mathematician might say, such protections are necessary, even if they are not sufficient.

Any suspension of communication privacy protections must occur only during periods of extreme emergency and must be for brief—and quite temporary— periods of time. "Temporary" should be a matter of days and weeks and not extend to months and years. A communications interception designed for such temporary use is much more likely to be used for a brief period and not become, as the system designed for the President's Surveillance Program did, part of communications infrastructure.

In line with the recommendations put forth by the 2007 National Research Council report on data mining and behavioral surveillance, any surveillance program that suspends privacy protections must be evaluated for effectiveness.[60] This implies that it should be designed in such a way that its effectiveness can be evaluated. No such program should be expanded unless there is a framework for evaluating its effectiveness.[61]

After a declaration of national emergency in which warrantless wiretapping of U.S. persons is temporarily permitted, there should be a deliberate and careful study of the circumstances under which the emergency was declared and any communications privacy violations that occurred. If privacy violations occurred, there should be a careful delineation of how investigative rules should change to prevent similar breaches in the future.

Communications surveillance should not impede the working of the press. This principle may seem less important than the other three. It is not. Journalists are society's guardians, and the security of their communications functions as the equivalent of canaries in the coal mine. The Founding Fathers understood that a free society rests on a free press. A nation is a democracy only so long as journalists' communications are secure.

Yet although the First Amendment provides an absolute right to publish, its protections of a reporter's right to investigate are less definitive.[62] Laws permit the wiretapping of journalists in the course of criminal investigations.[63] There is an important balancing act here.

Modern society is now heavily dependent on electronic communications. To be a journalist is to talk to sources by phone, email, Instant Messenger—and occasionally in person. The fact that reporters are so heavily dependent on electronic communications means they are particularly susceptible to wiretapping. At the time the U.S. Constitution was written, it was hard to track a journalist. Now it is both simple and cheap. Often it is not even necessary to listen to reporters' communications in order to discover what the reporter is uncovering: by exposing who is in a reporter's proximity, location information may reveal all.

There have been multiple times in U.S. history when journalists' communications were intercepted without legal authorization. Protecting the security of journalists' communication is necessary for ensuring the security of the nation. U.S. law allows government wiretapping under certain circumstances. Implementing this principle is almost entirely a matter of law and not one of technology.

Adhering to these principles cannot guarantee that we will secure "the Blessings of Liberty to ourselves and our Posterity," but failure to adhere to them will guarantee that we will not.

Epilogue

At the end of World War II, the United States entered into a period where it was at the height of its powers. Except for Pearl Harbor, the nation had experienced no serious attacks on U.S. territory, and its industrial strength was unparalleled. Meanwhile much of Europe lay in ruins, the Soviet Union had suffered the loss of 26 million people, and Japan had lost the war and saw much of its manufacturing base in ruins. China was impoverished and in the middle of a civil war. It was then that the paradigm for the next fifty years of U.S. military and diplomatic policy was established. While not every event in that fifty-year period went in favor of the United States—there were the Soviet atomic and hydrogen bombs, Sputnik, the loss in the Vietnam War—there can be little question that this was "the American century."

That is now slowly, but inexorably, changing. In the second decade of the new millennium the United States is still, to be sure, the sole superpower, but others are gaining economic power. By 2005, China's share of the world's GDP was 9.7 percent (the U.S. share was 22.5 percent); at one point, a mistaken calculation led economists to believe that China's GDP would overtake that of the United States in 2010.[1] When China's GDP exceeds that of the United States is not as important as the fact that it will, and most likely before the half-century mark. China is already the world's factory. The fact that the United States will not be the world's largest economy will have many implications for U.S. defense and diplomatic policy.

Cyber is now a critical aspect of U.S. defense, and an important strategic issue is whether it is possible to achieve overwhelming superiority in this domain. The answer is: almost surely not, for it is a domain where someone with a $40 Internet connection and a PC can create a great deal of havoc,[2] a situation unlikely to be alleviated soon. Multiply it by the size of the PLA and the issue becomes clear.

The communications infrastructure we build will persist for decades to come. Wiretapping is typically not debated except in times of high stress, when emotion takes over from rationality. Now, as we embark on a future network design, is the time to consider the issue thoughtfully.

When wiretapping is built into a communications infrastructure, all it takes to invoke surveillance against society is an insider misappropriating the technology; an outsider, including a foreign government, gaining unauthorized access and turning a switch; or a government invoking emergency powers and vastly expanding its reach.[3] The analysis concluding that the President's Surveillance Program was legal was done by a single attorney.[4] This experience, along with the Athens affair and the FBI misuse of exigent letters, clearly demonstrates that when surveillance mechanisms are easy to turn on, the chance of misuse is high.

Georgetown University law professor David Cole wrote that "the genius behind the Constitution is precisely the recognition that 'pragmatic' cost-benefit decisions will often appear in the short term to favor actions that may turn out in the long term to be contrary to our own best principles."[5] The founders sought to build a government that would act carefully and deliberately. They wanted to insulate the system from the potential that short-term decisions made in the heat of an "emergency" might limit freedom and justice, perhaps for the long term.[6] The checks and balances built into the U.S. form of government usually work to delay hasty action. This is not to say that during previous times of stress, the government has not acted against the rights of the people; such actions have included the 1798 Alien and Sedition Acts,[7] the suspension of habeas corpus during the Civil War, and the internment of Japanese-American citizens during World War II. The U.S. form of government was deliberately designed to slow such processes down; such a slowdown could cool the heat of the moment and sometimes prevent some of these actions from occurring.

It is easy to imagine that communications surveillance is imperative to the nation's security, but in fact, there is no right more important to democracy than the right of the public to communicate securely. Secure communication underlies freedom and the nation's and the people's security.

There are some who argue that the threat of catastrophic terrorism has changed everything.[8] So it also seemed to the United States during the Civil War, again with the development of modern warfare at the beginning of the last century, and when the Soviet Union acquired nuclear weapons. Building surveillance capabilities into communications infrastructure exposes our society to long-term risks. To establish justice, maintain domestic tranquility, and provide for the common defense, we must ensure that our communications are secure.

Notes

Preface

1. (p. xii) Angela Sasse, "Not Seeing the Crime for the Cameras," *Communications of the ACM* 53, no. 2 (February 2010): 22–25.

Acknowledgments

1. (p. xvi) John McPhee, "Checkpoints: Fact-Checkers Do It a Tick at a Time," *New Yorker*, February 9 and 16, 2009, 57–58.

Chapter 1

1. (p. 1) Whitfield Diffie, "Communications Revolution?", Program 10-94: "Crime and Chaos," KPFA Radio, September 6, 1994.

2. (p. 1) David Kahn, *The Codebreakers: The Comprehensive History of Secret Communication from Ancient Times to the Internet*, rev. ed. (New York: Scribner, 1996), 121–124.

3. (p. 1) Thomas Jefferson, letter to James Thomas Callender, October 6, 1799; in Thomas Jefferson, *The Works of Thomas Jefferson*, Federal ed., vol. 9 (New York: Putnam, 1904), 488.

4. (p. 2) Strong cryptography, meaning cryptography invulnerable to being broken using current technology, is a floating term. In the 1970s, 56-bit DES was considered strong, but since the late 1990s, DES-encrypted content can be easily decrypted through brute-force methods.

5. (p. 2) Customized equipment, especially if the purchaser is a government, continues to require an export license.

6. (p. 2) Stephen Levy, *Crypto: How the Code Warriors Beat the Government—Saving Privacy in the Digital Age* (New York: Viking Press, 2001).

7. (p. 2) Pub. L. 110-055.

8. (p. 2) J. Scott Marcus, affidavit in *Tash Hepting et al. v. AT&T Corporation et al.*, United States Second District Court for Northern California, Case 3:06-cv-0672-vrw, June 8, 2006, 12–15.

9. (p. 3) Steven M. Bellovin, Matt Blaze, Ernie Brickell, Clinton Brooks, Vinton Cerf, Whitfield Diffie, Susan Landau, Jon Peterson, John Treichler, "Security Implications of Applying the Communications Assistance to Law Enforcement Act to Voice over IP" (2006), 9, http://www.cs.columbia.edu/~smb/papers/CALEAVOIPreport.pdf.

10. (p. 3) Vassilis Prevelakis and Diomidis Spinellis, "The Athens Affair," *IEEE Spectrum*, July 2007, 18–25.

11. (p. 3) Alligator clips are spring-loaded clips with serrated jaws.

12. (p. 4) G. H. Johanessen, "Signaling Systems . . . An International Concern," *Bell Labs Record*, January 1970, 18.

13. (p. 4) Johanessen, "Signaling Systems," 13.

14. (p. 4) Railway gauges have become somewhat standardized. The Stephenson gauge, at 4'8 ½" separation, now accounts for about 60 percent of world's railway lines.

15. (p. 4) Johanessen, "Signaling Systems," 14.

16. (p. 5) In April 1963 overseas operators were able to dial directly to England, France, and West Germany. Shortly afterward this was extended to Australia, Belgium, the Netherlands, Italy, Japan, and Switzerland (Johannessen, "Signaling Systems," 14–15).

17. (p. 5) In 1964, the International Telegraph and Telephone Consultative Committee (later known as the International Telecommunications Union) recommended eleven digits as the preferred maximal length for international calls. This is prefixed by digits signaling that the call is international (e.g., "011" when dialing from the United States) (Bell Telephone Laboratories, *Engineering and Operations in the Bell System* (New York: Bell Telephone Laboratories, 1977), 117).

18. (p. 5) Johannessen, "Signaling Systems," 18.

19. (p. 5) A. E. Joel Jr. and other members of technical staff, *A History of Engineering and Science in the Bell System, Switching Technology (1925–1975)*, vol. 3 (New York: The Laboratories, 1982), 193–195.

20. (p. 5) The connection was "acoustical," with the handset of the operator's phone placed in a Carterfone device. The Carterfone switched on a radio transmitter whenever the telephone caller was speaking and returned to receiving mode when the voice stopped (Federal Communications Commission, In the Matter of Use of the Carterfone Device in Message Toll Telephone Service; In the matter of Thomas F. Carter and Carter Electronics Corp., Dallas, Tex. (complainants) v. American Telegraph and Telephone Co., Associated Bell System Companies, Southwestern Bell

Telephone Co., and General Telephone Co. of the Southwest (defendant); Docket No. 16942; Docket No. 17073; 13 F.C.C.2d 420 (1968); 13 Rad. Reg. 2d (P&F) 597; Release-Number: FCC 68–661; June 26, 1968 (adopted)).

21. (p. 5) This period had started with the phone company's interpretation of FCC tariff 132, which stated that "no equipment, apparatus, circuit or device not furnished by the telephone company shall be attached or connected with the facilities furnished by the telephone company, whether physically, by induction, or otherwise." After the Carterfone decision, this regulation was superseded by FCC tariff 263.

22. (p. 5) Federal Communications Commission, In the Matter of Use of the Carterfone Device in Message Toll Telephone Service.

23. (p. 6) Jason Oxman, *The FCC and the Unregulation of the Internet*, OPP Working Paper 31 (Washington, DC: Office of Plans and Policy, Federal Communications Commission, July 1999), 14.

24. (p. 6) David Halbfinger, "In Pellicano Case, Lessons in Wiretapping Skills," *New York Times*, May 5, 2008.

25. (p. 6) Wired How-To Wiki, *Tap a Phone Line*, http://howto.wired.com/wiki/Tap_a_Phone_Line.

26. (p. 6) United States Attorney's Office, Eastern District of Virginia, "Departments of Justice and Homeland Security Announced International Initiative against Traffickers in Counterfeit Network Hardware," February 28, 2008, http://www.justice .gov/criminal/cybercrime/Intl-Initiative.pdf.

27. (p. 6) Raul Roldan, "FBI Criminal Investigation: Cisco Routers," briefing, January 11, 2008.

28. (p. 6) John Markoff, "F.B.I. Says the Military Had Bogus Computer Gear," *New York Times*, May 9, 2008.

29. (p. 7) RFID tags are tiny microchips increasingly used to tag everything from the razors sold in Wal-Mart to U.S. military equipment deployed in a war zone. The tags have a small antenna and respond to a radio signal with their own ID code, alerting the scanner to their location.

30. (p. 7) This is only partially true; see chapter 8 for details.

31. (p. 7) The telephone was invented in 1876, but not until the 1920s was use widespread. The first major use of the telephone by criminals occurred during Prohibition (Ithiel de Sola Pool, Craig Decker, Stephen Dizard, Kay Israel, Pamela Rubin, and Barry Weinstein, "Foresight and Hindsight: The Case of the Telephone," in Ithiel de Sola, ed., *The Social Impact of the Telephone* (Cambridge, MA: MIT Press, 1977), 137). This was a period when law enforcement also found the telephone extremely valuable—but for wiretapping (Samuel Dash, Richard Schwartz, and Robert Knowlton, *The Eavesdroppers* (New Brunswick, NJ: Rutgers University Press, 1959), 28).

32. (p. 7) Widespread public utilization of a technology is also needed for criminals to use the technology; otherwise their usage marks them as "persons of interest" even before they commit an indictable offense.

33. (p. 8) During a 2007 American Bar Association panel discussion, an FBI associate deputy director complained that Skype puts "other people's data on *your* machine." While correct, that observation misses the point that this is core to peer-to-peer technology.

34. (p. 9) William A. Owens, Kenneth W. Dam, and Herbert S. Lin, *Technology, Policy, Law, and Ethics Regarding U.S. Acquisition and Use of Cyberattack Capabilities* (Washington, DC: National Academies Press, 2009), 5, 39.

35. (p. 9) Owens, Dam, and Lin, *Technology, Policy, Law, and Ethics*, 18.

36. (p. 9) In early 2009 Hathaway was appointed to do a sixty-day review of the nation's Internet and cybersecurity strategy.

37. (p. 9) Prepared remarks, 2009 RSA Conference, April 22, 2009.

38. (p. 9) Whitfield Diffie and Susan Landau, *Privacy on the Line: The Politics of Wiretapping and Encryption*, rev. ed. (Cambridge, MA: MIT Press, 2007), 129–131.

39. (p. 9) Diffie and Landau, *Privacy on the Line*, 130.

40. (p. 10) In recent years the courts have not supported unbridled investigations by journalists. During probes over the disclosure that Valerie Plame was a CIA agent, *New York Times* reporter Judith Miller was jailed for several months for refusing to release her sources.

41. (p. 10) *Jacobellis v. Ohio,* 378 U.S. 184, Stewart (concurring).

42. (p. 10) Herbert Danby, *The Mishnah* (Oxford: Oxford University Press, 1933), 233.

43. (p. 10) Samuel Warren and Louis Brandeis, "The Right to Privacy," *Harvard Law Review* IV, no. 5 (December 15, 1890): 193–220.

44. (p. 11) 357 U.S. 449 (1958).

45. (p. 11) 381 U.S. 479 (1965).

46. (p. 11) 410 U.S. 113 (1973).

47. (p. 11) In 1878 in *Ex Parte Jackson,* 96 U.S. 727, the Supreme Court ruled that the government could not open first-class mail without a search warrant.

48. (p. 11) 389 U.S. 347 (1967).

49. (p. 11) Note that this protection is for the contents of the call, not the transactional information of who called who when. Under U.S. law such information has lesser legal protection.

50. (p. 11) *Olmstead v. United States* 277 U.S. 438 (1928).

Chapter 2

1. (p. 13) 700 series.

2. (p. 13) In fact, both Bell and Elisha Grey submitted patent applications for the telephone on the same day; who was actually first remains controversial.

3. (p. 13) The telephone companies that began once Bell's telephone patent lapsed in 1894 did not interconnect their networks. Subscribers had to be on the same network in order to speak (Milton L. Mueller Jr., *Universal Service* (Cambridge, MA: MIT Press, 1997), 43). This led to the situation of households and offices having multiple telephones and multiple networks. Although some of those original companies remain extant to this day, systems interoperate and duplicate phones and networks are no longer needed.

4. (p. 13) Colin Cherry, "The Telephone System: Creator of Mobility and Social Change," in Ithiel de Sola Pool, ed., *The Social Impact of the Telephone* (Cambridge MA: MIT Press, 1977), 115.

5. (p. 13) Cherry, "The Telephone System," 115.

6. (p 13) Anton A. Huudeman, *The Worldwide History of Telecommunications* (Hoboken, NJ: Wiley, 2003), 59–60, 66–83.

7. (p. 14) Paul Starr, *The Creation of the Media: Political Origins of Modern Communications* (New York: Basic Books, 2004), 185.

8. (p. 14) Tom Standage, *The Victorian Internet: The Remarkable Story of the Telegraph and the Nineteenth Century's On-Line Pioneers* (New York: Walker and Company, 1998), 63.

9. (p. 14) Brenda Maddox, "Women and the Switchboard," in Ithiel de Sola Pool, ed., *The Social Impact of the Telephone* (Cambridge MA: MIT Press, 1977), 265–266.

10. (p. 14) The story is that the undertaker, Almon Strowger, did so because he believed that operators were shunting calls to his competitor (Maddox, "Women and the Switchboard," 272).

11. (p. 14) Van Jacobson, *A New Way to Look at Networking*, Google Video, 8:48.

12. (p. 16) In the case of rural areas with low phone usage, these three digits might represent a single town, while in cities the exchange would delineate a neighborhood. Originally names were used to describe these three digits. In the United Kingdom the names delineated the first three digits—thus Scotland Yard was WHItehall 1212 (or 944-1212)—while in the United States the names delineated only the first two digits. Ricky and Lucy Ricardo's number in the television show *I Love Lucy* was MUrray Hill 5–9975 (or 685–9975).

13. (p. 16) Bell Telephone Laboratories, *Engineering and Operations in the Bell System*, 31–38.

14. (p. 16) Katie Hafner and Matthew Lyon, *Where Wizards Stay Up Late: The Origins of the Internet* (New York: Simon and Schuster, 1996), 57; Stewart Brand, "Founding Father," *Wired* 9, no. 3 (2001): 145–153.

15. (p. 16) In practice, various Internet protocols limit maximum hop count to prevent messages from traveling infinite loops and using other unacceptably long routings.

16. (p. 17) Brand, "Founding Father," 149.

17. (p. 17) Brand, "Founding Father," 148.

18. (p. 17) Hafner and Lyon, *Where Wizards Stay Up Late: The Origins of the Internet,* 66.

19. (p. 17) Data traffic transmission patterns are very different from the PSTN pattern, where calls typically peak in midmornings and midafternoons of the business week (and on Mother's Day). The problem of peaks is of great importance to telephone companies, since such information informs pricing plans. Changing demographics and changing technologies have resulted in changing communication patterns, including a burst of traffic as people leave their jobs and announce they are on their way home.

20. (p. 17) Brand, "Founding Father," 149.

21. (p. 18) Brand, "Founding Father," 149.

22. (p. 18) Jacobson, *New Way*, 14:47.

23. (p. 18) Brand, "Founding Father," 149.

24. (p. 18) Hafner and Lyon, *Where Wizards Stay Up Late: The Origins of the Internet,* 67.

25. (p. 18) Brand, "Founding Father," 150.

26. (p. 19) Jacobson, *New Way*, 22:00.

27. (p. 19) There were multiple other responses to Sputnik as well.

28. (p. 19) The idea was an outgrowth of the work of J.C.R. Licklider, who had envisioned a "Galactic" model of interconnected "computers through which everyone could quickly access data and programs from any site" (Barry M. Leiner, Vinton G. Cerf, David D. Clark, Robert E. Kahn, Leonard Kleinrock, Daniel C. Lynch, Jon Postel, Larry G. Roberts, and Stephen Wolff, *A Brief History of the Internet,* version 3.32, December 10, 2003, Internet Society, http://www.isoc.org/internet/history/brief.shtml, 2).

29. (p. 19) In this respect the new network was a sharp break from the telephone network. Susan Crawford characterizes this view of what constitutes the Internet as "the engineers'" view; see Susan Crawford, "Internet Think," *Journal of Telecommunications and High Technology Law* 5, no. 6 (2007): 467–486 for an interesting characterization of the differing views of the Internet on the part of engineers, telcos, and netheads.

30. (p. 19) Leiner et al., *A Brief History of the Internet*, 4.

31. (p. 20) To explain the situation with somewhat more nuance: no network is completely decentralized, but the Internet is remarkably so. There is some centralization but only where it is really necessary (e.g., the DNS system). Otherwise all decisions are local. The PSTN's switches make local decisions from their router tables and, in that sense, also operate in a decentralized way. However, traditionally the PSTN local routing tables were determined by the phone company and this provided the centralized communications model. This difference is in large part due to the fact that the PSTN was a monopoly enterprise for much of its existence, while the Internet has always been an Internet of networks.

32. (p. 20) This can be expanded in various ways, including by connecting Network Address Translation (NAT) boxes to the Internet. These boxes show one address to the Internet but support multiple devices on a local network. NATs are widely used, for example, in home networks.

33. (p. 20) This is done using the Domain Name System, designed by Paul Mockapetris.

34. (p. 20) Routers are not infallible. When they make mistakes, the problems can be quite serious. In 1997 a small Florida ISP broadcast Sprint routes as its own. The Sprint routers added those routes to their tables; other routers followed suit. Soon there were loops in the routing paths, which led to a major breakdown in Internet communications (Javier Salido, Masanori Nakahara, and Yinhai Wang, "An Analysis of Network Reachability Using BGP Data," *Proceedings of the Third IEEE Workshop on Internet Applications* (Piscataway, NJ: IEEE, 2003), 17).

35. (p. 20) Leiner et al., *A Brief History of the Internet*, 6.

36. (p. 20) Andrew Odlyzko, "Content Is Not King," *First Monday* 6, no. 2–5 (February 2001), http://firstmonday.org/htbin/cgiwrap/bin/ojs/index.php/fm/article/view/833/742.

37. (p. 20) It is not surprising that email has such great value: email enables almost instantaneous communication. Unlike a telephone call, it is asynchronous. That asynchrony turns out to be extremely useful: email enables people to jointly make decisions without requiring that they be simultaneously present to do so. Email also leaves a written record, sometimes an advantage (and sometimes not). Human communication had never had a tool quite like this. Even the British post office in its heyday delivered mail only three times a day (Joseph Clarence Hemmeon, *The History of the British Post Office* (Cambridge, MA: Harvard University Press, 1912), 54).

38. (p. 21) Brand, "Founding Father," 151.

39. (p. 21) Jacobson, *New Way*, 29:00.

40. (p. 21) Only members of the military and ARPA contractors could use the ARPANET.

41. (p. 21) Leiner et al., *A Brief History of the Internet*, 7.

42. (p. 21) These were the Cornell National Supercomputer Facility (CNSF), John von Neumann Center (JVNC), National Center for Atmospheric Research (NCAR), National Center for Supercomputer Applications (NCSA) at the University of Illinois, Pittsburgh Supercomputer Center (PSC), and San Diego Supercomputer Center (SDSC).

43. (p. 21) National Science Foundation, "A Brief History of NSF and the Internet," http://www.nsf.gov/news/special reports/cyber/Internet.jsp.

44. (p. 22) National Science Foundation, "A Brief History."

45. (p. 22) National Science Foundation, "The Launch of NSFNET," http://www.nsf .gov/about/history/nsf0050/internet/launch.htm.

46. (p. 22) The expanded network reaches billions more users, is available in thousands more languages, and has millions more applications than NSFNET.

47. (p. 23) This is the level at which the Internet Control Message Protocol (ICMP), which can be used to provide information about network reliability, is located.

48. (p. 24) More precisely, a "mask" is associated with each IP address appearing in a table, indicating which parts of the address are significant for routing purposes. Recall that any IP address with an initial entry of 18 (that is, 18.x.y.z) denotes an address at MIT. A routing-table entry might use an entry of 18.0.0.0 and a mask that indicates that only the 18 is significant for routing. Once the packet reaches MIT, routers there will decide where on campus the packet will go. Those routers, in turn, are likely to use more specific masks on their routing-table entries that subdivide the network by buildings or departments.

49. (p. 24) Committee on the Internet in the Evolving Information Infrastructure, Computer Science and Telecommunications Board, Commission on Physical Sciences, Mathematics, and Applications, National Research Council, *The Internet's Coming of Age* (Washington, DC: National Academy Press, 2001), 36.

50. (p. 25) The other common transport-layer protocol, UDP, neither acknowledges the receipt of packets nor checks if all packets are present (Jon Postel, "RFC768—User Datagram Protocol," August 28, 1980, http://tools.ietf.org/html/rfc768). UDP is faster than TCP but also less reliable. In UDP the decision on what to do about a missing packet is left to the application.

51. (p. 25) There are a number of different algorithms to do this, each with somewhat different behaviors. TCP maintains a congestion window that measures the amount of data sent off but that lacks a "received" acknowledgment. What happens in the popular Tahoe algorithm, for example, is that each time a packet acknowledgment is received by TCP within the congestion window, TCP increases the window size. Thus if packets are flowing nicely, the number of packets sent out per time period doubles. At some point either a preset threshold is reached—in which TCP changes the congestion-window growth to linear—or acknowledgments are no

longer being received within the time window. If the latter happens, TCP halves the size of the congestion window. In this way, TCP is responsive to bandwidth conditions on the portion of the network for its current connection.

52. (p. 26) While it is only recently that cell phones can be used on airplanes, cell phone use on high-speed trains has always been permitted. Originally, however, the calls were dropped as the mobile phones transited the cell towers at high speed. So the cell phone companies added a twist to the algorithm: if a call was quickly passing through transmission towers along the route of a high-speed train, towers along the route would be preallocated to the call to enable it to be transmitted without being dropped (David Nacacche, personal communication, December 19, 2005).

53. (p. 26) Patrick Traynor, Patrick McDaniel, and Thomas La Porta, *Security for Telecommunications Networks* (New York: Springer, 2008), 27.

54. (p. 26) Steven M. Bellovin, Matt Blaze, Ernie Brickell, Clinton Brooks, Vinton Cerf, Whitfield Diffie, Susan Landau, Jon Peterson, John Treichler, "Security Implications of Applying the Communications Assistance for Law Enforcement Act to Voice over IP" (2006), http://www.cs.columbia.edu/~smb/papers/CALEAVOIPreport.pdf, 9.

55. (p. 27) The ISI team used the "Network Voice Protocol" (Danny Cohen, "Specification for the Network Voice Protocol (NVP) and Appendix 1: The Definition of Tables-Set-#1 (for LPC) and Appendix 2: Implementation Recommendations," NSC Note 68, Revision of NSC Notes 26, 40, and 43, NWG/RFC 741, Washington, DC, November 22, 1977).

56. (p. 27) This was later used in the LPC 10, a vocoding technique (a vocoder is a device that takes an analog voice signal and converts it to a digital signal), used by the government in the 1980s.

57. (p. 27) Danny Cohen, personal communication, December 17, 2008.

58. (p. 28) See http://www.skype.com.

59. (p. 28) This is not completely accurate: only clients that are not firewalled, and are thus on publicly routable IP addresses, may be used in the peer-to-peer communication (Skype, "P2P Telephony Explained—For Geeks Only," http://www.skype.com/help/guides/p2pexplained/).

60. (p. 28) Bellovin et al., "Security Implications," 3.

61. (p. 29) Although SMS, or Short Messaging System, is simply one form of texting, the term has come to stand for all forms of text messaging.

62. (p. 29) This channel, SS7, is a "store-and-forward" channel, meaning that if a communication using it does not go through, the message is stored and resent later.

63. (p. 29) The limit is 140 characters, though more modern versions allow longer messages by concatenating several shorter ones.

64. (p. 29) Charles Golvin, *Sizing the U.S. Mobile Messaging Market* (Forrester Research, 2004), 8.

65. (p. 29) Sadie Plant argues that "in much of Pacific Asia, where human interaction and interconnectivity are often more highly prized than any notions about privacy, the mobile is readily welcomed by people who have always liked to feel connected, constantly available, always within reach" (Sadie Plant, *On the Mobile: The Effects of Mobile Telephones on Social and Individual Life,* Motorola, October 2001, 40).

66. (p. 29) Gartner.com, *Gartner Says Mobile Messages to Surpass 2 Trillion Messages in Major Markets in 2008,* December 12, 2007, http://www.gartner.com/it/page.jsp?id=565124.

67. (p. 29) Norimitsu Onishi, "Thumbs Race as Japan's Best Sellers Go Cellular," *New York Times,* January 20, 2008.

68. (p. 29) Tradenet, a west African organization simplifying transborder trading by farmers, provides sellers with a platform to list their location and wares; users receive alerts on prices and information on market conditions via SMS messaging. In banking, SMS is the customer interface of choice at FNB Bank (Rebecca Sausner, "SMS Use Overtakes the Web at FNB," *Bank Technology News,* December 2007, http://www.americanbanker.com/btn_article.html?id=20071127OYQ8GGPT), a multinational bank also operating in Botswana, Lesotho, Mozambique, Namibia, and Swaziland.

69. (p. 30) Michael Bociurkiw, "Revolution by Cell Phone," *Forbes* 168, no. 6 (Fall 2001), http://www.forbes.com/asap/2001/0910/028.html.

70. (p. 30) In June 2007, text messages similarly summoned ten thousand people in Xiamen, China, to the streets to protest construction of a chemical plant; their efforts led to a delay pending further study (Edward Cody, "Text Messages Giving Voice to Chinese: Opponents of Chemical Factory Found Way around Censors," *Washington Post,* June 28, 2007).

71. (p. 30) Indeed, counterintuitively texting can cost more than voice communications. For example, in 2003 Verizon offered a cell plan that charged three hundred peak-time minutes and thirty-two hundred off-peak minutes for voice calls and ten cents per message sent, two cents per message received. As the National Communications System observed, this works out to having eleven hundred three-minute voice calls, or 291 SMS "conversations"—one message sent, one received (Office of the Manager, National Communications System, *SMS over SS7,* NCS Technical Information Bulletin 03-2, December 2003, 3–4). In 2009, AT&T charges its customers twenty cents a message ("AT&T Messaging FAQ," http://www.wireless.att.com/learn/messaging-internet/messaging/faq.jsp#pricing-text). By contrast, in the United Kingdom texting is about one-third the cost of voice calls (Alex Taylor and Jane Vincent, "An SMS History," in Lynne Hamill and Amparo Lassen, eds., *Mobile World: Past, Present, and Future* (New York: Springer, 2005), 84).

72. (p. 30) National Communications System, *SMS over SS7,* 39–41.

73. (p. 30) U.S. Bureau of the Census, *Statistical Abstract of the United States*, 83rd ed. (Washington, DC: U.S. Bureau of the Census, 1962), table 689.

74. (p. 30) U.S. Bureau of the Census, *Statistical Abstract of the United States*, 83rd ed., table 695.

75. (p. 30) U.S. Bureau of the Census, *Statistical Abstract of the United States: 2009,*128th ed. (Washington, DC: U.S. Census Bureau, 2008), table 1110.

76. (p. 30) U.S. Bureau of the Census, *Statistical Abstract of the United States: 2009*, table 1110.

77. (p. 30) CTIA, "Wireless Quick Facts: MidYear Figures," http://www.ctia.org/advocacy/research/index.cfm/AID/10323.

78. (p. 30) Pew Internet & American Life Project Surveys (March 2000–August 2008).

79. (p. 30) CTIA, "Wireless Quick Facts."

80. (p. 31) Jerome H. Saltzer, David P. Reed, and David D. Clark, "End-to-End Arguments in System Design," *ACM Transactions on Computer Systems* 2, no. 1 (November 1984): 278.

81. (p. 31) There are also secure browsers using https (http over an encrypted communications channel).

82. (p. 31) Susan Landau, "National Security on the Line," *Journal of Telecommunications and High Technology Law* 4, no. 2 (Spring 2006): 427.

83. (p. 31) The actual statement is as follows: "In the future, everyone will be world-famous for 15 minutes." (Of course, the issue then becomes: if everyone can be famous, who will be the audience?)

84. (p. 31) Teleconferencing services are possible on the PSTN but take work to arrange. On the Internet, one-to-many and many-to-many applications are readily available.

85. (p. 31) The 2004 Indian Ocean tsunami and 2006 London Underground and bus bombings gave multiple examples of this phenomenon. Descriptions of the events by eyewitnesses and photos by amateurs taken on cell phones appeared on blogs read around the world. These accounts and photos were then picked up by the popular press and were published in such standard news sources as the BBC.

86. (p. 31) In nations such as China and Singapore, where the government tightly controls Internet usage, the population does not have the same social and political freedoms that the Internet enables elsewhere (Shanthi Kalathil and Taylor Boas, *Open Networks, Closed Regimes: The Impact of the Internet on Authoritarian Rule* (Washington, DC: Carnegie Endowment for International Peace, 2003)). Sometimes the modicum of control is self-censorship rather than direct government control. The self-censorship is, of course, in order to avoid a punitive government response.

87. (p. 32) A notable instance occurred in the 2002 resignation of U.S. Senator Trent Lott from his position as Senate majority leader. Lott had made a racist comment at the one hundredth birthday party for former Senator Strom Thurmond. Although the comment was broadcast live by C-SPAN, it was originally ignored by the popular press. Bloggers kept the issue alive (Lawrence Lessig, *Free Culture: How Big Media Uses Technology and the Law to Lock Down Culture and Control Creativity* (New York: Penguin Press, 2004), 43), and the public fallout led to Lott's resignation as Senate majority leader.

88. (p. 32) Christopher Hayes, "MoveOn.org Is Not as Radical as Conservatives Think," *The Nation*, July 16, 2008. MoveOn's origins are a lesson in the power of the Internet. Frustrated by the prospect of Clinton's impeachment, two Silicon Valley entrepreneurs posted an online petition suggesting that Clinton be censured instead. They sent emails to a hundred friends about the petition, which was then mentioned in a *San Francisco Chronicle* news article. The petition quickly received a hundred thousand signatures.

89. (p. 32) Clay Shirky, *Here Comes Everybody: The Power of Organizing without Organization* (New York: Penguin Press, 2008), 143–160.

90. (p. 32) This is Voice of the Faithful.

91. (p. 32) It seems that the value of the network grows proportionally to $n \log n$ (Bob Briscoe, Andrew Odlyzko, and Benjamin Tilly, "Metcalfe's Law Is Wrong," *IEEE Spectrum Online*, July 2006, http://www.spectrum.ieee.org/jul06/4109/4).

92. (p. 32) In fact, the number of interesting groups, groups with more than one person, is $2^n - n - 1$; that is the refined version of Reed's law (David P. Reed, "The Law of the Pack," *Harvard Business Review*, February 2001, 23–24).

93. (p. 32) www.wikipedia.org.

94. (p. 33) Torvalds was developing a kernel for MINIX, an operating system created for academic purposes, to run on the Intel 386 chip.

95. (p. 33) The name *Linux* originally applied only to the operating-system kernel but has since been used to apply to the full operating system.

96. (p. 33) David Wheeler, *More Than a Gigabuck: Estimating GNU/Linux's Size*, July 29, 2002, http://www.dwheeler.com/sloc/redhat71-v1/redhat71sloc.html.

97. (p. 33) Supporting aspects of Linux's success include the GNU General Public License, a copyright license that requires that any derived works be licensed under the same copyright agreement as the original, thus preserving the freedoms of the original work if it is, for example, open source and sharable (Free Software Foundation, "GNU General Public License," http://firstmonday.org/htbin/cgiwrap/bin/ojs/index.php/fm/article/view/1479/1394).

98. (p. 33) Jae Yun Moon and Lee Sproull, "Essence of Distributed Work: The Case of the Linux Kernel," *First Monday*, October 3, 2005, http://firstmonday.org/htbin/cgiwrap/bin/ojs/index.php/fm/article/view/1479/1394.

99. (p. 33) There is an open-source effort in medicine, the Tropical Disease Initiative, which seeks to do open-source drug discovery. Much biological research is computational; a SARS protein was identified by scanning the SARS genome against a database of known proteins (Stephen Maurer, Arti Rai, and Andrej Sali, "Finding Cures for Tropical Diseases: Is Open Source an Answer?", *PLOS Medicine*, December 28, 2004). Given the wealth of publicly accessible biological data, open-source medical research is a real option for the future.

100. (p. 33) Yochai Benkler, *The Wealth of Networks: How Social Production Transforms Markets and Freedom* (New Haven, CT: Yale University Press, 2006), 3.

101. (p. 35) Federal Communications Commission, In the Matters of Formal Complaint of Free Press and Public Knowledge against Comcast Corporation for Secretly Degrading Peer-to-Peer Applications. Broadband Industry Practices Petition of Free Press et al. for Declaratory Ruling that Degrading an Internet Application Violates the FCC's Internet Policy Statement and Does Not Meet an Exception for "Reasonable Network Management," Memorandum Opinion and Order, File No. EB-08-III-1518, WC Docket No. 07–52, August 1, 2008 (adopted), 3.

Chapter 3

1. (p. 37) Cohen developed the first voice-over-the-Internet application.

2. (p. 38) Vinton Cerf and Robert Kahn, "A Protocol for Packet Network Intercommunication," *IEEE Transactions on Communications* 22, no. 5 (May 1974): 637–648.

3. (p. 38) Even six years after the original paper describing TCP/IP, in RFC761—DoD Standard Transmission Control Protocol, an updated version of the TCP specification based on eight earlier versions, the focus remained on robustness (Jon Postel, "RFC761—DoD Standard Transmission Control Protocol," January 1980, http://www.faqs.org/rfcs/rfc761.html).

4. (p. 38) Laura DeNardis, "A History of Internet Security," in Karl De Leeuw and Jan Bergstra, eds., *Handbook of the History of Information Security* (Amsterdam: Elsevier, 2007), 683.

5. (p. 38) This is codified in cryptography as Kerckhoffs' principle.

6. (p. 38) Dennis Jennings, personal communication, March 26, 2009.

7. (p. 39) In the early 1970s, BBN was asked to build packet encryption devices. The resulting devices were huge; they looked like "Darth Vader's refrigerators—black and seven feet tall" (Stephen Kent, personal communication, April 15, 2009).

8. (p. 39) Stephen Kent, personal communication, April 15, 2009.

9. (p. 39) Snow served as Technical Director for NSA's Information Assurance Directorate, one of three major technical components of NSA.

10. (p. 39) Research Day 2007: Interdisciplinary Studies in Information Security, Ecole Polytechnique Fédérale de Lausanne, July 5, 2007.

11. (p. 39) 2600 Hertz (Hz).

12. (p. 39) The user, often called a "phone phreak," either whistled at 2600 Hz or had a "blue box" that did so. The success relied on the fact that a PSTN trunk line would make its availability to transmit a call known by sending out a signal at 2600 Hz to the other lines in the network. The phone phreak would dial an 800 number. The sending end of the trunk line would be engaged and stop sending a 2600 Hz signal down the line. The phone company's accounting system would start the process of charging the call (to the party with the 800 number). But then the phone phreak would whistle a 2600 Hz signal down the line. That causes the far end of the trunk line to assume the user has disconnected and the trunk line stopped the dialing process. Instead, however, the user stopped the 2600 Hz signaling, causing the trunk to again wait for the dialed digits. But now the dialed digits could be anywhere—at least anywhere that was included in the automatic switching system at the time—and not just the expected 800 number. The accounting system is still engaged. Only at the actual end of the call would it make a notation, and that would be to charge the 800 number for the user's call, a call that never engaged the 800 number itself (Ron Rosenbaum, "Secrets of the Little Blue Box," *Esquire,* October 1971).

13. (p. 40) Human speech is often garbled, which is why it has a high level of redundancy. Furthermore, connections go down or become overloaded.

14. (p. 40) http://www.scientificamerican.com/article.cfm?id=magic-and-the-brain.

15. (p. 42) Of course, one could use a laptop's MAC address, the product's registered identification number. These addresses are intended to be globally unique identifiers, but on most current hardware, it is possible to change them. In any case, many computers have multiple users, so knowing the computer does not identify the user.

16. (p. 42) Dennis Jennings, personal communication, March 26, 2009.

17. (p. 43) One of the first British actions at the start of World War I involved cutting the five undersea cables connecting Germany to the rest of the world. Germany was forced to use easily intercepted radio communications, advantaging the British, who had a much larger and reliable wired network (Daniel Headrick, *The Invisible Weapon: Telecommunications and International Politics, 1851–1946* (Oxford: Oxford University Press, 1991), 141).

18. (p. 43) Whitfield Diffie and Susan Landau, *Privacy on the Line: The Politics of Wiretapping and Encryption,* rev. ed. (Cambridge, MA: MIT Press, 2007), 58.

19. (p. 44) The enciphering was really simple. Any alphanumeric message can be written as a string of 0s and 1s (this can be done, for example, by using Morse code, where "a" is 11000, "b" is 10011, etc.). Then the key is also a string of 0s and 1s, and the message is added to the key binary digit by binary digit using "XOR," in which 0+0=1, 1+0=0+1=1, and 1+1=0. The same key and algorithm were used at the other end for decoding, leading back to the original message (Kahn, *The Codebreakers: The Comprehensive History of Secret Communication from Ancient Times to the Internet*, rev. ed., New York: Scribner, 1996, 394–401).

20. (p. 44) In English, for example, the letter *e* appears 13 percent of the time, followed by the letter *t* (9.3 percent), *n* (7.8 percent), *r* (7.7 percent), and so on (Abraham Sinkov, *Elementary Cryptanalysis: A Mathematical Approach* (Washington, DC: Mathematical Association of America, 1966), 177). A more sophisticated approach also relies on the percentage of digraphs—pairs of letters—as well as the frequency with which particular letters appear at the beginning or end of a word to cryptanalyze a message.

21. (p. 44) Kahn, *The Codebreakers*, 394–401.

22. (p. 44) In a single rotor, the wiring between the contacts created a scrambled, but fixed substitution of the letters of the alphabet (e.g., a → D, b → M, c → T, . . . , z → V).

23. (p. 44) After encrypting a single letter, the first rotor would advance a single position, thus employing a new substitution alphabet for encoding the next letter. At that point the rotor machines had an added twist: the second rotor would only advance a position after the first had gone through all of its twenty-six positions, the third, only after the second had passed through all twenty-six of its positions (Kahn, *The Codebreakers*, 411–413). This change meant that the period—the number of letters encrypted before the machine would repeat the same configuration of alphabets was just under seventeen thousand. The four-rotor machines would take about four hundred thousand times before they would repeat the same series of alphabets, thus apparently thwarting frequency analysis.

24. (p. 44) At one point the British attacked a German boat solely to obtain the Enigma encryption keys it was carrying (Kahn, *The Codebreakers*, 977).

25. (p. 44) Ruth Davis, "The Data Encryption Standard in Perspective," *IEEE Communications Magazine* 16, no. 6 (November 1978): 6–7.

26. (p. 45) Whitfield Diffie and Martin Hellman, "Exhaustive Cryptanalysis of the NBS Data Encryption Standard," *IEEE Computer* 10, no. 6 (June 1977): 74–84.

27. (p. 45) If one is decrypting doing a brute-force search of the key space, on average this should take 2^{55} steps.

28. (p. 45) Electronic Frontier Foundation, *Cracking DES Secrets of Encryption Research, Wiretap Politics & Chip Design* (Sebastopol, CA: O'Reilly, 1998).

29. (p. 45) Kahn, *The Codebreakers*, 549–550.

30. (p. 45) Marks, Leo, *Between Silk and Cyanide: A Codemaker's Story 1941–1945* (New York: Free Press, 1998).

31. (p. 45) Whitfield Diffie and Martin Hellman, "New Directions in Cryptography," *IEEE Transactions in Information Theory* IT-22, no. 6 (1976): 644–654.

32. (p. 46) Multiplying two n–digit integers can be done in $n \log n$ steps.

33. (p. 46) Although it is believed that integer factorization has a high time complexity, no one has proved that factoring an integer must take more than a polynomial number of steps.

34. (p. 46) Diffie and Hellman, "New Directions."

35. (p. 46) Diffie and Landau, *Privacy on the Line,* 66–85, 205–206, 219–224, 229–246.

36. (p. 46) "The design and strength of all key lengths of the AES algorithm (i.e., 128, 192 and 256) are sufficient to protect classified information up to the SECRET level. TOP SECRET information will require use of either the 192 or 256 key lengths" (Committee on National Security Systems, National Security Agency, *National Policy on the Use of the Advanced Encryption Standard (AES) to Protect National Security Systems and National Security Information,* Policy No. 15, Fact Sheet No. 1 (Fort Meade, MD: June 2003)).

37. (p. 46) Serving the national-security market would, of course, require not just implementing AES but doing so in an approved implementation.

38. (p. 47) Hashes function as a way to compactly represent longer pieces of data. They are used to check whether data has been altered and for this reason are sometimes called a *digital fingerprint.* A hash is computed of a particular piece of data and compared to the hash of the data computed at a later date. If the two values are equal, with high probability, the data has not been changed. Sun Microsystems uses digital hashes to verify integrity of the binary files of the Solaris operating system; the hashes are available on Sun web pages.

39. (p. 47) Of course, such problems do occur. During the 2008 U.S. presidential election, Republican vice presidential candidate Sarah Palin thought she was speaking with French President Nicolas Sakozy. In fact, she was conversing with two Quebec comedians (who had previously done similar things to other public figures).

40. (p. 47) John Markoff, "'Virus' in Military Networks Disrupts Systems Nationwide," *New York Times,* November 4, 1988.

41. (p. 48) Morris was convicted of violating the Computer Fraud and Abuse Act and was sentenced to three years probation and a $10,000 fine.

42. (p. 48) John Markoff, "Author of Computer 'Virus' Is Son of N.S.A. Expert on Data Security," *New York Times,* November 5, 1988.

43. (p. 48) Hilarie Orman, "The Morris Worm: A Fifteen-Year Perspective," *IEEE Security and Privacy* 1, no. 5, (September/October 2003): 35.

44. (p. 48) As per note 41, Morris was convicted of violating the Computer Fraud and Abuse Act of 1986 (18 U.S.C. §1830) and sentenced to four hundred hours of community service and a fine of $10,000. The worm's effect on the Internet was indirect, but lasting; within a few years many organizations had barriers such as firewalls between their private networks and the public one (Steve Crocker, "Operational Security," in Daniel Lynch and Marshall Rose, eds., *Internet System Handbook* (Reading, MA: Addison-Wesley, 1993), 679).

45. (p. 48) Such routing misconfigurations may be propagated by accident; see note 34 in chapter 2.

46. (p. 49) Paul Mockapetris, "RFC 882—Domain Names: Concepts and Facilities," November 1983, http://tools.ietf.org/html/rfc882; "RFC 883—Domain Names: Implementation and Specification," November 1983, http://tools.ictf.org/html/rfc883.

47. (p. 49) Zones are a tree structure, with a root at the top that points to its *children*.

48. (p. 49) There is additional redundancy through replication: root servers and their IP addresses may name multiple physical servers around the world.

49. (p. 51) This is called time to live, or TTL.

50. (p. 51) It may pick the next one on its list, it may choose randomly, or it may do something else entirely.

51. (p. 51) Google maintains its own DNS servers, but many zones do not. Instead their ISPs provide the authoritative information for them.

52. (p. 51) The Google nameservers are ns1.google.com, ns2.google.com, etc.

53. (p. 51) The .com nameservers are a.gtld-servers.net., b.gtld-servers.net, etc.

54. (p. 51) The root servers are A.ROOT-SERVERS.NET, B.ROOT-SERVERS.NET, etc.

55. (p. 51) Steven M. Bellovin, "Using the Domain Name System for System Break-Ins," *Proceedings of the Fifth USENIX UNIX Security Symposium* (Berkeley, CA USENIX, 1995).

56. (p. 52) David Dagon, Chris Lee, Wenke Lee, and Niels Provos, "Corrupted DNS Resolution Paths: The Rise of a Malicious Resolution Authority," *Proceedings of the 15th Network and Distributed System Security Symposium (NDSS)* (Reston, VA: Internet Society, 2008).

57. (p. 52) Dagon et al., "DNS Resolution Paths."

58. (p. 52) Dagon et al., "DNS Resolution Paths."

59. (p. 52) There have been incidents in which criminals set up fake ATMs to steal users' passwords. Subsequently the criminals used counterfeit bankcards with account numbers and corresponding passwords and accessed the customer accounts at a real ATM.

60. (p. 52) This is actually an intrusion, not an attack.

61. (p. 52) Cisco, "Cisco Security Advisory: Malformed SNMP Message-Handling Vulnerabilities Document ID: 19294," Advisory ID: cisco-sa-20020212-snmp-msgs. Most router attacks focus on Cisco equipment for the same reason that most operating-system attacks are on Microsoft Windows. Cisco supplies well over half the routers used in the Internet.

62. (p. 53) If one network is larger than the other, the smaller network typically pays the larger one in order to be able to send communications over, or transit, the larger network.

63. (p. 54) Viruses had been developed in computer labs, but this was the first one "in the wild."

64. (p. 54) The Melissa virus affected machines running Microsoft Word 97 and Word 2000, as well as various versions of Microsoft Excel. Once the attachment was opened, the virus emailed itself to the first fifty addresses in the client's Microsoft Outlook address book. The ILOVEYOU virus also acted on the Windows operating system and also self-replicated by sending itself to *all* addresses in the client's Outlook address book.

65. (p. 54) Niels Provos, Dean McNamee, Panayiotis Mavrommatis, Ke Wang, and Nagendra Modadugu, "The Ghost in the Browser: Analysis of Web-Based Malware," *First Workshop on Hot Topics in Understanding Botnets (HotBots '07)* (Berkeley, CA: USENIX, 2007).

66. (p. 55) According to software safety expert Nancy Leveson, the shuttle code is about two hundred thousand lines of code. By contrast, the Boeing 777 airplane has five million lines of code, while the Linux operating system is over six million lines long and Microsoft's Vista operating system is even larger.

Leveson described NASA as heavily investing in the code correctness. In the mid-1990s, Leveson chaired a committee examining NASA's software processes. At the time, the agency was spending $100 million a year maintaining the code; it is undoubtedly spending even more today. The resulting software is highly successful—even if not fully error free (Nancy Leveson, personal communication, April 22, 2009).

67. (p. 55) The blocking is done through closing the "port" number through which the application travels.

68. (p. 55) This has been done several times by the Chinese government after protests in Tibet were shown on the video-sharing site.

69. (p. 55) James Fallows, "The Connection Has Been Reset," *Atlantic Monthly Online*, March 2008, http://www.theatlantic.com/doc/200803/chinese-firewall.

70. (p. 55) Open Net Initiative, "Telus Blocking of Labor Union Web Site Filters 766 Unrelated Sites," *Open Initiative Bulletin 010*, August 2005, http://opennet.net/bulletins/010/ONI-010-telus.pdf.

71. (p. 56) Van Jacobson, *A New Way to Look at Networking*, Google Video, 40:39.

72. (p. 56) Jonathan Zittrain, "The Generative Internet," *Harvard Law Review* 119 (2006): 1980.

73. (p. 56) There is an ongoing effort to create a legal system that enables such sharing. Creative Commons offers licenses that allow creators—artists, scientists, engineers—to delineate the restrictions that apply to the shared use of their content (e.g., "Attribution required," "No commercial reuse," etc.). Content licensed under Creative Commons license is allowed to be shared, but the creator can limit usage in certain ways; see http://www.creativecommons.org for more details.

74. (p. 57) Skype, "P2P Telephony Explained—For Geeks Only," http://www.skype .com/help/guides/p2pexplained/.

75. (p. 57) U.S. Congress, House of Representatives, House Committee on Oversight and Government Reform, *Inadvertent File Sharing over Peer-to-Peer Networks: Hearing before the Committee on Oversight and Government Reform, One Hundred and Tenth Congress, First Session, July 24, 2007,* Serial 110–39, 2.

76. (p. 57) The latter is already true in some countries. In Italy, for example, users in Internet cafés are required to show identification before being allowed to log on.

77. (p. 58) One could use an "overlay" anonymizing network such as Tor (short for "The onion routing").

78. (p. 58) Jeffrey Hunker, Bob Hutchinson, and Jonathan Margulies, *Role and Challenges for Sufficient Cyber-Attack Attribution* (January 2008) Hanover, NH: Institute for Infrastructure Protection, Dartmouth College.

79. (p. 58) T. Matsumoto, H. Matsumoto, K. Yamada, and S. Hoshino, "Impact of Artificial 'Gummy' Fingers on Fingerprint Systems," *Proceedings of SPIE,* vol. 4677, Optical Security and Counterfeit Deterrence Techniques IV (2002) San Jose, CA: SPIE.

80. (p. 58) One company that does this is Akamai; although it may look as if the IP address is cnn.com, in fact the IP address points to an Akamai server with the CNN content. This server is close to the user (where "close" is defined by network connectivity). Companies use Akamai to speed content delivery to their customers.

81. (p. 59) Siobhan Gorman, "Electricity Grid in U.S. Penetrated by Spies," *Wall Street Journal,* April 8, 2009.

82. (p. 59) Diffie and Landau, *Privacy on the Line,* 45–46.

83. (p. 59) See chapter 7 for a discussion of Soviet interception in Glen Cove, Long Island, and Washington, as well as in Lourdes, Cuba. The Lourdes station was capable of picking up satellite transmissions to locations all along the U.S. East Coast. The San Francisco trunk line was protecting communication from Lockheed Martin, which was working on the Poseidon missile.

84. (p. 60) One solution is Tor, an overlay network running on top of the Internet. This provides anonymity. It is discussed in chapter 6.

85. (p. 62) Meredith Baker, Acting Assistant Secretary for Communications and Information National Telecommunications and Information Administration, letter to Peter Dengate Thrush, "Public Comments: Improving Institutional Confidence in ICANN," http://www.ntia.doc.gov/comments/2008/ICANN_080730.html.

86. (p. 62) A signature guarantee is an authentication of your signature. It is usually performed at an authorized financial institution. Signature guarantees are considered more reliable than notarized signatures.

87. (p. 62) There are corresponding complexities in the infrastructure as well: at least for many states, the only infrastructure needed is that the notary files a form with the state and pays a fee, while signature guarantees require that the financial institution participates in a signature guarantee program.

88. (p. 62) This attack was discovered by Dan Kaminsky, who attempted to have patches installed in the DNS nameservers before the attack became publicly known. This did not happen, but most nameservers were patched fairly quickly after the vulnerability was made public.

The idea behind the attack is simple: set up a hacked DNS nameserver that stores bad IP addresses for various sites—that is, false addresses where the users can then be fooled into releasing valuable information (such as account numbers and passwords). Because the DNS protocol was set up to allow a response to a DNS query to return not only the IP address that was requested, but additional IP addresses for other sites, once the hacked DNS nameserver was queried, it would spread the false IP addresses to legitimate DNS nameservers, which would then cache them (David Schneider, "Fresh Phish," http://www.spectrum.ieee.org/print/6818).

89. (p. 62) J. Loughney, ed., *RFC 4294: IPv6 Node Requirements*, RFC 4294, April 2006, http://tools.ietf.org/html/rfc4294.

90. (p. 62) S. Kent and S. Seo, *RFC 4301: Security Architecture for the Internet Protocol*, December 2005, http://tools.ietf.org/html/rfc4301; R. Housely, *RFC 4309: Using Advanced Encryption Standard (AES) CCM Mode with IPsec Encapsulating Security Payload (ESP)*, December 2005, http://tools.ietf.org/html/rfc4309.

91. (p. 63) Sheila Frankel and David Green, "Internet Protocol Version 6," *IEEE Security and Privacy* 6, no. 3 (May/June 2008): 85.

92. (p. 63) Marjory Blumenthal and David D. Clark, "Rethinking the Design of the Internet: The End-to-End Arguments vs. the Brave New World," *ACM Transactions on Internet Technology* 1, no. 1 (August 2001): 70–109.

Chapter 4

1. (p. 65) 18 USC §2510–2521.

2. (p. 66) James Otis, "Against Writs of Assistance," February 1761.

3. (p. 66) 1 Stat. 232.

4. (p. 66) Whitfield Diffie and Susan Landau, *Privacy on the Line: The Politics of Wiretapping and Encryption*, rev. ed. (Cambridge, MA: MIT Press, 2007), 145–146.

5. (p. 66) *Ex Parte Jackson*, 96 U.S. 727, 733.

6. (p. 66) Heros von Borcke, *Memoirs of the Confederate War for Independence* (New York: P. Smith, 1938), 168.

7. (p. 66) Samuel Dash, Richard Schwartz, and Robert Knowlton, *The Eavesdroppers* (New Brunswick, NJ: Rutgers University Press, 1959), 25.

8. (p. 66) Dash, Schwartz, and Knowlton, *The Eavesdroppers*, 28.

9. (p. 67) *Olmstead v. United States*, 455–456.

10. (p. 67) Diffie and Landau, *Privacy on the Line*, 148–150.

11. (p. 67) Louis Brandeis, dissenting opinion in *Olmstead v. United States*, 475–476.

12. (p. 67) Pub. L. 416.

13. (p. 67) *Nardone v. United States*, 302 U.S. 379 (1937).

14. (p. 68) *Nardone v. United States*, 308 U.S. 338 (1939).

15. (p. 68) *Silverthorne Lumber Co., Inc. v. United States*, 251 U.S. 385 (1920).

16. (p. 68) *Weiss v. United States*, 302 U.S. 321 (1939).

17. (p. 68) U.S. Congress, Senate, Select Committee to Study Governmental Operations with Respect to Intelligence Activities, *Final Report of the Select Committee to Study Governmental Operations with Respect to Intelligence Activities: Supplementary Detailed Staff Reports on Intelligence Activities and the Rights of Americans: Book III*, Report 94-755 (Washington, DC: Government Printing Office, April 23, 1976), 278.

18. (p. 68) Franklin Delano Roosevelt, memo to Attorney General Jackson, May 21, 1940, in U.S. Congress, Senate, Select Committee to Study Governmental Operations with Respect to Intelligence Activities, *Final Report: Book III*, 279.

19. (p. 68) In the 1946 reauthorization request to President Truman, the limitation to aliens was removed (Tom Clark, letter to the president, July 17, 1946, in U.S. Congress, Senate, Select Committee to Study Governmental Operations with Respect to Intelligence Activities, *Final Report: Book III*, 282). It is unknown who removed that requirement: Attorney General Tom Clark or FBI Director J. Edgar Hoover.

20. (p. 68) U.S. Congress, Senate, Select Committee to Study Governmental Operations with Respect to Intelligence Activities, *Final Report: Book III*, 343.

21. (p. 68) One such case was that of Judith Coplon, a DoJ employee who was caught as she was about to give twenty-eight confidential FBI files to a Soviet UN employee.

Coplon's trial was dismissed after it was revealed that the FBI had been wiretapping her (Edward Ranzal, "Coplon Conviction Voided on Appeal: Court Declares Her 'Guilt Is Plain' in Spy Case but FBI Used Illegal Methods," *New York Times*, December 6, 1950).

22. (p. 68) This includes Martin Luther King, Ralph Abernathy, the Student Non-Violent Coordinating Committee, and the Jewish Defense League (U.S. Congress, Senate, Select Committee to Study Governmental Operations with Respect to Intelligence Activities, *Final Report of the Select Committee to Study Governmental Operations with Respect to Intelligence Activities: Supplementary Detailed Staff Reports on Intelligence Activities and the Rights of Americans: Book II*, Report 94-755 (Washington, DC: Government Printing Office, April 23, 1976), 105).

23. (p. 68) U.S. Congress, Senate, Select Committee to Study Governmental Operations with Respect to Intelligence Activities, *Final Report: Book III*, 320.

24. (p. 68) U.S. Congress, Senate, Select Committee to Study Governmental Operations with Respect to Intelligence Activities, *Final Report: Book III*, 339–340; *Final Report: Book II*, 63.

25. (p. 68) Athan Theoharis, "FBI Wiretapping: A Case Study of Bureaucratic Autonomy," *Political Science Quarterly* 107, no. 1 (Spring 1992): 108–109; U.S. Congress, Senate, Select Committee to Study Governmental Operations with Respect to Intelligence Activities, *Final Report, Book III*.

26. (p. 68) The latter list includes Supreme Court Justices Hugo Black, Stanley Reed, William O. Douglas, Abe Fortas, and Potter Stewart (Alexander Charns, *Cloak and Gavel: FBI Wiretaps, Bugs, Informers, and the Supreme Court* (Urbana: University of Illinois Press, 1992), 17, 25, 87; J. Edgar Hoover, Letter to H. R. Haldeman, June 25, 1970, in U.S. Congress, Senate, Select Committee to Study Governmental Operations with Respect to Intelligence Activities, *Final Report: Book III*, 345). The list also includes the clerk for the House of Representatives Committee on Agriculture (*Final Report: Book III*, 64) as well as members of the Nixon administration. Many of the taps that occurred during the Nixon administration were at the request of the president.

27. (p. 68) FBI files included transcripts of an affair during World War II that John Kennedy had with a woman briefly suspected of being a German spy. These files were transferred to Hoover's office on July 14, 1960, the day after Kennedy won the Democratic nomination for president (Theoharis, "FBI Wiretapping," 111).

28. (p. 69) Diffie and Landau, *Privacy on the Line*, 185–186.

29. (p. 69) U.S. Congress, Senate, Select Committee to Study Governmental Operations with Respect to Intelligence Activities, *Final Report: Book III*, 173–174.

30. (p. 69) U.S. Congress, Senate, Select Committee to Study Governmental Operations with Respect to Intelligence Activities, *Final Report: Book III*, 123.

31. (p. 69) U.S. Congress, Senate, Select Committee to Study Governmental Operations with Respect to Intelligence Activities, *Final Report: Book III*, 326.

32. (p. 69) This was the wiretapping of a well-connected Washington lobbyist: Thomas Corcoran.

33. (p. 70) 316 U.S. 129 (1942).

34. (p. 70) 347 U.S. 128 (1954).

35. (p. 70) 365 U.S. 505 (1961).

36. (p. 70) 389 U.S. 347 (1967).

37. (p. 70) *Charles Katz v. United States*, 349.

38. (p. 70) *Charles Katz v. United States*, 352.

39. (p. 70) *Charles Katz v. United States*, 359.

40. (p. 70) Six months earlier the Court examined *Berger v. New York*, 388 U.S. 41 (1967), in which state-authorized wiretaps formed an important part of the evidence. The Court found the New York statute insufficiently "precise and discriminate" in granting warrants and reversed the conviction. The ruling was a clear hint that a sufficiently "precise and discriminate" warrant procedure for wiretapping would be constitutionally acceptable.

41. (p. 71) Diffie and Landau, *Privacy on the Line*, 131.

42. (p. 71) Diffie and Landau, *Privacy on the Line*, 132.

43. (p. 71) Steven M. Bellovin, Matt Blaze, Ernie Brickell, Clinton Brooks, Vinton Cerf, Whitfield Diffie, Susan Landau, Jon Peterson, John Treichler, "Security Implications of Applying the Communications Assistance for Law Enforcement Act to Voice over IP" (2006), http://www.cs.columbia.edu/~smb/papers/CALEAVOIPreport.pdf, 5.

44. (p. 72) If the subscriber has caller ID, then the *numbers* of the calling parties would be available to the wiretap; the content *would not* be (Bellovin et al., "Security Implications," 5).

45. (p. 72) Electronic Switching System #4. This is AT&T's major toll switch that can handle 130 thousand trunk lines (trunk lines connect telephone switchboards). This switch was introduced in 1976 and is still the way most long-distance calls are handled in the United States.

46. (p. 73) Diffie and Landau, *Privacy on the Line*, 190–192.

47. (p. 73) *Sneak-and-peek* warrants, authorized under §213 of the 2001 USA PATRIOT Act, allow law enforcement officers to surreptitiously search private areas (e.g., a home, a car, an office) for evidence without notice. Law enforcement is not allowed to seize property but can take photographs, which may be used to apply for a regular

search warrant. The suspect is informed about the sneak-and-peek warrant after the search has occurred.

48. (p. 73) The 2006 German film, *The Lives of Others,* captures that aspect extremely well.

49. (p. 73) These included President John Kennedy in 1963, Malcolm X in 1965, and Martin Luther King Jr. and presidential candidate Robert Kennedy in 1968.

50. (p. 73) 18 U.S.C. §2510–2521 (1968).

51. (p. 74) The law originally listed twenty-six such crimes. The law has been amended several times, and the number of crimes for which a wiretap warrant can be obtained now stands at just under one hundred.

52. (p. 74) §2518 (3)(a–d). Wiretaps need not be the "last resort" for investigators, but must be close to that standard. The Department of Justice manual on conducting electronic surveillance states, "The application for a Title III order also (1) must show that normal investigative procedures have been tried and failed, or that they reasonably appear to be unlikely to succeed or to be too dangerous" (U.S. Department of Justice, Computer Crime and Intellectual Property Section, Criminal Division, *Searching and Seizing Computers and Obtaining Electronic Evidence in Criminal Investigations,* July 2002).

53. (p. 74) If a warrant was not obtained within the forty-eight hours, then the intercepted information could not be used in evidence (or even divulged, as per the *Nardone* decision) (*Omnibus Crime Control and Safe Streets Act* §515).

54. (p. 74) Administrative Office of the United States Courts, James C. Duff, Director, *2009 Wiretap Report,* 25.

55. (p. 74) Administrative Office of the United States Courts, James C. Duff, Director, *2009 Wiretap Report,* 7.

56. (p. 74) Wiretap applications for criminal investigations at the federal level must be approved by a member of the Department of Justice at least at the level of deputy assistant attorney general; orders submitted by state investigators need approval by the "principal prosecuting attorney of [the] state, or the principal prosecuting attorney of the political subdivision thereof." The latter was most recently codified in the 1986 Electronic Communications Privacy Act 45, 18 U.S.C. §2516(2)).

57. (p. 74) In the case of multiple crimes being investigated, the most serious one is listed.

58. (p. 74) This resulted in a change in the market, with most companies no longer offering products with weak cryptography.

59. (p. 74) Diffie and Landau, *Privacy on the Line,* 192–193.

60. (p. 74) U.S. Congress, House of Representatives, Subcommittee No. 5, *Anti-Crime Program,* Hearings on HR 5037, 5038, 5384, 5385, and 5386, March 15, 16, 22, 23, April 5, 7, 10, 12, 19, 20, 26, and 27, 1967, Ninetieth Congress, First Session, 545, 547, 554, and 560.

61. (p. 75) U.S. Congress, House of Representatives, Subcommittee No. 5, *Anti-Crime Program*, Hearings on HR 5037, 5038, 5384, 5385, and 5386, March 15, 16, 22, 23, April 5, 7, 10, 12, 19, 20, 26, and 27, 1967, Ninetieth Congress, First Session, 545, 547, 554, and 560, 320.

62. (p. 75) *Congressional Quarterly Weekly* 25, Washington, DC, February 10, 1967, 222.

63. (p. 75) 407 U.S. 297 (1972).

64. (p. 75) William Funk, "Electronic Surveillance of Terrorism: The Intelligence/Law Enforcement Dilemma—a History," *Lewis and Clark Law Review* 11, no. 4 (2007): 1105.

65. (p. 75) The tools involved include open-source intelligence, operations intelligence, human intelligence (HUMINT), signals intelligence (SIGINT), photo intelligence (PHOTINT), measurement and signatures intelligence (MASINT), and communications intelligence (COMINT) (Diffie and Landau, *Privacy on the Line*, 88–93).

66. (p. 76) Funk, "Electronic Surveillance of Terrorism," 1116–1117.

67. (p. 76) These are, respectively, Robert Woodward and Carl Bernstein, John Sirica, Sam Ervin, and Samuel Dash.

68. (p. 77) U.S. Congress, Senate, "A Resolution to Establish a Committee to Study Government Operations with Respect to Intelligence," Senate Resolution 21, Ninety-Fourth Congress, First Session, 1975.

69. (p. 77) U.S. Congress, Senate, Select Committee to Study Governmental Operations with Respect to Intelligence Activities, *Final Report: Book II*, 291.

70. (p. 77) 50 U.S.C. 1801 *et seq*

71. (p. 77) In 2004 this was extended to allow a FISA tap if the target was believed to be a "lone wolf" engaging in international terrorism even if not a member of a recognized group (Intelligence Reform and Terrorism Prevention Act, Pub. L. No. 108–458).

72. (p. 77) §1802(a).

73. (p. 78) §1805(f).

74. (p. 78) §1805(a)(3)(A).

75. (p. 78) For FISA, these are assistant to the president for national security and other national security or defense executive branch officials designated by the president. The latter are typically the FBI director for FBI applications and the secretary or deputy secretary of defense for applications originating at the NSA (David Kris, *Modernizing the Foreign Intelligence Surveillance Act*, Working Paper of the Series on Counterterrorism and American Statutory Law, a joint project of the Brookings Institution, the Georgetown University Law Center, and the Hoover Institution, 493–494).

76. (p. 78) In 2008, 2, 083 were approved and none denied. Two needed changes (Ronald Weich, assistant attorney general, letter to Senate Majority Leader Harry Reid, May 14, 2009).

77. (p. 78) The requirement is not explicit in the law, which says only that "the purpose of the surveillance is to obtain foreign intelligence information" (§1804(a) (7)(B)). However, this formulation appears in the history of the bill as well as in a series of court cases that uphold this interpretation (Funk, "Electronic Surveillance of Terrorism," 1112–1123).

78. (p. 79) 425 U.S. 435 (1976).

79. (p. 79) *Miller v. United States*, 440.

80. (p. 79) 442 U.S. 735 (1979).

81. (p. 79) *Miller v. United States*, 443.

82. (p. 79) Daniel Solove and Marc Rotenberg, *Information Privacy Law* (New York: Aspen, 2003), 305.

83. (p. 80) Pub. L. 99-508; 18 U.S.C. §2510.

84. (p. 80) Kenneth Dam and Herbert Lin, *Cryptography's Role in Securing the Information Society* (Washington, DC: National Academy Press, 1996), 397.

85. (p. 80) The "electronic communication" definition also excluded tone-only paging devices, communications from tracking devices, and electronic funds transfer (§2510(12)).

86. (p. 80) There was an exception if they were voice communications partially carried by radio and partially by wire or switches, in which case they were considered wire communications.

87. (p. 81) 18 U.S.C. §2518(4).

88. (p. 81) U.S. Congress, House of Representatives, Committee on the Judiciary, *Telecommunications Carrier Assistance to the Government: Report Together with Additional Views (to accompany H.R. 4922)*, One Hundred and Third Congress, Second Session, Report 103-827, Part 1 (October 4, 1994), 15.

89. (p. 81) U.S. Department of Justice, Federal Bureau of Investigation, "Benefits and Costs of Legislation to Ensure the Government's Continued Capability to Investigate Crime with the Implementation of New Telecommunication Technologies," in David Banisar, ed., *1994 Cryptography and Privacy Sourcebook: Documents on Wiretapping, Cryptography, the Clipper Chip, Key Escrow, and Export Controls* (Upland, PA: Diane Publishing Co., 1994).

90. (p. 81) There were two different ways that doubts were cast in the claims. See Betsy Anderson and Todd Buchholz, "Memo for Jim Jukes," May 22, 1992; in Banisar,

1994 Cryptography and Privacy Sourcebook, and Diffie and Landau, *Privacy on the Line*, 218–219.

91. (p. 81) Speech by FBI Director Louis Freeh to the Executives' Club of Chicago, February 17, 1994.

92. (p. 81) Diffie and Landau, *Privacy on the Line*, 219–220.

93. (p. 81) U.S. General Accounting Office, Briefing Report to the Chairman, Subcommittee on Telecommunications and Finance, Committee on Energy and Commerce, House of Representatives, *FBI: Advanced Telecommunications Technologies Pose Wiretapping Challenges*, July 1992.

94. (p. 81) U.S. Congress, *Telecommunications Carrier Assistance*, 17.

95. (p. 82) U.S. Congress, *Telecommunications Carrier Assistance*, 17.

96. (p. 82) Pub. L. 103-414; 47 U.S.C. 1001 *et seq.*

97. (p. 82) U.S. Congress, *Telecommunications Carrier Assistance*, 18.

98. (p. 82) Pub. L. 103-414, §107 (a)(1).

99. (p. 82) Such documents often guide court decisions on the intent of legislation.

100. (p. 82) U.S. Congress, *Telecommunications Carrier Assistance*, 20.

101. (p. 82) Administrative Office of the United States Courts, *Wiretap Report* (Washington, DC: Government Printing Office, 1994); Diffie and Landau, *Privacy on the Line*, 221.

102. (p. 82) Diffie and Landau, *Privacy on the Line*, 222–223.

103. (p. 84) *United States Telecom Association v. FCC* (277 F.3d 450 D.C. Cir. 2000). The case was against the FCC because that agency was in charge of setting the actual regulations and determining service-provider compliance.

104. (p. 84) Federal Communications Commission, In the matter of Communications Assistance for Law Enforcement Act, CC Docket No. 97-213, Order on Remand (adopted: April 5, 2002), 34.

105. (p. 84) Pub. L. 103-414, §103(a)(2)(B).

106. (p. 84) U.S. Department of Justice, Office of the Inspector General, Audit Division, *The Implementation of the Communications Assistance for Law Enforcement Act by the Federal Bureau of Investigation*, Audit Report 08-20, March 2008, 4.

107. (p. 84) U.S. Department of Justice, Office of the Inspector General, Audit Division, *Implementation of the Communications Assistance for Law Enforcement Act*, 16.

108. (p. 84) Freeh said, "Well, the computer companies would widen that hole. You're correct, we are excluding them, excluding them for a couple of reasons; one, to narrow the impact and focus of the legislation. We could have incorporated in

there [sic], as we did in the proposal two years ago, which was rejected out of hand" (U.S. Congress, Senate, Technology and Law Subcommittee of the Senate Judiciary Committee, and House of Representatives, Civil and Constitutional Rights Subcommittee of the House Judiciary Subcommittee of the House Judiciary Committee, and House of Representatives, *Wiretapping: Joint Hearing*, One Hundred and Third Congress, Second Session (March 18, 1994)).

109. (p. 84) §103(b)(2)(A).

110. (p. 84) Specifically, in §102(8), CALEA says that the term "'telecommunications carrier'—(A) means a person or entity engaged in the transmission or switching of wire or electronic communications as a common carrier for hire; and (B) includes– (i) a person or entity engaged in providing commercial mobile service (as defined in section 332(d) of the Communications Act of 1934 (47 U.S.C. 332(d))); or (ii) a person or entity engaged in providing wire or electronic communication switching or transmission service to the extent that the Commission finds that such service is a replacement for a substantial portion of the local telephone exchange service and that it is in the public interest to deem such a person or entity to be a telecommunications carrier for purposes of this title; but (C) does not include– (i) persons or entities insofar as they are engaged in providing information services; and (ii) any class or category of telecommunications carriers that the Commission exempts by rule after consultation with the Attorney General."

111. (p. 85) *American Council of Education v. Federal Communications Commission*, 371 U.S. App. D.C. 307; 451 F.3d 226; 2006 U.S. App., Edwards, dissenting.

112. (p. 85) Federal Communications Commission, Enforcement Bureau, "Enforcement Bureau Outlines Requirements of November 28, 2005 Interconnected Voice Over Internet Protocol 911 Compliance Letters WC Docket No. 04-36 WC Docket No. 05-196" (November 7, 2005). The VoIP provider had to do this or else inform their customer of their inability to do so.

113. (p. 85) Neil King Jr. and Ted Bridis, "FBI Wiretaps to Scan E-Mail Spark Concern," *Wall Street Journal*, July 11, 2000.

114. (p. 85) As with CALEA, the device had been designed by the government rather than the ISPs. The latter include user privacy as part of their business model.

115. (p. 85) This was EarthLink. This dispute caused Carnivore's existence to come to light (Diffie and Landau, *Privacy on the Line*, 382, note 30).

116. (p. 85) Beryl Howell, "Seven Weeks: The Making of the USA PATRIOT Act," *George Washington Law Review* 72 (August 2004): 1153.

117. (p. 86) Despite strong concerns in the summer of 2001 that Al-Qaeda was poised to attack the United States, the CIA was slow to inform the FBI of the U.S. presence of two suspected terrorists (National Commission on Terrorist Attacks upon the United States, *The 9/11 Commission Report: Final Report of the National Commission*

on Terrorist Attacks upon the United States (New York: Norton, 2004), 269–272). A Phoenix FBI agent wrote FBI headquarters about a possible Bin Laden effort to send people to train in U.S. aviation schools, noting an unexpected number of "individuals of investigative interest" doing so (p. 273). The FBI discovered a suspicious individual "with little knowledge of flying" seeking to learn how to take off and land Boeing 747s, but the suspect's background, which included clear connections to Al-Qaeda, was not adequately probed (p. 273). No one "put the dots together" and the plan was not averted.

118. (p. 86) Howell, "Seven Weeks," 1148.

119. (p. 86) Howell, "Seven Weeks," 1159–1161. It took thirty days for a bill to pass the Senate, thirty-one for the House of Representatives (p. 1173). Normally there would have been a conference between the legislative bodies to reconcile the bills, but with Democrat Senator Patrick Leahy chairing the meeting and other liberal senators likely to attend, House Republicans maneuvered to prevent that conference. A Senate staff member observed that ironically the resulting bill, which included portions of the House version, was more protective of civil liberties than the Senate's version of the bill had been (Howell, "Seven Weeks," 1174–1177).

120. (p. 86) This section also required that the court that issued the order have jurisdiction over the case, and made explicit that laws governing pen registers and trap-and-trace devices exclude the interception of communication content. In addition, it required that if a wiretapping device was installed by law enforcement (as was the case with Carnivore), it must provide an audit trail of who accessed the device, what the configuration was at the time of operation, and what data was collected.

121. (p. 86) Such permission was needed because the computer owner was not part of the communication and therefore could not simply grant permission.

122. (p. 86) Howell, "Seven Weeks," 1997.

123. (p. 86) Daniel A. Bryant, assistant attorney general, letter to Patrick J. Leahy, chair, Committee on the Judiciary, November 29, 2001 (on file with *George Washington Law Review*).

124. (p. 86) Howell, "Seven Weeks," 1202–1203.

125. (p. 86) These included §203(b), 206, 214, and 217.

126. (p. 87) U.S. Senate, Committee of the Judiciary, *Legislative History P.L. 95–511 Foreign Intelligence Surveillance Act*, Report 95-604, Ninety-Fifth Congress, First Session (15 Nov. 1977), 34.

127. (p. 87) At least a third of overseas communications went by transoceanic cable (Kris, "Modernizing," 11–12).

128. (p. 87) Steven M. Bellovin, Matt Blaze, Whitfield Diffie, Susan Landau, Peter Neumann, and Jennifer Rexford, "Risking Communications Security: Potential

Hazards of the 'Protect America Act,'" *IEEE Security and Privacy* 6, no. 1 (January/February 2008): 25.

129. (p. 88) James Risen and Eric Lichtblau, "Bush Lets U.S. Spy on Callers without Courts," *New York Times*, December 16, 2005.

130. (p. 88) Eric Lichtblau and James Risen, "Eavesdropping Efforts Began Soon After Sept. 11 Attacks," *New York Times*, December 18, 2005.

131. (p. 88) Leslie Cauley, "NSA Has Massive Database of Americans' Phone Calls," *USA Today*, May 11, 2006.

132. (p. 89) Pub. L. 104-104.

133. (p. 89) Whitfield Diffie and Susan Landau, "Communications Surveillance: Privacy and Security at Risk," *Communications of the ACM* 52, no. 11 (November 2009): 42–47

134. (p. 89) Mark Klein, affidavit in *Tash Hepting et al. v. AT&T Corporation et al.*, United States Second District Court for Northern California, Case 3:06-cv-0672-vrw (June 8, 2006), 4.

135. (p. 89) Marcus, affidavit in *Hepting*, 24.

136. (p. 89) Mark Klein, *Wiring Up the Big Brother Machine . . . And Fighting It* (Charlestown, SC: BookSurge, 2009), 42.

137. (p. 90) President Bush referred to the program publicly as the "Terrorist Surveillance Program." Within the administration the program was known as the "President's Surveillance Program" (Offices of the Inspector General of the Department of Defense, Department of Justice, Central Intelligence Agency, National Security Agency, Office of the Director of National Intelligence, *Unclassified Report on the President's Surveillance Program,* Report 2009-0013-AS, July 10, 2009, 1).

138. (p. 90) U.S. Foreign Intelligence Surveillance Court, *Memorandum Opinion*, May 17, 2002, 11, in U.S. Congress, Senate, Committee on the Judiciary, *USA PATRIOT Act in Practice: Shedding Light on the FISA Process. Hearing,* Serial No. J107102, One Hundred and Seventh Congress, Second Session (September 10, 2002), 145–171.

139. (p. 90) U.S. Foreign Intelligence Surveillance Court, *Memorandum Opinion,* 12.

140. (p. 90) U.S. Foreign Intelligence Surveillance Court, *Memorandum Opinion,* 2–3.

141. (p. 90) U.S. Foreign Intelligence Surveillance Court of Review, In re: Sealed Case No. 02-001, Consolidated with 02-002, *On Motions for Review of Orders of the United States Foreign Intelligence Surveillance Court (Nos. 02-662 and 02-968)* (November 18, 2002).

142. (p. 90) The term "read into" means being approved for access to particularly sensitive and restricted information about a classified program (Offices of the Inspector General of the Department of Defense, Department of Justice, Central Intelligence

Agency, National Security Agency, Office of the Director of National Intelligence, *Unclassified Report on the President's Surveillance Program*, Report 2009-0013-AS, July 10, 2009, 10).

143. (p. 90) John Yoo and Robert Delahunty, U.S. Department of Justice, Office of Legal Counsel, *Memorandum for Alberto R. Gonzales, Counsel to the President* (October 23, 2001), 25.

144. (p. 90) 343 U.S. 579 (1952).

145. (p. 91) Eric Lichtblau, *Bush's Law: The Remaking of American Justice* (New York: Pantheon, 2008), 173–174.

146. (p. 91) Lichtblau, *Bush's Law,* 179–183, and Offices of the Inspector General, *Unclassified Report on the President's Surveillance Program.*

147. (p. 91) Out of 1,758 applications submitted in 2004, the court asked for substantive changes in 94 (William Moschella, assistant attorney general, letter to Speaker of the House Dennis Hastert, April 1, 2005). In 2005, the situation was slightly better: the court asked for substantive changes in 61 of the 2,074 applications (William Moschella, letter to Speaker of the House Dennis Hastert, April 28, 2006, http://www.fas.org/irp/agency/doj/fisa/2005rept.html). Again in 2006, it asked for substantive changes in 73 of the 2,181 applications (Richard A. Hertling, acting assistant attorney general, letter to Speaker of the House Nancy Pelosi, April 27, 2007).

148. (p. 91) David Johnston and Neil A. Lewis, with Eric Lichtblau contributing, "Domestic Surveillance: The White House; Defending Spy Program, Administration Cites Law," *New York Times,* December 23, 2005.

149. (p. 91) Jarrett Murphy, "Error in Albany 'Terror' Case: Terror Camp Document Said Defendant Was 'Brother,' Not 'Commander,'" CBSNews.com, August 18, 2004.

150. (p. 91) Lowell Bergman, Eric Lichtblau, Scott Shane, and Don Van Natta Jr., "Spy Agency Data After Sept. 11 Led FBI to Dead Ends," *New York Times,* January 17, 2006.

151. (p. 91) In *Bush's Law,* Eric Lichtblau states that it was between 10 and 20 percent (p. 163), but other sources (Carol Leonnig, "Secret Court's Judges Were Warned about NSA Spy Data," *Washington Post,* February 9, 2006) report a lower number.

152. (p. 92) In 2007 he said, "[FISA] worked in the 20th century; it works today" (James Baker, "Spying on the Home Front," PBS Frontline, March 2, 2007).

153. (p. 92) Leonnig, "Secret Court's Judges Were Warned about NSA Spy Data."

154. (p. 92) Lichtblau, *Bush's Law,* 173.

155. (p. 92) *American Civil Liberties Union et al. v. National Security Agency et al.* (United States District Court, Eastern District of Michigan, Southern Division, Case No. 06-CV-10204), Anna Diggs Taylor, *Memorandum Opinion.*

156. (p. 92) American Civil Liberties Union et al., v. National Security Agency et al., Nos. 06-2095/2140, Appeal from the United States District Court for the Eastern District of Michigan at Detroit, No. 06-10204, Anna Diggs Taylor, District Judge, Decided and Filed: July 6, 2007.

157. (p. 92) Yale law professor Jack Balkin characterized the situation in the following way: "We won't answer hypothetical questions about what we can do legally or constitutionally. We also won't tell you what we've actually done or plan to do; hence every question you ask will [*sic*] about legality be in effect a hypothetical, and therefore we can refuse to answer it" (Balkinization blog, http://balkin.blogspot.com/2006/02/shorter-attorney-general-gonzales.html).

158. (p. 92) In *United States v. Reynolds*, 345 US 1 (1953), the Supreme Court ruled that there did indeed exist a state-secrets privilege, but its role was left unclear, "Judicial control over the evidence in a case cannot be abdicated to the caprice of executive officers. Yet we will not go so far as to say that the court may automatically require a complete disclosure to the judge before the claim of privilege will be accepted in any case." In the particular case at hand, it turned out that the Air Force accident report describing a plane crash had no classified material but rather demonstrated negligence on the part of the military. The report was withheld until 1996.

159. (p. 92) *Tash Hepting et al. v. AT&T Corporation,* United States District Court for the Northern District of California, Case 3:06-cv-00672-vrw.

160. (p. 93) Pub. L. 107-40, 115 Stat. 224.

161. (p. 93) Arlen Specter, "The Need to Roll Back Presidential Power Grabs," *New York Review of Books*, May 11, 2009, 50.

162. (p. 93) Pub. L. 110-55, 121 Stat. 552.

163. (p. 93) Four former senior officials including the former head of counterterrorism at the National Security Council, Richard A. Clarke, wrote the director of national intelligence, Mike McConnell, saying that it was not clear that "the immunity debate will affect our surveillance capabilities. . . . The intelligence community currently has the tools it needs to acquire surveillance of new targets and methods of communication" (letter from Rand Beers, Richard A. Clarke, Don Kerrick, and Suzanne Spaulding to Mike McConnell, February 25, 2008, http://www.nsnetwork.org/node/727).

164. (p. 93) Pub. L. 110-261. The official name is "Foreign Intelligence Surveillance Act of 1978 Amendments Act of 2008," but it is rarely used.

165. (p. 94) In Re: National Security Agency Telecommunications Record Litigation, *Memorandum of Decision and Order*, United States District Court for the Northern District of California, MDL Docket No 06-1791 VRW, Case No C 07-0109 VRW.

166. (p. 94) Charles Savage and James Risen, "Federal Judges Finds N.S.A. Wiretaps Were Illegal," *New York Times*, March 31, 2010.

167. (p. 94) *New Signal Surveillance Act.*

168. (p. 94) Spiegel Staff, "How German Spies Eavesdropped on an Afghan Ministry," Spiegel Online, April 28, 2008, http://www.spiegel.de/international/germany/0,1518,550212-2,00.html.

169. (p. 94) At the end of World War II, the occupying powers, which included the United States, required that the German constitution include protections of fundamental human rights.

170. (p. 94) Von Holger Stork, "BND infiltrierte Tausende Computer im Ausland," Spiegel Online, March 7, 2009, http://www.spiegel.de/netzwelt/web/0,1518,611954,00.html.

171. (p. 94) Russell Tice, interview with Keith Olbermann, "Countdown: NSA Whistleblower—Bush Administration Spying on Journalists—Recording 'Everything'." http://www.youtube.com/watch?v=osFprWnCjPA, 5:00–5:26.

172. (p. 94) Interview with Lawrence Wright, *On the Media,* National Public Radio, http://www.onthemedia.org/transcripts/2009/02/06/01.

173. (p. 94) Kim Zetter, "NSA Whistleblower: Wiretaps Were Combined with Credit Card Records of U.S. Citizens," *Wired,* January 23, 2009, http://www.wired.com/threatlevel/2009/01/nsa-whistlebl-1/.

174. (p. 94) James Risen, interview, http://www.youtube.com/watch?v=IRCm4077qos&feature=related, 3:48–4:17.

175. (p. 95) Mark Mazzeti and Neil A. Lewis, "Wiretap Said to Be Viewed as Serious in Late 2005," *New York Times,* April 24, 2009; Neil A. Lewis and David Johnston, "U.S. to Drop Spy Case against Pro-Israeli Lobbyists," *New York Times,* May 1, 2009.

176. (p. 95) Mazzeti and Lewis, "Wiretaps Said to Be Viewed as Serious in Late 2005."

177. (p. 95) Mazzeti and Lewis, "Wiretaps Said to Be Viewed as Serious in Late 2005."

178. (p. 95) Siobhan Gorman, "House Panel Chief Demands Details of Cybersecurity Plan," *Baltimore Sun,* October 24, 2007.

Chapter 5

1. (p. 97) This includes pulse rate and sweat, for example. Such measurements are the principle behind lie detectors.

2. (p. 97) One exception was the Total Information Awareness program, whose funding was eliminated by Congress because of negative publicity surrounding the program.

3. (p. 97) The specific recommendation was: "U.S. government agencies should be required to follow a systematic process . . . to evaluate the effectiveness, lawfulness, and consistency with U.S. values of every information-based program, whether

classified or unclassified, for detecting and countering terrorism before such a system can be deployed and periodically thereafter" (National Research Council, *Protecting Individual Privacy in the Struggle against Terrorists: A Framework for Program Assessment* (Washington, DC: National Academies Press, 2008), 5).

4. (p. 98) Administrative Office of the United States Courts, James C. Duff, director, *2008 Wiretap Report,* http://www.uscourts.gov/wiretap08/contents.html, 8.

5. (p. 98) Wiretaps showed that Ames's wife knew about his illegal activities. The government used this to pressure Ames into revealing information in exchange for a reduced sentence for his wife.

6. (p. 98) Don Van Natta Jr. and Desmond Butler, "How Tiny Swiss Cellphone Chips Helped Track Global Terror Web," *New York Times,* March 4, 2004.

7. (p. 98) Van Natta and Butler, "How Tiny Swiss Cellphone Chips." Fighters in Somalia and Bosnia also stayed off the airwaves once they discovered that the NSA was monitoring them (Matthew Aid, *Secret Sentry: The Untold History of the National Security Agency* (New York: Bloomsbury Press, 2009), 202).

8. (p. 98) Kenneth Dam and Herbert S. Lin, *Cryptography's Role in Securing the Information Society* (Washington, DC: National Academy Press, 1996),, 4.

9. (p. 99) Right to Financial Privacy Act, Pub. L. 99-569, §404, 100 Stat. 3197 (1986).

10. (p. 99) Charles Doyle, *National Security Letters in Foreign Intelligence Investigations: Legal Background and Recent Amendments,* CRS Report for Congress, RS33320 (March 28, 2008), CRS-3.

11. (p. 99) Pub. L. 107-56, §505, 115 Stat. 365–366 (2001).

12. (p. 100) U.S.C. §2709. This provision was struck down in 2008 (*John Doe, Inc., John Doe, American Civil Liberties Union, American Civil Liberties Union Foundation Plaintiffs-Appellees, v. Michael B. Mukasey, Robert Mueller, Valerie Caproni,* United States Court of Appeals for the Second Circuit, Docket No. 07–4943-cv, December 15, 2008). Under the current ruling, there can still be a "gag" order on an NSL, but it is not automatic; the FBI has to go to court to obtain one.

13. (p. 100) U.S. Department of Justice, Office of the Inspector General, *A Review of the FBI's Use of National Security Letters: Assessment of Corrective Actions and Examination of NSL Usage in 2006* (March 2008), 9.

14. (p. 100) U.S. Department of Justice, Office of the Inspector General, *A Review of the FBI's Use of National Security Letters,* 110.

15. (p. 100) U.S. Department of Justice, Office of the Inspector General, *A Review of the FBI's Use of National Security Letters,* 28.

16. (p. 100) U.S. Department of Justice, Office of the Inspector General, *A Review of the FBI's Use of National Security Letters* (March 2007), 48. The DoJ Inspector General

has characterized the NSLs as an "important tool" in FBI national-security investigations (DoJ OIG, *Assessment and Examination of NSL Usage in 2006,* 114). That description appears to be based on anecdotal evidence rather than a careful comparison of potential alternatives.

17. (p. 100) U.S. Department of Justice, Federal Bureau of Investigation, *FOIA: DCS-3000 and Red Hook, Other Documents Released* (July 2, 2007), part 6 (agency emails), http://www.eff.org/directory/3673/228 082707_dcs01.pdf, 41.

18. (p. 100) Heather Timmons, "London Suspect Betrayed by Cellphone," *New York Times*, August 2, 2005. Adus also used the alias Hussain Osman.

19. (p. 101) Over three weeks in October 2002, a sniper in the Washington, D.C., metropolitan area killed ten people and critically wounded three others; the attacks occurred in parking lots, gas stations, and schools, and terrified area citizens until the perpetrators were found.

20. (p. 101) On April 10, 2009, a paid escort was bound and robbed in a room at the Westin Copley Place Boston after an arrangement made through craigslist. On April 14, 2009, a masseuse who had also made such an arrangement through craigslist was found murdered in a room at the Boston Marriott Copley Place.

21. (p. 101) Al Gidari, personal communication, July 27, 2009.

22. (p. 101) Al Gidari, personal communication, July 27, 2009.

23. (p. 101) Al Gidari, personal communication, July 27, 2009.

24. (p. 101) Actually they scan all Subscriber Identity Module (SIM) cards—electronic cards that provide a unique ID for the phone to enable billing and so on. This is the actual phone identifier.

25. (p. 101) Vanessa Gratzer and David Naccache, "Cryptography, Law Enforcement, and Mobile Communications," *IEEE Security and Privacy* 4, no. 6 (November/December 2006): 68.

26. (p. 101) The user may have shut the phone "off," but it may still be able to transmit and receive radio signals. The only thing "off" is the user interface.

27. (p. 101) Gratzer and Naccache, "Cryptography, Law Enforcement, and Mobile Communications."

28. (p. 101) 18 U.S.C. §3126(8).

29. (p. 101) This report was found by Patricia Bellia of the University of Notre Dame Law School (Paul Schwartz, "Reviving Telecommunications Surveillance Law," *University of Chicago Law Review* 75 (2008): 296).

30. (p. 102) William Moschella, assistant attorney general, letter to Representative John Conyers, November 3, 2004, http://www.paulschwartz.net/penregister-report.pdf.

31. (p. 102) While the official number of approved pen-register plus trap-and-trace orders were 5,007, 4,972, 4,579, 5,778, and 7,323 and the number of approved Title III warrants for 1994–1998 were 1,154, 1,058, 1,149, 1,186, and 1,329, respectively, gives a 5:1 ratio of pen-register and trap-and-trace orders to Title III wiretaps (Electronic Privacy Information Center, "Approvals for Federal Pen Register and Trap and Trace Devices 1987–1998," http://epic.org/privacy/wiretap/stats/penreg.html), this represents a major understatement of the number of pen registers actually implemented. Each wiretap order applies only to a single telephone number, while a pen-register order may—and usually does—result in records for multiple numbers. This one order for multiple lines has been the pen-register experience of the telephone companies; its prevalence is further corroborated by the estimates made by the FBI for CALEA capacity requirements (U.S. Department of Justice, Federal Bureau of Investigation, "Implementation of the Communications Assistance for Law Enforcement Act," *Federal Register* 60, no. 199: 53643–53646).

32. (p. 102) Marc Rotenberg, John Verdi, and Christopher Soghian, letter to Senator Patrick Leahy, April 29, 2009, 4.

33. (p. 102) Rotenberg, Verdi, and Soghian, letter to Senator Patrick Leahy.

34. (p. 102) U.S. Department of Justice, Federal Bureau of Investigation, *FOIA: DCS-3000 and Red Hook, Other Documents Released,* July 2, 2007, part 6 (agency emails; miscellaneous statements and reports), 148.

35. (p. 103) *Judicious Use of Surveillance Tools in Counterterrorism Efforts (JUSTICE) Act,* S. 1686.

36. (p. 103) *JUSTICE Act,* §101 (b)(1)(B)(i)(ii).

37. Specifically, "someone who has been in contact with a suspected agent of a foreign power or an individual who is the subject of a national-security investigation . . . or if they pertain to the activities of a suspected agent of a foreign power, where those activities are the subject of an ongoing and authorized identified national security investigation (other than an assessment)," *JUSTICE Act,* §101 (b)(1)(B)(i)(ii).

38. (p. 103) U.S. Department of Justice, *Electronic Surveillance Manual: Procedures and Case Law Forms,* (2005), 40.

39. (p. 103) U.S. Department of Justice, *Electronic Surveillance Manual: Procedures and Case Law Forms,* (2005), 40.

40. (p. 103) Triggerfish technology can also easily obtain call content; of course, a wiretap order is required if this is to be done.

41. (p. 103) http://www.pathintelligence.com/website-demo/ui-demo.html.

42. (p. 104) *On Lee v. United States,* 343 U.S. 747 (1952).

43. (p. 104) Administrative Office of the United States Courts, Leonidas Ralph Mecham, director, *2001 Wiretap Report,* 11.

44. (p. 104) Administrative Office of the United States Courts, *Wiretap Report* (Washington, DC: Government Printing Office, 1998), 11.

45. (p. 105) Herman Schwartz, *The Costs and Benefits of Electronic Surveillance*, ACLU Report, 1973, 185–186.

46. (p. 105) Herman Schwartz, testimony in National Commission for the Review of Federal and State Laws Relating to Wiretapping and Electronic Surveillance, *Commission Hearings*, vol. 2 (Washington, DC: Government Printing Office, 1976), 1098.

47. (p. 105) Herman Schwartz, "Reflections on Six Years of Legitimated Electronic Surveillance," in National Commission for the Review of Federal and State Laws Relating to Wiretapping and Electronic Surveillance, *Commission Hearings*, vol. 1 (Washington, DC: Government Printing Office, 1976), 1141.

48. (p. 105) Arlen Specter, testimony in National Commission for the Review of Federal and State Laws Relating to Wiretapping and Electronic Surveillance, *Commission Hearings*, vol. 1, 257.

49. (p. 106) Administrative Office of the United States Courts, *Wiretap Report* (Washington, DC: Government Printing Office, 1979), xiv.

50. (p. 106) Whitfield Diffie and Susan Landau, *Privacy on the Line: The Politics of Wiretapping and Encryption*, rev. ed. (Cambridge, MA: MIT Press, 2007), 211.

51. (p. 106) Patrick Fitzgerald, testimony at the Twelfth Public Hearing, National Commission on Terrorist Attacks on the United States, June 16, 2004.

52. (p. 106) Because the suspects were speaking Arabic, the FBI was allowed to tape the conversation and minimize collection afterward. The surveillance tapes captured the sounds of the young woman being murdered (Tim Bryant, "4 Indicted Here as Terrorists, FBI: Tina Isa Killing Part of Conspiracy," *St. Louis Post-Dispatch*, April 2, 1993).

53. (p. 106) The police heard that a murder was being planned, but they could not figure out against whom because of the jargon (Dam and Lin, *Cryptography's Role*, 89).

54. (p. 107) A 1999 investigation listed "bombing" as the most serious crime (Administrative Office of the United States Courts, *Wiretap Report* (Washington, DC: Government Printing Office, 1999, 42), but three years later the three convictions in the case were for narcotics (Administrative Office of the United States Courts, Leonidas Ralph Mecham, director, *2002 Wiretap Report*, 90).

55. (p. 107) This is from Administrative Office of the United States Courts, James C. Duff, director, *2009 Wiretap Report*, 25. The numbers in 2007 and 2008 were higher, at 1809 and 1764 respectively (Administrative Office of the United States Courts, James C. Duff, director, *2007 Wiretap Report*, 15; Administrative Office of the United States Courts, James C. Duff, Director, 2008 Wiretap Report, 25).

56. (p. 107) This is required by Pub. L. 106–197.

57. (p. 107) There were twenty-two such cases in 2000, thirty-four in 2001, seventeen in 2002, one in 2003, forty-one state and one federal case in 2004, thirteen in 2005, none in 2006–2008, and one in 2009.

58. (p. 107) Administrative Office of the United States Courts, James C. Duff, director, *2009 Wiretap Report*, 8.

59. (p. 107) David Kahn, *The Codebreakers: The Comprehensive History of Secret Communication from Ancient Times to the Internet* (revised and updated) (New York, NY: Scribner, 1996), 594–601.

60. (p. 107) James Bamford, *The Shadow Factory: The Ultra-Secret NSA from 9/11 to the Eavesdropping on America* (New York: Doubleday, 2008), 135–136.

61. (p. 108) David Johnston and Paul Zielbauer, "A Nation Challenged: The Investigation; 3 Held in Detroit After Aircraft Diagrams Are Found," *New York Times*, September 20, 2001.

62. (p. 108) Eric Lichtblau and William Glaberson, "Threats and Responses: Financing Terror; Millions Raised for Qaeda in Brooklyn, U.S. Says," *New York Times*, March 5, 2003.

63. (p. 108) Scott Shane and Andrea Zarate, "FBI Killed Plot in Talking Stage, a Top Aide Says," *New York Times*, June 24, 2006.

64. (p. 108) Damien Cave and Carmen Gentile, "Five Convicted in Plot to Blow Up Sears Tower," *New York Times*, May 12, 2009.

65. (p. 108) These definitions are all laid out in Transactional Records Access Clearinghouse, "Who Is a Terrorist? Government Failure to Define Terrorism Undermines Enforcement, Puts Civil Liberties at Risk," September 2009, 3–4.

66. (p. 108) Transactional Records Access Clearinghouse, "Who Is a Terrorist?", 2.

67. (p. 108) Transactional Records Access Clearinghouse, "Who Is a Terrorist?", 6.

68. (p. 109) Saul Horwtiz, "Cigarette Smuggling Tied to Terrorism," *Washington Post*, June 8, 2004.

69. (p. 109) If one uses the federal-prosecutor definition of terrorism, then in recent years the government has prosecuted just over a quarter of the suspects charged during a terrorism investigation. While in 2002 prosecutors filed in 69 percent of terrorism investigations, by 2008 that number had dropped to 27 percent (TRAC, "Who Is a Terrorist?", figure 2).

70. (p. 109) TRAC, "Who Is a Terrorist?", table 7.

71. (p. 109) TRAC, "Who Is a Terrorist?", 6.

72. (p. 109) U.S. Department of Justice, Federal Bureau of Investigation, "Federal Judge Hands Down Sentences in Holy Land Foundation Case," May 27, 2009, http://www.justice.gov/opa/pr/2009/May/09-nsd-519.html.

73. (p. 109) U.S. Department of Justice, U.S. Attorney, Southern District of New York, "Naji Antoine Abi Khalil Sentenced to 60 Months' Imprisonment for Attempting to Export Military Night-Vision Equipment to Hezbollah," February 13, 2006, http://www.justice.gov/usao/nys/pressreleases/February06/khalilsentencingpr.pdf.

74. (p. 109) U.S. Department of Justice, Federal Bureau of Investigation, "Jury Finds Former Member of U.S. Navy Guilty of Terrorism and Espionage Charges," March 5, 2008, http://www.ice.gov/pi/news/newsreleases/articles/080305newhaven.htm.

75. (p. 109) U.S. Department of Justice, Federal Bureau of Investigation, "Al Qaeda Supporter and Organizer of Jihad Training Camp in Oregon Sentenced in Manhattan Federal Court to Life in Prison," September 15, 2009, http://newyork.fbi.gov/dojpressrel/pressrel09/nyfo091509.htm.

76. (p. 109) U.S. Department of Justice, Federal Bureau of Investigation, "Jury Finds Former Member of U.S. Navy Guilty."

77. (p. 110) U.S. Department of Justice, Federal Bureau of Investigation, "Illinois Man Pleads Guilty in Foiled Plan to Set Off Grenades in Shopping Mall," November 28, 2007, http://www.justice.gov/usao/iln/pr/chicago/2007/pr1128_01.pdf.

78. (p. 110) The Tamil Tigers are extremely violent and pioneered the use of suicide bombings. In separate incidents, the Tamil Tigers assassinated former Indian Prime Minister Rajiv Gandhi and Sri Lankin President Ranasinghe Premadasa.

79. (p. 110) TRAC, "Who Is a Terrorist?", table 3.

80. (p. 110) TRAC, "Who Is a Terrorist?", figure 7.

81. (p. 111) A. G. Sulzberger and William K. Rashbaum, "Guilty Plea Made in Plot to Bomb New York Subway," New York Times, February 22, 2010; Associated Press, "Najibullah Zazi's Plea in Court to Terror Charges," New York Times, February 22, 2010; U.S. District Court, Eastern District of New York, United States of America v. Najibullah Zazi, Memorandum of Law in Support of the Government's Motion for a Permanent Order of Detention, Case 1:09-cr-00663-RJD (filed September 24, 2009).

82. (p. 111) United States of America v. Najibullah Zazi, 7.

83. (p. 111) United States of America v. Najibullah Zazi, 6–7.

84. (p. 111) United States of America v. Najibullah Zazi, 8.

85. (p. 111) Associated Press, "Najibullah Zazi's Plea."

86. (p. 111) Although federal agents tracked Zazi as he drove across the country on September 9–10, when he was stopped on his entrance to Manhattan, his car was not carrying explosives, and he was not arrested until September 19. Even then officials found the situation unclear; one was quoted as saying this was a "possible plot to detonate explosives in the United States" (David Johnston and William Rashbaum, "Terror Suspect Had Bomb Guide," New York Times, September 20, 2009).

87. (p. 111) U.S. Department of Justice, Federal Bureau of Investigation, "Jury Finds Former Member of U.S. Navy Guilty."

88. (p. 112) Eric Lichtblau, "Bank Data Sifted by U.S. in Secret to Block Terror," *New York Times*, June 23, 2006.

89. (p. 112) In 2010, the European Parliament first rescinded, and then reinstated, United States access to European Union banking data. James Kanter, "Europe Resumes Sharing Financial Data with U.S.," *New York Times*, July 9, 2010.

90. (p. 112) Lichtblau, "Bank Data Sifted by U.S. in Secret."

91. (p. 112) Lichtblau, "Bank Data Sifted by U.S. in Secret."

92. (p. 112) U.S. Department of Justice, Office of the Inspector General, *A Review of the FBI's Use of National Security Letters*, 32–33.

93. (p. 112) U.S. Department of Justice, Office of the Inspector General, *A Review of the FBI's Use of National Security Letters*, 34–35.

94. (p. 112) U.S. Department of Justice, Office of the Inspector General, *A Review of the FBI's Use of National Security Letters*, 36.

95. (p. 114) Whitfield Diffie and Susan Landau, "The Export of Cryptography in the 20th Century and the 21st," in Karl De Leeuw and Jan Bergstra, eds., *Handbook of the History of Information Security* (Amsterdam: Elsevier, 2007), 725–736.

96. (p. 114) The government also controlled the sale of products that had a "hole" for inserting cryptographic functionality once the product had been shipped overseas.

97. (p. 114) U.S. Department of Commerce, "NIST Announces Voluntary Escrowed Encryption Standard to Promote Secure Telecommunications," NIST 94-8, February 4, 1994.

98. (p. 115) Hal Abelson, Ross Anderson, Steven M. Bellovin, Josh Benaloh, Matt Blaze, Whitfield Diffie, John Gilmore, Peter G. Neumann, Ronald L. Rivest, Jeffrey I. Schiller, and Bruce Schneier, *The Risks of Key Recovery, Key Escrow, Trusted Third Party and Encryption: a Report by an Ad Hoc Group of Cryptographers and Computer Scientists* (1998) http://www.crypto.com/papers/escrowrisks98.pdf.

99. (p. 115) Diffie and Landau, *Privacy on the Line*, 239.

100. (p. 116) U.S. Bureau of Export Administration, Appl. Ref. No: Z066051/G006298.

101. (p. 116) Philip R. Karn Jr., Plaintiff, v. United States Department of State and United States Department of Commerce, and William A. Reinsch, Undersecretary of Commerce for the Bureau of Export Administration, United States District Court of Appeals, Civ. A. No. 95-1812(LBO).

102. (p. 116) Appl. Ref. No: Z066051/G006298.

103. (p. 116) Lee Tien, letter to William Reinsch in reference to Appl. Ref. No.: Z066051/G006298.

104. (p. 116) Stephen Levy, *Crypto: How the Code Warriors Beat the Government—Saving Privacy in the Digital Age* (New York, NY: Viking Press, 2001), 162–163.

105. (p. 117) Levy, *Crypto*, 162.

106. (p. 117) Ozzie explained that "we asked the government to generate a special RSA key pair, and to make known their RSA Public Key. We asked them to keep their private key classified, compartmentalized—as secret as they'd keep the keys to their own military and diplomatic communication systems—and to never disclose it to anyone. Then, we changed Notes so that whenever the product generates an encrypted 64-bit bulk data key, bound to that key is a small package—a 'workfactor reduction field'—containing 24 bits of the bulk data key encrypted with the U.S. government's public key. So the U.S. government has exclusive access to 24 of the 64 bits. That's 64 bits against the cracker, 40 bits for the government." ("Prepared Remarks," RSA Data Security Conference, 1996).

107. (p. 117) Frederik Laurin, "Secret Swedish E-Mail Can Be Read by the U.S.A.," *Calle Froste*, November 18, 1997.

108. (p. 117) Sowing *fear, uncertainty, and doubt (FUD)* is a well-known tactic to influence public perception without necessarily having a firm basis in facts.

109. (p. 118) Diffie and Landau, "Export of Cryptography," 732–733.

110. (p. 118) Diffie and Landau, "Export of Cryptography," 732.

111. (p. 118) Network exploitation employs a combination of techniques to collect, monitor, and falsify information on an adversary's networked system. It may include infiltration of the target system, placing code to be activated at a later date, and exfiltration of data.

112. (p. 119) GOTS equipment is typically developed by a government agency.

113. (p. 119) Former NSA general counsel Stewart Baker testified in Congress in 2004 on behalf of an industry association and described the situation this way: "While American innovators are still cooling their heels in Quantico, waiting to explain a new technology to the FBI Lab, their competitors in Singapore, China, Japan, and Europe will be manufacturing already. The U.S. market will end up a laggard, getting technologies after they've been sufficiently proven in the rest of the world to justify the engineering and lobbying costs needed to get an assurance of CALEA compliance" (Stewart Baker, written testimony in U.S. Congress, House of Representatives, Committee on Energy and Commerce, Subcommittee on Telecommunications and the Internet, *Law Enforcement Access to Communications Systems in the Digital Age*, One Hundred and Eighth Congress, Second Session, Serial No. 108-115, September 8, 2004).

114. (p. 119) DoJ OIG, "Implementation of CALEA, Audit Report," 16.

115. (p. 119) Landau, "National Security on the Line," *Journal of Telecommunications and High Technology Law* 4, no. 2 (Spring 2006): 419.

116. (p. 119) AOL has, for example, made its Instant Messaging product surveillance compliant.

117. (p. 119) Siobhan Gorman, "NSA to Defend against Hackers: Privacy Fears Raised as Spy Agency Turns to Systems Protection," *Baltimore Sun*, September 20, 2007.

118. (p. 120) This was also known as Homeland Security Presidential Directive 23.

119. (p. 120) U.S. Department of Homeland Security, National Cyber Division, U.S. Computer Emergency Readiness Team, "Privacy Impact Assessment: Einstein Program. Collecting, Analyzing, and Sharing Computer Security Information across the Federal Civilian Government," September 2004.

120. (p. 120) U.S. Department of Homeland Security, National Cyber Division, U.S. Computer Emergency Readiness Team, "Privacy Impact Assessment: Einstein Program."

121. (p. 120) U.S. Department of Homeland Security, National Cyber Division, U.S. Computer Emergency Readiness Team, "Privacy Impact Assessment: Einstein Program."

122. (p. 121) In *Stengart v. Loving Care Agency* (A-16-09), the New Jersey Supreme Court affirmed a lower court decision that an employee using a work-supplied computer to access a private email account has a reasonable expectation of privacy. Marina Stengart had been communicating with her lawyer through a password-protected yahoo account using a laptop supplied by her employer, the Loving Care Agency. The company had a clear policy that while employees could occasionally use company equipment for personal purposes, communications (email, Internet, etc.) transmitted over the machine would not be considered private. The system had been set up so that every web page Stengart viewed on the laptop was automatically saved to the computer's hard drive.

Stengart left the company and filed suit over employment discrimination. Loving Care had the laptop's hard drive searched and found the communications, which it sought to use in the subsequent court case. Emphasizing the lawyer-client privilege aspect of the communications between Stengart and her attorneys and the "equivacol" nature of Loving Care's personal use policy, the court found for Stengart; it ruled that Loving Care and its lawyers had no right to use the communications between Stengart and her attorneys in preparation of their case.

123. (p. 121) Specifically the Court wrote, "Prudence counsels caution before the facts in this case are used to establish far-reaching premises that define the existence, and extent, of privacy expectations of employees using employer-provided communication devices. Rapid changes in the dynamics of communication and information transmission are evident not just in the technology itself but in what society accepts as proper behavior. At present, it is uncertain how workplace norms, and the law's treatment of them, will evolve." (*City of Ontario v. Quon*, 130 S. Ct. 2619 (2010)).

124. (p. 121) Steven Bradbury, "Legal Issues Relating to the Testing, Use, and Deployment of an Intrusion-Detection System (Einstein 2.0) to Protect Unclassified Computer Networks in the Executive Branch: Memorandum Opinion for the Counsel to the

President," January 9, 2009; David Barron, "Legality of Intrusion-Detection System to Protect Unclassified Computer Networks in the Executive Branch: Memorandum Opinion for an Associate Deputy Attorney General," August 14, 2009.

125. (p. 121) 130 S. Ct. 2619 (2010).

126. (p. 121) Prudence counsels caution before the facts in this case are used to establish far-reaching premises that define the existence, and extent, of privacy expectations of employees using employer-provided communication devices. Rapid changes in the dynamics of communication and information transmission are evident not just in the technology itself but in what society accepts as proper behavior. At present, it is uncertain how workplace norms, and the law's treatment of them, will evolve." (*City of Ontario v. Quon*, 130 S. Ct. 2619 (2010)).

127. (p. 121) Ellen Nakashima, "Cybersecurity Plan Doesn't Breach Employee Privacy, Administration Says," *Washington Post*, September 19, 2009; Department of Homeland Security, *Privacy Impact Assessment for the Initiative Three Exercise*, March 18, 2010, 2, 4.

128. (p. 121) Department of Homeland Security, *Privacy Impact Assessment for Initiative Three*, 5.

129. (p. 121) Siobhan Gorman, "Troubles Plague Cyberspy Defense," *Wall Street Journal*, July 3, 2009.

130. (p. 121) Gorman, "Troubles Plague Cyberspy Defense."

131. (p. 122) Nakashima, "Cybersecurity Plan."

Chapter 6

1. (p. 123) Open source predates the Internet, but became significantly more successful after widespread use of the network.

2. (p. 124) Fermat numbers are integers of the form $2^{2^k} + 1$. The first several Fermat numbers, $F_1 = 5$, $F_2 = 17$, $F_3 = 257$, $f_4 = 65537$, are prime. The Fermat numbers have various interesting properties; Gauss showed, for example, that if F_n is a prime p, then a regular p-gon (a polygon with p equal sides and all equal angles) can be inscribed in a circle using just compass and straight edge. Fermat conjectured that all F_i were prime, but F_5 was shown not to be.

3. (p. 124) Arjen K. Lenstra, Hendrik W. Lenstra Jr., Mark Manasse, and John Pollard, "The Factorization of the Ninth Fermat Number," *Mathematics of Computation* 61, no. 203 (July 1993): 339.

4. (p. 125) Adam L. Beberg, Daniel L. Ensign, Guha Jayachandran, Siraj Khaliq, and Vijay S. Pande, "Folding@home: Lessons from Eight Years of Volunteer Distributed Computing," *Eighth IEEE International Workshop on High Performance Computational Biology* (Piscataway, NJ: IEEE Press, 2009).

5. (p. 125) These include a better understanding of the "misbehavior" of a protein thought to be responsible for Huntington's disease and a model for predicting mutations in p53, a protein that in a healthy state protects against developing cancer (Folding @home distributed computing, http://folding.stanford.edu/English/Papers/#ntoc6).

6. (p. 125) http://www.google.com/trends.

7. (p. 125) Jeremy Ginsberg, Matthew Mohebbi, Rajan Patel, Lynette Brammer, Mark Smolinski, and Larry Brilliant, "Detecting Influenza Epidemics Using Search Engine Query Data," *Nature*, February 19, 2009, 1011.

8. (p. 125) Diagrams of the Internet often represent the network as a cloud, the fuzzy area being the area in which the user cannot predict the path through which packets pass on their way from source to destination.

9. (p. 127) *Miller v. United States,* 425 U.S. 435 (1976).

10. (p. 127) *Miller v. United States,* 443.

11. (p. 127) Network Address Translation (NAT) boxes connect to the Internet and enable multiple devices to share a single address. They do this by showing one address to the Internet, while actually supporting multiple devices on a local network. NATs are widely used in home networks.

12. (p. 128) Elizabeth Wasserman, "Beaver Street Fisheries Catch RFID," *RFID Journal*, April 1, 2005, http://www.rfidjournal.com/article/purchase/1546.

13. (p. 128) Michael Totty, "Business Solutions: New Ways to Use RFID," *Wall Street Journal*, June 2, 2009, http://online.wsj.com/article/SB10001424052970203771904574175882366028604.html.

14. (p. 128) Ari Juels, "RFID Security and Privacy: A Research Survey," *Journal of Selected Areas in Communications* 24, no. 2 (February 2006): 382.

15. (p. 128) This was done through hydrophones—long acoustic sensors—placed on the ocean floor.

16. (p. 128) Three hundred sensors were embedded in the new I-35 bridge over the Mississippi River (Henry Petrowski, "The Minneapolis Bridge," *American Scientist* 97, no. 6 (November/December 2009): 447).

17. (p. 128) Voice communications have different requirements than other applications: the "unreliability" centered on delay, jitter (time variation of delay), and packet loss due to network congestion.

18. (p. 128) Federal Communications Commission, In the Matters of Formal Complaint of Free Press and Public Knowledge against Comcast Corporation for Secretly Degrading Peer-to-Peer Applications. Broadband Industry Practices Petition of Free Press et al. for Declaratory Ruling that Degrading an Internet Application Violates the FCC's Internet Policy Statement and Does Not Meet an Exception for

"Reasonable Network Management," Memorandum Opinion and Order, File No. EB-08-IH-1518, WC Docket No. 07–52, August 1, 2008 (adopted), 19.

19. (p. 129) Another is in wiretaps, a situation I will revisit in chapter 8.

20. (p. 129) Dale Hatfield, *A Report on Technical and Operational Issues Impacting the Provision of Wireless Enhanced 911 Services* (2002), 4. Report prepared for the FCC.

21. (p. 129) Hatfield, *Report on Technical and Operational Issues*, 9–10.

22. (p. 129) Susan Crawford, "The Ambulance, the Squad Car, and the Internet," *Berkeley Technology Law Journal* 21, no. 2 (2006): 895–896.

23. (p. 130) NET Improvement Act of 2008, Pub. L. 110–283, §6.

24. (p. 130) *United States v. John Tomero et al.*, S2 06 Crim. 0008(LAK) (U.S. District Court, S.D. New York).

25. (p. 130) *In re: In the Matter of the Application of the United States for an Order Authorizing the Roving Interception of Oral Communications*, 2003 U.S. App LEXIS 23433.

26. (p. 130) 18 U.S.C. §2518(4).

27. (p. 131) Gmail inspects user mail in order to target ads on the Gmail pages. Although there were initial objections to this, Gmail has proved a major success. There are more differences than similarities in the two situations: Gmail is a service in the cloud, while Charter Communications is functioning as a communications provider.

28. (p. 132) Federal Communications Commission, "Formal Complaint against Comcast," 4.

29. (p. 132) Peter Eckersley, Fred von Lohmann, and Seth Schoen, *Packet Forgery by ISPs: A Report on the Comcast Affair*, Electronic Frontier Foundation, November 28, 2007, http://www.eff.org/wp/packet-forgery-sps-report-comcast-affair.

30. (p. 132) It is worth noting that telephone companies cannot discriminate in this way because they are "common carriers"; cable companies are not under such a jurisdiction. In Europe such discrimination against dial-up modem users did occur. Calls were blocked or interrupted if the phone company noticed that a modem was in use. The rationale for this was that users stayed on the line longer when they used modems, causing congestion. In some cases, there was also the argument that the caller had not paid for modem use, which involved an additional charge. Finally there were concerns that the digital signal sent by the modem might be encrypted, to which the state security agencies of some European countries objected.

31. (p. 132) Adam Liptak, "Verizon Reverses Itself on Abortion Messages," *New York Times*, September 28, 2007.

32. (p. 132) Federal Communications Commission, "Formal Complaint against Comcast," 31.

33. (p. 132) Federal Communications Commission, "Formal Complaint against Comcast," 31.

34. (p. 133) There was controversy over whether the FBI needed the stronger wiretap warrant for the keystroke logger.

35. (p. 133) The password was nds09813–050; Nds09813–050 was the federal prison identification number for Nicodemo D. Scarfo, Scarfo's father.

36. (p. 133) George Anastasia, "Big Brother and the Bookie," *Mother Jones*, January/ February 2002, http://motherjones.com/politics/2002/01/big-brother-and-bookie.

37. (p. 133) Ted Bridis, "FBI Is Building a 'Magic Lantern'; Software Would Allow Agency to Monitor Computer Use," *Washington Post*, November 23, 2001, A15.

38. (p. 133) U.S. District Court, Western District of Washington, Application and Affidavit for Search Warrant, MJ07-5114, June 12, 2007.

39. (p. 133) CIPAV documents released under FOIA to *Wired*, April 16, 2009.

40. (p. 134) Median duration is two minutes (Federal Communications Commission, Wireline Competition Bureau, Industry Analysis and Technology Division, *Trends in Telephone Service,* August 2008, p. 11–8). In recent years median duration on wireline phones has dropped to two minutes but average duration remains higher than for cell phones (p. 14–4).

41. (p. 134) As of September 2009, 56 percent of devices on wireless networks were capable of browsing the web ("100 Wireless Facts," http://www.ctia.org/advocacy/research/index.cfm/AID/10382).

42. (p. 134) Jo Rabin, *Guidelines for Web Content Transformation Proxies 1.0,* W3C Working Draft, February 11, 2010.

43. (p. 134) David Kahn, *The Codebreakers: The Comprehensive History of Secret Communication from Ancient Times to the Internet* (rev. ed.) (New York: Scribner, 1996), 299–300.

44. (p. 134) Kahn, *The Codebreakers*, 300.

45. (p. 135) Kahn, *The Codebreakers*, 578.

46. (p. 135) Even when the United States could not acquire signals from within the Soviet Union, the NSA could listen to Soviet communications to its embassies and military deployed abroad (e.g., in Afghanistan).

47. (p. 135) These were Geoffrey Arthur Prime and Ronald Pelton, respectively.

48. (p. 135) Matthew Aid, *The Secret Sentry: The Untold History of the National Security Agency,* (New York: Bloomsbury Press, 2009), 152–153.

49. (p. 135) Aid, *The Secret Sentry*, 143–144.

50. (p. 135) Aid, *The Secret Sentry*, 168–170.

51. (p. 135) Aid, *The Secret Sentry*, 48.

52. (p. 136) Aid, *The Secret Sentry*, 58.

53. (p. 136) Aid, *The Secret Sentry*, 110–111.

54. (p. 136) Aid, *The Secret Sentry*, 106–107.

55. (p. 136) One example occurred when Intel researchers studying ambient Bluetooth technology had staff members wear Bluetooth-enabled devices. Two such devices were in close proximity each night, disclosing a previously unknown relationship between a pair of researchers (George Danezis and Richard Clayton, "Introducing Traffic Analysis," in Alessandro Acquisti, Stefanos Gritzalis, Costos Lambrinoudakis, and Sabrina di Vimercati, eds., *Digital Privacy: Theory, Technologies, and Practices* (Boca Raton, FL: Auerbach Publications, 2007), 95–116).

56. (p. 136) Mark Klein, affidavit in *Tash Hepting et al., v. AT&T Corporation et al.*, United States Second District Court for Northern California, Case 3:06-cv-0672-vrw, June 8, 2006, 7.

57. (p. 136) Corinna Cortes, Daryl Pregibon, and Chris Volinsky, "Communities of Interest," *Intelligent Data Analysis* 6, no. 3 (2002): 105–114.

58. (p. 136) The issue was not simply storing the records, but storing them in "live" storage so that they would quickly be accessible.

59. (p. 137) Directive 2006/24EC.

60. (p. 137) The directive specifically exempted requiring retention of unsuccessful call attempts (European Union, "Directive 2006/24/EC of the European Union and the Council of 14 March 2006," *Official Journal of the European Union*, April 4, 2006, §1.2).

61. (p. 137) European Union, "Directive 2006/24/EC," Article 5.

62. (p. 137) The law would require communications providers to retain traffic data for six to twenty-four months, with each member state determining its own data retention period within those parameters.

63. (p. 137) Daniel Soar, "Short Cuts," *London Review of Books* 30, no. 16 (August 14, 2008):24.

64. (p. 138) Nathan Eagle, Alex Pentland, and David Lazer, "Inferring Social Network Structure Using Mobile Phone Data," *Proceedings of the National Academy of Sciences* 106, no. 36 (2009): 15274–15278.

65. (p. 138) Joseph Bonneau, Jonathan Anderson, Frank Stajano, and Ross Anderson, "8 Friends Are Enough: Social Graph Approximation via Public Listings," *ACM Workshop on Social Network Systems* (New York: ACM, 2009).

66. (p. 138) Shishir Nagaraja, "The Economics of Covert Community Detection and Hiding," WEIS 2008—Seventh Workshop on Economics of Information Security, Hanover, NH, June 25–28, 2008, 7–8.

67. (p. 138) "Suspect Tracked by Phone Calls," BBC News, August 1, 2005.

68. (p. 139) "Profile: Hussain Osman," BBC News, July 9, 2007.

69. (p. 139) Some of the material in this section originally appeared in Whitfield Diffie and Susan Landau, *Privacy on the Line: The Politics of Wiretapping and Encryption*, rev. ed. (Cambridge, MA: MIT Press, 2007), 272–274.

70. (p. 139) This was said by Scott McNealy, the CEO of Sun Microsystems. McNealy has a much more nuanced view of privacy than would appear from this flip and oft-quoted comment.

71. (p. 139) A simple example is as follows: Let the mix network have three intermediary servers. Assume Alice, Charlotte, Emily, Gilda, and Irina are sending messages to Bob, David, Ferdinand, Henryk, and John respectively. Each of Alice, Charlotte, Emily, Gilda, and Irina encrypt their messages, including the email address, using the public keys of the three servers. This is done "Russian-doll" style, in which the encryption is done first using the key of the last server, then encrypting the message with the key of the intermediate server, and then finally encrypting using the key of the initial server one. These five messages are put in a batch—in practice a batch should be very large—and delivered to the first server. This server decrypts the messages using its private key, mixes up the order of the messages, and sends them on to the next server, which repeats the process. The process continues through all the servers in the mix network. If there are many messages in the batch, it is difficult for an eavesdropper to trace a message in order to determine who is communicating with whom.

72. (p. 139) Tor: Overview, https://www.torproject.org/overview.html.en#thesolution.

73. (p. 140) In addition, the Tor path keys are deleted.

74. (p. 140) Roger Dingledine and Nick Mathewson, "Anonymity Loves Company: Usability and the Network Effect," *Fifth Workshop on the Economics of Information Security (Pre-proceedings)*, June 26–28, 2006, 533–544.

75. (p. 141) http://metrics.torproject.org/consensus-graphs.html#networksize-30d.

76. (p. 141) Tor is recommended by Reporters without Borders for use by journalists and their sources.

77. (p. 141) http://www.torproject.org/torusers.html.en.

78. (p. 142) Harold Kwalwasser, "Internet Governance," in Franklin Kramer, Stuart Starr, and Larry Wentz, eds., *Cyberpower and National Security* (Washington, DC: NDU Press, 2009), 497.

79. (p. 142) Alexa.com, http://www.alexa.com/topsites.

80. (p. 142) These data are from the second quarter of 2009 (Internet World Stats, http://www.internetworldstats.om/stats3.htm).

81. (p. 143) Patrick Leahy, Charles Grassley, and Arlen Specter, *Interim Report on FBI Oversight in the 107th Congress by the Senate Judiciary Committee: FISA Implementation Failures*, February 2003, 11.

82. (p. 143) James McGroddy and Herbert Lin, eds., *A Review of the FBI's Trilogy Information Technology Modernization Program* (Washington, DC: National Academies Press, 2004), 35.

83. (p. 143) McGroddy and Lin, *A Review of the FBI's Trilogy Information Technology Modernization Program*, 36.

84. (p. 143) Clive Thompson, "Open-Source Spying," *New York Times Magazine*, December 3, 2006.

85. (p. 143) Thompson, "Open-Source Spying."

86. (p. 143) In November 2006, FBI Special Agent Bobby Flaim commented at the Security and Privacy session of the Global Forum in Paris that the FBI could sometimes find information online that subpoenas could not uncover.

87. (p. 143) His father had explicitly warned the United States about the son's radical turn. In addition, NSA had picked up Yemenese intercepts discussing using a Nigerian in an attack. Nonetheless, Abdulmutallab was allowed to board a Northwest Airlines plane flying from Amsterdam to Detroit (Scott Shane, "Shadow of 9/11 Is Cast Again," *New York Times*, December 31, 2009).

Chapter 7

1. (p. 145) Rainer Böhme and Thorsten Holz, "The Effect of Stock Spam on Financial Markets," Workshop on the Economics of Information Security, Cambridge, U.K., 2006.

2. (p. 145) The term *bots* comes from *robots*; these are also sometimes called *zombies*.

3. (p. 145) William A. Owens, Kenneth W. Dam, and Herbert S. Lin, *Technology, Policy, Law, and Ethics Regarding U.S. Acquisition and Use of Cyberattack Capabilities* (Washington, DC: National Academies Press, 2009), 353.

4. (p. 146) Evan Cooke, Farnam Jahanian, and Danny McPherson, "The Zombie Roundup: Understanding, Detecting, and Disrupting Botnets," *Usenix Workshop on Steps to Reducing Unwanted Traffic on the Internet (SRUTI 2005)* (Berkeley, CA: USENIX), July 2005, 2.

5. (p. 146) "Botnets for Rent," PBS, http://www.pbs.org/kcet/wiredscience/story/12-botnets for rent.html.

6. (p. 146) Böhme and Holz, "Stock Spam," 16.

7. (p. 146) Michael Lesk, "The New Frontline: Estonia under Cyberassault," *IEEE Security and Privacy* 5, no. 4 (July/August 2007): 76.

8. (p. 146) Jose Nazario, "Security to the Core: The Arbor Networks Security Blog," May 17, 2007, http://assert.arnetworks.com/2007/05/estonian-ddos-attacks-a-summary-to-date/.

9. (p. 146) Lesk, "New Frontline," 77.

10. (p. 146) Eneken Tikk, Kadri Kaska, Kristel Rnnimeri, Mari Kert, Anna-Maria Talihrm, and Liis Vihul, *Cyber Attacks against Georgia: Legal Lessons Identified*, Cooperative Cyber Defense Center of Excellence, Tallinn, Estonia, NATO Unclassified, Version 1.0 (November 2008), 15–16.

11. (p. 146) Owens, Dam, and Lin, *Use of Cyberattack Capabilities*, 81.

12. (p. 147) Thomas R. Johnson, *United States Cryptologic History: The NSA Period, 1952–Present. Volume 5: American Cryptology during the Cold War, 1945–1989; Book III, Retrenchment and Reform: 1972–1980* (Fort Meade, MD: Center for Cryptologic History, National Security Agency, 1995), 145.

13. (p. 147) Johnson, *United States Cryptologic History*, vol. 5, book III, 145.

14. (p. 147) Johnson, *United States Cryptologic History*, vol. 5, book III, 145–146.

15. (p. 148) Laura Rocchio, "Protecting the Price of Bread," National Aeronautics and Space Administration, April 2, 2007, http://landsat.gsfc.nasa.gov/news/news-archive/soc_0010.html.

16. (p. 148) Susan Landau, Stephen Kent, Clinton Brooks, Scott Charney, Dorothy Denning, Whitfield Diffie, Anthony Lauck, Douglas Miller, Peter Neumann, and David Sobel, *Codes, Keys, and Conflicts: Issues in U.S. Crypto Policy: Report of a Special Panel of the ACM U.S. Public Policy Committee (USACM)* (New York: ACM, June 1994), 1.

17. (p. 148) Kenneth Dam and Herbert Lin, *Cryptography's Role in Securing the Information Society* (Washington, D.C.: National Academy Press, 1996), 68.

18. (p. 148) Lourdes was active until early in this century, when most overseas U.S. communications began traveling by fiber-optic cable and the station no longer served a useful function.

19. (p. 148) Matthew Aid, *Secret Sentry: The Untold History of the National Security Agency* (New York: Bloomsbury Press, 2009), 62.

20. (p. 148) Johnson, *United States Cryptologic History*, vol. 5, book III,148.

21. (p. 148) Johnson, *United States Cryptologic History*, vol. 5, book III, 146.

22. (p.149) U.S. Interagency OPSEC Support Staff, *Intelligence Threat Handbook* (June 2004), 37.

23. (p. 149) U.S. General Accounting Office, *Economic Espionage: Information on Threat from U.S. Allies*, T-NSIAD-96–114 (February 1996), 3.

24. (p. 149) (p. 149) U.S. General Accounting Office, *Economic Espionage*, 3.

25. (p. 149) Dam and Lin, *Cryptography's Role*, 33.

26. (p. 149) Peter Schweizer, "The Growth of Economic Espionage," *Foreign Affairs* 75, no. 1 (January/February 1996): 12.

27. (p. 149) William Carley, "A Chip Comes in from the Cold: Tales of High-Tech Spying," *Wall Street Journal*, January 19, 1995.

28. (p. 149) The GAO report does not actually name the nations, calling them instead "Country A," "Country B," and so on. These countries have been identified, respectively, as Israel, France, Germany, and Japan (http://fas.org/irp/gao/nsi96114.htm).

29. (p. 149) U.S. General Accounting Office, *Economic Espionage*, 2.

30. (p. 149) John Flaka, *War by Other Means: Economic Espionage in America* (New York: Norton, 1997), 181–182.

31. (p. 149) This was previously known as the Ministry of Industrial Trade and Industry (MITI).

32. (p. 149) Peter Schweizer, *Friendly Spies: How America's Allies Are Using Economic Espionage to Steal Our Secrets* (New York: Atlantic Monthly Press, 1993), 64.

33. (p. 150) Interagency OPSEC Support Staff, *Intelligence Threat Handbook* (April 1996; rev. May 1996), section 5.

34. (p. 150) Schweizer, *Friendly Spies*, 88–90.

35. (p. 150) Schweizer, "Growth of Economic Espionage," 9.

36. (p. 150) Interagency OPSEC, *Intelligence Threat Handbook* (1996), section 5.

37. (p. 150) Office of the National Counterintelligence Executive, *Annual Report to the Congress on Foreign Economic Collection and Industrial Espionage*, FY07, September 10, 2008, 2.

38. (p. 150) Louis Freeh, testimony before the Subcommittee on Crime, Judiciary Committee, House of Representatives, *Economic Espionage*, May 9, 1996.

39. (p. 151) Robert Mueller, "The FBI: Meeting New Challenges" (speech), National Press Club, June 20, 2003.

40. (p. 151) Office of the National Counterintelligence Executive, *Annual Report to the Congress on Foreign Economic Collection and Industrial Espionage—2005*, August 2006, 1.

41. (p. 151) Schweizer, *Friendly Spies*, 92.

42. (p. 151) Flaka, *War by Other Means*, 152.

43. (p. 151) Soviet agents touring a Grumman aircraft plant in 1987 had adhesive tape on their shoes to pick up slivers of metal for analyzing the planes (Daniel Patrick Moynihan, "How the Soviets Are Bugging America," *Popular Mechanics*, April 1987, 104).

44. (p. 151) Two men in a van belonging to the French consul general in Houston were seen removing garbage bags filled with trash at the home of an executive for a major U.S. defense company; the FBI was called in (Flaka, *War by Other Means*, 87).

45. (p. 151) Schweizer, *Friendly Spies*, 17.

46. (p. 151) Frank Greve, "French Techno-Spies Bugging U.S. Industries," *San Jose Mercury News*, October 21, 1992.

47. (p. 151) Schweizer, *Friendly Spies*, 19, 84.

48. (p. 151) Stansfield Turner, "Intelligence for a New World Order," *Foreign Affairs* 70, no. 4 (Fall 1991): 151.

49. (p. 151) David Sanger and Tim Weiner, "Emerging Role for the C.I.A.: Economic Spy," *New York Times*, October 15, 1995.

50. (p. 152) Alan Cowell, "Bonn Said to Expel U.S. Envoy Accused of Economic Espionage," *New York Times*, March 10, 1997.

51. (p. 152) Nicky Hager, *Secret Power: New Zealand's Role in the International Spy Network* (Nelson, New Zealand: Craig Potton Publishing, 1996); Duncan Campbell, *Interception Capabilities 2000: Development of Surveillance Technology and Risk of Abuse of Economic Information*, Report to the Director General for Research of the European Parliament, Luxemburg (April 1999).

52. (p. 152) The company is now called Thales.

53. (p. 152) James Woolsey, "Why We Spy on Our Allies," *Wall Street Journal*, March 17, 2000.

54. (p. 152) This includes bribes paid to receive a contract. While in many nations, bribery to obtain a contract is legal, in the United States it is illegal.

55. (p. 153) Pub. L. 104-294, Title 18 U.S.C. 1831 et seq.

56. (p. 153) Under §1832 of the act, it is also a criminal offense if a trade secret is misappropriated with intent to create economic benefit for someone other than the owner of the secret.

57. (p. 153) This makes enforcement of the Economic Espionage Act difficult. Even though the law has an extraterritorial aspect, a suspect will not be extradited to the United States to face charges under the act unless economic espionage is a crime in the foreign nation.

58. (p. 153) Owens, Dam, and Lin, *Use of Cyberattack Capabilities*, 26.

59. (p. 153) David A. Espie, "The Domain Program and the InfraGard Program," FBI briefing, slides 10 and 39.

60. (p. 153) U.S. Department of Defense, Defense Security Service, *Targeting U.S. Technologies* (2008), 4.

61. (p. 154) World Trade Organization, *Annual Report 1998* (Geneva: World Trade Organization, 1999), 36.

62. (p. 154) Hal Varian, "An iPod Has Global Value. Ask the (Many) Countries That Make It," *New York Times*, June 28, 2007.

63. (p. 154) Greg Linden, Jason Dedrick, and Kenneth Kraemer, "Who Profits from Innovation in Global Value Chains? A Study of the iPod and Notebook PCs," *Industrial and Corporate Change* (published online June 22, 2009), 33–34, http://icc .oxfordjournals.org/cgi/content/abstract/dtp032.

64. (p. 154) Linden, Dedrick, and Kraemer, "Who Profits from Innovation in Global Value Chains?", 17.

65. (p. 154) Greg Linden, Jason Dedrick, and Kenneth Kraemer, "Innovation and Job Creation in a Global Economy," (UC Irvine: Personal Computing Industry Center, January 2009), 6.

66. (p. 154) Thomas Friedman, *The World Is Flat: A Brief History of the Twenty-first Century* (New York: Farrar, Straus and Giroux, 2005), 134.

67. (p. 154) Friedman, *The World Is Flat*, 136.

68. (p. 155) Benetton's innovations are not just in IT. The company first knits and then dyes the fabric; this is contrary to the way most clothing is manufactured. This change is much to Benetton's advantage. Sewing is slow, dyeing is fast, and doing the process in this order enables the company to respond quickly to customer demand (Peter Dapiran, "Benetton—Global Logistics in Action," *International Journal of Physical Distribution and Logistics Management* 22, no. 6 (1992): 7–11).

69. (p. 155) Kuldeep Kumar, "Technology for Supporting Supply Chain Management," *Communications of the ACM* 44, no. 6 (June 2001): 57–61.

70. (p. 155) The export trading arm of Li and Fung employs fourteen thousand people across three continents (North America, Europe, and Asia).

71. (p. 155) Kasra Ferdows, "New World Manufacturing Order: Supply Chain Management Goes Global in a Dispersed Manufacturing Environment," *All Business*, February 1, 2003.

72. (p. 155) Disclosure: Sun was my employer between 1999 and 2010.

73. (p. 156) Sun's hardware break-fix service was outsourced in the 1990s.

74. (p. 156) This is probably the most frequently asked question of system administrators.

75. (p. 157) In recognition of the leveling resulting from such intellectual capital being available around the globe, journalist Tom Friedman has proclaimed the world *flat*.

76. (p. 157) USA PATRIOT Act of 2001, §1016(e).

77. (p. 157) U.S. Department of Homeland Security, *National Infrastructure Protection Plan* (Washington, DC: U.S. Department of Homeland Security, 2006), 3.

78. (p. 157) U.S. Department of Justice, *Juvenile Computer Hacker Cuts Off FAA Tower at Regional Airport* (March 18, 1998), http://www.justice.gov/criminal/cybercrime/juvenilepld.htm.

79. (p. 158) Committee on Science and Technology for Countering Terrorism, National Research Council, *Making the Nation Safer: The Role of Science and Technology in Countering Terrorism* (Washington, DC: National Academies Press, 2002), 141.

80. (p. 158) Committee on Science and Technology for Countering Terrorism, National Research Council, *Making the Nation Safer*, 141.

81. (p. 158) Markus Brändle and Martin Naedle, "Security for Process Control Systems: An Overview," *IEEE Security and Privacy* 6, no. 6 (November/December 2008): 26.

82. (p. 159) The disruption of others, such as food supply, would create a national crisis that would play out over a much longer period of time.

83. (p. 159) National Infrastructure Protection Center, *Highlights,* vol. 3-02 (June 15, 2002): 5.

84. (p. 159) "Sources: Staged Cyber Attack Reveals Vulnerability in Power Grid," CNN, September 26, 2007.

85. (p. 159) In January 2008 the U.S. government acknowledged that attacks had occurred in an unnamed foreign country.

86. (p. 160) U.S. Department of Justice, Office of Public Affairs, *Alleged International Hacking Ring Caught in $9 Million Fraud* (November 10, 2009); U.S. District Court, Northeastern District of Georgia, Atlanta Division, United States v. Viktor Pleshchuk, Sergei Tsbrikov, Hacker 3, Oleg Covelin, Igor Grudijev, Ronald Tsoi, Evelin Tsoi, and Mikhail Jevgenov, Defendants, Criminal Indictment 1–09-CR-491 (November 10, 2009), 3–5.

87. (p. 160) Kevin Poulsen, "Card Processor Admits to Large Data Breach," *Wired,* January 20, 2009, http://www.wired.com/threatlevel/2009/01/card-processor/.

88. (p. 160) U.S. Department of Justice, Office of Public Affairs, *Alleged International Hacker Indicted for Massive Attack on U.S. Retail and Banking Networks* (August 17, 2009).

89. (p. 160) Saul Hansell, "Citibank Fraud Case Raises Computer Security Questions," *New York Times,* August 19, 1995.

90. (p. 161) U.S.-Canada Power System Outage Task Force, *Final Report on the August 14, 2003 Blackout in the United States and Canada: Causes and Recommendations* (April 2004), 45.

91. (p. 161) U.S.-Canada Power System Outage Task Force, *Final Report,* 65.

92. (p. 161) Gorman, "Electricity Grid in U.S. Penetrated by Spies," *Wall Street Journal* (April 8, 2009).

93. (p. 161) Hackers were employed in the DDoS attack on Georgia.

94. (p. 161) Barton Gellman, "Cyber-Attacks by Al Qaeda Feared," *Washington Post*, June 27, 2002.

95. (p. 161) U.S. General Accountability Office, testimony before the Subcommittee on Emerging Threats, Cybersecurity, and Science and Technology, Committee on Homeland Security, House of Representatives, "Critical Infrastructure Protection: Multiple Efforts to Secure Control Systems Are Under Way, but Challenges Remain," September 2007, 13.

96. (p. 162) U.S. Congress, Senate, Senate Select Committee on Intelligence, *An Assessment of the Aldrich H. Ames Espionage Case and Its Implications for U.S. Intelligence, Part One*, (Washington, DC: Government Printing Office, November 1, 1994).

97. (p. 162) Howard had been under twenty-four-hour-a-day watch by the FBI. With his wife driving, he jumped out of his car as it rounded a turn. Howard's wife then pushed a dummy into Howard's seat, fooling the watchers (Tim Weiner, David Johnston, and Neil A. Lewis, *Betrayal: The Story of Aldrich Ames, an American Spy* (New York: Random House, 1995), 53).

98. (p. 162) U.S. Congress, Senate, *An Assessment of the Aldrich H. Ames Espionage Case*.

99. (p. 162) Weiner, Johnston, and Lewis, *Betrayal*, 74.

100. (p. 162) One CIA source described the Soviets "wrapping up our cases with reckless abandon" (Senate, *An Assessment of the Aldrich H. Ames Espionage Case*).

101. (p. 162) U.S. Congress, Senate, *An Assessment of the Aldrich H. Ames Espionage Case*.

102. (p. 162) U.S. Congress, Senate, *An Assessment of the Aldrich H. Ames Espionage Case*.

103. (p. 162) The five were Kim Philby, Donald Maclean, Guy Burgess, John Cairncross, and Anthony Blunt. Maclean, Burgess, and Philby defected to the USSR, while Blunt, who was unmasked in 1979, served as director of the Courtauld Institute in London. British intelligence discovered Cairncross's spying in 1951 but he was never prosecuted, and his activities were not made public until many years later.

104. (p. 163) Hanssen was uncovered only when his voice was recognized on a tape during an investigation of another agent.

105. (p. 163) Interagency OPSEC, *Intelligence Threat Handbook* (2004), 39–40.

106. (p. 163) U.S. Department of Justice, U.S. Attorney's Office, District of Delaware, *Guilty Plea in Secrets Case*, February 15, 2006.

107. (p. 163) Dam and Lin, *Cryptography's Role*, 32.

108. (p. 164) Marisa Reddy Randazzo, Michelle Keeney, Eileen Kowalski, Dawn Cappelli, and Andrew Moore, *Insider Threat Study: Illicit Cyber Activity in the Banking*

and Finance Sector, Technical Report CMU/SEI-2004-TR-021 ESC-TR-2004-021 (Pittsburgh, PA: Software Engineering Institute, Carnegie, Carnegie Mellon, June 2005).

109. (p. 164) See, for example, Schweizer, *Friendly Spies,* 169–172.

110. (p. 164)According to annual surveys conducted by the Computer Security Institute, between 2004 and 2008, insider attacks account for 44 to 59 percent of all security incidents (Robert Richardson, *2008 CSI Computer Crime & Security Survey,* New York: Computer Security Institute, 2008, 15).

111. (p. 164) This is not the only place in which organized crime has entered the picture. Organized crime has also begun more sophisticated attacks on data. The theft at RBS involved decrypting the stolen data. Another type of attack involves targeting "transient" data. Typically, if stored data are at all sensitive, it will be encrypted, while data in transient storage is not encrypted. Criminals have been targeting the data in transient storage, which is more difficult to access (Verizon Business RISK Team, Verizon Business, *2009 Data Breach Investigations Report,* 22). Verizon reports that such malware is increasingly customized. The customization requires a major investment in time, money, and expertise, but the potential gains make it worth it to organized crime.

112. (p. 164) Dam and Lin, *Cryptography's Role,* 470.

113. (p. 164) Dan Schutzer, "Research Challenges for Fighting Insider Threat in the Financial Services Industry," in Salvatore J. Stolfo, Steven M. Bellovin, Shlomo Hershkop, Angelos D. Keromytis, Sara Sinclair, and Sean W. Smith, eds., *Insider Attack and Cyber Security: Beyond the Hacker* (New York: Springer, 2008), 215.

114. (p. 164) Piero Colaprico, "'Da Telecom dossier sui Ds' Mancini parla dei politici," *La Repubblica,* January 26, 2007.

115. (p. 164) The number is surely higher. As Supreme Court Justice Louis Brandeis observed in 1928, "Whenever a telephone line is tapped, the privacy of the persons at both ends of the line is invaded and *all conversations between them* upon any subject, and, although proper, confidential and privileged, may be overheard" (*Olmsted v. United States,* 476; emphasis added). Many people were undoubtedly wiretapped who were not among the 6,000.

116. (p. 165) Schutzer, "Research Challenges," 215.

117. (p. 165) U.S. Department of Justice, Commission for Review of FBI Security Programs, *A Review of FBI Security Programs* (Washington, DC: U.S. Department of Justice, March 2002), 1.

118. (p. 165) U.S. General Accountability Office, *Information Security: FBI Needs to Address Weaknesses in Critical Network* (Washington, DC: U.S. General Accountability Office, April 2007), 19.

119. (p. 165) Richelson, Jeffrey, *A Century of Spies* (Oxford: Oxford University Press, 1995), 377.

120. (p. 165) Interagency OPSEC, *Intelligence Threat Handbook* (2004), 32–33.

121. (p. 165) Matthew French, "Tech Sabotage during the Cold War," *Federal Computer Week*, April 26, 2004, 2.

122. (p. 165) French, "Tech Sabotage during the Cold War," 3.

123. (p. 165) Richelson, *A Century of Spies*, 378.

124. (p. 166) William Safire, "The Farewell Dossier," *New York Times*, February 4, 2004.

125. (p. 166) Years later Glenn Gaffney, Deputy Director for National Intelligence for Collection, Office of the Director of National Intelligence, observed that "you don't have to corrupt any information to corrupt all of it. . . . Just the fact that your adversary has been present in your system makes the entire system suspect" (James Gosler, "Counterintelligence: Too Narrowly Practiced," in Jennifer Sims and Burton Gerber, eds., *Vaults, Mirrors, and Masks: Rediscovering U.S. Counterintelligence* (Washington, DC: Georgetown University Press, 2009), 193–194).

126. (p. 166) Walter Pincus, "Russian Spies on Rise Here; Administration Worried about 'Aggressive' Economic Espionage," *Washington Post*, September 21, 1999.

127. (p. 166) These data come from CNNIC, whose survey methods are disputed ("China Statistics and Related Data Information and Links," ChinaToday.com, http://www.chinatoday.com/data/data.htm#int). Since CNNIC numbers tend, if anything, to be high, and the report I am citing says that by 1997 0.62 million Chinese were Internet users, I believe "under a million" is accurate.

128. (p. 166) Nathan Thornborough, "Inside the Chinese Hack Attack," *Time Magazine*, August 25, 2005, http://www.time.com/time/nation/article/0,8599,1098371,00.html.

129. (p. 166) Nathan Thornborough, "The Invasion of the Chinese Cyberspies (And the Man Who Tried to Stop Them)," *Time Magazine*, August 29, 2005, 4.

130. (p. 167) Dawn Onley and Patience Wait, "Red Storm Rising," *Government Computer News*, August 17, 2006, 3.

131. (p. 167) Peter Warren, "Smash and Grab, the Hi-Tech Way," *Guardian*, January 19, 2006.

132. (p. 167) Oak Ridge National Laboratory, "Potential Identity Theft," http://www.ornl.gov/identitytheft.

133. (p. 167) Bryan Krekel, *Capability of the People's Republic of China to Conduct Cyber Warfare and Computer Network Exploitation*, prepared for the U.S.-China Economic and Security Review Commission, 2009, 72–74.

134. (p. 167) One researcher, Shishir Nagaraja, was from Cambridge University.

135. (p. 167) Information Warfare Monitor, Munk Center for International Studies, University of Toronto, *Tracking Ghostnet: Investigating a Cyber Espionage Network* (Toronto: Munk Center for International Studies, University of Toronto, March 29, 2009), 40.

136. (p. 167) This included the ministries of Bangladesh, Barbados, Bhutan, Brunei, Iran, and Latvia (Information Warfare Monitor, *Tracking Ghostnet*, 43).

137. (p. 167) This included the Indian embassies to Belgium, Serbia, Germany, Italy, Kuwait, the United States, and Zimbawe (Information Warfare Monitor, *Tracking Ghostnet*, 40).

138. (p. 167) Information Warfare Monitor, *Tracking Ghostnet*, 5.

139. (p. 167) Information Warfare Monitor, *Tracking Ghostnet*, 31–32.

140. (p. 168) Information Warfare Monitor, *Tracking Ghostnet*, 28.

141. (p. 168) Shishir Nagaraja and Ross Anderson, "The Snooping Dragon: Social-Malware Surveillance of the Tibetan Movement," University of Cambridge Computer Laboratory, UCAM-CL-TR-746 (Cambridge: University of Cambridge Computer Laboratory, March 2009), 5.

142. (p. 168) Nart Villineuve, *Breaching Trust: An Analysis of Surveillance and Security Practices on China's Tom-Skype Platform*, Information Warfare Monitor (Toronto: Munk Center for International Studies, University of Toronto, October 1, 2008).

143. (p. 168) Krekel, *Capability of the People's Republic of China*, 6.

144. (p. 168) James Mulvenon, "Chinese Defense Agencies and the 'Digital Triangle' Paradigm," Statement before the U.S.-China Economic and Security Review Commission Hearing on "China's Proliferation and the Impact of Trade Policy on Defense Industries in the United States and China" (Washington, DC: July 12, 2007), 2–3. http://www.uscc.gov/pressreleases/2007/agenda/07_07_12_13agenda.php.

145. (p. 168) Kevin O'Brien, "Upstart Chinese Telecom Company Rattles Industry as It Rises to No. 2," *New York Times*, November 30, 2009.

146. (p. 168) The quote is from *Information War* by Zhu Wenguan and Chen Taiyi and is in Timothy L. Thomas, "China's Electronic Long-Range Reconnaissance," *Military Review*, November/December 2008, 48.

147. (p. 168) Thomas, "China's Electronic Long-Range Reconnaissance."

148. (p. 168) Thomas, "China's Electronic Long-Range Reconnaissance," 49–50.

149. (p. 168) Thomas, "China's Electronic Long-Range Reconnaissance," 50.

150. (p. 168) David Barboza, "Hacking for Fun and Profit in China's Underworld," *New York Times*, February 1, 2010.

151. (p. 169) Krekel, *Capability of the People's Republic of China*, 38–39.

152. (p. 169) Mak did so for over twenty years. He was aided by his younger brother, who immigrated to the United States in 2001 (Office of the National Counterintelligence Executive, *Annual Report to the Congress on Foreign Economic Collection and*

Industrial Espionage, FY08, July 23, 2009, 5). The espionage stopped with the men's arrest in 2005. The quality of the operational methods—data, encrypted and hidden within other files, indirect flights to China, use of code words during conversations—demonstrated expert tradecraft and was a strong indication of government involvement in the espionage.

153. (p. 169) Keith Epstein and Ben Elgin, "Network Security Breaches Plague NASA," *Business Week,* November 20, 2008.

154. (p. 169) Confidential source.

155. (p. 169) Onley and Wait, "Red Storm Rising," 1.

156. (p. 169) Owens, Dam, and Lin, *Use of Cyberattack Capabilities,* 198.

157. (p. 170) Krekel, *Capability of the People's Republic of China,* 59–66.

158. (p. 170) Krekel, *Capability of the People's Republic of China,* 52.

159. (p. 170) Since the attack occurs before any vulnerability has been announced by the vendor, this is called a *zero-day exploit.*

160. (p. 170) According to Google, the information observed was account information, such as the date the account was created, and the subject line; mail contents were not accessed (David Drummond, "A New Approach to China," January 12, 2010, http://googlepublicpolicy.blogspot.com).

161. (p. 170) David Drummond, "A New Approach to China."

162. (p. 170) John Markoff and David Barboza, "2 China Schools Said to Be Tied to Online Attacks," *New York Times,* February 18, 2010.

163. (p. 170) Rhys Blakely, Jonathan Richards, James Rossiter, and Richard Beeston, "MI5 Alert on China's Cyberspace Threat," *Times Online,* December 1, 2007.

164. (p. 171) Interagency OPSEC, *Intelligence Threat Handbook* (2004), 18.

165. (p. 171) Nicholas Eftimiades, *Chinese Intelligence Operations* (Annapolis, MD: Naval Institute Press, 1994), 27.

166. (p. 171) Owens, Dam, and Lin, *Use of Cyberattack Capabilities,* 173–174.

167. (p. 171) Owens, Dam, and Lin, *Use of Cyberattack Capabilities,* 328–329.

168. (p. 171) Owens, Dam, and Lin, *Use of Cyberattack Capabilities,* 332.

169. (p. 171) Timothy Thomas, "Like Adding Wings to the Tiger: Chinese Information War and Practice," *Military Intelligence Professional Bulletin,* July-September 2003, http://www.iwar.org.uk/iwar/resources/china/iw/chinaiw.htm.

170. (p. 171) Gorman, "Electricity Grid in U.S. Penetrated by Spies."

171. (p. 172) Steve Chabinsky, personal communication, December 14, 2009.

172. (p. 172) David Leppard, "Fraudsters' Bugs Transmit Credit Card Details to Pakistan," *Times Online*, October 12, 2008.

173. (p. 172) Henry Samuel, "Chip and Pin Scam 'Has Netted Millions from British Shoppers,'" *Telepgrah.co.uk*, October 10, 2008.

174. (p. 173) U.S. Immigration and Customs Enforcement, U.S. Department of Homeland Security, "ICE, CBP, DOJ Announce International Initiative against Traffickers in Counterfeit Network Hardware" (February 28, 2008), http://www.ice.gov/pi/news/newsreleases/articles/080228washington.htm.

175. (p. 173) Raul Roldan, "FBI Criminal Investigation: Cisco Routers," briefing, January 11, 2008.

176. (p. 173) The damage caused to Cisco's reputation, on the other hand, would not have been minor if the activity had not been uncovered.

177. (p. 173) Roldan, "FBI Criminal Investigation: Cisco Routers."

178. (p. 173) Presumably confidential communications would be encrypted but even the transactional information, who is communicating with whom when, is potentially quite revealing.

179. (p. 173) This is known as 4G LTE.

180. (p. 173) In the end, AT&T went with Alcatel-Lucent and Ericsson.

Chapter 8

1. (p. 175) Under the SHAMROCK Program, between August 1944 and May 1975 RCA Global and ITT World provided copies to the NSA of essentially all international communications from the United States, while Western Union International gave copies of only certain telegrams to the surveillance agency. The NSA estimated that by the final months of the program it was reviewing one hundred fifty thousand telegrams a month (U.S. Congress, Senate, *Final Report of the Select Committee to Study Governmental Operations with Respect to Intelligence Activities: Supplementary Detailed Staff Reports on Intelligence Activities and the Rights of Americans: Book II* (Washington, DC: Government Printing Office, 1976), 765).

2. (p. 175) U.S. Congress, Senate, *Final Report of the Select Committee to Study Governmental Operations with Respect to Intelligence Activities*, 749.

3. (p. 175) The First Amendment reads as follows: "Congress shall make no law respecting an establishment of religion, or prohibiting the free exercise thereof; or abridging the freedom of speech, or of the press; or the right of the people peaceably to assemble, and to petition the Government for a redress of grievances."

4. (p. 175) U.S. Congress, Senate, *Final Report of the Select Committee to Study Governmental Operations with Respect to Intelligence Activities*, 749–750.

5. (p. 175) The interception ended in the fall of 1973 (U.S. Congress, Senate, *Final Report of the Select Committee to Study Governmental Operations with Respect to Intelligence Activities*, 756–757).

6. (p. 176) There was no evidence of illegal activities. In 1989 FBI Director William Sessions said: "The broadening of the investigation in October 1983, in essence, directed all field offices to regard each CISPES chapter, wherever located, as a proper subject of investigation. Based on the documentation available to the FBI by October 1983, there was no reason ... to expand the investigation so widely" (U.S. Senate, *Senate Select Committee on Intelligence Inquiry into the FBI Investigation of the Committee in Solidarity with the People of El Salvador* (Washington, DC: Government Printing Office, 1989), 122). See also James Dempsey and David Cole, *Terrorism and the Constitution* (Los Angeles: First Amendment Foundation, 1999), 22–24.

7. (p. 176) Its purpose was described in an FBI memo as providing "assistance to Palestinian students in their education and settlement in the United States and to report, explain, correct and spread the Palestinian cause to all people" (Dempsey and Cole, *Terrorism and the Constitution*, 44–45).

8. (p. 176) U.S. Department of Justice, Executive Office for Immigration Review, Immigration Court, Los Angeles, *In the Matters of: Khader Musa Hamde and Michel Ibrahim Nasif Shehaldeh, in Deportation Proceedings Files A19 262 560 Los Angeles CA A30 650 528 respectively; Order of the Immigration Judge* (October 29, 2007).

9. (p. 176) The organization, the Popular Front for the Liberation of Palestine (PFLP), provided support for social services—day care, healthcare, and so on—as well as for terrorist activities. Material support for the terrorist side of the organization would be grounds for prosecution, but the LA 8's efforts were directed toward the social service side of the PFLP.

10. (p. 176) *Tash Hepting et al. v. AT&T Corporation*, U.S. District Court for the Northern District of California, Case 3:06-cv-00672-vrw, Exhibit C, Klein-C3.

11. (p. 176) J. Scott Marcus, affidavit in *Tash Hepting et al. v. AT&T Corporation et al.*, United States Second District Court for Northern California, Case 3:06-cv-0672-vrw (June 8, 2006), 21.

12. (p. 177) Mark Klein, personal communication, December 16, 2009.

13. (p. 177) Susan Landau, "National Security on the Line," *Journal of Telecommunications and High Technology Law*, 4, no. 2 (Spring 2006): 411.

14. (p. 177) Vassilis Prevelakis and Diomidis Spinellis, "The Athens Affair," *IEEE Spectrum*, July 2007, 18–25.

15. (p. 177) For a PSTN or cellular call, the phone number might reveal who is communicating with whom; on the Internet, the equivalent, which is an IP address,

may be quite revelatory, or it might simply signify an Internet café with two dozen users. Of course, the IP address may be combined with other information that may, in fact, identify the user.

16. (p. 178) *Wired How-To Wiki, Tap a Phone Line,* http://howto.wired.com/wiki/Tap a Phone Line.

17. (p. 178) Adam Clymer, "Gingrich is Heard Urging Tactics in Ethics Case," *New York Times,* January 10 1997.

18. (p. 178) Office of the Manager, National Communications System, *SMS over SS7,* NCS Technical Information Bulletin 03-2 (December 2003), 41–42.

19. (p. 178) D. Richard Kuhn, Thomas J. Walsh, and Steffen Fries, *Security Considerations for Voice over IP Systems,* National Institute for Standards and Technology Special Publication 800-58 (Gaithersberg, MD: National Institute for Standards and Technology, January 2005), 4.

20. (p. 178) Kuhn, Walsh, and Fries, *Security Considerations for Voice over IP Systems,* 82–83.

21. (p. 179) One estimate is fifteen to twenty systems other than those of the sender and receiver (Kuhn, Walsh, and Fries, *Security Considerations for Voice over IP Systems,* 18).

22. (p. 179) Patrick Traynor, Patrick McDaniel, and Thomas La Porta, *Security for Telecommunications Networks* (New York: Springer, 2008), 144–145.

23. (p. 179) Tom Berson, *Skype Security Evaluation* (October 18, 2005), 11, http://www.anagram.com/berson/abskyeval.html.

24. (p. 179) Nart Villineuve, *Breaching Trust: An Analysis of Surveillance and Security Practices on China's Tom-Skype Platform,* Information Warfare Monitor (Toronto: Munk Center for International Studies, University of Toronto, October 1, 2008). The insecurity of the logging servers was corrected after the report was issued.

25. (p. 179) Kuhn, Walsh, and Fries, *Security Considerations for Voice over IP Systems,* 77.

26. (p. 179) This phenomenon results from the distinctive packet lengths for each of the phonemes, which arises from compression used to save communications bandwidth. If padding, which adds bits so that all packets are a longer common length, is used, then it becomes much more difficult to recognize words or phrases within the encrypted communications (Charles V. Wright, Lucas Ballard, Scott E. Coull, Fabian Monrose, Gerald M. Masson, "Spot Me If You Can: Uncovering Spoken Phrases in Encrypted VoIP Conversations," Proceedings of the 2008 IEEE Symposium on Security and Privacy, Piscataway, NJ: IEEE, 2008).

27. (p. 179) Even when sessions are encrypted through SSL, through examining the number and length of the encrypted http responses, it is possible to determine which web pages are being viewed.

28. (p. 180) Asoke Talukder, "Clean and Tidy," *Communications Engineer* 3, no. 4 (2005): 39.

29. (p. 180) Traynor, McDaniel, and La Porta, *Security for Telecommunications Networks*, 77.

30. (p. 180) Finding active phone numbers from which to launch the assault is the main problem in this space (Traynor, McDaniel, and La Porta, *Security for Telecommunications Networks*, 80–81, 83–86).

31. (p. 181) BluFlo, "Handheld SCADA," http://www.bluflo.com/ndex.php?option =comcontent&taks=view&id=27&itemid=42.

32. (p. 181) Traynor, McDaniel, and La Porta, *Security for Telecommunications Networks*, 59–60.

33. (p. 181) Pub. L. 104–104, 110 Stat. 56.

34. (p. 181) Traynor, McDaniel, and La Porta, *Security for Telecommunications Networks*, 59.

35. (p. 181) The fee of $2,000 was AT&T's fee in the state of California, which should be representative. This included a $590 nonrecurring fee, a $100 monthly charge, and a small mileage charge.

36. (p. 181) AT&T was advertising "Talk and surf the Web at the same time on 3G."

37. (p. 181) Jenna Wortham, "AT&T Urges Customers to Use Less Wireless Data," *New York Times*, December 10, 2009.

38. (p. 182) Wayne Jansen and Karen Scarfone, *Guidelines on Cell Phone and PDA Security*, National Institute of Standards and Technology Special Publication 800-124 (Gaithersberg, MD: National Institute of Standards and Technology, October 2008), 3–8.

39. (p. 182) All it takes to be able to track a user is for them to register their cell number with a website and agreeing via text to their phone that "X" is their "buddy" and allowed to have their location information. A *Guardian* newspaper reporter described the system, whose security rests on responding to a text message sent to the cell of the person being tracked (Ben Goldacre, "How I Stalked My Girlfriend," guardian.co.uk, February 1, 2006, http://www.guardian.co.uk/technology/2006/ feb/01/news.g2). Such a system is easy to subvert.

40. (p. 183) The discussion in this section relies heavily on Steven M. Bellovin, Matt Blaze, Ernie Brickell, Clinton Brooks, Vinton Cerf, Whitfield Diffie, Susan Landau, Jon Peterson, John Treichler, "Security Implications of Applying the Communications Assistance for Law Enforcement Act to Voice over IP" (2006), http://www.cs.columbia .edu/~smb/papers/CALEAVOIPreport.pdf

41. (p. 183) This is interconnected VoIP.

42. (p. 187) Steven M. Bellovin et al., "Security Implications," 15.

43. (p. 187) Steven M. Bellovin, Matt Blaze, Whitfield Diffie, Susan Landau, Peter Neumann, and Jennifer Rexford, "Risking Communications Security: Potential Hazards of the 'Protect America Act,'" *IEEE Security and Privacy*, 6, no. 1 (January/February 2008): 29.

44. (p. 188) Steven M. Bellovin et al., "Security Implications," 15.

45. (p. 188) Bellovin et al., "Security Implications," 16–17.

46. (p. 188) U.S. Department of Justice, Office of Inspector General, Audit Division, *The Implementation of the Communications Assistance for Law Enforcement Act*, Audit Report 06–13 (Washington, DC: U.S. Department of Justice, March 2006), 54.

47. (p. 188) U.S. Department of Justice, Office of Inspector General, Audit Division, *Implementation of the Communications Assistance for Law Enforcement Act*, 54–55.

48. (p. 188) The bill was not introduced; Senator Mike DeWine, who had been planning to do so, lost his reelection bid and chose not to introduce the bill late in the term. That does not mean that the FBI will not try a variation of the bill at a later date. CALEA itself was first proposed by the FBI in 1992 as the "Digital Telephony" bill. It was reintroduced in the 1994 session and passed in the waning days of the term.

49. (p. 188) Bellovin et al., "Security Implications," 17.

50. (p. 189) U.S. Department of Justice, Office of Inspector General, Audit Division, *The Implementation of the Communications Assistance for Law Enforcement Act*, 23–30.

51. (p. 189) Bellovin et al., "Security Implications," 17.

52. (p. 189) Center for Democracy and Technology, *Balancing the Location Needs of E911 with Privacy and Innovation* (Washington, DC: Center for Democracy and Technology, May 2007).

53. (p. 189) Yochai Benkler, *Wealth of Networks: How Social Production Transforms Markets and Freedom* (New Haven, CT: Yale University Press, 2006), 370.

54. (p. 189) Jed Rubenfeld, "The End of Privacy," *Stanford Law Review* 61, no. 1 (October 2008): 118–199.

55. (p. 190) James Otis, "Against Writs of Assistance," February 1761, http://www .constitution.org/bor/otis_against_writs.txt.

56. (p. 190) Otis, "Against Writs of Assistance."

57. (p. 190) Rubenfeld, "The End of Privacy," 124–125.

58. (p. 190) Rubenfeld, "The End of Privacy," 158–160.

59. (p. 190) Al Gidari, personal communication, July 27, 2009.

60. (p. 191) Steven M. Bellovin, personal communication, January 6, 2009.

61. (p. 191) Sun Microsystems Inc., Proxy Statement, June 8, 2009.

62. (p. 191) I believe that despite the study's limited sample size, the conclusions hold much more broadly.

63. (p. 191) Shishir Nagaraja, "The Economics of Covert Community Detection and Hiding," *WEIS 2008—Seventh Workshop on Economics of Information Security* (Hanover, NH, June 25–28, 2008), 8–9.

64. (p. 191) This description is vague, which is in fact one of the problems in anonymization research. What Narayanan and Shmatikov show is that for any reasonable definition of privacy, reidentification is possible (Arvind Narayanan and Vitaly Shmatikov, "Deanonymizing Social Networks," *Proceedings of the 2009 IEEE Computer Society Symposium on Research in Security and Privacy* (Piscataway, NJ: IEEE, 2009), 173–187).

65. (p. 191) Arvind Narayanan and Vitaly Shmatikov, "Deanonymizing Social Networks."

66. (p. 191) This statement is true as of this writing (September 22, 2009). Obviously Facebook may change its policies at any time.

67. (p. 192) Steven Bellovin et al., "Risking Communications Security," 30.

68. (p. 192) Eric Lichtblau and James Risen, "Officials Say U.S. Wiretaps Exceeded Law," *New York Times*, April 15, 2009.

69. (p. 192) James Risen and Eric Lichtblau, "E-Mail Surveillance Renews Concern in Congress," *New York Times*, June 16, 2009.

70. (p. 192) U.S. Department of Justice, Office of the Inspector General, Oversight and Review Division, *A Review of the Federal Bureau of Investigation's Use of Exigent Letters and Other Informal Requests for Telephone Records* (Washington, DC: U.S. Department of Justice, January 2010), 16.

71. (p. 192) 18 U.S.C. §2709(b)(2).

72. (p. 192) U.S. Department of Justice, Office of the Inspector General, Oversight and Review Division, *Federal Bureau of Investigation's Use of Exigent Letters,* 10.

73. (p. 192) U.S. Department of Justice, Office of the Inspector General, *A Review of the Federal Bureau of Investigation's Use of the National Security Letters* (Special Report) (Washington, DC: U.S. Department of Justice, March 2007), 22.

74. (p. 192) U.S. Department of Justice, Office of the Inspector General, Oversight and Review Division, *Federal Bureau of Investigation's Use of Exigent Letters,* 65.

75. (p. 193) U.S. Department of Justice, Office of the Inspector General, Oversight and Review Division, *Federal Bureau of Investigation's Use of Exigent Letters,* 20.

76. (p. 193) As often happens with people who work together, the two groups also socialized together. This further brought down barriers (U.S. Department of Justice, Office of the Inspector General, Oversight and Review Division, *Federal Bureau of Investigation's Use of Exigent Letters,* 25–26).

77. (p. 193) U.S. Department of Justice, Office of the Inspector General, Oversight and Review Division, *Federal Bureau of Investigation's Use of Exigent Letters,* 13.

78. (p. 193) U.S. Department of Justice, Office of the Inspector General, Oversight and Review Division, *Federal Bureau of Investigation's Use of Exigent Letters*, 41–42.

79. (p. 193) U.S. Department of Justice, Office of the Inspector General, Oversight and Review Division, *Federal Bureau of Investigation's Use of Exigent Letters*, 65.

80. (p. 193) U.S. Department of Justice, Office of the Inspector General, Oversight and Review Division, *Federal Bureau of Investigation's Use of Exigent Letters*, 137–138.

81. (p. 193) U.S. Department of Justice, Office of the Inspector General, Oversight and Review Division, *Federal Bureau of Investigation's Use of Exigent Letters*, 70.

82. (p. 193) U.S. Department of Justice, Office of the Inspector General, Oversight and Review Division, *Federal Bureau of Investigation's Use of Exigent Letters*, 70.

83. (p. 193) U.S. Department of Justice, Office of the Inspector General, Oversight and Review Division, *Federal Bureau of Investigation's Use of Exigent Letters*, 46–47.

84. (p. 193) U.S. Department of Justice, Office of the Inspector General, Oversight and Review Division, *Federal Bureau of Investigation's Use of Exigent Letters*, 70.

85. (p. 193) In fact, after May 2006 the community-of-interest requests appeared in boilerplate language in NSLs (U.S. Department of Justice, Office of the Inspector General, Oversight and Review Division, *Federal Bureau of Investigation's Use of Exigent Letters*, 56–57).

86. (p. 193) U.S. Department of Justice, Office of the Inspector General, Oversight and Review Division, *Federal Bureau of Investigation's Use of Exigent Letters*, 60.

87. (p. 193) U.S. Department of Justice, Office of the Inspector General, Oversight and Review Division, *Federal Bureau of Investigation's Use of Exigent Letters*, 74.

88. (p. 194) U.S. Department of Justice, Office of the Inspector General, Oversight and Review Division, *Federal Bureau of Investigation's Use of Exigent Letters*, 44, 182–184.

89. (p. 194) U.S. Department of Justice, Office of the Inspector General, Oversight and Review Division, *Federal Bureau of Investigation's Use of Exigent Letters*, 44.

90. (p. 194) U.S. Department of Justice, Office of the Inspector General, Oversight and Review Division, *Federal Bureau of Investigation's Use of Exigent Letters*, 47.

91. (p. 194) U.S. Department of Justice, Office of the Inspector General, Oversight and Review Division, *Federal Bureau of Investigation's Use of Exigent Letters*, 48.

92. (p. 194) U.S. Department of Justice, Office of the Inspector General, Oversight and Review Division, *Federal Bureau of Investigation's Use of Exigent Letters*, 70.

93. (p. 194) U.S. Department of Justice, Office of the Inspector General, Oversight and Review Division, *Federal Bureau of Investigation's Use of Exigent Letters*, 74.

94. (p. 194) U.S. Department of Justice, Office of the Inspector General, Oversight and Review Division, *Federal Bureau of Investigation's Use of Exigent Letters*, 82, 84, 88.

95. (p. 194) U.S. Department of Justice, Office of the Inspector General, Oversight and Review Division, *Federal Bureau of Investigation's Use of Exigent Letters*, 82.

96. (p. 194) U.S. Department of Justice, Office of the Inspector General, Oversight and Review Division, *Federal Bureau of Investigation's Use of Exigent Letters*, 86.

97. (p. 194) U.S. Department of Justice, Office of the Inspector General, Oversight and Review Division, *Federal Bureau of Investigation's Use of Exigent Letters*, 124–127.

98. (p. 194) The use of exigent letters grew out of experience in the New York field office. One telephone company analyst who worked with them there briefed the CAU, which adopted them without question. Analysts from the other companies were pressed to accept them (U.S. Department of Justice, Office of the Inspector General, Oversight and Review Division, *Federal Bureau of Investigation's Use of Exigent Letters*, 40–42).

99. (p. 194) U.S. Department of Justice, Office of the Inspector General, Oversight and Review Division, *Federal Bureau of Investigation's Use of Exigent Letters*, 191.

100. (p. 195) U.S. Department of Justice, Office of the Inspector General, Oversight and Review Division, *Federal Bureau of Investigation's Use of Exigent Letters*, 276.

101. (p. 195) Bellovin et al., "Security Implications," 15.

102. (p. 195) Sometimes buildings are erected before such issues are brought to light. A striking one occurred with New York's Citicorp Center. A year after the tower was built in 1977, it was discovered to be at risk of collapse if strong hurricane winds came at a 45-degree angle. It was retrofitted with steel plates, which corrected the problem (Joseph Morgenstern, "The Fifty-Nine Story Crisis," *New Yorker*, May 29, 1995, 45–53).

103. (p. 195) Network Working Group, *RFC 2804—IETF Policy on Wiretapping*, May 2000, http://www.faqs.org/rfcs/rfc2804.html.

104. (p. 195) Network Working Group, *RFC 2804—IETF Policy on Wiretapping*.

105. (p. 196) Whitfield Diffie and Susan Landau, *Privacy on the Line: The Politics of Wiretapping and Encryption*, rev. ed. (Cambridge, MA: MIT Press, 2007), 232–239.

106. (p. 196) Matt Blaze, "Protocol Failure in the Escrowed Encryption Standard," *Proceedings of the Second ACM Conference on Computer and Communications Security* (New York: ACM, November 1994), 59–67.

107. (p. 196) Micah Sherr, Eric Cronin, Sandy Clark, and Matt Blaze, "Signaling Vulnerabilities in Wiretapping Systems" (*IEEE Security and Privacy* 3, no. 6 (November/December 2005): 13–25.

108. (p. 196) Sherr et al., "Signaling Vulnerabilities in Wiretapping Systems."

109. (p. 196) A 2007 system was using MD5 for hashing even though the algorithm had already been shown to be weak.

110. (p. 196) Tom Cross, "Exploiting Lawful Intercept to Wiretap the Internet," *Black Hat DC 2010* (February 2010); the architecture is from F. Baker, B. Foster, and C. Sharp, *RFC 3924: Cisco Architecture for Lawful Intercept in IP Networks* (October 2004), http://www.faqs.org/rfcs/rfc3924.html.

111. (p. 197) The first problem in the architecture was that the system error messages stated whether the request had an incorrect username or an incorrect password. This simplifies finding a valid username. The second problem was with implementations. The system was designed to compare the hash of the interception request with the hash of the expected response, and the protocol called for message digests shorter than 12 bytes to be discarded. Many implementations did not do that, allowing a small brute-force attack to find an appropriate credential (Cross, "Exploiting Lawful Intercept," 4–6).

112. (p. 197) Tom Cross, personal communication, March 7, 2010.

113. (p. 197) David G. Boak, *A History of U.S. Communications Security (Volume I); the David G. Boak Lectures, National Security Agency* (Fort Meade, MD: National Security Agency, 1973), 59.

114. (p. 197) The Chinese-manufactured smartcard readers were discovered before the damage was devastating, and the consequences of the fake Cisco routers was minor. The equipment did not have secret back doors (John Markoff, "F.B.I. Says the Military Had Bogus Computer Gear," *New York Times*, May 9, 2008), and the counterfeiting appeared to have been done solely for profit. Genuine routers cost $1,300, while the fakes sold for a little under a fifth of that. (These are low-end routers; high-end Cisco routers designed to work in the Internet backbone run to millions of dollars.) There was a real market for the fakes, which came into the United States through a variety of suppliers.

115. (p. 197) Seagate, "Maxtor Basics Personal Storage 3200," http://www.seagate .com/www/en-us/support/downloads/personal storage/ps3200-sw.

116. (p. 197) John Flaka, *War by Other Means: Economic Espionage in America* (New York: W.W. Norton and Company, 1997), 117.

117. (p. 198) David Kahn, *The Codebreakers: The Comprehensive History of Secret Communication from Ancient Times to the Internet,* rev. ed. (New York: Scribner, 1996), 33.

118. (p. 198) David G. Boak, *A History of U.S. Communications Security (Volume II); the David G. Boak Lectures, National Security Agency* (Fort Meade, MD: National Security Agency, 1973), 10.

119. (p. 198) Boak, *A History of U.S. Communications Security (Volume II)*, 10.

120. (p. 199) http://www.crypto.com/blog/wiretap_risks.

121. (p. 199) That is why web-based financial transactions are secured through SSL.

122. (p. 199) Boak, *A History of U.S. Communications Security (Volume I)*, 59.

123. (p. 199) This was the credo of the Mountain States Telephone and Telegraph Company in the early years of the twentieth century.

124. (p. 200) Andrew Hetherington, "Constitutional Purpose and Interclause Conflict: The Constraints Imposed on Congress by the Copyright Clause," *Michigan Telecommunications Technical Law Review* 9 (2003): 479.

125. (p. 200) 206 U.S. 46 (1907).

126. (p. 200) *Kansas v. Colorado*, 90.

127. (p. 200) 514 U.S. 779 (1995).

128. (p. 201) *U.S. Terms Limits, Inc. v. Thornton*, 838.

129. (p. 201) The 1786–1787 Shay's Rebellion was an insurgency mounted by poor farmers in western Massachusetts objecting to paying taxes needed to repay Revolutionary War debts.

130. (p. 201) As Supreme Court Justice Robert Jackson observed, the Constitution is not a suicide pact (*Terminiello v. Chicago*, 337 U.S. 1 (1949), Robert Jackson, dissenting).

131. (p. 201) These include, respectively, President Lincoln's suspension of habeas corpus, the internment of Japanese-American citizens, and denial of civil liberties, including freedom of association and freedom of speech, among others.

132. (p. 201) Richard Posner, *Not a Suicide Pact: The Constitution in a Time of National Emergency* (Oxford: Oxford University Press, 2006), 44.

133. (p. 201) *Woods v. Cloyd W. Miller* Co., 333 U.S. 138 (No. 486) 74 F.Supp. 546, reversed, Jackson (concurring).

134. (p. 202) *Woods v. Cloyd W. Miller Co.* 333 U.S. 138 (No. 486) 74 F.Supp. 546, reversed, Jackson (concurring).

135. (p. 202) Larry Lessig named this the "West Coast code" in deference to Silicon Valley.

136. (p. 202) Windows 3.1 was introduced in 1992. Vista was released in stages, first to hardware and software manufacturers, then businesses, and finally in retail; worldwide distribution was in 2007.

137. (p. 202) Windows 3.1 had been built on the model of a single user, not as part of a network.

138. (p. 202) QWERTY, the absurd and counterintuitive keyboard layout, dates from 1874. It was adopted to prevent the most frequently typed letters from hitting each other as they were pressed. Mechanical typewriters are long gone, but the QWERTY keyboard, with its less-than-optimal layout, endures.

Chapter 9

1. (p. 203) Laura Donohue, *The Cost of Counterterrorism: Power, Politics, and Liberty* (Cambridge: Cambridge University Press, 2008), 3.

2. (p. 203) The Universal Declaration of Human Rights was passed by the UN General Assembly on December 10, 1948; Article 12 states:

"No one shall be subjected to arbitrary interference with his privacy, family, home or correspondence, nor to attacks upon his honor and reputation. Everyone has the right to the protection of the law against such interference or attacks."

3. (p. 204) In the 1970s, investigative work by *New York Times* reporter David Burnham uncovered massive graft in the New York City Police Department (David Burnham, "Graft Paid to Police Here Said to Run into Millions," *New York Times,* April 25, 1970). The Knapp Commission conducted a major investigation into police corruption, and there were multiple changes in the administration of the New York City Police Department.

4. (p. 204) 406 U.S. 665 (1972).

5. (p. 204) 406 U.S. 665 (1972), 707.

6. (p. 204) 406 U.S. 665 (1972), 705.

7. (p. 204) 406 U.S. 665 (1972), 705–706.

8. (p. 205) Code of Federal Regulations §50.10.

9. (p. 205) U.S. Department of Justice, Office of the Inspector General, Oversight and Review Division, *A Review of the Federal Bureau of Investigation's Use of Exigent Letters and Other Informal Requests for Telephone Records* (January 2010), 92–95.

10. (p. 205) Oversight and Review Division, *FBI Use of Exigent Letters*, 116–121.

11. (p. 205) Jed Rubenfeld, "The End of Privacy," *Stanford Law Review,* 61, no. 1 (October 2008), 129.

12. (p. 206) In 1914 the U.K. Parliament passed home rule for Ireland; World War I intervened before the law was implemented. The Protestant counties in the north of the country objected and instead the nation was partitioned. There was home rule for the Republic of Ireland (the southern two-thirds of Ireland), while the northern counties were to be part of the United Kingdom.

13. (p. 206) On August 9, 1971, the Northern Ireland security forces arrested 342 people; on February 14, 1972, they arrested an additional 2,447 (Donohue, *Cost of Counterterrorism,* 37).

14. (p. 206) Donohue, *Cost of Counterterrorism,* 38.

15. (p. 206) Dermot Walsh, *Bloody Sunday and the Rule of Law in Northern Ireland* (New York: St. Martin's Press, 2000), 12.

16. (p. 207) John F. Burns, "British Premier Apologizes for 'Bloody Sunday' Killings in 1972," *New York Times,* June 15, 2010.

17. (p. 207) Donohue, *Cost of Counterterrorism,* 26.

18. (p. 207) Steven M. Bellovin, Matt Blaze, Whitfield Diffie, Susan Landau, Peter Neumann, and Jennifer Rexford, "Risking Communications Security: Potential Hazards of the 'Protect America Act,'" *IEEE Security and Privacy* 6, no. 1 (January/February 2008), 30.

19. (p. 207) Lichtblau and Risen, "Officials Say U.S. Wiretaps Exceeded Law," *New York Times,* April 15, 2009, A1.

20. (p. 207) This occurred during a meeting on the Protect America Act, October 25, 2007.

21. (p. 207) A particularly striking example of this occurred in the United Kingdom, where the Regulation of Investigatory Powers Act (RIPA), which, while greatly expanding the scope of the government's ability to conduct surveillance, still limited it to criminal and national-security cases. RIPA was applied to a family that the local government believed had given a false address in order to enroll their three-year-old in a favored nursery school. The family's daily car trips and sleeping habits were monitored by police to determine the family's actual place of residence ("Spying on You for Your Own Good," *The Guardian Weekly,* April 18, 2008, 14).

22. (p. 207) James Duff, *Report of the Director of the Administrative Office of the United States Courts on Applications for Delayed-Notice Search Warrants and Extensions* (July 2, 2009), 8.

23. (p. 207) This decision was made by the National Security Division, the FBI's counter foreign intelligence division. The 2010 Inspector General report expressed concern: "We believe that inaccurate statements to the FISA Court are serious matters. They also affect the credibility of representations made by the government." (Oversight and Review Division, *FBI Use of Exigent Letters,* 128).

24. (p. 208) James Baker, "Spying on the Home Front," PBS Frontline (March 2, 2007).

25. (p. 208) Matthew Aid, *Secret Sentry: The Untold History of the National Security Agency* (New York: Bloomsbury Press, 2009), 249.

26. (p. 208) Samantha Power, "The Democrats and National Security," *New York Review of Books,* August 14, 2008, http://www.nybooks.com/articles/archives/2008/aug/14/the-democrats-national-security/.

27. (p. 208) William A. Owens, Kenneth W. Dam, and Herbert S. Lin, *Technology, Policy, Law, and Ethics Regarding U.S. Acquisition and Use of Cyberattack Capabilities* (Washington, DC: National Academies Press, 2009), 18.

28. (p. 208) Henry Landau, *The Enemy Within* (New York: Putnam, 1937), 77–91.

29. (p. 209) Mitchell Silber and Arvin Bhatt, *Radicalization in the West: The Home-grown Threat* (New York: New York City Police Department, 2007), 82.

30. (p. 209) Christopher Dickey, *Securing the City: Inside America's Best Counterterror Force—the NYPD* (New York: Simon & Schuster, 2009), xi.

31. (p. 209) Michael Cooper, "Ex-CIA Spy Chief to Run Police Intelligence," *New York Times*, January 25, 2002.

32. (p. 209) Mitchell Silber and Arvin Bhatt, *Radicalization in the West: The Home-grown Threat* (New York City Police Department, 2007), 5.

33. (p. 209) Silber and Bhatt, *Radicalization*, 84.

34. (p. 209) Silber and Bhatt, *Radicalization*, 22–53.

35. (p. 210) Silber and Bhatt, *Radicalization*, 7–8.

36. (p. 210) Susan Landau, "National Security on the Line," *Journal of Telecommunications and High Technology Law*, 4, 2 (Spring 2006), 442.

37. (p. 210) Dickey, *Securing the City*, 213–214.

38. (p. 210) (p. 210) Dickey, *Securing the City*, 212.

39. (p. 210) Silber and Bhatt, *Radicalization*, 49.

40. (p. 210) Dickey, *Securing the City*, 272.

41. (p. 211) Dickey, *Securing the City*, 96.

42. (p. 211) Dickey, *Securing the City*, 64–65.

43. (p. 211) Don Van Natta Jr., Elaine Sciolino, and Stephen Grey, "In Tapes, Receipts, and a Diary, Details of a British Terror Case," *New York Times*, August 28, 2006.

44. (p. 211) Christopher Caldwell, "Counterterrorism in the U.K.; After Londonistan," *New York Times*, June 25, 2006.

45. (p. 211) Scott Shane, "Pakistan Detains Five Americans in Raid Tied to Militants," *New York Times*, December 9, 2009.

46. (p. 212) Landau, *National Security on the Line*, 442.

47. (p. 212) Jane Mayer, "The Trial: Eric Holder and the Battle over Khalid Sheikh Mohammed," *New Yorker*, February 15 and 22, 2010, 56.

48. (p. 212) Paul Starr, *The Creation of the Media of the Media: Political Origins of Modern Communications* (New York: Basic Books, 2004), 3.

49. (p. 212) Starr, *Creation of the Media*, 159.

50. (p. 212) Landau, "National Security on the Line," 446.

51. (p. 212) Landau, "National Security on the Line," 446.

52. (p. 213) David Fromkin, *A Peace to End All Peace* (New York: Holt, 1989), 240.

53. (p. 213) Ashok Bardhan and Cynthia Kroll, "Competitiveness and an Emerging Sector: The Russian Software Industry and its Global Linkages," *Industry and Innovation* 13, no. 1 (March 2006), 69–95:

54. (p. 213) Jagdish Bhagwati, "Made in China," *New York Times*, February 18, 2007.

55. (p. 214) Will Hutton, "Power, Corruption, and Lies," guardian.co.uk, January 8, 2007.

56. (p. 214) Bhagwati, "Made in China."

57. (p. 214) Edward Wong, "After Long Ban, Western China Is Back Online," *New York Times* (May 14, 2010).

58. (p. 214) Richard Stone, "Internet Blockade Puts a Strain on Science," *Science* 326 (December 11, 2009): 1471.

59. (p. 214) Bhagwati, "Made in China."

60. (p. 215) Bruce Berkowitz and Allan Goodman, *Best Truth: Intelligence in the Information Age* (New Haven, CT: Yale University Press, 2000), 75.

61. (p. 215) Joseph Nye, "Peering into the Future," *Foreign Affairs*, July/August 1994, 86–88.

62. (p. 215) Berkowitz and Goodman, *Best Truth*, 4.

63. (p. 215) Nye, "Peering into the Future," 86–88.

64. (p. 216) Nye, "Peering into the Future," 4. While the United States was taken by surprise by the Indian nuclear tests in 1998, not everyone else was. An "obscure anti-Indian newsletter," *Charhdi Kala International*, reported "feverish" activity at the site (Nye, "Peering into the Future," 2).

65. (p. 216) Bobby Inman, in a hearing on January 19, 1996, of the Commission on the Roles and Responsibilities of the United States Intelligence Community, *Preparing for the 21st Century: An Appraisal of U.S. Intelligence* (Washington, DC: Government Printing Office, March 1, 1996), http://www.fas.org/irp/commission/testinma.htm.

66. (p. 217) Treverton, *Reshaping National Security*, 215.

67. (p. 217) Treverton, *Reshaping National Security*, 113.

68. (p. 217) Treverton, *Reshaping National Security*, 133.

69. (p. 217) Patrick Ball, affidavit in *Atlanta Division of the American Civil Liberties Union of Georgia et al. v. Zell Miller, in his official capacity as Governor of the State of Georgia, et al.*, File No. 96-CV-2475-MHS (October 9, 2003).

70. (p. 217) U.S. Department of Justice, *The Electronic Frontier: The Challenge of Unlawful Conduct Involving the Use of the Internet: A Report of the President's Working*

Group on Unlawful Conduct on the Internet (March 2000), http://www.justice.gov/criminal/cybercrime/unlawful.htm.

71. (p. 218) Shirin Ebadi, *Iran Awakening* (New York: Random House, 2007), 194.

72. (p. 218) Alexa.com, http://www.alexa.com/siteinfo/google.com.

73. (p. 218) U.S. Department of State, "Global Internet Freedom Task Force (GIFT) Strategy: A Blueprint for Action," December 20, 2006.

74. (p. 219) Kenneth Dam and Herbert Lin, *Cryptography's Role in Securing the Information Society* (Washington, DC: National Academy Press, 1996), 6.

75. (p. 219) Ellen Nakashima, "Cybersecurity Plan to Involve NSA Doesn't Breach Employee Privacy Administration Says," *Washington Post* (September 19, 2009).

76. (p. 219) Siobhan Gorman, "U.S. Plans Cyber Shield for Utilities, Companies," *Wall Street Journal*, July 8, 2010.

77. (p. 219) Paul Ohm, "The Rise and Fall of Invasive ISP Surveillance," *University of Illinois Law Review* 2009 Volume, no. 5 (2009): 1433.

78. (p. 219) Ohm, "The Rise and Fall of Invasive ISP Surveillance," 1432, 1439–1440.

79. (p. 220) British Telecom ran such experiments using Phorm. For an explanation of the technology, see Richard Clayton, "The Phorm 'Webwise' System," May 18, 2008, www.cl.cam.ac.uk/~rnc1/080518-phorm.pdf.

80. (p. 220) Clayton, "The Phorm 'Webwise' System," 1450.

81. (p. 220) The one exception to this is that some people may use a different ISP at home and at the office. In that case, each ISP will have a remarkably detailed record of your behavior.

82. (p. 221) Timothy Garton Ash, "The Stasi Could Only Dream of Such Data," *Manchester Guardian Weekly*, February 8, 2008, 19.

83. (p. 221) 18 U.S.C. §2511(2)(a)(i).

84. (p. 221) Robert Mueller, testimony before U.S. Congress, House of Representatives, Committee on the Judiciary, *Federal Bureau of Investigation, Part II,* One Hundred and Tenth Congress, Second Session, April 23, 2008, Serial No. 110–99.

85. (p. 221) Ohm, "The Rise and Fall of Invasive ISP Surveillance," 487.

86. (p. 222) Landau, *The Enemy Within,* 77–91.

87. (p. 222) Landau, *The Enemy Within,* 92.

88. (p. 223) Tony Judt, "What Have We Learned, If Anything?", *Washington Post*, May 1, 2008.

Chapter 10

1. (p. 225) Hurricanes are classified by their maximum sustained wind speed. A category 3 storm has wind speeds of 111–130 miles an hour; a category 4, 131–155; and a category 5, in excess of 156. The recent severe hurricanes to hit the United States include: 1992, Andrew, category 5; 1995, Opal, category 3; 1996, Fran, category 3; 2004, Charley, Ivan, and Jeanne, all category 3.

2. (p. 225) Even mundane weather events like ice storms can have remarkably severe effects.

3. (p. 225) Paul Parmofak, *Vulnerability of Concentrated Critical Infrastructure: Background and Policy Options,* CRS Report for Congress, RL33206 (updated: September 12, 2008), 9.

4. (p. 225) Katrina sharply intensified when passing over the warm waters in the Gulf of Mexico.

5. (p. 226) One can plausibly argue that the flooding of New Orleans after Hurricane Katrina was a human-made disaster; whether it was or not (and I side with those who say it was) does not matter for this analysis.

6. (p. 226) Committee on the Internet under Crisis Conditions, Computer Science and Telecommunications Board, National Research Council, *The Internet under Crisis Conditions: Learning from September 11* (Washington, DC: National Academies Press, 2003), 23–24.

7. (p. 226) John Rendleman, "Despite Its Losses, Verizon Went Right Back to Work Restoring Communications Services," *Information Week,* October 29, 2001.

8. (p. 226) Committee on the Internet under Crisis Conditions, *The Internet under Crisis Conditions,* 36–37.

9. (p. 226) Committee on the Internet under Crisis Conditions, *The Internet under Crisis Conditions,* 38.

10. (p. 227) Committee on the Internet under Crisis Conditions, *The Internet under Crisis Conditions,* 38.

11. (p. 227) Committee on the Internet under Crisis Conditions, *The Internet under Crisis Conditions,* 23–24.

12. (p. 227) A peculiar exception—peculiar only to those who do not know the network fiber-optic cable topology—affected South African users seeking access to Internet domains ending in "za" (South Africa). If the cached entry in the local servers had expired, the South African servers queried the root server, which could not be reached (Committee on the Internet under Crisis Conditions, *The Internet under Crisis Conditions,* 32–33).

13. (p. 227) Rendleman, "Verizon Went Right Back to Work."

14. (p. 227) Committee on the Internet under Crisis Conditions, *The Internet under Crisis Conditions*, 29–30.

15. (p. 227) Committee on the Internet under Crisis Conditions, *The Internet under Crisis Conditions*, 3.

16. (p. 227) Peter Meyers, "In Crisis Zone, a Wireless Patch," *New York Times*, October 4, 2001.

17. (p. 227) U.S. Congress, House of Representatives, Select Bipartisan Committee to Investigate the Preparation for and Response to Hurricane Katrina, *A Failure of Initiative*, One Hundred and Ninth Congress, Second Session, February 15, 2006, 164.

18. (p. 227) Kenneth P. Moran, written testimony, U.S. Congress, Senate, Committee on Commerce, Science and Transportation, *Hearing on Hurricane Katrina and Communications Interoperability* (September 29, 2005), 3–4.

19. (p. 228) Christopher Rhoads, "Cut Off: At Center of Crisis, City Officials Faced Struggle to Keep in Touch," *Wall Street Journal*, September 9, 2005.

20. (p. 228) UN News Center, "Communications between 'First Responders' in Haiti to Be Strengthened—U.N. Agency," February 16, 2010.

21. (p. 228) U.S. Congress, House of Representatives, Select Bipartisan Committee, *A Failure of Initiative*, 172.

22. (p. 229) Jim Dwyer, Kevin Flynn, and Ford Fessenden, "Fatal Confusion: A Troubled Emergency Response; 9/11 Exposed Deadly Flaws in Rescue Plan," *New York Times*, July 7, 2002.

23. (p. 229) National Commission on Terrorist Attacks, *The 9/11 Commission Report*, 310.

24. (p. 229) National Commission on Terrorist Attacks, *The 9/11 Commission Report*, 301.

25. (p. 229) National Commission on Terrorist Attacks, *The 9/11 Commission Report*, 307.

26. (p. 229) Dwyer, Flynn, and Fessenden, "Fatal Confusion."

27. (p. 229) Dwyer, Flynn, and Fessenden, "Fatal Confusion."

28. (p. 229) Meyers, "In Crisis Zone, a Wireless Patch."

29. (p. 230) Gerald Faulhaber, "Solving the Interoperability Problem: Are We All on the Same Channel? An Essay on the Problems and Prospects for Public Safety Radio," *Federal Communications Law Journal* 59 (June 2007): 496.

30. (p. 230) Department of Homeland Security, *National Emergency Communications Plan* (rev. August 7, 2008), 11.

31. (p. 230) Faulhaber, "Solving the Interoperability Problem," 497.

32. (p. 231) Faulhaber, "Solving the Interoperability Problem," 509.

33. (p. 231) Jerry Brito, "Sending Out an S.O.S.: Public Safety Communications Interoperability as a Collective Action Problem," *Federal Communications Law Journal* 59 (2007): 479.

34. (p. 231) Charles Werner, personal communication, March 3, 2010.

35. (p. 231) Chris Essid, personal communication, March 4, 2010.

36. (p. 231) "The nation does not have unlimited resources to address deficiencies in emergency communications" (Department of Homeland Security, *National Emergency Communications Plan*, ES-2).

37. (p. 231) Department of Homeland Security, *National Emergency Communications Plan*, ES-2, 24.

38. (p. 231) Dickie George, personal communication, February 26, 2010.

Chapter 11

1. (p. 233) Helen Nissenbaum, "Where Computer Security Meets National Security," in Jack Balkin, James Grimmelmann, Eddan Katz, Nimrod Kozlovski, Shlomit Wagman, and Tal Zarsky, eds., *Cybercrime: Digital Cops in a Networked Environment* (New York: New York University Press, 2007), 63.

2. (p. 233) Nissenbaum, "Where Computer Security Meets National Security," 63.

3. (p. 233) Einstein 3's "checking the road" is limited to examining communications bound for federal systems.

4. (p. 233) Nissenbaum, "Where Computer Security Meets National Security," 75.

5. (p. 234) This included plans for rocket-engine designs, for the design and testing of satellite command-and-control software, for the shuttle-engine design, and for rockets for intercontinental missiles.

6. (p. 235) Bernard Esambert, former French cabinet minister, said, "We are living in a state of world economic war and this is not just a military metaphor . . . the companies are training the armies and the unemployed are the casualties" (Wanja Eric Naef, "Economic and Industrial Espionage: A Threat to Corporate America," *Infocon Magazine* 1 (October 2003): http://www.iwar.org.uk/infocon/economic -espionage.htm.

7. (p. 235) The U.S. Cyber Command is a multibillion dollar effort to develop U.S. cyberwarfare capabilities. Part of the offensive work being proposed and worked on is actually defensive. One example is developing the capability to enter a foreign system and destroy the command-and-control system for botnets poised to attack U.S. sites (David Sanger, John Markoff, and Thom Shanker, "U.S. Steps Up Effort on Digital Defenses," *New York Times*, April 27, 2009).

8. (p. 235) William A. Owens, Kenneth W. Dam, and Herbert S. Lin, *Technology, Policy, Law, and Ethics Regarding U.S. Acquisition and Use of Cyberattack Capabilities* (Washington, DC: National Academies Press, 2009), 1.

9. (p. 235) Bryan Krekel, Capabilities of the People's Republic of China to Conduct Cyber Warfare and Computer Network Exploitation, Prepared for the US-China Economic and Security Review Commission (2009), http://www.uscc.gov/researchpapers/ 2009/NorthropGrumman_PRC_Cyber_Paper_FINAL_Approved%20Report _16Oct2009.pdf, 72–74.

10. (p. 235) David Barboza, "Hacking for Fun and Profit in the Chinese Underworld," *New York Times* (February 1, 2010).

11. (p. 236) David D. Clark, "Toward the Design of a Future Internet," Version 7.0, October 10, 2009, http://groups.csail.mit.edu/ana/People/DDC/Working%20Papers.html, 7.

12. (p. 236) Jerome H. Saltzer, David P. Reed, and David D. Clark, "End-to-End Arguments in System Design," ACM Transactions on Computer Systems, 2, no. 4, (November 1984), 278.

13. (p. 237) Committee on Science and Technology for Countering Terrorism, National Research Council, *Making the Nation Safer* (Washington, DC: National Research Council, 2002), 150.

14. (p. 237) Tom Cross, "Exploiting Lawful Intercept to Wiretap the Internet," Black Hat DC 2010 (February 2010).

15. (p. 237) Cross, "Exploiting Lawful Intercept," 11.

16. (p. 237) Cross, "Exploiting Lawful Intercept," 8–9.

17. (p. 237) Cross, "Exploiting Lawful Intercept," 4–6.

18. (p. 237) State crimes were a different matter.

19. (p. 238) Clark, "Future Internet," 15.

20. (p. 238) One example of this is that not all packets are created equal. Quality of Service (QoS)—whether a packet should have priority in traversing the network—can make or break an application; VoIP and streaming video are two examples of this. VoIP packets should not take longer than 150 milliseconds to traverse the network; more delay than that disrupts conversation flow (D. Richard Kuhn, Thomas J. Walsh, and Steffen Fries, *Security Considerations for Voice over IP Systems,* National Institute for Standards and Technology Special Publication 800-58, Gaithersberg MD: National Institute for Standards and Technology, January 2005, 19). With the minor exception that NSFNet gave priority to remote login packets, Internet 1.0—the Internet designed by the DARPA project—did not discriminate on the basis of content type. In a future Internet, QoS will need to be more deeply embedded in network protocols; at the same time, carriers will need to be able to determine content type to determine whether a packet should have priority treatment.

21. (p. 238) Nick McKeown, Tom Anderson, Hari Balakrishnan, Guru Parulkar, Larry Peterson, Jennifer Rexford, Scott Shenker, and Jonathan Turner, "Open Flow: Enabling Innovation in Campus Networks," *CCR Online* March 14, 2008, http://ccr.sigcomm.org/online/?q=node/328.

22. (p. 239) Martin Casado, Michael J. Freedman, Justin Pettit, Jianying Luo, Natasha Gude, Nick McKeown, and Scott Shenker, "Rethinking Enterprise Network Control," *IEEE/ACM Transactions on Networking* 17, no. 4 (August 2009): 1271.

23. (p. 239) Casado et al., "Rethinking Enterprise Network Control," 1283.

24. (p. 239) "When we consider the problem of attacks on hosts, we must accept that general purpose end-node operating systems such as Windows or Unix will always have flaws that present vulnerabilities" (Clark, "Future Internet," 18).

25. (p. 239) Clark, "Future Internet," 19–20.

26. (p. 240) This includes building trustworthy components, creating modifications in application-level communications, and developing controls on connectivity (Clark, "Future Internet," 19).

27. (p. 240) Clark, "Future Internet," 21.

28. (p. 240) Steven M. Bellovin, Whitfield Diffie, Susan Landau, Peter Neumann, and Jennifer Rexford, "Risking Communications Security: Potential Hazards of the Protect America Act," *IEEE Security and Privacy* 6, no. 1 (January/February 2008), 30.

29. (p. 240) This was the case with the collection resulting from the FISA Amendments Act (Lichtblau and Risen, "Officials Say U.S. Wiretaps Exceeded Law," *New York Times*, April 16, 2009); whether it was the case from the PSP is unclear.

30. (p. 240) U.S. Department of Justice, Office of the Inspector General, Oversight and Review Board, *A Review of the Federal Bureau of Investigation's Use of Exigent Letters and Other Informal Requests for Telephone Records,* (January 2010), 33.

31. (p. 241) Note that the Greek system involved eavesdropping on a cellular network, while the Cisco architecture was an IP-based surveillance system.

32. (p. 241) Tom Cross made this point as well (Cross, "Exploiting Lawful Intercept.").

33. (p. 241) Protecting against an individual intent on such violent activities requires an inordinate amount of surveillance. This is different from protecting against a complex plot involving dozens of participants.

34. (p. 241) As the size of the community increases, more third-party software becomes available, making the system more attractive, and in turn, this helps increase the number of users.

35. (p. 242) Ross Anderson, "Closing the Phishing Hole—Fraud, Risk and Non-banks," Conference on Nonbanks in the Payment System: Innovation, Competition, and Risk, Santa Fe, NM, May 2007.

36. (p. 242) Hal Varian, "Managing Online Security Risks," *New York Times*, June 1, 2000.

37. (p. 242) The classic case regarding standard of care concerns two oceangoing tugboats traveling between Norfolk, Virginia, and New York during a gale. Each tug was towing three barges loaded with coal. The tugs lacked working radios and the captains did not know of the approaching weather; they did not put into harbor. Each tug lost its final barge. Although having a radio was not yet standard industry practice, Circuit Court Judge Learned Hand ruled that "there are precautions so imperative that even their universal disregard will not excuse their omission" (*The T. J. Hooper v. Northern Barge Corporation; N. Hartwell & Son, Inc. v. Same,* Circuit Court of Appeals, Second Circuit 60 F.2d 737, 1932, 740).

38. (p. 242) Seymour Goodman and Herbert Lin, eds., *Toward a Safer and More Secure Cyberspace* (Washington, DC: National Academies Press, 2007), 165–166.

39. (p. 242) In "two-party" states such as Maryland, both parties must consent before the interception is permitted.

40. (p. 242) 18 U.S.C. §2511 (2).

41. (p. 243) Under the Bush administration warrantless wiretapping and the subsequent Protect America Act and FISA Amendments Act, no purely domestic calls were supposed to be targeted; some were, however (Lichtblau and Risen, "Officials Say U.S. Wiretaps Exceeded Law").

42. (p. 244) Pub. L. 100-235.

43. (p. 244) At the time of the passage of the act, NIST was known as the National Bureau of Standards.

44. (p. 244) Whitfield Diffie and Susan Landau, *Privacy on the Line: The Politics of Wiretapping and Encryption,* rev. ed. (Cambridge, MA: MIT Press, 2007), 74–85.

45. (p. 244) Diffie and Landau, *Privacy on the Line*, 78.

46. (p. 245) Infragard is one such.

47. (p. 246) Notable examples of secure communications include ssh for securing data exchange between two networked devices (used for remote login, secure file transfer, etc.); secure browser communication or https, which is used for passwords for secure login and for financial transactions (although in January 2010 Google started employing it for Gmail); and Skype. VPNs are securely encrypted between an end host and gateway rather than securing the communication end to end.

48. (p. 246) U.S. Congress, House of Representatives, Committee on Energy and Commerce, Subcommittee on Telecommunications and the Internet, *Law Enforcement Access to Communications Systems in the Digital Age,* One Hundred and Eighth Congress, Second Session, Serial No. 108-115 (September 8, 2004).

49. (p. 246) Bellovin et al., "Security Implications."

50. (p. 247) Bellovin et al., "Security Implications."

51. (p. 248) Administrative Office of the United States Courts, James C. Duff, Director, *2009 WiretapReport,* 8.

52. (p. 249) The ability to capture sound at a distance means that parabolic microphones are used for collecting nature recordings.

53. (p. 249) This works through aiming a laser beam at a glass window; if there is a mirror in the room, the beam is aimed at that. Otherwise the window provides ample reflection. Voices in the room bounce off hard surfaces including the window; the modulations are picked up by the reflected beam. The slight disruption of the reflected beam is analyzed and reveals the communication.

54. (p. 250) Jed Rubenfeld, "The End of Privacy," *Stanford Law Review* 61, no. 1 (October 2008): 122.

55. (p. 251) I use the word *substantively* because, as the IETF RFC 2804 notes, "Wiretapping, even when it is not being exercised, therefore lowers the security of the system" (Network Working Group, *RFC 2804: IETF Policy on Wiretapping,* http://www.ietf.org/rfc/rfc2804.txt 7). By definition, any form of wiretapping intrudes on the security of a communication.

56. (p. 251) In this and what follows in this section, I use the term *must* as in the "MUST" of IETF RFCs: "This word, or the terms 'REQUIRED' or 'SHALL,' mean that the definition is an absolute requirement of the specification" (Scott Bradner, *RFC 2119: Key Words for Use in RFCs to Indicate Requirement Levels,* (http://www.ietf.org/rfc/rfc2119.txt, March 1997), 1).

57. (p. 251) The Cisco architecture used a hashing algorithm, MD5, that is now known to have weaknesses. Periodic review of systems in place will catch such security changes.

58. (p. 251) "The system is less secure . . . [and] more complex. Being more complex, the risk of unintended security flaws in the system is larger" (Network Working Group, *RFC 2804: IETF Policy on Wiretapping,* 7).

59. (p. 251) Cross, "Exploiting Lawful Intercept," 2, 5, 7.

60. (p. 252) National Research Council, *Protecting Individual Privacy in the Struggle Against Terrorists: A Framework for Program Assessment* (Washington, DC: National Academies Press, 2008), 5.

61. (p. 252) National Research Council, *Protecting Individual Rights,* 5.

62. (p. 252) In *Branzburg v. Hayes,* the Supreme Court held that requiring journalists to testify before state or federal grand juries does not violate the First Amendment.

63. (p. 252) The issue is not can a wiretap order be placed on a journalist, for the answer is yes if there is a probable cause that the journalist is involved in the commission of a serious crime, an agent of a foreign power, and so on. Rather the concern

is whether a subpoena to place a pen register on a journalist is legitimate during the course of a criminal or foreign-intelligence investigation of *another party*. The government takes the issue very seriously and requires, for example, that the subpoena be approved by the attorney general.

Epilogue

1. (p. 255) Wayne M. Morrison and Michael F. Martin, *How Large Is China's Economy? Does It Matter?*, Congressional Research Service Report for Congress, RS22808 (February 13, 2008), CRS3-CRS4.

2. (p. 255) Franklin D. Kramer, "Cyberpower and National Security: Policy Recommendations for a Strategic Framework," in Franklin D. Kramer, Stuart H. Starr, and Larry K. Wentz, eds., *Cyberpower and National Security* (Washington, DC: National Defense University Press, 2009), 12.

3. (p. 256) The U.S. government found no evidence that the warrantless wiretapping of the President's Surveillance Program had been intentionally misused (Offices of the Inspector General of the Department of Defense, Department of Justice, Central Intelligence Agency, National Security Agency, Office of the Director of National Intelligence, *Unclassified Report on the President's Surveillance Program*, Report 2009-0013-AS, July 10, 2009, 15).

4. (p. 256) The Department of Justice Inspector General report concluded that "it was extraordinary and inappropriate that a single DOJ attorney" could conduct such a critical legal analysis working entirely on his own (Offices of the Inspector General, *Unclassified Report on the President's Surveillance Program*, 30).

5. (p. 256) David Cole, "How to Skip the Constitution," *New York Review of Books*, November 16, 2006, 21.

6. (p. 256) Cole, "How to Skip the Constitution," 21.

7. (p. 256) The Sedition Act, which criminalized publishing "false, scandalous, and malicious writing" against the government and government officials, expired in 1801; it is assumed that had the act been tested in court, it would have been found unconstitutional. The Alien Act, which remains in effect today as 50 U.S.C. §21–24, authorizes the president to deport resident aliens if their native country is at war with the United States.

8. (p. 256) Cole, "How to Skip the Constitution," 22.

Bibliography

Administrative Office of the United States Courts. *Wiretap Report*. Washington, DC: Government Printing Office, 1999.

Afanasyev, Mikhail, Tadayoshi Kohno, Justin Ma, Nick Murphy, Stefan Savage, Alex Snoeren, and Geoffrey Voelker. *Network Support for Privacy-Preserving Forensic Attribution*. University of California San Diego Technical Reports, CS2009–0940, March 2009.

AT&T Messaging FAQ. http://www.wireless.att.com/learn/messaging-internet/messaging/faq.jsp#pricing-text.

Bernstein, Nina. "In American Mill Towns, No Mirror Image of the Muslims in Leeds." *New York Times*, July 21, 2005

Bobbit, Philip. *The Shield of Achilles: War, Peace, and the Course of History*. New York. Knopf, 2003.

Byres, Eric, and Justin Lowe. "The Myths and Facts behind Cyber Security Risks for Industrial Control Systems." *Proceedings of the VDE Kongress*, 213–217. Berlin: VDE, 2004.

Center for Democracy and Technology. *Einstein Intrusion Detection Systems: Questions That Should Be Addressed*. Washington, DC: Center for Democracy and Technology, July 2009.

Clarke, Richard. Interview on *Frontline*, http://www.pbs.org/wgbh/pages/frontline/shows/cyberwar/interviews/clarke.html, March 18, 2003.

Cooper. Michael. "Ex-CIA Spy Chief to Run Police Intelligence." *New York Times*, January 25, 2002.

Commission of the European Communities. Brussels, "Protecting Europe from Large Scale Cyber-Attacks and Disruptions: Enhancing Preparedness, Security and Resilience." Communication from the Commission to the European Parliament, the Council, the European Economic and Social Committee and the Committee of the Regions on Critical Information Infrastructure Protection. SEC 2009 Brussels, 2009.

"Cyber War: Sabotaging the System." *Sixty Minutes*, CBS, November 8, 2009. http://www.cbsnews.com/stories/2009/11/06/60minutes/main5555565.shtml?tag=cont.

Dagon, David, Cliff Zou, and Wenke Lee. "Modeling Botnet Propagation Using Time Zones." *Proceedings of the 13th Annual Network and Distributed System Security Symposium (NDSS 2006)*, San Diego, CA, February 2006.

Doyle, Charles. *The USA PATRIOT Act: A Sketch*. CRS Report for Congress, RS21203, April 18, 2002.

Droma, R. *RFC 2131—Dynamic Host Configuration Protocol*. March 1997. http://tools.ietf.org/html/rfc2131.

EFF v. Department of Justice. Civil Action No. 06-1708—CKK (D.D.C.) (filed 3 Oct. 2006). www.eff.org/ issues/foia/061708CKK.

European Union, Council of the European Union. *Report from Working Party on Cooperation in Criminal Matters to Article 36 Committee, 6566/05*. Copen 35, Telecom 10. Brussels, February 24, 2005.

Exhibit A. *Tash Hepting et al. v. AT&T Corporation et al.* United States Second District Court for Northern California, Case 3:06-cv-0672-vrw, June 8, 2006.

Fildes, Jonathan. "Wikipedia 'Shows CIA Page Edits.'" BBC News, August 15, 2007. http://news.bbc.co.uk/2/hi/technology/6947532.stm.

Froehlich, Fritz E., and Allen Kent. *The Froehlich/Kent Encyclopedia of Telecommunications*, vol. 15, 231–255. New York: Marcel Dekker, 1997. http://www.cert.org/encyc_article/tocencyc.html.

Frost, Mike, as told to Michael Gratton. *Spyworld: Inside the Canadian and American Intelligence Establishments*. Toronto: Doubleday Canada, 1994.

Gellman, Barton, Dafna Linzer, and Carol Leonnig. "Surveillance Net Yields Few Suspects." *Washington Post*, February 5, 2006.

Goldberg, Ian. "Privacy-Enhancing Technologies for the Internet, II: Five Years Later." In Roger Dingledine and Paul Syverson, eds., *Proceedings of the Privacy Enhancing Technologies Workshop (PET 2002)*, April 2002. New York: Springer, 2003.

Golle, Philipe, and Kurt Partridge. "On the Anonymity of Home/Work Location Pairs." Proceedings of the 7th *International Conference, Pervasive 2009*, New York: Springer 2009.

Hadian, Nasser, Shaul Bakhash, Henry Precht, and Gary Sick. "The Shah and Revolution." World Feature, *BBC News*, October 26, 2004. http://www.theworld.org/?q=node/3567.

Helm, Sarah. *A Life in Secrets: Vera Atkins and the Lost Agents of SOE*. London: Little, Brown, 2005.

Heymann, Phillip. *Terrorism and America: A Commonsense Strategy for a Democratic Society*. Cambridge, MA: MIT Press, 1998.

Hussain, Zahid, Siobhan Gorman, and Neil King, Jr. "Students Linked to Al Qaeda." *Wall Street Journal,* December 11, 2009.

"Internet Infrastructure Security: A Taxonomy." *IEEE Network* (November/December) (2002): 13–21.

Johnson, Thomas R. *American Cryptology during the Cold War, 1945–1989; Book II, Centralization Wins: 1960–1972.* vol. 5. United States Cryptologic History: The NSA Period, 1952–Present. Fort Meade, MD: Center for Cryptologic History, National Security Agency, 1995.

Johnston, David, and James Risen. "Traces of Terrorism: The Intelligence Series: Series of Warnings." *New York Times,* May 17, 2002.

Jones, Seth, and Martin Libiki. *How Terrorist Groups End: Lessons for Countering Al Qa'ida.* Santa Monica, CA: Rand Corporation, 2008.

Kahn, David. "The Rise of Intelligence." *Foreign Affairs,* September/October 2006.

Kennedy, Charles, and Peter Swire. "State Wiretaps and Electronic Surveillance after September 11th." *Hastings Law Journal* 54 (2003): 971.

Kent, Stephen. "Architectural Security." In Daniel Lynch and Marshall Rose, eds., *Internet System Handbook,* 369–419. Reading, MA: Addison-Wesley, 1993.

Kent, Stephen, and Lynette Miller. *Who Goes There? Authentication through the Lens of Privacy.* Washington, DC: National Academies Press, 2003.

Kepel, Gilles. *The Battle for Muslim Minds: Islam and the West.* Cambridge, MA: Harvard University Press, 2004.

Kohlmann, Evan. "The World of Warcraft." *Foreign Affairs,* September/October 2006.

Kosta, Eleni, and Peggy Valcke. "Telecommunications, the EU Data Retention Directive: Retaining the Data Retention Directive." *Computer Law & Security Report* 22 (2006): 370–380.

Kris, David. "The Rise and Fall of the FISA Wall." *Stanford Law & Policy Review* 17 (2006): 487–528.

Landau, Susan. "Standing the Test of Time: The Data Encryption Standard." *Notices of the American Mathematical Society* (March) (2000): 341–349.

Leibovich, Mark. "Strom of the Century; The Hill Sings 'Happy Birthday' as Sen. Thurmond Turns 100." *Washington Post,* December 6, 2002, A1.

Lockhart, Gregory. "Ohio Man Pleads Guilty to Conspiracy to Bomb Targets in Europe and the United States." Press release, United States Attorney General, Southern District of Ohio, June 3, 2008.

Lynch, Daniel, and Marshall Rose, eds. *Internet System Handbook.* Reading, MA: Addison-Wesley, 1993.

Markoff, John. "Before the Gunfire, Cyberattacks." *New York Times*, August 13, 2009.

McMillan, Robert. "The NSA Wiretapping Story That Nobody Wanted." *New York Times*, July 17, 2009.

Nakashima, Ellen. "Cybersecurity Plan to Involve NSA, Telecoms." *Washington Post*, July 3, 2009.

Office of the Manager, National Communications System. *The Electronic Intrusion Threat to National Security and Emergency Preparedness Telecommunications.* 2nd ed. Arlington, VA: Office of the Manager, National Communications System, December 5, 1994.

Packer, George. "Knowing the Enemy." *New Yorker* December 18, 2006, 61–69.

Parfomak, Paul W. *Vulnerability of Concentrated Critical Infrastructure: Background and Policy Options.* CRS Report for Congress. Washington, DC: Congressional Research Service, September 12, 2008.

Parker, Geoffrey, and Edward Anderson, Jr. "From Buyer to Integrator: The Transformation of the Supply-Chain Manager in the Vertically Integrating Firm." *Production and Operations Management* 11 (1) (Spring 2002): 75–91.

Pew Research Center. *Muslim Americans: Middle Class and Mostly Mainstream.* Washington, DC: Pew Research Center, May 22, 2007.

Research and Development Committee, Financial Services Coordinating Council for Critical Infrastructure Protection and Homeland Security. *Research Agenda for the Banking and Finance Sector.* September 2008. https://www.fsscc.org/fsscc/reports/2008/RD_Agenda-FINAL.pdf.

Rheingold, Howard. *Smart Mobs: The Next Social Revolution.* Cambridge, MA: Perseus Press, 2002.

Risen, James, and Eric Lichtblau. "Rice Defends Bush Eavesdropping." *New York Times*, December 19, 2005.

Rishikof, Harvey. "Economic and Industrial Espionage." In Jennifer Sims and Burton Gerber, eds., *Vaults, Mirrors, and Masks: Rediscovering U.S. Counterintelligence,* 199–222. Washington, DC: Georgetown University Press, 2009.

Rosenthal, Elizabeth, with David Sanger. "U.S. Plane in China After It Collides with Chinese Jet." *New York Times*, April 2, 2001, A1.

Rosenzweig, Paul. *"National Security Threats in Cyberspace: A Workshop Jointly Conducted by the American Bar Association Standing Committee on Law and National Security and National Strategy Forum,"* Post Workshop Report, September 2009.

Savage, Stefan. Comments on "CCC BLOG." February 25, 2009. http://www.cccblog.org/2009/02/21/does-better-security-depend-on-a-better-internet/.

Schwartz, John. "Blogs Provide Raw Details from Scene of Disaster." *New York Times*, December 28, 2004.

Shapiro, Samantha M. "Revolution, Facebook-Style." *New York Times Magazine*, January 25, 2009, 34–39.

Shea, Dana. *Critical Infrastructure: Control Systems and the Terrorist Threat*. Congressional Research Service, Library of Congress, February 21, 2003.

Spafford, Eugene. *The Internet Worm Program: An Analysis*. Purdue Technical Report CSD-TR-823, December 8, 1988.

Standage, Tom. "The Internet Untethered." *The Economist* (October 13, 2001).

Tribe, Lawrence, and Michael Dorf. *On Reading the Constitution*. Cambridge, MA: Harvard University Press, 1991.

U.S. Congress. Senate, Committee on the Judiciary. USA PATRIOT Act in Practice: Shedding Light on the FISA Process. Hearing, Serial No. J107102, One Hundred and Seventh Congress, Second Session, September 10, 2002.

U.S. Department of Commerce, National Institute of Standards and Technology. *Escrowed Encryption Standard. Federal Information Processing Standards Publication 185*. Gaithersberg, MD: Department of Commerce, 1994.

U.S. Department of Justice. *Chapter 3: Electronic Surveillance—Non-Wiretap*. Obtained through htpp://www.aclu.org/pdfs/freespeech/cellfoia release 074130 20080812.pdf.

U.S. Department of Justice. *Electronic Surveillance Manual: X V: Mobile Tracking Devices*. May 27, 2004. http://10.173.2.12/usao/eousa/ole/usabook/elsu15elsu.htm. Obtained through htpp://www.aclu.org/pdfs/freespeech/cellfoia release 074130 20080812.pdf.

U.S. Department of Justice, United States Attorney's Office, Northern District of Georgia. "Former IRS Employee Pleads Guilty to Disclosing Taxpayer Info." June 7, 2005, http://www.justice.gov/usao/gan/press/2005/06-07-2005.htm.

U.S. Department of State, Bureau of International Organizational Affairs. *Clinton Administration Policy on Reforming Multilateral Peace Operations (PDD 25)*. Washington, DC, February 22, 1996.

U.S. Foreign Intelligence Surveillance Court. In Re: All Matters Submitted to the Foreign Intelligence Surveillance Court, Docket Numbers: Multiple, Order, as Amended, May 17, 2002. In U.S. Senate, Committee on the Judiciary, *USA PATRIOT Act in Practice: Shedding Light on the FISA Process*, Hearing, September 10, 2002, Serial No. J–107–102, One Hundred and Seventh Congress, Second Session, 172–175.

U.S. General Accountability Office. Testimony before the Subcommittee on Emerging Threats, Cybersecurity, and Science and Technology, Committee on Homeland Security, House of Representatives. Critical Infrastructure Protection: DHS Needs to

Better Address Its Cybersecurity Responsibilities: Statement of David Powner, director, GAO-08–1157T, September 16, 2008.

U.S. Senate, Select Committee on Intelligence. Senate Select Committee on Intelligence Inquiry into the FBI Investigation of the Committee in Solidarity with the People of El Salvador. Hearings on February 23, April 13, September 14 and 29. One Hundredth Congress, Second Session, 1988.

Index